Cost Accounting

W M Harper ACMA

THE M & E HANDBOOK SERIES

Pitman Publishing
128 Long Acre, London WC2E 9AN

A Division of Longman Group UK Limited

First published as *Cost and Management Accounting Vol I Cost Accounting* 1982
Second edition published as *Cost Accounting* 1987
Reprinted 1989, 1990
Reprinted in this format 1991 (twice)

© Macdonald & Evans Ltd 1982
© Longman Group UK Ltd 1987

British Library Cataloguing in Publication Data
Harper, W.M.
   Cost and management accounting. – 2nd ed.
   – (M & E handbooks, ISSN 0265–8828).
   Cost accounting
   1. Cost accounting
   I. Title
   657′.42   HF5686.C8

ISBN 0 7121 1015 1

Founding Editor: P.W.D. Redmond

Printed and bound in Singapore

Contents

Preface

In this new edition of *Cost Accounting* a return is made to the policy of having separate stand-alone volumes for cost accounting and management accounting as against covering the combined subjects in a single two-volume work. Consequently a number of topics previously covered in the management accounting texts are now to be found in this book.

As students will know, there have been recent revisions of virtually all the syllabuses of the accounting bodies. This new edition has been written so as to cover these new syllabuses – although in the event the necessary changes have been more of emphasis than content.

Progress tests are divided, where appropriate, into *Principles* (testing ideas, definitions, etc.) and *Practice* (testing the application of the principles). Answers to the Practice questions are contained in Appendix 3. Students should note that I have sometimes used the answers to illustrate points which are not illustrated in the chapter.

Acknowledgements

I gratefully acknowledge permission to quote from the past examination papers of the following bodies:

Association of Accounting Technicians (AAT)
Chartered Association of Certified Accountants (ACCA)
Chartered Institute of Management Accountants (CIMA)
Institute of Chartered Accountants in England and Wales (ICA)

W M Harper
July 1987

1

Introduction

Accountancy work can be divided into two categories. The first involves handling monetary figures in order to comply with legal requirements – this is the world of tax computations, published accounts, liquidations, executorships and the like. The second involves handling monetary figures in order to quantify business activities and plans.

This book is concerned solely with the second of these two categories.

Background

1. Dual role of money. Fundamental to a clear understanding of the whole field of management accounting is the appreciation that *money* in business plays a dual role – firstly as a physical economic factor of production and secondly as an abstract economic measure of performance.

(*a*) *Money as an economic factor of production.* Money in its physical form of currency is as necessary to an enterprise as any other economic factor such as materials or labour. In this form it is usually referred to as *cash* and consists, of course, of coins, bank notes and cheques. Without cash (or credit, which is essentially a form of cash to a businessman) an enterprise would quickly grind to a halt.

(*b*) *Money as a measure of economic performance.* Basically, the object of an enterprise is to combine a variety of economic factors (materials, labour, land, machines, etc.), so that from the combination some utility emerges which can be exchanged for cash.

Since the combination can be varied (e.g. machines can be used in lieu of labour) it is necessary to be able to measure the economic value involved in any combination together with the value of the utility. Unfortunately, tonnes of material cannot be added to hours of labour nor compared with units of production. To make measurements in such circumstances, therefore, calls for the use of a common denominator, and money is the chosen measure.

NOTE: In some ways the use of money as such a measure is unfortunate. People may confuse *money* used in this way with *cash*, and learning that on average it costs thirty pence a mile to run a particular type of vehicle, wrongly assume that by running the vehicle ten miles less they will have £3 more cash in their pockets. Moreover, money is an unstable unit, continuously affected by inflation, so the same economic performance one year has a different monetary value from an identical performance another year. Despite these serious disadvantages, however, it is the most practical measure we have.

In cost accounting it is important that the two roles are kept separate. In the main this is not difficult but in certain circumstances (and particularly where inflation arises, for then one must undertake the conceptually complex task of valuing cash in monetary terms) a clearheaded approach is essential.

2. History of cost and management accounting. It is probably fair to say that, historically speaking, in the beginning there was costing, not accounting. Book-keeping at that time was concerned solely with money as an economic resource and no real attempt was made by accountants to use it to measure economic performance. When ultimately measurement in the form of ascertaining profit was called for one gains the impression that the accountants of the day complied with little enthusiasm for either accuracy or consistency.

However, although the enterprise owners (usually owner-managers in those days, of course) were understandably more interested in cash than profit, the reverse was true for the enterprise engineers. Needing to quote a price for their work, much of which was done then on a job basis, they required accurate measurements of the value of the resources entering into each project. To this end they engaged cost clerks whose places were firmly alongside the engineer within the production function. There was no link between the cost clerk and the accountant, the clerk being left to dig around on his own initiative for the monetary figures which would enable him to prepare his cost statements.

As the deficiencies in this approach became more obvious, and as overheads which had previously been only a small percentage of the total costs grew in significance, the cost clerk moved more and more towards a full accounting approach to his tasks, and eventually the increasing complexity of his work led him and other similarly engaged clerks to claim professional status. Out of this came the founding of the Institute of Cost and Works Accountants. Cost accounting, however, still concentrated in the main on tracing costs, and this state of affairs continued until the Second World War, the literature of the 1930s debating such matters as how to define capacity and whether interest was a cost.

After the Second World War the emphasis began to change. Now the *managerial* significance of the figures began to be more appreciated and the preparation of statements that were useful to managers became emphasised. The term 'management accountant' was eventually coined and the Institute of Cost and Works Accountants became the Institute of Cost and Management Accountants (now the Chartered Institute of Management Accountants). With the change of emphasis came a change in the approach to the accounting – no longer was it a matter of tracing past figures to jobs and departments but rather of predicting future costs and analyzing these in terms of enterprise profitability. Moreover, the whole arc of the accountant's influence widened. No longer was he merely reporting costs but instead considerably influencing top management decisions. From his corner in the works engineer's office he had risen to a seat at the boardroom table.

3. Financial, management and cost accounting. With this brief history of management accounting before us it will be clear that the distinctions between financial, management and cost accounting are more historical than logical. In reality there is only one function – that of the economic management of the enterprise. This function can be divided into managing cash (which includes accounting for its use and planning its economic manipulation) and measuring performance (which includes both past and planned performance). Because of its historical development the division of this basic function is slightly different in practice. The following is an attempt to make some logical distinctions between the actual divisions that have evolved.

(*a*) *Financial accounting.* This is concerned with *money as a physical economic resource*, i.e cash. Consequently cheques, coins and notes, bank balances and overdrafts, debtors and creditors feature largely in this type of accounting. Just as managers of any other physical resource must know the sources, varieties and economic value of their resource, so financial accountants must know the source of their finances, the varieties of finance available and the economic value (in interest terms) of that finance. Financial accounting is, then, primarily concerned with resource management and as such it is a rather specialist function.

(*b*) *Management accounting.* This is concerned with *measuring the economic consequences and implications of management decisions.* It concerns itself particularly with money as a measure of economic performance, and with using that measure to help managers manage. In truth, its 'accounting for' function is only one of its minor aspects and the management accountant has far more in common with the economist than with the traditional accountant.

(*c*) *Cost accounting.* This is really that aspect of management accounting which is concerned with *measuring the economic performance of departments, methods and equipment and of measuring the value of the resources consumed in producing goods and services.*

Clearly, in places the accounting categories overlap, but as broad definitions of the work of the modern accounting department these divisions suffice.

In this book financial accounting will be discussed as little as possible. It is a specialist field and only that part of it which impinges on the enterprise's need for cash will be considered. And only that aspect of management accounting that is important to cost accounting will be included here – discussion of the further and wider aspects may be found in *Management Accounting*, Harper, M&E Handbook series.

4. Management accounting and management. Management accounting is concerned with *management*. Students should imagine themselves as equal members of a top management team which has been set the collective task of managing an enterprise.

Members of the team will naturally undertake specialist activities – one may manage the factory, another handle research. The management accountant's particular task will be to provide information to colleagues relating to the economic aspects of the operation of the enterprise. While he will take from the field of accountancy such techniques as will be useful, he will always look at the enterprise with the eyes of a manager, conscious of management's problems, responsibilities, opportunities, limitations, hopes and fears.

5. Management in the ultimate – decision-making. Managing involves an extensive and complex range of skills but at the end of the day all these culminate in a management decision. Management accounting, then, is concerned with assisting managers to make decisions.

6. The role of the future. At all times managers must, in effect, live in the future. They must always be looking ahead, for the instructions they issue in the present must be based on what they envisage the future will bring. This continual involvement with the future affects everything management accountants do. They are constantly concerned with what *will be* and every aspect of their work is orientated ultimately to enabling them to predict the future. Past and present figures only have value in so far as they foreshadow the future – although their potential to do just that should never be underestimated, for in the absence of definite information to the contrary the best predictor as to what will happen next time is what happened last time. It is, incidentally, for this reason that cost accounting is a part of management accounting and not merely a disassociated technique ploughing its own separate furrow.

NOTE: The student may wonder how the presentation of a priced past job cost (an obviously important if lowly task in the management accounting department) can have anything to do with future figures. The fact is, however, that there are a number of ways of pricing jobbing work and past jobs enable any existing pricing strategy to be tested for effectiveness – the result clearly affecting *future* pricing strategy.

7. The basic principle of data selection and arrangement. It must be emphasized at this point that management accounting statements should always be prepared with the following question in mind: *for what purpose is the information required?* In management accounting you are continually faced with the problem of choosing which pieces of data you should use and if at every point you consider whether or not use of the data will help achieve the purpose, then it becomes much easier to pass through the labyrinth of alternative treatments of data that are a feature of management accounting. Remember, too, that there are no definitive rules or statute laws that make the choice for you; books may point the way but always the final decision must be left to the judgment of the individual accountant.

Cost accounting

Although cost accounting is a part of management accounting it can perhaps be distinguished from the other parts of that subject by its considerable attention to actual past cost figures. Despite the fact that management accounting concentrates on future figures there is no doubt that much of the insight into what the figures will be in future circumstances is obtained by a careful consideration of what they actually were in the present or immediately past circumstances. In looking to actual figures, cost accounting is much more an 'accounting for' function than management accounting. As a result it concerns itself with far more detail than the latter function and so tends to need more space for its exposition than the other aspects of management accountancy. This allocation of space (virtually this whole book) is not, however, to be regarded as indicative of its importance. As has already been pointed out, past and present figures are only of value in predicting future figures, which are the real raw data for the management accountant.

8. Costing. Strictly speaking, cost accounting involves accounting for costs, i.e. explaining how they arose and detailing where they went. *Costing*, on the other hand, involves indicating to managers the *economic consequences of carrying out, or having carried out, any specified activity.* If a manager is, for example, considering the acceptance of a contract, he or she needs to know whether or not an adequate profit will arise from it – and if the contract is accepted, he or she will need to know how much profit was actually made (or lost) so that future actions can benefit from past experience.

From a management accounting point of view, then, our main interest in this field is in costing rather than cost accounting.

9. Cost. A cost is the value of economic resources used as a result of producing or doing the thing costed. Note the word 'value'. In a majority of cases the value of the economic resources used is the amount of money spent in acquiring or producing them, but this is not always so. For instance, if the market price of an article were £5 at the time of purchase and rose to £7 by the time it was actually used in production, then one could well say that the cost is £7, since this is the *value* of the article used.

Some people would probably disagree with this view of cost, and would regard cost as simply what was paid for an economic resource. Yet clearly in the foregoing example, if the article were sold in its unmanufactured state for £6, then £5 as the cost means there would be £1 profit. But this is not a valid measure of management's *manufacturing* performance (though it may be a good measure of their speculative performance). This simpler concept of cost relates really to measuring excess of receipts over payments, that is, we are back to the financial accounting concept of money as cash. In cost accounting one should, however, always bear in mind the ultimate need to consider economic values for measuring economic performance rather than cash expenditure. (A word of warning: costing evolved as a practical business technique. As a result the practice is not always consistent with the theory. For example, a number of methods of costing stores issues aim only to recover the amount spent on purchasing the stores and not to show the value of the issues (*see* 2: **16–21**).)

10. Cost = usage × price. Cost has been defined as 'the value of economic resources used'. Note that for each resource the 'value' is always made up of two components: the units of the resource used and the resource price per unit. Cost, therefore, can be mathematically stated as:

$$\text{Cost} = \text{usage} \times \text{price}.$$

This means that costing involves ascertaining both a usage figure and a price figure. Students will find this double-component value arises throughout costing theory, and it is particularly significant in standard costing and variance analysis.

It should, incidentally, be appreciated that in costing it is the economic resources used that are really important – multiplying by price to give cost is only the conversion to the common denominator of money. Improvement by management of economic performance hinges on the more economical use of resources or the substitution of cheaper resources for more expensive resources. A management accountant should never forget, then, that it is the *resources* underlying the £ figures that are really significant.

11. Cost units. We cannot have 'costs' unless there are things being costed (such as cars, theatre performances, forests or herds of cows) and when these are the things that the enterprise or department is set up to provide, then such 'things' are termed 'cost units'. A cost unit, then, can be defined as *a unit of quantity of produce, service or time in relation to which costs may be ascertained or expressed.* These cost units may be:

(*a*) units of production, e.g. cars, tonnes of material, litres of liquid, books, pairs of shoes, construction contracts;

(*b*) units of service, e.g. kilowatt-hours, cinema seats, passenger-miles, consultancy hours.

NOTE: Students should learn and understand this definition as the term is frequently used in costing. In most cases cost units are simply the individual items of production, and provided the wider meaning (e.g. service units) is appreciated, students may regard them as such for study purposes.

12. Cost centres. Costs can relate to things other than cost units. They can refer to individual parts of the enterprise. Such parts can range from an entire factory (in the case of a company with a group of factories) down to a single machine or salesperson. *Any part of an enterprise to which costs can be charged* is called a *cost centre.* A cost centre can be:

(*a*) *geographical*, i.e. an area such as a department, store-yard or sales area;

(*b*) *an item of equipment*, e.g. a lathe, fork-lift truck or delivery vehicle;

(*c*) *a person*, e.g. a salesperson.

Charging costs to a cost centre simply involves charging to that centre those costs which relate to it. Thus a lathe can be charged with the cost of its depreciation, maintenance, power and cleaning and also with a share of the rent, rates and heat and light costs of the enterprise.

13. Current, past and sunk costs. Costs are sometimes quite subtle concepts. At this point it is necessary to distinguish between three kinds of 'costs', namely:

(*a*) *Current cost.* A current cost is one you incur as you carry out an activity. Thus, if you are paying someone £4 an hour to carry out an activity your current cost is £4 per hour.

(*b*) *Past cost.* A past cost is one you incurred in the past but which still has benefit or value to you. Thus, if last month you paid a man £40 on the understanding he would supply you this month with 10 hours work then the work he does this month carries a past cost of £4 per hour.

(*c*) *Sunk cost.* A sunk cost is one you incurred in the past and which now has no benefit or value to you. So if the man to whom you paid £40 last month fulfils his contract by digging a hole so that you can put down the foundations for a heavy machine, then (since a hole in the ground has no benefit or value in itself) the cost is a sunk cost.

Note that a cost can be both a past and a sunk cost, depending on the circumstances. Fixed assets almost always fall into this category for if you paid £10,000 for a machine that would last ten years, then each year you use the machine you incur a past cost of (have benefit worth) £1,000, but if the day you bought it you find you have no work for it and can only re-sell it for £3,000, you are faced with a sunk cost of £7,000. Generally speaking, past costs enter performance measurement and sunk costs enter decision making (or, to put it in its more usual form, only the re-sale value of a past cost is used to make decisions – sunk costs being ignored). This distinction, of course, is paralleled in accountancy by the distinction between the going-concern historical cost value of an asset and its realizable value.

14. Cost data as building bricks. Unlike most financial accounting data, cost data is not destined for a single accounting statement. In financial accounting an expenditure of £4 on a tin of paint would, for instance, normally simply form part of the 'purchases' figure in the profit and loss account and nothing else. In a costing system, however, the £4 could appear as a charge to the stores, to the cost centre using it, to the cost unit or activity on which it was used, and perhaps also to the persons who authorized its purchase and use respectively. In costing, then, each element of cost data – and the elements should be kept as small as is reasonably possible – is to be regarded as a building brick which is available to construct statement 'buildings' of whatever design is required. These bricks, moreover, are re-usable for as many occasions as is required.

15. Methods and techniques. The different ways of arranging cost data fall into two main categories: methods and techniques (*see* Fig. 1.1).

(*a*) Cost *methods* depend upon *the nature of production*. There are really only two basic ways, one where production results in cost units that are different from each other and the other where the cost units are all identical (*see* 6: **8** and **9**).

(*b*) Cost *techniques* depend upon *the purpose for which management require the information*. Management need information for a variety of purposes, such as control, decision-making, predicting profits and price determination, and the exact purpose determines the technique to be used.

16. Basic costing principles.

(*a*) *A cost should be related as closely as possible to its cause.* A foreman's salary, for instance, cannot usually be pinned down to a single cost unit, but it should be recorded in such a way that the cost can be shared only among the cost units passing through that foreman's department and not among any units remaining outside his department. This relating of cost to cause, pinning the cost down so that it covers neither more nor less than the cost units or cost centres which caused it, is an important aspect of good costing. Grouping overheads into one single 'general expenses' category is to be avoided.

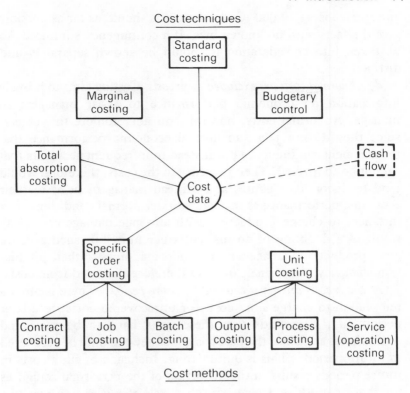

Figure 1.1 *Costing methods and techniques*

(*b*) *A cost is not to be charged until it is incurred.* This appears obvious, but is often forgotten. For instance, care should be taken that a cost unit is not charged with any selling costs while it is still in the factory, since units cannot incur selling costs until they are sold. Similarly, when the cost of lost units must be carried by good units such a charge cannot be imposed on units which have not passed the point of loss.

(*c*) *The 'prudence' convention should be ignored.* One of the historical functions of accounting is to value assets conservatively in order to avoid the risk of paying dividends out of capital. This results in the 'prudence' convention of accounting. This convention must be ignored in cost accounting, otherwise there is a danger than management appraisal of the profitability of projects may be vitiated. For instance, to fail to take advantage of a project which would in the event net £20,000 means that in effect the enterprise loses £20,000. Cost statements should as far as possible give the facts with no known bias. If a contingency sum needs to be taken into consideration it should be shown separately and distinctly.

(d) *Abnormal costs are excluded from costs.* Costing aims to provide information on economic performance to assist managers to manage. Abnormal costs, however, do not promote this object, since they do not relate to normal economic performance that management can influence but instead to infrequent accidents that cannot be controlled. Their presence in the costs, therefore, would tend to distort cost figures and mislead management as to their economic performance as managers under normal conditions. For instance, to charge Production with any gale damage costs may result in a doubling of normal costs per unit, but such a figure gives production managers no real information as to their production efficiency. Abnormal costs are therefore excluded from costs.

(e) *Sunk costs are never charged to future periods.* There is often a temptation to charge sunk costs, or unrecovered costs, to a later period on the grounds that these costs have to be recovered somewhere, and since the past has gone they can only be recovered in future periods. This is quite wrong. Inclusion of sunk costs in future periods results in the distortion of the performance figures for those periods and gives rise to a risk of misleading management. This, of course, does not mean that a past cost cannot be charged to a future period. If the object of a costing exercise is to *measure performance* then the benefit of any past cost should be brought in to the analysis. For instance, you cannot accurately measure this month's performance of a sales manager if you ignore the fact that he or she has the benefit of a £1M advertising campaign incurred the previous month – even though for *decision-making* the whole of the £1M is sunk.

(f) *Profit appropriations are excluded from costs.* In costing, profit appropriations are always excluded from the costs. Thus, dividends and taxes arising from profits are never included in costing statements. This is because such appropriations are not deemed economic resources which are consumed by an activity. But, again, in the case of *decision-making* it sometimes happens that different alternatives do not have the same tax incidence (e.g. different types of capital outlays may result in different capital allowances) and since management accounting is concerned with economic consequences, the consequential taxes must be shown on the comparative statements that detail the alternatives. (It should, incidentally, be noted that traditionally *interest* is also treated as a profit appropriation.)

17. Classification of costs. There are numerous ways of classifying costs, the way chosen being determined by the purpose for which they are required. In a well-organized system of cost accounting it should always be easy to re-classify costs when desired, since it is rare (and inefficient) to prepare costs for one purpose only. The following are the main forms of classification:

(*a*) *Direct and indirect costs.* All costs fall into one of the two categories of direct and indirect costs.

(*i*) A *direct cost* may be defined as a cost that arises *solely* from the existence of whatever is being costed. With a direct cost there can be no suggestion of sharing the cost between the things being costed. If the individual 'thing' – cost unit, cost centre or whatever – being costed had not existed the cost would not have arisen at all.

(*ii*) An *indirect cost* does not depend solely on what is being costed. It therefore implies some element of sharing a cost that is common to or jointly incurred by two or more things being costed. When the things being costed are cost units, indirect costs can also be referred to as *overheads*.

This distinction between direct and indirect costs will be taken up again later (*see* Chapter 4), but it should be noted in passing that the definitions refer to 'whatever is being costed'. If departments, sales areas or even customer classifications are being costed, then the definitions should be applied with these in mind. For example, a departmental manager's salary is a direct cost if the department is being costed, though indirect if costing the cost units in the department. However, the terms direct and indirect costs are used far more often in relation to the costing of cost units, and so, unless the context clearly indicates differently, they should normally be regarded as relating to cost units.

(*b*) *Nature.* A further classification relates to the nature of the costs (i.e. what they are), the basic categories here being material, labour and expenses. These three categories can be further broken down as required, e.g. material can be subdivided into raw materials, components and maintenance materials, etc.; labour into supervision, cleaning and clerical work, etc.; and expenses into rent, power, depreciation, postage, etc.

(*c*) *Function.* Costs may also be classified according to the function to which they relate, typical categories being production, selling, distribution, administration, finance, and research and development. The category into which a given cost should be placed under this system of classification is sometimes uncertain. This is not particularly important: classification of costs by function is a traditional classification and is becoming less and less significant in modern costing, as the entire business process is rapidly becoming a single, integrated function. (For instance, if the sales manager insists on the factory placing an elaborate name plate on the product which acts mainly as a form of advertisement, is the cost of affixing this plate a production cost or a selling cost? The distinction is neither possible nor important.)

18. Elements of costs. Traditionally the cost of a cost unit can be regarded as being built up of a number of elements of cost. Such a build-up can be shown diagrammatically as follows:

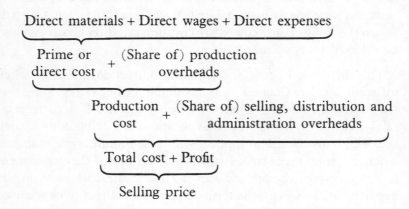

The definitions of these terms are as follows.

(*a*) *Direct materials.* Materials that actually become part of the cost unit.

(*b*) *Direct wages.* Wages paid to employees for the time they are engaged in working on the direct materials.

(*c*) *Direct expenses.* Expenses incurred specifically on behalf of the cost unit.

NOTE: The traditional term given to the sum of these three direct costs is *prime cost*.

(*d*) *Production overheads.* Overheads incurred in production, i.e. generally speaking, overheads incurred within the four walls of the factory proper.

(*e*) *Selling overheads.* Overheads incurred in inducing customers to place orders.

(*f*) *Distribution overheads.* Overheads incurred in getting finished production from the factory to the customer. It includes warehouse, packing and transport costs.

(*g*) *Administration overheads.* Overheads incurred in managing the enterprise. It includes top management costs, accounts, legal and (usually) personnel department costs, audit fees and other such general enterprise costs.

(*h*) *Profit.* The difference between the selling price and the total cost.

NOTE: This profit is not quite the same as the accountant's profit (which means the amount available for appropriation), since the total cost does *not* include an allowance for abnormal costs (*see* 16(*d*)), unrecovered sunk costs (*see* 16(*e*)), unabsorbed overheads (*see* 5: 23(*c*)), discounts and bank charges (*see* 4: 7) and interest (*see* 16).

These definitions represent the traditional concept of costs, and differ slightly from the more modern concept. For instance, a salesperson's commission for selling a cost unit would be regarded as a selling overhead in the above definitions, but in modern costing it would be classed as a direct cost.

It should be appreciated that the above scheme relates only to costing cost units and that cost accounting extends far beyond this traditional task.

General considerations

19. Cost and management accounting reports. Whatever invaluable data accountants may collect, whatever inspired ideas they may have, unless they can present the data and their conclusions in a lucid and meaningful manner they will have wasted their time. And it should be appreciated that the onus of effective reporting is wholly on the person reporting – not the person reported to.

NOTE: Examination questions frequently call for a report and to assist the student to deal with this form of question, Appendix I includes an outline on how to write such a report.

20. Reliability of cost data. Cost accountants should never forget that data relating to actual circumstances may not always be reliable. Much of it comes from the shop-floor – time-sheets, material requisitions, material returned notes, transfer notes, piecework tickets and scrap returns – and it should be appreciated that many shop-floor employees:

(*a*) are not clerks, nor are they really paid for their clerical ability;

(*b*) rarely have good clerical facilities (either office desks or even proper pencils);

(*c*) often regard paperwork as an unnecessary obstacle to 'getting the job out' (it should be noted, however, that the accountant who thinks the paperwork should have priority makes an even graver error);

(*d*) often have to record information from memory, because no written reference exists or because it is not at hand;

(*e*) may deliberately falsify the data.

This last possibility may be common where time-sheets are involved, particularly if an incentive scheme is in operation. Two points should be noted here. Firstly, if management uses a single record for both computing bonuses and preparing costs, it cannot really complain if the employees use them as instruments to maximize their bonuses in preference to recording accurate cost information. Secondly, attempts to enforce accurate time-recording usually prove abortive; loopholes are almost invariably found unless the scheme is so elaborate that it is uneconomic.

In view of such possible unreliability in much of their basic data, accountants must be cautious about jumping to conclusions from such data. For instance, when booking time to a mixture of small and large jobs employees may easily forget they worked on some small jobs. Moreover, they are conscious that their excessive time is much more noticeable on a small job than a large job involving a number of other employees. As a result, small jobs are almost always underbooked and large jobs overbooked and the accountant should allow for this.

21. Book-keeping in cost and management accounting. Neither cost accounting nor management accounting are essentially recording techniques (although in cost accounting a certain degree of recording is a prerequisite of an effective costing system). Both aim to make economic assessments of the past and future activities of the enterprise in which they are practised, and these assessments rarely call for any formal accounting procedure. However, some such formal procedure, even if it is kept to a minimum, is usually necessary because:

(*a*) certain valuations form part of the final accounts of the enterprise (e.g. stock and work-in-progress) and it is desirable that these should be linked with the enterprise accounts;

(*b*) it is desirable on occasions to ensure that all the costs incurred by the enterprise have been incorporated into the cost and management analyses (e.g. in cost and profit control).

The book-keeping associated with the two subjects will, therefore, be discussed occasionally in this book. The technique adopted will be that of conventional double entry, partly because this form will be most familiar to the student but more importantly because this is the form needed for the examinations. It should, perhaps, be observed that the system of database accounting should soon become widespread, although it is suspected that examiners will continue to require a knowledge of double-entry methods for some time yet.

22. Historical cost. The student should note in passing that the adjective 'historical' when applied to a cost (or any other term in the field of cost accounting) merely indicates that past actual amounts are being referred to.

23. Profitability and productivity. These are two terms used in the measurement of economic performance which are frequently misunderstood, but which it is vital for the cost accountant to understand thoroughly. The important thing to note is that they are *relative* measures and so must not be confused with profit and production, which are *absolute* measures.

(a) *Profitability*. When we use the concept of profitability we are concerned only with which of two or more alternatives is the *more* profitable. Note that we do *not* need to find the profit from each alternative to do this. For example, if an article can be sold to A for £40 or to B for £50, then, other things being equal, it is clearly more profitable to sell to B. This is true whatever the costs are (provided they are the same in either case), and so we know which alternative is the more profitable without knowing the profit to be earned from either. Indeed, even if the costs exceed £50 (so that we make a loss either way) it is still more 'profitable' to sell to B since this results in a smaller loss than selling to A. Profitability, then, is a relative measure – it indicates the *most profitable alternative*. Profit, on the other hand, is an absolute measure – it indicates the overall amount of profit earned by a transaction or enterprise.

(b) *Productivity*. Productivity is a ratio of economic output to economic input, i.e.:

$$\text{Productivity} = \frac{\text{Economic output}}{\text{Economic input}}$$

Thus if the same goods can be produced (i.e. output unchanged) for less labour hours (i.e. input reduced) then productivity has increased. Note that in this example the *production* has remained unchanged although the productivity has altered, and indeed it is obviously possible for production to fall while productivity increases (e.g. if output drops by 20 per cent but labour hours drop by 30 per cent).

Although discussions on productivity usually revolve round labour hours, the input can be any economic resource. For example, if one is considering those resources the consumption of which remains unaltered for small changes of output (e.g. land), then an increase in output clearly leads to increased productivity (since the input remains constant in this respect). Actually, of course, a number of input factors usually change from one situation to another so a common denominator is again required to enable the different forms of consumption to be added together. Hence more sophisticated productivity measurements tend to use the formula: productivity = output/cost (i.e. output per £ cost), while situations where the forms of output themselves differ and change require a sales/cost type of formula.

24. Conversion cost and added value. These two terms can relate to any aspect of costing and need to be carefully distinguished.

(*a*) *Conversion cost* is the cost of converting raw materials to the finished state, or to the next stage of production. It includes direct wages, direct expenses and production overheads.

(*b*) *Added value* is the market value of a product less the costs of bought-out materials and services.

The main difference between conversion cost and added value is that added value includes profit. The importance of this concept can be seen if one appreciates that the function of an enterprise is to take economic resources in the form of raw materials and services and create utilities having as great a value as possible. Added value measures the increase in value of the resources used as a result of the creation of such utilities.

Use of computers in cost accounting

25. Strengths of a computer. A computer is:

(*a*) *very fast.* With a computer all calculations, even the most complex, can be carried out with great rapidity. You do not have to wait very long for answers even though the computer is called upon to perform calculations on thousands of items of data (as in the case of a payroll).

(*b*) *untiring.* A computer can be run day and night without any loss of effectiveness. This enables it to process considerable amounts of work.

(*c*) *very accurate.* Only a computer that is malfunctioning generates errors – and these are almost always so bizarre that the malfunction is immediately observable.

(*d*) *discerning.* Providing it has been programmed properly, a computer can make comparisons between elements in the data it is given and, on the basis of such comparisons, direct itself into whichever procedure is appropriate in the circumstances of the moment.

26. Weaknesses of a computer. On the other hand a computer has the following weaknesses:

(*a*) *Data invisibility.* Computer data is invisible – except on a specific order to print it on paper or display it on a VDU. This means that any search for data outside the established procedure is rather like looking, blindfolded, for a randomly placed needle in a monstrous haystack of near-infinite dimensions.

(*b*) *Liability to breakdown.* Because of their considerable power, computers are often given immense workloads. As a result a computer breakdown can create major problems – particularly if a deadline is involved (e.g. a payroll). Moreover, arising from weakness (*a*) it can mean that with a breakdown not only the means to process data is lost but also, to all intents and purposes, the data may be lost, too, since it cannot be retrieved from the system.

(*c*) *Program incomprehensibility.* It is astonishing how incomprehensible a program can look – even to its creator. Should it prove necessary to amend the program then in the absence of very comprehensive program documentation the task will be found to be on a par with correctly positioning all the available pieces of a jigsaw in which half the pieces are missing.

(*d*) *Training requirements.* Since computers have to be precisely instructed – either in terms of programming or in terms of keyboard operations – poor training can lead to a non-operating computer system.

(*e*) *Information swamping.* In the past, management has tended to suffer from too little information. Now it may find that the useful information computers can provide may be swamped by masses of trivia. More does not mean better when it comes to information and since a computer has no innate ability to decide what is useful and what is not, it must be intelligently programmed to supply only relevant information.

27. Computer packages. For the majority of standard computer applications there exist *packages* which are no more than prewritten programs that can be bought. With a package and its documentation it should be possible for relatively inexperienced personnel to run very complex programs. Such packages in the majority of cases involve either spread-sheets or databases.

(*a*) *Spread-sheets.* These are programs which in effect create a table out of the user's data. Each column and row can carry such titles as the user gives them and each entry is either an entered value or is computed from already entered data according to such a formula as the user designates. Column and row totalling is automatically carried out and the totals entered on the spreadsheet. A feature of these programs is that a change of any entry by the user results in a re-computation of the whole table. The table, incidentally, is not limited to the dimension of the computer's VDU – indeed, the table really exists in the computer's memory and the VDU merely displays that section of the overall table that the user directs it to.

(b) *Databases*. A database program is one that holds units of data in its memory, each unit carrying pieces of information. Once a database has been created the user can extract required information relating to all units which hold a specified piece of information (e.g. the names of all debtors owing over £1,000) or can combine the information relating to each unit in a prescribed way (e.g. draw a graph showing how the total stock value of any specified class of stores has changed over the months).

28. Packages v. own programming. Whereas a package probably exists for any computer for any common application (e.g. payroll, debtors ledger, job costing), they can never, despite the ingenious adaptability built into them by their designers, do anything which they are not programmed to do. And so cost accountants who want something a little different will find that they are left to their own skills. It is then that it is necessary for accountants to be able to design their own programs – and, if they do not write them themselves, to have them written by one of their staff. There is no doubt that the need to design one's own programs brings a fresh approach to the solution of old problems. Indeed, methods which would never be viable manually become absurdly simple with a computer. For example, the assumption in budgeting that for interest computations cash is received or paid at the month end can be dispensed with and the daily budgeted amounts can be incorporated instead in a simple program. So, if interest is 12 per cent per annum nominal, i.e. effectively 0.0310537 per cent per day, £3,225 is banked for the first four days of any week in the year with £4,500 on the fifth day – when simultaneously £13,500 is withdrawn – then the program X = 1.000310537: FOR W = 1 TO 52: FOR D = 1 TO 4: S = S*X + 3225: NEXT D: S = S*X + 4500 – 13500: S = S*X↑2: NEXT W: PRINT S will display the year-end cash balance on the basis that interest is calculated on the daily balance.

Here for each of 52 weeks and for each of 4 days in each week, the computer updates the current balance, S, by one day's interest and then adds the usual day's receipts – and then, after updating the balance again, it adds the fifth day's receipts less the weekly payments before updating the balance by the two remaining days of the week.

Currently, computer development is at the railway train stage of transport. Just as catching a train is both the simplest, most comfortable, and, over distances of 100–200 miles, usually the quickest method of travel, so packages are the simplest, most comfortable and, within limits, quickest methods of solution. However, like trains, they lack flexibility and just as motor transport has far greater flexibility at the cost of greater effort, so writing one's own programs gives greater flexibility but again only as the result of greater effort. And just as one looks at train timetables to see where trains go to, so accountants look up package lists to see what packages do (and, like railway timetables, a few months see these lists become very out of date). However, computers will really come of age in cost accounting only when cost accountants design the majority of their own programs.

29. Conclusion. As indicated, this is about as much space as can be given to the topic of computers in a book on the principles of cost accounting. As you read the book, however, you should reflect on how a computer could be of assistance for the topic being studied. And to help you see the role of the computer in such circumstances, here and there short programs that incorporate the procedures under discussion will be given.

Progress test 1

Principles
1. How does money take on a dual role? (**1**)
2. How do financial, management and cost accounting divide up in practice? (**3**)
3. What is the basic principle of data selection and arrangement? (**7**)
4. What two components are always found in a cost? (**10**)
5. Why is cost data often unreliable? (**20**)

6. Distinguish between: (*a*) cost unit and cost centre; (**11, 12**) (*b*) current cost, past cost and sunk cost; (**13**) (*c*) direct and indirect cost; (**17**(*a*)) (*d*) profit and profitability; (**23**(*a*)) (*e*) production and productivity. (**23**(*b*))

7. Define: (*a*) cost; (**9**) (*b*) direct materials and direct wages; (**18**) (*c*) prime cost; (**18**) (*d*) historical cost; (**22**) (*e*) conversion cost; (**24**(*a*)) (*f*) added value. (**24**(*b*))

8. What costing principles do the terms 'prudence', 'abnormal', 'appropriations' and 'sunk' call to your mind? (**16**)

9. What are the strengths and weaknesses of computers when used in cost accounting? (**25, 26**)

10. Distinguish between spread-sheets and databases. (**27**)

Part one

Cost ascertainment

2

Cost data: materials

Before any cost methods or techniques can be examined it is necessary to be fully conversant with the different types of cost data. It must always be remembered that a cost statement can never be more accurate or reliable than the cost data upon which it is based. Appreciation of the sources of such data and the background from which they originate is a vital part of the cost accountant's know-how.

Acquisition and issue of materials

The sources of cost data relating to materials lie almost wholly in the documents and routines relating to the acquisition and issue of materials.

1. **Purchase and receipts routines.** The routines which are commonly followed when purchasing and receiving materials can be summarized as follows:

(a) *Purchase initiated.* A purchase is initiated when one of the following events occurs.

(i) The level of a material held in stock falls below its reorder level (*see* 5(c)).

(ii) The production control department foresees the need for a material not held in stock.

(iii) A departmental manager requires a material not held in stock in order to run the department.

(b) *Purchase requisition raised.* Any person requiring materials raises a requisition requesting the purchase office to purchase the wanted materials. This document is called a *purchase requisition* (not to be confused with a materials requisition, *see* 2(b)).

(c) *Purchase order raised.* On receipt of the purchase requisition the purchasing officer selects a suitable supplier and sends a *purchase order* which is simply an order to a supplier to supply specified materials.

(d) *Goods received note raised.* On receipt of the materials a *goods received note* is raised by the goods inwards department recording all details relating to the receipt of the materials. This document may also incorporate an *inspection note* which details the results of any inspection made of the materials.

(e) *Invoice passed for payment.* On receipt of the supplier's invoice, it is:

(i) checked against the purchase order to ensure that the invoiced materials are as ordered;

(ii) checked against the goods received note to ensure the invoiced materials have been received;

(iii) checked to ensure prices, discounts and computations are all correct.

After this the invoice is 'passed for payment' and in due course the supplier is paid.

2. Stores receipt and issue routines. The routines which are commonly followed when receiving and issuing materials in a store can be summarized as follows.

(a) *Materials received in stores.* The goods inwards department forwards the materials received from the supplier to the stores together with a copy of the goods received note. The materials are then suitably stored and the receipt recorded on the appropriate materials stores record card (*see* 3).

(b) *Materials issued.* Anyone requiring materials from the stores raises a *materials requisition* which details the materials wanted. This requisition is then exchanged for the materials, and the issue recorded on the appropriate stores record card. It should be appreciated that a materials requisition is a key document in virtually all costing systems and that it is both:

(*i*) an authorization to issue materials; and
(*ii*) a record of usage.

(*c*) *Materials returned.* The return of any materials to stores should be accompanied by a *materials returned note* which is, in effect, a 'reverse' materials requisition, usually of identical design but coloured differently (generally red) to aid rapid identification.

3. Stores record cards and bin cards. The most important records in a stores are as follows.

(*a*) *Stores record cards.* These are cards prepared for *each item of material* and they normally show:

(*i*) full identification of the material and its location in the stores;

(*ii*) quantities on order, received, issued, reserved and free together with a running balance of the quantity in stock;

(*iii*) prices and values of all receipts and issues;

(*iv*) all material control quantities (*see* 5).

(*b*) *Bin cards.* These are cards prepared for *each bin* or other storage location so that the material held there can be identified and the quantity quickly ascertained. The data recorded is, therefore, usually limited to:

(*i*) the location code of the bin;

(*ii*) full identification of the material;

(*iii*) the receipts, issues and remaining balance of the material held in that location.

It should be appreciated that as there may be two or more bins for the same material (one at the front of the stores for ease of issue and others at the back to hold the bulk supplies) the same material may appear on more than one bin card, though never on more than one stores record card.

4. Stores control. It is very important that management avoids both the costs of overstocking (e.g. interest on the capital unnecessarily tied up) and the costs of understocking (e.g. profit on orders lost because of failure to deliver). To this end control quantities are predetermined for each item of material and recorded on the stores record cards. By basing all purchasing action on these quantities the stock levels of all items can be held between acceptable limits.

5. Stores control quantities. The four most important control quantities are as follows.

(*a*) *Maximum level.* The maximum level of a given material is the maximum quantity that may be held in store. It is essentially an uppermost limit that the buyer must ensure is not exceeded (unless an excess is specifically authorized by higher management; for example, when unusually favourable purchasing conditions arise). It is set after consideration of:

    (*i*) rate of consumption;
    (*ii*) risks of obsolescence;
    (*iii*) risks of deterioration;
    (*iv*) costs of storing above-normal stocks;
    (*v*) storage space available.

(*b*) *Minimum level.* The minimum level is the lowest level to which stocks should fall. It is essentially a *buffer stock* which will not normally be touched. In the event of any item falling to its minimum level management is immediately alerted and the acquisition of new supplies given top priority. It is set after consideration of:

    (*i*) rate of consumption;
    (*ii*) the time required in a top priority situation to acquire enough supplies to avoid a production stoppage.

(*c*) *Reorder level.* The reorder level is the level at which a purchase requisition is made out (*see* **1**(*b*)). The level selected is such that, in the normal course of events, by reordering when the stock falls to the reorder level, *new supplies will be received just before the minimum level is reached.* It is set after consideration of:

    (*i*) rate of consumption;
    (*ii*) minimum level;
    (*iii*) delivery time;
    (*iv*) variations in delivery time.

(*d*) *Reorder quantity.* The reorder quantity is the quantity to be reordered in normal circumstances. By setting this quantity the buyer is saved the task of recalculating how much he should buy each time he orders. He may, of course, disregard this order quantity if he deems circumstances warrant it. It is set after consideration of:

(i) rate of consumption;

(ii) cost of holding stock as against cost of purchasing (the quantity that minimizes the sum of these costs is termed the *economic order quantity* and is discussed in **28–33** below);

(iii) bulk discounts;

(iv) transport costs (half a load involves virtually the same transport costs as a whole load);

(v) obsolescence and deterioration risks.

6. Two-bin and periodic review systems. Reordering of materials can be initiated using one of the following two systems:

(a) *Two-bin.* This is the most usual system, described in 5(c), where materials are reordered when their levels fall to predetermined reorder levels.

(b) *Periodic review.* Under the periodic review system material balances are inspected on a schedule basis (i.e. at pre-determined periodic intervals) and if a balance indicates the probability of running out of stock before the next review plus lead-time span of time then the material is reordered. The *advantage* of this method is that reordering is spread more equally over the working days than in the case of the two-bin system under which it is possible for a large number of reorder levels to be reached more or less simultaneously. The *disadvantage* is that materials tend to be ordered sooner (to avoid the risk of stocks becoming dangerously low before the stock balances are reviewed again) so that the average stock held is a little higher than under the two-bin system.

7. Reserved and free stock. There are sometimes occasions when it is necessary to reserve some items of stock for specified future production. Where this is so it is important that a careful note of the reserved stock is made on the stores record card in such a way that the quantity of unreserved *free* stock is known at any time. It is, of course, this free stock that is subject to the control levels.

To illustrate the workings on such a record card assume that on

6 May and June respectively 1,200 units are reserved for a special job, issues of 800 units being made to this job on 1 June, July and August. The reorder level is 1,200 units.

The following is a typical record incorporating these details within the ordinary receipts and issues record:

Date	Receipts	Issues	Reserved	Balance Free stock	
1 April	Opening balance			1,500	
20 April		700	–	800	(Reorder)
1 May	2,500		–	3,300	
6 May			1,200	2,100	(Free stock reduced by reservation)
25 May		1,000	1,200	1,100	(Reorder)
1 June		800	400	1,100	(Issue made from reserved stock)
6 June			400 ⎫ 1,200 ⎭	– 100*	(Free stock reduced by reservation)
8 June		500	1,600	– 600*	
15 June	2,500		1,600	1,900	
1 July		800	800	1,900	(Issue made from reserved stock)
15 July		500	800	1,400	
1 August		800	–	1,400	(Issue made from reserved stock)

*There is of course, no negative holding of stock. All the minuses indicate is that issues to 'free stock' work have been made from the reserved stock, the 100 and 600 following the minuses respectively showing the extents to which the reserved stocks have been depleted.

Note that the sum of the free stock and the reserved stock gives the total actual number of units in the store.

Under an alternative method of accounting the materials on order are included in the free stock. It is a matter of personal preference which method is selected but the one illustrated here does have the advantage of showing as free stock material which is immediately available.

8. Pareto (80/20) phenomenon. In a stores one will very often observe that a minority of materials comprise the bulk of the stores value – indeed, frequently to the extent that some 80 per cent of the stores value can be attributed to around a mere 20 per cent of the materials (e.g. in a store of 20 different materials worth

£50,000, just 4 materials could have a value of £40,000). This imbalance is referred to as the Pareto (or, for obvious reasons, the 80/20) phenomenon. This being so, a storekeeper should not carry out his work on the basis that all types of material are equal for, clearly, a material which comprises a significantly high proportion of the total stores value must be given more attention than another the value of which is relatively insignificant.

9. Costs of storage. In setting any control figure the costs of storage should be borne in mind. These costs include the following:

(a) *Capital costs.* The loss of return which could be obtained if the capital tied up in stock were employed elsewhere usually results in this cost being the highest one of all.

(b) *Space costs* (rent, heating, lighting, etc.).

(c) *Equipment costs* (bins, racks, material handling equipment, etc.).

(d) *Personnel costs* (storing, stocktaking, security, etc.).

(e) *Insurance.*

(f) *Deterioration.*

(g) *Obsolescence.*

10. Perpetual inventory and continuous stocktaking. A system of stores recording under which the up-to-date stock balances are always known is called a *perpetual inventory* system. Where a perpetual inventory exists it is possible to carry out *continuous stocktaking*, which is the continuous taking of stock, quantities counted being checked against the perpetual inventory balances. In the operation of the system a few items are checked each day so that all items are checked two or three times a year. Continuous stocktaking can often render the usual annual stocktaking unnecessary since if it confirms the accuracy of the perpetual inventory balances then at the year end those balances can be taken as the actual stock figures.

Continuous stocktaking has a number of important advantages over annual stocktaking. These include the facts that since there is less time pressure counting and identification is more accurate and also that any failure in the stores system is disclosed much sooner.

11. Stock turnover. It is of considerable value to managers if they can devise measures of the efficiency of their stockholding practices. One such measure is *stock turnover* which can be computed as the *ratio of average stock held to annual usage*. For instance, if 1,000 units of a material are used each year and on average 200 units are held in stock, then the stock turnover is five times a year, i.e. the average stock in effect is used and replenished five times in a year. Clearly, the higher the stock turnover, the better this is (providing expensive stock-outs do not result) since the less the material held in stock the lower the stockholding costs.

NOTE: (1) If the materials are valued then it is possible to compute the stock turnover of classes of materials by dividing the total value of the class average stock into the total value of the class annual usage. (2) Stock turnover is sometimes expressed as the length of time the average stock would last if there were no further receipts. So in the example above the stock turnover could be expressed as $200/1{,}000 \times 52 =$ just under $10\frac{1}{2}$ weeks.

Materials classification and coding

12. Classification of materials. Materials may be classified in the following groups:

(*a*) *Raw materials.* Those which are worked on in the course of manufacture (e.g. timber, sheet metal).

(*b*) *Components.* Finished parts which are attached to the product during manufacture (e.g. instruments, locks).

(*c*) *Consumable materials.* Those used in running the factory generally (e.g. soap, cotton waste, brushes).

(*d*) *Maintenance materials.* Those required for the maintenance of plant and buildings (e.g. spare parts, door hinges).

(*e*) *Tools.* All forms of tools including jigs and fixtures.

Frequently separate stores are used for some or all of these groups, though this is not essential.

13. Need for material codes. Material descriptions are often vague, e.g. 'paper-clips,' of which there are a number of different kinds, or they may be ambiguous as to their main word for the purpose of filing, e.g. should 'stepladders' be filed under 'step' or 'ladder'? Descriptions may also be very long. In order to avoid these disadvantages materials are coded. The purpose of coding may therefore be summarized as:

(a) To *avoid ambiguity* in description.

(b) To *minimize length* in description.

14. Principles of coding. A *code* has been defined as 'A system of symbols designed to be applied to a classified set of items, to give a brief accurate reference facilitating entry, collation and analysis' (CIMA Terminology). The actual form the code takes is, of course, a matter of individual choice, although there are certain basic principles that require the code to be:

(a) *Exclusive.* Each code number should relate to one type of material, and one only. There must be no duplication (e.g. if code 6666 relates to a certain size of steel rod it must not also relate to a similar size of brass rod).

(b) *Certain.* The code number must identify the material without any ambiguity or uncertainty whatsoever.

(c) *Elastic.* The code should be such that new materials can be added easily and logically.

(d) *Brief.* Large code numbers take longer to write and are more subject to error. Numbers, therefore, should be as brief as possible without violating the other principles.

(e) *Mnemonic,* if possible (i.e. assisting the memory, such as MSB for 'mild steel bar'). Mnemonic codes are both easier to remember and less subject to error.

(f) *Computer friendly.* Because computers are almost invariably used for stores accounting it is necessary to ensure that the coding is in the form that facilitates computer data-processing. On the whole, most typical codes meet this requirement although sometimes a computer does need each section of the code to be of a fixed length. Also one should remember that computers cannot see conceptual relationships between codes or descriptions, e.g. if it were looking at 'nuts, almond' it would consider 'nuts, brass' to be more closely related than 'nuts, brazil' since alphabetically 'brass' falls between 'almonds' and 'brazil'.

15. Coding material sizes. One of the more confusing aspects of material classification arises because a number of material items may be identical in every respect other than dimension. Thus there may be a whole range of copper flat sections in a store running from $1 \text{ m} \times 1 \text{ cm} \times 2.5 \text{ cm}$ to $3 \text{ m} \times 3 \text{ cm} \times 10 \text{ cm}$. To enable an exclusive, certain, elastic and mnemonic system to be employed a code can be such that the final digits incorporate these dimensions. For example, if all section lengths increased in 10 cm steps, thicknesses in 0.25 cm steps, and widths in 0.5 cm steps, then the first two digits of the code can be used to indicate the length by stating the number of 10 cm steps that make up the length. Similarly the second two digits can indicate the thickness in 0.25 cm steps and the final two the width in 0.5 cm steps. Our smaller size section, the $1 \text{ m} \times 1 \text{ cm} \times 2.5 \text{ cm}$, will, therefore, be coded 100405 and our largest, the $3 \text{ m} \times 3 \text{ cm} \times 10 \text{ cm}$, will be 301220. (The student should check that this code *is*, with respect to dimensions, exclusive, certain, elastic and mnemonic as claimed above.)

Pricing stores issues

When pricing stores issues (i.e. charging out materials issued from store) there is always the problem as to whether the original purchase price or the immediate current price should be used. In times of inflation there is a danger that by using the original purchase price when costing a product the profit *from manufacturing* will be confused with the *paper profit* arising as a result of charging materials bought much earlier at a low price to a product whose market price reflects the newly inflated material price. If a radio is bought for £100 and the price then rises to £110, to sell it for £110 does not really bring in a £10 profit, since if the radio is to be replaced in stock this £10 cannot be distributed as a dividend. (This replacement involves no expansion, only a return to the original stock position.) If, on the other hand, issues are priced at current (replacement) prices many people may argue that this is not costing, since the original cost price is not being used.

This dilemma has led to a number of methods of pricing stores issues, all aimed at some form of compromise. The six most important of these are: FIFO; LIFO; simple average; weighted average; replacement price; standard price. Using the basic data given in Fig. 2.1, so that the methods can be compared, these six are discussed and illustrated below.

Issue price method	Date	RECEIPTS			ISSUES			BALANCE	
		Quantity	Price £	Value £	Quantity	Price £	Value £	Quantity	Value £
FIFO	1/1	200 ~~100~~	10.25	2,050				200	2,050
	23/1	150 ~~120~~ 20	12.00	1,800				350	3,850
	4/2				100	10.25	1,025	250	2,825
	16/2				130[1]		1,385	120	1,440
	25/2	80	12.50	1,000				200	2,440
	4/3				100	12.00	1,200	100	1,240
LIFO	1/1	200 ~~120~~ 100	10.25	2,050				200	2,050
	23/1	150 ~~50~~	12.00	1,800				350	3,850
	4/2				100	12.00	1,200	250	2,650
	16/2				130[2]		1,420	120	1,230
	25/2	~~80~~	12.50	1,000				200	2,320
	4/3				100[3]		1,205	100	1,025
Weighted average	1/1	200	10.25	2,050				200	2,050
	23/1	150	12.00	1,800				350	3,850
	4/2				100	11.00	1,100	250	2,750
	16/2				130	11.00	1,430	120	1,320
	25/2	80	12.50	1,000				200	2,320
	4/3				100	11.60	1,160	100	1,160
Replacement price	1/1	200	10.25	2,050				200	
	23/1	150	12.00	1,800				350	
	4/2				100	12.25	1,225	250	Not
	16/2				130	12.50	1,625	120	used
	25/2	80	12.50	1,000				200	
	4/3				100	13.00	1,300	100	
Standard price (£12)	1/1	200	12	2,400[4]				200	2,400
	23/1	150	12	1,800[4]				350	4,200
	4/2				100	12	1,200	250	3,000
	16/2				130	12	1,560	120	1,440
	25/2	80	12	960[4]				200	2,400
	4/3				100	12	1,200	100	1,200

Figure 2.1 *Issue price methods*

The five main methods of pricing stores issues are illustrated together using the following data:

Date	Units purchased	Purchase price	Units issued	Replacement price
1/1	200	£10.25		£10.25
23/1	150	£12.00		£12.00
4/2			100	£12.25
16/2			130	£12.50
25/2	80	£12.50		£12.50
4/3			100	£13.00

(Standard price = £12)

16. FIFO (First in, first out). The FIFO method uses *the price of first batch received* for all issues until all units from this batch have been issued – after which the price of the next batch received becomes the issue price. Upon that batch being fully issued the price of the next batch received is used, and so on.

Note the following (*see* Fig. 2.1).

(*a*) The need to record units left in each batch after an issue.

(*b*) The balance cross-check: the 100 units left in stock at the end must comprise the last 80 received at £12.50 and the 20 remaining from the previous batch at £12, i.e.:

$(80 \times £12.50) + (20 \times £12)$
$$= £1,240 = \text{amount in the balance-value column.}$$

17. LIFO (Last in, first out). The LIFO method uses *the price of the last batch received* for all issues until all units from this batch have been issued, when the price of the previous batch received is used. If, however, a new delivery is received before the first batch is fully issued, the new delivery price at once becomes the 'last-in' price and is used for pricing issues until either the batch is exhausted or a new delivery received.

Note the following.

(*a*) The method can result in many batches being only partially 'written off'.

(*b*) This is a book-keeping method and must not be confused with the physical method of issue used by the store-keeper, who will always issue the oldest stock first.

(*c*) The balance cross-check (*see* Fig. 2.1): the 100 units remaining in stock must now relate to the very first batch received and

---

The figures in bold type indicate the differences in each method. Note that under the LIFO and FIFO methods the storekeeper needs to amend the RECEIPTS column continually by crossing out quantities as units are issued so that the remaining balance in respect of each individual batch of material received can be identified. For the standard price method, the unnecessary figures are italicized (*see* **21**).

NOTES:
(1) Split issue: 100 at £10.25 + 30 at £12.00.
(2) Split issue: 50 at £12.00 + 80 at £10.25.
(3) Split issue: 80 at £12.50 + 20 at £10.25.
(4) Gain or loss on purchasing written off in the accounts.

Figure 2.1 *Continued*

the value, therefore, is:

$$100 \times £10.25 = £1,025 = \text{amount in balance-value column.}$$

18. Simple average. The simple average method involves *adding all the different prices and dividing by the number of prices.* For instance, the simple average of the first two prices in Fig. 2.1 is:

$$(10.25 + 12.00) \div 2 = £11.125.$$

This is a crude and usually unsatisfactory method. If, for example, 1,000 units were bought at £1 and 1 unit at £9 the whole 1,001 units would be issued at an 'average' price of £5 each!

This method is used only where the value of the issues is trivial.

19. Weighted average. The weighted average method *averages prices after weighting (i.e. multiplying) by their quantities.* Thus, the weighted average for the first two prices in Fig. 2.1 is:

$$\frac{(10.25 \times 200) + (12 \times 150)}{350} = £11.$$

Students are sometimes puzzled as to how to calculate a weighted average where there are units already in stock, but they need only remember that the average price *at any time* is simply the *balance-value* figure divided by the *balance-units* figure, e.g. in Fig. 2.1 after the February receipt there are 200 units, value £2,320, in stock and the weighted average, therefore, is:

$$\frac{£2,320}{200} = £11.60.$$

Note the following.

(*a*) Issue prices need only be computed on the *receipt* of new deliveries, not at the time of each issue as with FIFO and LIFO.

(*b*) The balance cross-check: the 100 in stock in Fig. 2.1 is at the average price of £11.60, i.e. the value is:

$$100 \times £11.60 = £1,160 = \text{amount in balance-value column.}$$

20. Replacement price. This method simply uses *the current replacement price* to value issues. Note the following.

(*a*) The replacement price *at the time of each issue* must be found. This may involve considerable work.

(*b*) The *balance-value* column cannot be used in the same way as in the methods described above (**16–19**); such use would quickly give rise to ridiculous figures.

21. Standard price. The standard price method uses *the planned purchase (standard price) for all valuations.* Note the following.

(*a*) Purchases are also valued at standard, the gain or loss following such a valuation being written-off in the accounts.

(*b*) Since all quantities are valued at the same price, there is no need to record money figures at all (other than a single statement of the standard price). This means records can be kept in quantity only. (In Fig. 2.1 the unnecessary figures are italicized.)

(*c*) Much less clerical work is required.

(*d*) The value of the method is greatly improved if a complete system of standard costing is in operation (*see* Chapters 17–20).

22. Base stock method. This is essentially a method of *valuing stock.* It assumes that the very first purchases were made solely to provide a working buffer stock. Since in theory this 'base stock' is never issued, it is always in stock, and therefore should *appear in every stocktaking at its original cost.* Excess stock above this base stock is then valued using one of the methods discussed earlier.

It should be appreciated, incidentally, that this method of stock valuation is not acceptable under SSAP 9.

Comparison of the methods of pricing stores issues

Throughout the following comparison it should be appreciated that in the valuation of stock SSAP 9 lays down that such valuation should always be at net realizable value where this is less than cost (and, indeed, SSAP 9 should be referred to for any figures likely to form part of the enterprise's formal final accounts).

23. FIFO.

(*a*) *Advantages.*

(*i*) Realistic, i.e. based on actual physical issuing of items to the shop-floor in order of receipt.

(*ii*) Valuation of stock balance is a fair commercial valuation of stock.

(*iii*) No profits or losses arise (i.e. value of issues after allowing for stock exactly equals cost of purchases).

(b) *Disadvantages.*

(i) Cumbersome.

(ii) Issue price may not reflect current economic value.

(c) *Effect on costs.* Costs lag behind current economic values.

(d) *Effect on stock valuation.* Value based on most recently acquired items.

24. LIFO.

(a) *Advantages.*

(i) Keeps value of issues close to current economic values.

(ii) Valuation of stock balance usually very conservative.

(iii) No profits or losses arise.

(b) *Disadvantages.*

(i) Cumbersome.

(ii) Not realistic, i.e. assumes physical issue principle to be opposite of that actually followed by the storekeeper.

(iii) Valuation of stock balance is not acceptable under SSAP 9 and may not be acceptable for corporation tax assessments.

(iv) Should issues 'dip into old stock' then they will be valued at out-of-date prices.

(c) *Effect on costs.* Very slight lag only behind current economic values.

(d) *Effect on stock valuation.* Completely out of line with current values.

25. Weighted average.

(a) *Advantages.*

(i) Logical, i.e. assumes values of identical items are all equal.

(ii) Since receipts are much less frequent than issues, not so cumbersome as LIFO or FIFO.

(iii) Smooths out fluctuations in purchase price.

(iv) No profits or losses arise.

(b) *Disadvantages.*

(i) Issues may not be at current economic values.

(*ii*) Issue price is usually a fiction since it may have never existed in the market, e.g. the £11 in Fig. 2.1.

(*iii*) Issue price may run to a number of decimal places.

(*c*) *Effect on costs.* In between FIFO and LIFO.

(*d*) *Effect on stock valuation.* Usually satisfactory, though slightly out of date relative to FIFO.

26. Replacement price.

(*a*) *Advantages.*

(*i*) Issues are at current economic values.

(*ii*) Calculations are simple.

(*b*) *Disadvantages.*

(*i*) Difficult to be continually up to date with replacement prices.

(*ii*) Profits or losses arise.

(*iii*) Not a traditional 'cost' price.

(*c*) *Effect on costs.* Costs are at current economic values.

(*d*) *Effect on stock valuation.* Valuation at current economic values, but can be used only with full understanding of inflation accounting.

27. Standard price.

(*a*) *Advantages.*

(*i*) Very simple to apply.

(*ii*) Provides a check on efficiency of purchasing department.

(*iii*) Eliminates price fluctuations from costs, enabling satisfactory manufacturing cost comparisons to be made.

(*iv*) Does not change over accounting period.

(*b*) *Disadvantages.*

(*i*) Requires careful initial determination.

(*ii*) Profits and losses arise (under full standard costing this is not a disadvantage).

(*iii*) Issues may not be at current economic values.

(*iv*) Disregards price trends.

(*c*) *Effect on costs and stock valuation.* Standardized; not necessarily in line with current economic value or even past market values.

Economic order quantity

A problem that frequently faces managers responsible for the control of materials relates to the quantity of any item which should be ordered at the time of purchase.

28. The costs of purchasing and holding stock. The following two kinds of costs are always involved in a purchase order decision.

(a) *Costs of purchasing.* Making a purchase always results in costs, which include the cost of the time involved in negotiating the order and completing the paperwork, together with the costs of telephone calls, stationery, postage, etc. There are also the costs of receiving the goods on delivery. Although these costs are rarely the same each time there is a purchase, it is nevertheless often possible to compute the average cost of making a purchase.

(b) *Costs of holding stock.* Holding stock also results in costs (*see* **9**), particularly the interest cost on the money tied up in the stock held, e.g. a £100 item held for six months when the interest rate is 14 per cent will have an interest cost of £7. These stock-holding costs can often be added together and expressed collectively as an annual percentage rate of the value of the goods in stock.

29. The economic order quantity (EOQ). Clearly, these two kinds of costs vary inversely with each other over a given period of time; the smaller the quantities ordered the greater the costs of purchasing (for more purchases will need to be made during the period), but the less the costs of holding stock (as on average fewer units will be in stock) and vice versa. Equally clearly, it would be prohibitively expensive to order an item twice a day on the one hand, or only once in ten years on the other. Somewhere in between there is a point at which the total cost of purchasing and holding stock is at a minimum. The order quantity at this point is called the *economic order quantity.*

30. Illustrative figures. To illustrate the computation of an economic order quantity the following figures and symbols will be used.

Costs of placing a purchasing order (P): £5 per order.

Costs of holding stock (H): 20 per cent per annum of the value held.

Annual usage (N): 1,000 units.

Purchase price per unit (U): £20.

Order quantities will be symbolized as Q and the economic order quantity as EOQ.

31. Finding the EOQ by graphical methods. To find the EOQ by graphical methods the following steps should be taken (*see* Fig. 2.2).

(a) Prepare a graph showing:

(i) on the vertical axis, the *total annual cost of purchasing and holding stock;*

(ii) on the horizontal axis, the *range of possible order quantities.*

(b) Select a number of order quantities and compute for each the following.

(i) *The annual cost of purchasing.* This is found by multiplying the cost per purchase order (P) by the number of orders that would be placed in a year (which is the annual usage divided by the quantity ordered at each purchase, i.e. N/Q). So the purchasing cost is $P \times N/Q = PN/Q$.

(ii) *The annual cost of holding stock.* This is found by multiplying the annual cost of holding one unit in stock (HU) by the average number of units held in stock. Since it is usual for units to be withdrawn from stock at an even rate, the average stock held between the receipt of one ordered quantity and the receipt of the next is half that quantity (and so this will be the stock held on average over the year). In other words, the average stock is $\frac{1}{2}Q$, and the annual cost of holding stock is, therefore, $\frac{1}{2}Q \times HU = QHU/2$.

(iii) *The total annual cost of purchasing and holding stock.* This is found by adding the costs in (i) and (ii).

(c) Plot on the graph the total annual cost of purchasing and holding stock against each selected order quantity and draw a smooth curve through the points.

(d) Find the minimum point of this curve. This point identifies the economic order quantity (in our illustration, 50 units).

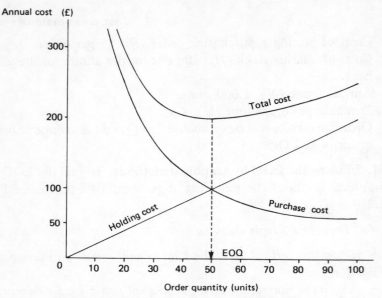

Figure 2.2 *Identifying the economic order quantity*

NOTES:

(1) Illustrative figures (*see* **30**):

$$P = £5; \quad H = 20 \text{ per cent}; \quad N = 1,000; \quad U = £20;$$
$$\therefore HU = £4 \text{ and } PN = £5,000.$$

(2) Selected point for graph (*see* **31**):

Order quantity (Q)	Purchasing $\left(\dfrac{PN}{Q}\right)$	Holding ($\frac{1}{2}QHU$)	Total
		Costs	
20	$\dfrac{£5,000}{20} = £250$	$\frac{1}{2} \times 20 \times £4 = £40$	£290
40	$\dfrac{£5,000}{40} = £125$	$\frac{1}{2} \times 40 \times £4 = £80$	£205
60	$\dfrac{£5,000}{60} = £83.3$	$\frac{1}{2} \times 60 \times £4 = £120$	£203.3
80	$\dfrac{£5,000}{80} = £62.5$	$\frac{1}{2} \times 80 \times £4 = £160$	£222.5
100	$\dfrac{£5,000}{100} = £50$	$\frac{1}{2} \times 100 \times £4 = £200$	£250

(3) So that the cost pattern can be better appreciated the purchase cost curve and the holding cost curve are both shown in addition to the total purchase and holding cost curve. Notice, incidentally, that the point where these two component curves intersect identifies the EOQ (*see* also **32**).

32. Finding the EOQ by formula. Fig. 2.2 shows that the total annual cost curve falls to a minimum at a point immediately above the intersection of the two component curves. This is no coincidence for it can be mathematically shown that the minimum total cost is achieved when the annual purchasing cost equals the annual holding cost (*see* note below). Consequently we can say that when the quantity ordered equals the economic order quantity then:

$$\frac{QHU}{2} = \frac{PN}{Q}$$

Cross-multiplying we have:

$$Q^2 HU = 2PN$$

$$\therefore Q^2 = \frac{2PN}{HU} \quad \text{and} \quad Q = \sqrt{\frac{2PN}{HU}}$$

Since HU is frequently written as S, i.e. the annual cost of holding one unit in stock for a year, the formula becomes:

$$\text{EOQ} = \sqrt{\frac{2PN}{S}}$$

Using the formula to find the economic order quantity then simply involves substituting actual values for the symbols, e.g. in the case of our illustration (where $S = HU = 20$ per cent of £20 = £4):

$$\text{EOQ} = \sqrt{\frac{2PN}{S}} = \sqrt{\frac{2 \times 5 \times 1,000}{4}} = 50 \text{ units}$$

NOTE: Students with a knowledge of differential calculus may appreciate the following proof of our initial equation above:

$$\text{Total costs} = PN/Q + QHU/2 = PNQ^{-1} + Q^1 HU/2$$
$$\therefore d(\text{Total costs})/dQ = d(PNQ^{-1} + Q^1 HU/2)/dQ$$
$$= -PNQ^{-2} + HU/2$$

The total costs are therefore minimized when $-PNQ^{-2} + HU/2 = 0$, that is, when $HU/2 = PN/Q^2$, which (after multiplying each side by Q) is when $QHU/2 = PN/Q$.

33. Limitations of the economic order quantity technique. Although a popular concept, the economic order quantity technique has distinct limitations. These include the following.

(*a*) The fact that in practice the total annual cost curve is relatively flat in the vicinity of the economic order quantity means that quite significant divergences from the quantity result in only minor cost increases. The economic order quantity, then, is by no means a critical figure.

(*b*) The actual optimum order quantity is, in fact, often much more crucially dependent on the storage space and facilities available, work-load of the purchase office, economics of delivery and overall convenience of all involved in the purchase, than it is on the potential saving of a few pounds.

(*c*) The costs of purchasing and holding stock are often difficult to quantify with any accuracy. Consequently even when the economic order quantity has been calculated there is little certainty that the result is particularly accurate.

(*d*) Changing prices or usage rates in theory require a recomputation of the economic order quantity, with the consequential need to alter all the relevant records in the purchase office and the stores office. If interest rates change then the order quantities and records of *all* materials bought and stocked will need to be changed.

(*e*) The formula presumes that the purchase of the material will continue for eternity. The shorter, then, the total time the material will be purchased the less valid the formula will be.

All in all, the technique is perhaps best used simply to check that some more convenient existing rule-of-thumb order quantity is not proving significantly more expensive than necessary.

Progress test 2

1. Outline a purchase routine. (**1**)
2. What are the functions of a materials requisition? (**2**)
3. What is the difference between a stores record card and a bin card? (**3**)
4. What factors must be considered when setting the following stores control quantities: (*a*) maximum level; (*b*) minimum level; (*c*) reorder level; (*d*) reorder quantity? (**5**)
5. Distinguish between the *two-bin* and the *periodic review* systems of material reordering. (**6**)
6. What are the costs of storage? (**9**)

7. Define: (*a*) perpetual inventory; (**10**) (*b*) continuous stocktaking; (**10**) (*c*) stock turnover. (**11**)

8. List the principles of material coding. (**14**)

9. How does the value of the stores balance differ under each of the following issue pricing methods: FIFO; LIFO; weighted average; replacement price; standard price? (**23-7**)

10. What is meant by the economic order quantity? (**29**)

11. What is the EOQ formula and what are its limitations (**32, 33**)

Practice

12. From the following data compute the value of the 20 units closing stock under (*a*) the FIFO method, (*b*) the LIFO method, and (*c*) the weighted average method.

Receipts: 1/6/... 40 units at £25 each;
　　　　　 8/6/... 40 units at £30 each.
Issues: 　2/6/... 30 units;
　　　　　 9/6/... 30 units.

13. A company uses 60,000 electronic units a year, each of which costs £10, although when orders of 14,000 units or more are placed a quantity discount of 2 per cent is given. If it costs the company £105 to place a purchase order for such units and the annual storage cost is 25 per cent of the value held, what is the economic order quantity?

3
Cost data: labour

Methods of remuneration

1. Basic methods of remuneration. Although there are a multitude of different wage schemes, nearly all are variants of only three basic methods, namely dayrate, piecework and premium bonus. These methods are discussed below, the following illustrative data being used to enable comparisons to be made:

Hourly rate	£5 per hour
Agreed rate of production	100 units per hour
Hours worked	8 hours
Units produced	1,200 units

2. Dayrate (daywork; time rate). Under the dayrate method the employee is paid on the *basis of time worked*. The formula is:

$$\text{hours worked} \times \text{dayrate per hour.}$$

Using the data given in **1**, the dayrate earnings would be 8 hours × £5 = £40.

Dayrate wages have the advantages that they are easy to compute and understand and avoid the frequent and often complex negotiations that seem to be inherent in incentive schemes. However, the method has the grave disadvantage that there is no incentive for employees to work harder than is absolutely necessary – and, indeed, there is a direct incentive to work more slowly if this will result in a greater opportunity for them to work overtime.

3. Circumstances under which dayrate is applicable. Dayrate is particularly suitable where:

(a) quality is more important than production, e.g. toolroom work which involves expensive tools and where hurried workmanship can result in costly errors;

(b) the work is such that there is no basis for an incentive scheme, e.g. a night-watchman;

(c) the rate of production is outside the employee's control, e.g. an oil-refinery operation.

4. High dayrate plan. This is a dayrate variant that aims to avoid the complications and negotiations involved in incentive schemes while at the same time providing the employee with an incentive to work hard. The principle is that all work is carefully studied and timed. On the basis of each timing the employee is then offered a dayrate well above average for undertaking to complete a workload which, while reasonable in itself, is nevertheless well above that which would be completed by an employee working under normal dayrate conditions. In this way employees can earn high wages while at the same time the employer gains from high productivity.

This type of scheme in also referred to as *measured daywork*.

5. Incentive schemes. An incentive scheme is a scheme that relates remuneration to *performance*. Although an occasional scheme aims at improving punctuality or reducing material waste, the majority aim at increasing production. These fall into two groups, piecework schemes and premium bonus schemes, and are discussed below.

6. Piecework (P/W). Under the piecework method the employee is paid on a *basis of production*. The formula is:

units produced × rate per unit.

Sometimes each unit is given a 'piecework hours' value. This use of 'hours' is particularly applicable where units of production are varied. In these circumstances piecework earnings are the sum of all 'piecework hours' earned multiplied by the rate per 'piecework hour'. It should be appreciated that 'piecework hours' are in the nature of production 'points' and are *not* the same as worked hours.

The figures given in **1** indicate that management is prepared to pay £5 per 100 units produced.

∴   Piecework earnings = 1,200 units at £5 per 100 = £60.

Alternatively, from the P/W hours aspect, the figures show that management allows 0.01 hours per unit.

∴   P/W hrs earned = 0.01 × 1,200 = 12 P/W hours.
∴   Earnings = 12 P/W hrs at £5 per hr = £60.

7. Piecework variants. There are a number of variations on the simple scheme outlined in **6**. The two most important are as follows.

(a) *Piecework with guaranteed dayrate.* Under this method a dayrate is guaranteed, so that if at any time piecework earnings fall below the amount that would have been earned on dayrate, then the dayrate earnings are paid instead. This avoids an employee being poorly paid on account of low production which arose through no fault of the employee, e.g. poor materials. Virtually all modern piecework schemes carry a guaranteed dayrate.

(b) *Differential piecework.* In this type of scheme the piecework rate changes at different levels of efficiency, e.g. £0.40 a unit when efficiency is below 7 units an hour; £0.60 a unit when 7–10 units an hour; and £0.80 a unit when above 10 units an hour. The object is to provide a strong incentive to reach the maximum rate of production.

It should be appreciated that in such a scheme it is important to distinguish between paying the increased rate on *all* production or on only the *excess* production, e.g. if 11 units were produced under the above scheme, either the 11th unit *only* would be paid for at £0.80 or all 11, depending upon a more detailed definition of the scheme.

8. Disadvantages of piecework. While superficially attractive on the grounds that performance and pay are directly linked, piecework does suffer from the following disadvantages.

(a) Establishing piecework *rates* can involve protracted and expensive negotiations with the employees.

(b) Establishing *allowances* that management must give when the production rate falls as a result of matters outside the control of employees (e.g. shortage of materials or machine breakdowns) can also involve complicated negotiations.

(c) Piecework negotiations can lead to bad feelings between employees and management.

(d) An error on the part of management when setting the rate can prove very expensive.

(e) Piecework often involves a much more complex recording system than is required for straight daywork.

(f) Management is compelled to set up control systems to avoid abuse of the scheme. (It is not, for example, unknown for employees to: present the same work twice for payment; book times incorrectly when claiming waiting-time allowances; disguise defective work on which no payment would otherwise be made; or throw oil over work where payment is based on weight, such as in washer production.)

These disadvantages (which, incidentally, in the main apply to all incentive schemes) are often so serious that many managers believe they outweigh the advantages.

9. Premium bonus. Under the premium bonus method a time allowance (TA) for a job is given, the time taken (TT) is recorded and *a bonus is paid on the basis of the time saved* (TS). It is important to remember that this method relates to the *bonus*; the employee's basic pay is normal dayrate. The formula, therefore, for the employee's *total pay* is:

dayrate wage + bonus based on time saved.

If the time taken exceeds the time allowed, there is no time saved. There is, then, no bonus and dayrate only is paid for the time taken.

10. Formulae for premium bonus schemes. The formulae for the bonuses earned under the three most well-known schemes are as follows.

(a) Halsey: Bonus = $\frac{1}{2}$ TS × dayrate.

(b) Halsey–Weir: Bonus = $\frac{1}{3}$ TS × dayrate.

(c) Rowan: Bonus = $\dfrac{TT}{TA}$ × TS × dayrate.

EXAMPLE:
(Based on data given in **1**.)

Hours

$$\text{Time allowed for 1,200 units } (TA) = \frac{1,200}{100} = 12$$

Time taken (TT) $\qquad\qquad\qquad = 8$

$\therefore$ Time saved (TS) $\qquad\qquad\quad = 4$

Earnings under Halsey:
Bonus $= \frac{1}{2} \times 4 \times £5 = £10$.
$\therefore$ Total earnings = dayrate wage + bonus
$$= [8 \times £5] + £10 = £50.$$

Earnings under Rowan:
Bonus $= \frac{8}{12} \times 4 \times £5 = £13.33$
$\therefore$ Total earnings = dayrate wage + bonus
$$= [8 \times £5] + £13.33$$
$$= £53.33$$

NOTE: In some schemes the bonus is not calculated on the dayrate but on a separate *bonus rate*. Since there can be a number of dayrates in a department the use of a single bonus rate simplifies bonus calculations and ensures that bonuses paid out are independent of the dayrate of the employee.

11. Setting time allowances. The following is a summary of the procedure adopted in setting time allowances.

(*a*) The work study department determines the length of time required by the average worker to do the job.

(*b*) Personal allowances are added to this time to give the expected time.

(*c*) The expected time is then increased by a set proportion laid down by management to give the *allowed time*. Such an increase is added so that employees who complete the job in the expected time earn a wage which is distinctly above the dayrate wage, a condition usually made necessary as a result of trade union negotiations.

12. Labour remuneration and overheads. Under some schemes the labour cost per unit actually *increases* as efficiency improves. At first sight this may appear to involve management in a loss, but it should be realized that many factories have high fixed overheads, and a doubling of efficiency naturally halves the cost per unit of these costs. In consequence, the increased labour cost per unit is more than counterbalanced by this reduction in the fixed overhead cost per unit.

13. Value-added incentive scheme. A somewhat different kind of incentive scheme is one based on the added value arising from an employee's, or group of employees', efforts. As we have seen, added value is the difference between the market value of a product and the cost of bought-out materials and services (*see* 1: **24**) which, on the shop floor, is often, to all intents and purposes, the difference between market price and the cost of materials converted. On occasion this difference is considerable, particularly if highly-skilled labour or expensive machinery is involved. So when using such scarce resources it pays management to try and obtain the maximum possible output. To encourage this, an added-value bonus can be offered, and this bonus can be very generous. For instance, take the following figures:

Market cost per unit	£30
Material cost per unit	£5
Normal labour time per unit	1 hour
Labour dayrate	£6 per hour
Maximum working hours per day	10

Under normal conditions the daily profit before deduction of overheads is

$$10 \times 30 - 10 \times (5 + 6) = £190.$$

If, though, a bonus of 10% added value (i.e. 10% of $30 - 5 = £2.5$ per unit) is offered and this increases production by 40%, then the employee earns $10 \times 6 + 14 \times 2.5 = £95$ a day as against previous earnings of $10 \times 6 = £60$. And the new daily profit before overheads is $14 \times 30 - (14 \times 5 + 95) = £255$, i.e. an extra £65. Such are the bones of a simple value-added scheme. Unfortunately, as it stands a bonus would be paid even if only 1 unit were produced in the whole day! To ensure that above-average performance must be achieved before a bonus is paid a slightly different approach needs to be taken. This approach calls for a standard ratio of added value to gross wages to be set on the basis of average performance. Then the difference between the actual added value in a period and the expected added value in view of the actual wages paid gives a gain out of which a group bonus can be paid. Thus, if £100,000 wages at average performance gave £250,000 added value the standard ratio would be 2.5. If subsequently £120,000 wages gave an actual added value of £340,000 then the gain would be 340,000 − (120,000 × 2.5) = £40,000. If the scheme laid down this was to be split 50/50 between employees and company then the group bonus would be £20,000.

14. Overtime (O/T) premium. An overtime premium (or *penalty*) is an extra amount over and above dayrate earnings paid to an employee who works longer than a normal working day. It is almost invariably calculated as a percentage of the extra hours worked, usually 50 per cent, called 'time and a half', or 100 per cent, called 'double time'.

For instance, if four hours of overtime is worked at time and a half, a total of six hours (4 + 50 per cent of 4) is paid, of which the payment for the *extra two hours* is called the overtime premium.

15. In lieu bonus. When it is desired to give an employee a bonus but the work is not suitable for an incentive scheme the management may make agreed payments in lieu of a normal bonus. Such a payment is termed an *in lieu bonus*. It is particularly made when an employee who is normally on bonus is temporarily transferred to non-bonus work.

16. Idle-time payments. If employees on an incentive scheme are held up for any reason outside their control they record their 'idle time' quite separately from their normal working time. They are then paid normal dayrate for such time plus, in some cases, an in lieu bonus. Obviously such 'idle time' recording must be countersigned by some appropriate authority.

17. Individual *v*. group incentive schemes. Under normal circumstances a scheme that rewards each employee on a basis of his or her own individual performance is better in all respects than one that rewards group performance. Individual incentive schemes, therefore, should normally be employed.

18. Circumstances requiring group incentives. Despite the superiority of an individual incentive scheme, group schemes should be employed in the following circumstances.

(a) *When workforce flexibility is required.* Some forms of work require employees to switch quickly from job to job so that the *individual's* performance cannot be measured, although the *group's* performance can.

(b) *When team-work is necessary*, e.g. in a coal-mine.

(c) *When production is on a continuous production-line basis*, so that extra production depends upon *all* employees increasing their speeds.

19. Computation of group bonuses. Computing the bonus under a group incentive scheme falls into two parts:

(a) finding the group bonus;
(b) sharing the group bonus.

Finding the group bonus depends upon the scheme selected by the management and can be group piecework, premium bonus, added-value bonus, saving on cost target or another form of incentive scheme. Sharing the group bonus should be left as far as possible to the members of the group to decide themselves.

Labour time and wage routines

We turn now to seeing how labour time is recorded and wages compiled and paid. Recording labour time falls into two quite distinct categories: first, recording the time the employee is at work (gate timekeeping), and second, recording the time the employee is engaged on different activities.

20. Gate timekeeping. It is very important that the time an employee spends on the factory premises during any week is known. Employees on dayrate are obviously paid for all the hours they are on the premises, but even pieceworkers must record their hours, if only to be correctly paid for overtime. In practice, the actual hours spent on the premises by such workers are also needed to ensure regular and punctual attendance, for it is necessary to keep production not only at a high level but also flowing steadily.

Irregular production by one employee, high though his or her overall production may be, leads to stresses at other parts of the production line which result in an unnecessary lowering of efficiency.

The recording of the time when employees enter and leave the premises is known as *gate timekeeping*.

21. Clock cards. In the past a variety of systems were used for gate timekeeping, but today the clock card is almost universal. A *clock card* is simply a stiff card that is inserted into a clock at the 'gate' and the time of insertion stamped. Nowadays most 'gate' clocks are situated in the employee's department. All employees have their own clock card and 'clock in' and 'clock out' every time they enter and leave the department. Clock cards normally record clockings for a full week.

22. Clock numbers. On joining an enterprise an employee is given an individual clock number which is printed on the clock card. To avoid ambiguity, employees are identified in all enterprise procedures by their clock numbers.

23. Prevention of gate timekeeping frauds. Modern clocks assist in preventing the following two types of fraud.

(*a*) *Manipulating times*. To prevent employees clocking the current day's time in spaces relating to other days, the clocks print an indication of both the day and period (a.m. or p.m.). In addition, the design of many clocks and clock cards is such that it is virtually impossible to clock a time into the space of an earlier day.

(*b*) *Employees clocking unofficially*. Employees sometimes wish to clock the cards of their absent friends. Clocks therefore ring a bell when a clocking is made so that attention is drawn to such a clocking. Prevention of this kind of fraud, however, also depends upon close supervision, which may or may not exist.

24. Necessity for recording times on activities. Since labour is a major cost in most factories, it is essential that a detailed analysis is made showing the activities on which the cost was incurred. Such an analysis can be made only if every employee records his or her activities in detail and the time spent on each one.

25. Time sheets. The most common method of recording labour times is for each employee to fill in a *time sheet*, i.e. a sheet detailing the employee's activities and the time spent on each. There are two kinds of time sheet, as follows.

(a) *Weekly time sheets.* These record the activities day by day of an employee for a complete week, each employee filling in one sheet a week. The *disadvantage* of weekly sheets is that since most employees do not start to fill them in until they are obliged to, i.e. at the very end of the week, the times spent earlier in the week on activities have often been forgotten, and consequently the sheets are inaccurate. Sometimes, in fact, the activity itself is forgotten and appears in the cost records as having been completed without the aid of any labour at all!

(b) *Daily time sheets.* These are similar to weekly time sheets, except that they are completed and sent to the cost office each day. The *disadvantage* of daily sheets is that they result in a considerable volume of paper – in the case of a small factory with 100 employees, for example, some 2,000 pieces per month. They do have the *advantage*, however, that this risk of times being forgotten or manipulated is considerably lessened.

26. Job cards. Another method of recording labour times is by means of job cards. A job card is a card made out *for each job*, unlike time sheets, which are made out for each employee. When an employee works on a job he or she records on the job card the time spent on that job. There are two kinds of job card.

(a) *One card per complete job.* The card travels round with the job and labour times are recorded upon it after each operation. This has the advantage that when the card reaches the cost office all labour times are listed, and the cost clerks have merely to insert the labour rates, multiply and add to obtain the full labour cost. It has, however, a serious disadvantage: until the job is fully completed none of the times are known in the cost office. As some jobs may be weeks being completed, it is virtually impossible to reconcile labour time with gate times each week (*see* **27**).

(b) *One card per operation.* This method of recording means that a single job will have a number of job cards, one for each operation. This involves considerable paperwork, but it does enable time bookings to reach the cost office quickly.

NOTE: Students should appreciate that no matter what method is used, there is always a possibility that in practice the times recorded are unreliable (*see* I, **20**).

27. Reconciling booked time to gate time. Clearly, the total employee time booked to activities must equal the total gate time paid for (*see* **20**) and it is necessary to insert in the wages routine a check that ensures those two totals do, in fact, agree. As part of this routine each employee must make sure that the total hours he or she books in a period are equal to the total hours he or she is paid for. Such time booked will be within one or a combination of the following categories.

(*a*) Production jobs, each with its own job number (*see* 6: **3**).

(*b*) Process work (*see* 8: **1** (*a*)).

(*c*) Overhead activities (*see* 5: **1–2**).

(*d*) Idle (waiting) time. If employees have no work to do they must record the time they are 'idle' and indicate the reason (e.g. breakdown; waiting for material, tools or instructions).

28. Wage computations. Once all the timekeeping records have been prepared the wages office can compute the wages of the employees. This computation is recorded on a *payroll* (or *wage sheet*) which lists all the employees and shows the major details relating to their pay.

Preparation of the payroll falls into the following two parts.

(*a*) *Computation of gross wages.* The gross wage of each employee is computed by reference to the following documents.

(*i*) Clock cards: these are required, of course, for dayrate and premium bonus workers and also to compute overtime and minimum guaranteed wages for pieceworkers.

(*ii*) Piecework tickets: these are tickets recording each piece-worker's production.

(*iii*) Job cards: these are needed in order to compute premium bonuses, since bonuses depend upon total time spent on individual jobs.

(*iv*) Employee's record card: this is a document recording remuneration details of the individual employee, e.g. rate of pay; holidays taken or outstanding; PAYE code number and earnings summary.

(*b*) *Computation of net wages.* From each employee's gross pay all the statutory and voluntary deductions are then made and the net pay for each employee is found.

29. Prevention of payroll fraud. Payrolls are a favourite target for fraud. Prevention is helped by the following measures.

(*a*) Arranging for different clerks to carry out the different steps of computation, and on payday changing the clerks around yet again, so that no clerk who compiled the wages on any given wage sheet handles the wage packets relating to that sheet.

(*b*) Ensuring that each employee's insurance and tax documents are in order. This prevents non-existent people being entered on the payroll.

(*c*) Insisting on overtime or loans being properly authorized before payment.

(*d*) Using 'see-through' wage packets so that employees can check their wages before breaking the packet seal. (Too much blind trust should not be put in this device. It is not as foolproof as it might initially appear.)

Needless to say, the increasing trend towards paying all wages by cheque or bank transfer is eliminating many kinds of payroll fraud, although other, more computer orientated, frauds are countering this gain to some extent.

30. Labour turnover. This refers to the rate at which employees who have to be replaced leave the enterprise. It is often closely linked to the level of remuneration – the lower the remuneration the higher the turnover. It can be measured in various ways, the simplest way being by use of the following formula:

$$\text{Labour turnover} = \frac{\text{No. of employees leaving who have to be replaced}}{\text{Average no. of employees}}$$

Progress test 3

Principles

1. What are the three basic methods of labour remuneration and how do they differ? (**2, 6, 9**)

2. What are the principles underlying the high dayrate plan? (**4**)

3. What are the disadvantages of piecework? (**8**)

4. How is overtime premium calculated? (**14**)

5. What is an in lieu bonus? (**15**)

6. When should a group incentive scheme be employed? (**18**)

7. Why is gate timekeeping necessary? (**20**)

8. What are the most important gate timekeeping frauds and what steps can be taken to guard against them? (**23**)

9. What are the relative advantages and disadvantages of daily and weekly time sheets? (**25**)

10. Why are job cards sometimes needed to compute an employee's gross pay? (**28**)

11. What steps can be taken to guard against payroll frauds? (**29**)

12. How can labour turnover be analyzed? (**30**)

Practice

13. Jobs are issued to operative X, to make 189 units, and to operative Y, to make 204 units, for which a time allowance of 20 standard minutes and 15 standard minutes per unit respectively is credited. For every hour saved, bonus is paid at 50 per cent of the base rate, which is £4 per hour for both employees. The basic working week is 42 hours. Hours in excess are paid at time and a half.

X completes her units in 45 hours and Y completes his in 39 hours (but works a full week). Because of defective material, six of X's units and four of Y's units are subsequently scrapped although all units produced are paid for.

You are required to calculate for each of X and Y:

(*a*) the amount of bonus payable;

(*b*) the total gross wage payable;

(*c*) the wages cost per good unit made.

(*CIMA, adapted*)

4

Cost data: expenses

Finally we look at the cost data relating to expenses which are costs that are neither materials nor labour. They include, therefore, such items as rent, rates, power, royalties, advertising, depreciation, printing, telephones, heating, lighting, subcontracts, machine hire, freight, etc.

Expenses in general

1. Direct and indirect expenses. In 1: **17**(*a*) a direct cost was defined as a cost that results solely from the existence of whatever is being costed. A *direct expense*, therefore, is an expense that results solely from the existence of whatever is being costed. An *indirect expense* is, of course, any expense that is not a direct expense.

2. Types of cost unit direct expenses. Cost unit direct expenses are relatively few, most expenses being indirect. However, the possibility of an expense being direct should always be kept in mind, and care taken not to form a habit of regarding all expenses as indirect. The following are examples of cost unit direct expenses.

(*a*) *Royalties*, since royalties charged are based on a rate per unit.

(*b*) *Plant hire*, if the plant is hired solely in order to manufacture a specific cost unit.

(*c*) *Subcontract or outside work*, if jobs are sent out for special processing, e.g. plating.

(*d*) *Salesmen's commissions*, since these are usually based on the sales value of units sold.

(*e*) *Freight*, if the goods are handled by an outside carrier whose charges can be related to individual units, e.g. rate per unit or per kg.

3. Minor direct expenses treated as indirect. In practice there are frequently a number of costs which are direct, but the amounts chargeable, particularly to different cost units, may be both small and difficult to ascertain. To avoid needless petty analysis such costs are usually treated as indirect expenses. Examples of such expenses are: sewing cotton; nails and glue; material-handling labour; and labour time spent on paperwork.

One direct expense which is often far from small but is nevertheless treated as indirect is *power*. The reason is that to charge out this cost as a direct expense would involve placing a meter on every machine and in every cost centre, and in the case of cost units, moreover, taking readings in respect of every unit processed. This, of course, is not practical, and so for convenience power is treated as an indirect expense.

4. The borderline between direct and indirect costs. Although we have carefully distinguished between direct and indirect costs (*see* 1: **17**(*a*)), in practice it is sometimes difficult to classify an individual cost. For example, a company may accept an order that requires a special tool which is bought and used. If no other work will ever require the use of the tool, then clearly it is a direct cost to the order. If, on the other hand, the tool is to be used on future work the cost cannot really be said to result solely from the existence of the order, since future work would ultimately have given rise to the cost. In this case the cost is indirect, and the current order should only bear at most a proportionate share of it. Sometimes, however, it is very difficult to determine whether or not the tool will be of use in future work, and so it is virtually impossible to say whether or not the cost is truly indirect.

5. Indirect costs that appear as direct costs. Sometimes what appears to be an indisputable direct cost turns out to be wholly or partially indirect. For instance, direct wages were earlier defined as wages paid to employees working on the direct materials (*see*

1: **18**(*b*)). Now assume that 200,000 such hours were booked against the first of a group of aircraft. Clearly this particular aircraft would be charged with 200,000 hours' direct wages. However, it could almost certainly be argued that part of this total included time spent clearing up production queries that would never be incurred again and which would, in fact, benefit all future aircraft (e.g. minor blueprint errors). Such labour costs would be akin to design costs, which are, of course, indirect. Thus part of the wages paid for the 200,000 hours is an indirect cost.

A similar case arises when a trainee works on a job. The labour cost here is, in fact, partially a training cost. Rather, then, than regard the whole wage cost as a direct wage cost it would be better to charge the job with the estimated direct wages which would otherwise have been incurred, and then charge the balance of the trainee's wage to training costs.

6. Effect of changes in cost analysis detail. If the cost unit is very large, say a new factory building, then many costs that are normally regarded as indirect become direct, e.g. supervision, site clerical labour, power, etc. However, if the cost accountant decides to cost each *part* of the building separately, such costs become indirect in respect of the individual parts.

Whether a cost is classified as direct or indirect, therefore, depends upon the extent of detail required in the cost analysis.

7. Financial costs traditionally excluded from expenses. It should be noted in passing that according to the traditional concept of cost expenses all financial costs are excluded. These costs include interest (which has already been referred to, *see* 1: **16**(*f*)), discounts both received and given, and bank charges.

Depreciation and obsolescence

8. Depreciation. Depreciation is the loss in value of an asset due to wear and tear and deterioration. Usually the loss in value is due primarily to wear and tear, but an unused asset will lose value on account of deterioration.

9. Obsolescence. Obsolescence is the loss in value of an asset due to its supersession, i.e. the loss due to the development of a technically superior asset. There are degrees of obsolescence, since it is rare that the technical improvement is so dramatic that an existing asset is reduced to scrap value only.

Needless to say, the major problem with obsolescence is predicting its occurrence.

10. Depreciation and obsolescence. As obsolescence involves loss of asset value, it is often considered to be a part of depreciation, which is then defined as 'loss of value due to effluxion of time', but as the loss of value is due to quite another reason than wear and tear and the circumstances are so very different, it is considered advisable to keep the two concepts quite separate.

11. Life of an asset. When discussing depreciation, reference is often made to the 'life' of an asset. This is often assumed to be its potential physical life. This is not always true; assets may well be used by the enterprise for a period less than their normal physical life (e.g. when bought for use on a particular contract only). To avoid error, therefore, the life of an asset should be regarded as *the length of time such an asset will be used*. It may be measured in years, production hours or units of production.

12. Revision of asset life. As time passes the original estimate of asset life may well be seen to be erroneous. In such a case the asset life should be revised and depreciation amounts adjusted accordingly. Although this may well cause some alteration of previously accepted figures, it is better to admit an error and minimize its effects than to ignore the error and allow some future period to carry large and inappropriate losses or gains.

13. Asset cost. The full loss of value that must be accounted for by depreciation and obsolescence charges should be computed as follows:

$$\text{Total loss in value} =$$

$$\begin{pmatrix} \text{Asset} \\ \text{purchase} \\ \text{price} \end{pmatrix} + \begin{pmatrix} \text{Purchase and} \\ \text{installation} \\ \text{charges} \end{pmatrix} - \begin{pmatrix} \text{Scrap} \\ \text{value} - \begin{matrix} \text{Dismantling} \\ \text{and removal} \\ \text{charges} \end{matrix} \end{pmatrix}$$

This overall charge is normally simply referred to as 'asset cost'.

EXAMPLE:

Data:

Purchase price	£10,300
Freight and purchase costs	£80
Installation costs	£320
Scrap value	£800
Disposal costs	£100

Method:

Asset cost is, therefore:

$$£10,300 + £80 + £320 - £(800 - 100) = £10,000$$

14. Replacement value. Should depreciation charges for any given period be based on the original purchase cost of an asset or upon current replacement price? The answer to this question hinges upon whether the object of depreciation is to recover the cost of a capital outlay over the life of the asset, or to make an assessment of the true economic worth of the service given by the asset. In financial accounting one may well be primarily concerned with recovering the original cost, and therefore this figure will be used for calculating depreciation, but since the basic object of costing is to provide economic assessments, to adopt original cost in the depreciation calculations may well lead to serious error. In cost accounting, therefore, replacement values should be used.

15. Depreciation methods. The two most popular methods of charging depreciations are as follows.

(a) *Straight line*, in which *equal amounts* of depreciation are charged each period throughout the life of the asset.

(b) *Reducing balance*, in which an *equal percentage* is applied each period to the written-down value of the asset at the beginning of the period to obtain the depreciation amount.

The straight-line method is usually preferred in cost accounting; since all periods benefit from the existence of the asset, it is felt that all should share the depreciation charge equally. Where, however, one wishes to select a method that results in written-down values more closely equating to market values, the reducing-balance method is usually chosen.

16. Straight-line depreciation. The formula for the straight-line depreciation charge is:

$$\frac{\text{Asset cost}}{\text{Asset life}}$$

Thus, if the asset cost is £10,000 and the asset life 10 years, the depreciation is:

$$\frac{10,000}{10} = £1,000 \text{ per year}$$

17. Reducing-balance depreciation. The formula for the reducing-balance depreciation charge is:

$$\frac{\text{Written-down value at}}{\text{beginning of period}} \times \text{Fixed percentage}$$

The fixed percentage is the percentage which must be written off the written-down value each year so that ultimately the written-down asset value is reduced to its net residual value (i.e. scrap value less disposal costs) by the end of its life. This percentage can be found from the formula:

$$\text{Percentage} = \left(1 - \sqrt[n]{\frac{R}{A}}\right) \times 100,$$

where A = asset cost, R = residual value and n = life in years.

EXAMPLE:

If A = £10,700, R = £700 and n = 10 years, then the depreciation percentage is:

$$\left(1 - \sqrt[10]{\frac{700}{10,700}}\right) \times 100 \approx 24\%$$

Using this rate of depreciation for, say, the first three years gives the following depreciation figures:

	£
Original total installed asset cost	10,700
1st year's depreciation = 24% × £10,700	2,568
Reduced balance	8,132
2nd year's depreciation = 24% × £8,132	1,952
Reduced balance	6,180
3rd year's depreciation = 24% × £6,180	1,483
Reduced balance	4,697

Note that rather than calculate the appropriate percentage every time an asset is purchased, it is common practice for an arbitrary percentage, determined by custom, to be used.

18. Other depreciation methods. It should be appreciated that the following other methods of depreciation are sometimes used.

Method	Formula: depreciation for period
Production unit:	$\dfrac{\text{Asset cost}}{\text{Life (units of production)}} \times \begin{array}{l}\text{Units produced}\\\text{during period}\end{array}$
Production hour:	$\dfrac{\text{Asset cost}}{\text{Life (production hours)}} \times \begin{array}{l}\text{Production hours}\\\text{for period}\end{array}$
Repair reserve:	$\dfrac{\text{Asset cost} + \begin{array}{l}\text{Estimated total maintenance}\\\text{costs during life}\end{array}}{\text{Life}}$
Annuity:*	$\dfrac{\begin{array}{l}\text{Asset}\\\text{cost}\end{array} + \begin{array}{l}\text{Total of all yearly interest charges}\\\text{to be charged on written-down value}\end{array}}{\text{Life}}$
Sinking fund:*†	$\dfrac{\text{Asset cost} - \begin{array}{l}\text{Total interest to be received}\\\text{from depreciation funds invested}\end{array}}{\text{Life}}$
Endowment policy:†	Annual premium required to provide endowment at end of asset life equal to asset cost
Revaluation:	Difference between the value of the asset at the beginning of the year and its revalued value at the end of the year

*These methods require the selection of an interest rate.

†These methods require the depreciation amount to be actually withdrawn in cash, which must then be used for buying an investment or paying a premium according to the method involved.

Progress test 4

Principles

1. How can a direct expense be distinguished from an indirect expense? (1)

2. In what circumstances is plant hire a direct expense? (2)

3. Distinguish between depreciation and obsolescence. (8–10)

4. When considering depreciation charges, what is meant by:

(a) asset life; (11)
(b) asset cost? (13)

5. Distinguish between the straight-line and the reducing-balance methods of depreciation. (15)

6. What are the other methods of depreciation? (18)

5

Absorption costing: overheads

Absorption costing is the traditional form of cost ascertainment. It is based on the principle that costs should be charged to (or 'absorbed into') whatever is being costed – be it cost unit, cost centre or enterprise function – on the basis of the benefit received from those costs. In this context direct costs give little in the way of theoretical difficulty since anything which gives sole rise to a cost must be the sole beneficiary. However, the indirect costs do create problems of analysis and in this chapter the traditional manner of solving these problems is explained.

Overheads

1. **Definition of overheads.** Overheads are, broadly speaking, all those costs that are not charged directly to cost units. They equate, then, very closely to indirect costs and indeed the CIMA defines overhead cost as the 'total cost of indirect materials, indirect labour and indirect expenses'. However, some costs which are direct, such as sales commission, are nevertheless not charged to cost units but treated as if they were indirect costs and so classed as overheads. What is and is not an overhead depends to some extent on the accountant, and past practice has usually limited direct cost unit charges to production costs involving materials booked on a material requisition, wages booked on a time sheet or job card, and expenses booked on a supplier's invoice or other obvious source of direct charging – all other costs being regarded as overheads.

2. **Overhead code numbers.** All overhead categories are given

accounting code numbers as a matter of course. These numbers are sometimes called *standing order numbers*. They are given this name to contrast them with the normal works order numbers which identify the production passing through the factory. Use of this name facilitates shop-floor recordings, since all employees are instructed to book all work times and materials to order numbers, either normal works order numbers or standing order numbers.

3. Notional charges. Sometimes an enterprise is able to avoid incurring a particular cost in the cost ledger, e.g. if the premises are owned by the enterprise there will be no rent. If in these sort of circumstances the cost accountant wants his costs to reflect the true economic position he will make a notional charge to his overheads for the missing item. Such a step is often taken where an enterprise owns some factories and rents others and wishes all its factory costs to be comparable (*see* 6: **9**).

> NOTE: Cost book-keeping is dealt with later (*see* 7), but it should be mentioned here that to bring notional charges in the accounts, it is necessary to debit overheads with the charge and credit either the financial or the cost profit and loss account.

Allocation and apportionment of overheads

Since overheads are not charged direct to cost units, they must be shared equitably among them. Needless to say, cost accountants often have different opinions on what is equitable. Such differences of opinion are permissible, providing they are based on an intelligent understanding of the circumstances.

In this section the manner in which overheads are charged to cost units is explained.

4. Summary of overhead charging procedure. The overhead charging procedure involves the following steps.

(*a*) Abstracting all the overheads (*see* 5).

(*b*) Allotting overheads to cost centres (overhead analysis) (*see* **6–15**):

(*i*) allocation of overheads to cost centres;

(*ii*) apportionment of overheads to cost centres;

(*iii*) allocation and apportionment of service cost centres' costs to production cost centres.

(*c*) Absorbing overheads into cost units (overhead absorption) (*see* **20–26**):

(*i*) computation of overhead absorption rates;
(*ii*) application of overhead absorption rates to cost units.

5. Abstracting overheads. The first step is the abstraction of all the overheads of the enterprise. Traditionally these are divided into production, selling, distribution and administration overheads. Only the production overheads, however, then move on to the more elaborate overhead analysis and absorption routine, the other overheads being dealt with more simply, as indicated in **26**.

6. Overhead analysis. Once the production overheads have been abstracted the next step is the preparation of an overhead analysis which allots these overheads to cost centres. It is essentially an analysis sheet listing the overheads vertically and the cost centres horizontally.

A complete worked example of an overhead analysis is shown in Fig. 5.1. Here the overheads are seen listed on the left-hand side together with the total amounts. In this example three service cost centres (Stores, Maintenance, and Production Control and Inspection) and two production cost centres (departments X and Y) have been assumed for the purpose of illustration.

When compiling an overhead analysis there are two ways of allotting overheads to cost centres, *allocation* and *apportionment*.

7. Allocation. This is allotting to a cost centre those overheads that result *solely* from the existence of that cost centre. (Note the similarity to the 'direct cost' definition, i.e. if the overhead is a direct cost to the cost centre it is allocated.)

Overheads should always be allocated if possible. However, allocation can be made only if the exact amount incurred is known without any need to have recourse to any form of sharing. Where the amount is not known in this unambiguous manner, the total amount must be *apportioned*.

In Fig. 5.1 only indirect materials and labour have been allocated (from the materials and wages analyses respectively, *see*

Overheads	Total £	Apportionment		
		Basis	Units	Rate per unit
Rent	8,000	Area	80	£100
Indirect materials	1,740	*Allocation*		
Indirect labour	54,630	*Allocation*		
Factory admin o'h'ds.	21,840	No. of employees	546	£40
Machine depreciation	4,400	Value £000s	400	£11
Power	5,500	Kwh 000s	550	£10
Heat and light	800	Area	80	£10
Machine insurance	400	Value £000s	400	£1
Extraction (fumes) plant	1,200	No. of extraction points	40	£30
Total	98,510			
Service Depts.				
Stores		No. of material requisitions	1,750	£2
Maintenance {		*Allocation*		
		Allocated wages	£6,300	£0.50 per £
Production Control and Inspection		No. of employees	500	£37
Total	98,510			

Figure 5.1 *Overhead analysis*
The italicized figures are allocations as opposed to apportionments.
Total of X and Y = £40,280 + £58,230 = £98,510, i.e. the grand
total of all overheads. This cross-check proves the arithmetical
accuracy of the analysis

Stores		Maintenance		Production Control and Inspection		Production Dept. X		Production Dept. Y	
Units	£	Units	£	Units	£	Units	£	Units	£
3	300	4	400	1	100	30	3,000	42	4,200
	110		*250*		*440*		*310*		*630*
	2,870		*6,710*		*16,600*		*10,400*		*18,050*
4	160	12	480	30	1,200	200	8,000	300	12,000
—	—	80	880	—	—	200	2,200	120	1,320
—	—	20	200	—	—	320	3,200	210	2,100
3	30	4	40	1	10	30	300	42	420
—	—	80	80	—	—	200	200	120	120
1	30	2	60	—	—	14	420	23	690
	3,500		9,100		18,350		28,030		39,530
	−3,500	175	350	—	—	1,000	2,000	575	1,150
	Nil		9,450		18,350		30,030		40,680
			−6,300		*100*		*1,900*		*4,300*
			−3,150	100	50	1,900	950	4,300	2,150
			Nil		18,500		32,880		47,130
					−18,500	200	7,400	300	11,100
					Nil		£40,280		£58,230

7: **20**(*b*), **23**). If, however, a plant register is available then depreciation and possibly machine insurance can also be allocated.

8. Apportionment. This is allotting to a cost centre a fair *share* of an overhead on the basis of the *benefit* received by the cost centre in respect of the facilities provided by the overhead.

If an overhead cannot be allocated to cost centres then it must be apportioned. This involves finding some basis, called the *basis of apportionment*, that will enable the overhead to be equitably shared between cost centres.

9. Bases of apportionment. The following are the most usual bases of apportionment and the overheads using them.

Basis	*Overheads apportioned on this basis*
Area	Rent, rates, heat and light, building depreciation
Number of employees	Personnel office, welfare, administration, canteen, supervision, time and wages offices, safety
Book value	Depreciation, insurance
Weight of materials	Materials handling, storekeeping
Space (volume)	Heating, building depreciation
Number of radiators	Heating
Direct (to cost centres) maintenance costs	Indirect maintenance costs
Technical estimate	Power, steam consumption

NOTE: A technical estimate is an estimate of usage made by a technically qualified person.

10. Choice of basis. Students will notice that some overheads in the above list can be apportioned on more than one basis. The choice of an appropriate basis is really a matter of judgment; it is necessary to ask oneself what factor is most closely related to the benefit received by the cost centres. For example, 'number of employees' is a good basis for apportioning time and wages office overheads, since the more employees there are in a cost centre, the larger the proportional benefit received in respect of the clerical salaries and stationery necessary to arrange their wage payments.

The choice of basis, therefore, is left to the judgment of the accountant – who is not compelled, of course, to select one of the more conventional bases. If an unusual basis is more suitable it should be chosen and, indeed, the bases that can be devised are limited only by human ingenuity.

11. Illustrative example. Apportionments clearly depend on factory statistics, and in order that the student may be able to work through the overhead analysis given in Fig. 5.1 thoroughly, the statistics on which that analysis is based are given below.

Factory statistics

	Total	Stores	Main-tenance	Prodn. Control & Insp.	Prodn. X	Prodn. Y
Area – sq. ft. (000s)	80	3	4	1	30	42
Indirect material issues	£1,740	£110	£250	£440	£310	£630
Indirect labour bookings	£54,630	£2,870	£6,710	£16,600	£10,400	£18,050
Employees	546	4	12	30	200	300
Machine values	£400,000	–	£80,000	–	£200,000	£120,000
Estimated kwh (000s)	550	–	20	–	320	210
Fume extraction points	40	1	2	–	14	23
Materials requisitions issued	1,750	–	175	–	1,000	575
Maintenance labour bookings	£6,300	–	–	£100	£1,900	£4,300

12. Service cost centre costs. Once the overheads have been analyzed to cost centres and totalled, the next step is to charge service cost centre costs to production cost centres. This is necessary since our ultimate object is to charge overheads to cost units, and as no cost units pass through service departments the costs of such departments are, in effect, themselves overheads and so must be charged to those cost centres where there are cost units, i.e. the production cost centres.

The method of analyzing service cost centre costs is similar to that of the main analysis; where possible costs are allocated (e.g. wages of maintenance workers actually engaged in production cost centres), otherwise they are apportioned on some basis that reflects the work done by the service department for each of the production cost centres.

13. Service department charges illustrated. In Fig. 5.1 the first service department that must be charged out is Stores. A typical basis of apportionment for Stores, materials requisitions, has been selected and the £3,500 Stores cost charged in proportion to the number of requisitions used by each of the other cost centres.

In the case of Maintenance, £6,300 can be immediately allocated from the maintenance labour bookings. The balance of £3,150 must be apportioned on some basis that reflects the work done by Maintenance for other centres. Clearly, the maintenance labour bookings provide an excellent measure of work done by this centre, and the £3,150 is charged in proportion to the wages previously allocated. Since this allocation totalled £6,300, it can be seen that for every £1 maintenance wages allocated there must be £0.50 charged for apportionment of the remaining maintenance costs.

Finally, Production Control and Inspection overheads must be apportioned. A reasonable measure of the work done by this centre is the number of employees whose work is controlled and inspected. Since this centre only does work for the two production centres, the total overhead of £18,500 must be shared on the basis of the total of 500 employees engaged in the two production centres. This gives a charge of £37 per employee (£18,500 divided by 500).

14. Services working for other service departments. If a service department carries out work for a second service department, then clearly part of the former's costs are allotted to the latter department. Care should be taken, therefore, not to analyze the second department's costs until it has first been allotted its charges from all the other departments whose services it called upon (e.g. in Fig. 5.1 the Maintenance department is allotted its £350 share of Stores costs before its own charges are allotted).

15. Analysis by computer. Clearly, this form of analysis is ideal for a computer method of solution and in Fig. 5.2 a typical program is shown. After asking for the number of overheads and departments (instruction 20), the computer calls on the user to enter for each overhead the total overhead cost and then the amount *allocated* to each department (instruction 26) and the number of base units applicable to each department where some apportionment is needed (instruction 27). Once entries have been made in respect of all the overheads the computer automatically apportions the non-allocated costs for each overhead pro-rata to the entered base figures, and adds up each department's costs – these totals being printed out department by department (instruction 30).

```
20   INPUT "NO. OF OVERHEAD COSTS";N1: INPUT "NO. OF DEPTS.";N2
24   PRINT "TOTAL PERIOD COSTS TO BE ALLOCATED:"
25   FOR J=1 TO N1: PRINT: PRINT "O'H'D"J"TOTAL COST";: INPUT C: T=0
26   FOR K=1 TO N2: A=0: PRINT "DEPT."K;: INPUT "ALLOCATION";A: D(K)=D(K)+A: C=C-A
27   A=0:  INPUT "          APPORTIONMENT UNITS";A: AU(K)=A: T=T+A: NEXT
28   FOR K=1 TO N2: IF T>0 THEN D(K)=D(K)+C*AU(K)/T
29   NEXT K,J
30   PRINT "ALLOTMENTS:": FOR J=1 TO N2: PRINT "DEPT."J" "D(J): NEXT
```

Figure 5.2 *Overhead analysis computer program*

Reciprocal services

A problem arises when two or more service departments do work for each other. Thus if the departments are A and B, then until B's charge to A is known, A cannot apportion any cost to B. But similarly until A's charge to B is known, B cannot apportion that initial cost to A.

There are three methods of breaking this vicious circle which are explained in **16–18** below. Worked examples are given using the following basic data.

The overhead analysis prior to allotment of service cost centre costs shows the following overhead charges:

Service department A	£3,200
Service department B	£4,100
Production department 1	£8,000
Production department 2	£6,000

These overheads are to be apportioned as follows:

	To A	To B	To Production 1	To Production 2
Dept. A's costs	—	10%	50%	40%
Dept. B's costs	50%	—	10%	40%

16. Continuous allotments. In this method the costs of the first service department are apportioned in the normal way. This 'closes off' the first department. However, subsequent apportionment of the costs of other service departments results in new charges to the first department and so 'reopens' it. The total of these new charges is then apportioned back to the other service departments in the same manner as the original costs. This in turn 'reopens' the other service departments. This process is continued until the amounts involved become insignificant.

NOTE: By deferring apportionments to production cost centres until after the overall cost for each service department has been found, some saving of time can be made. This has been done in the example below.

EXAMPLE:

Step	Dept. A	Dept. B	Dept. 1	Dept. 2
	(All amounts rounded to the nearest £)			
	£	£	£	£
Opening centre costs	3,200	4,100	Ignore initially	
Apportion A (10% to B)	−3,200	320		
		4,420		
Apportion B (50% to A)	2,210	−4,420		
Apportion A	−2,210	221		
Apportion B	110	−221		
Apportion A	−110	11		
Apportion B	6	−11		
Apportion A	−6	1		

| Step | *(All amounts rounded to the nearest £)* | | | |
	Dept. A	*Dept. B*	*Dept. 1*	*Dept. 2*
Apportion B	0	−1		
∴ Total cost centre overheads (add all apportionments to opening costs)	5,526	4,653		
Final apportionments:				
Original apportionments	3,200	4,100	8,000	6,000
Apportion A total	−5,526	553	2,763	2,210
Apportion B total	2,326	−4,653	465	1,862
Total	*Nil*	*Nil*	£11,228	£10,072

17. Algebraic method. Here the *total* service costs of each department are expressed as algebraic equations. The unknowns can then be found either by solving the simultaneous equations or by substitution, whichever is preferred.

EXAMPLE:

Let a = *total* overhead cost of Dept. A after apportionment
     from B.

Let b = *total* overhead cost of Dept. B after apportionment
     from A.

so $a = 3,200 + 0.5b$

∴ $a - 0.5b = 3,200$ . . . . . . (1)

and $b = 4,100 + 0.1a$

∴ $b - 0.1a = 4,100$ . . . . . . (2)

Solving (1) × 2: $2.0a - b = 6,400$

$\quad\quad$ (2) × 1: $-0.1a + b = 4,100$

Add: $1.9a = 10,500$

∴ $a = £5,526$ (to nearest £).

Substituting in (2): $b - 0.1 \times 5,526 = 4,100$

∴ $b = 4,100 + 553 = £4,653$ (to nearest £).

(Alternatively, using substitution, $a = 3,200 + 0.5b = 3,200 + 0.5 (4,100 + 0.1a)$, and solve for a.)

Knowing these amounts, the formal apportionment can be made as in the previous method of continuous allotment.

18. Specified order of closing. The order of closing departments is carefully determined so that the services that do the most work for other service departments are closed first. The departments are then closed off in this order in the normal manner, and *no return charges from other service departments are made.* Although this method gives a theoretically inaccurate result, it has the advantage of ease. Moreover, the word 'accuracy' has little meaning within the context of apportionment so objections under this head tend to be pedantic.

EXAMPLE:
B, apportioning 50 per cent of its cost to A, affects A more than A, apportioning only 10 per cent of its costs to B, affects B. Therefore, B is closed off first, and A's apportionment to B omitted.

Step	Dept. A	Dept. B	Dept. 1	Dept. 2
Opening centre costs	3,200	4,100	8,000	6,000
Apportion B	2,050	−4,100	410	1,640
Apportion A	−5,250	—	2,917*	2,333*
Total	*Nil*	*Nil*	£11,327†	£9,973†

*Since the 10 per cent apportionment to B is omitted, Depts. 1 and 2 must share all A's costs in the ratio of 50 : 40.

†Note that the relative error in this instance is only 1 per cent.

19. Reciprocal services computations and the computer. Once again the nature of the problem calls for a computer solution – though in this instance it must be appreciated that the best approach is not necessarily the most obvious one for at first glance it would seem sensible to hand over to the computer the complexities of the algebraic method. But in actual fact the method of continuous allotment is the best. True, in an extensive problem there will be a great deal of allotting but computers love this kind of work. And it is much easier to write a continuous allotment program than an algebraic program.

Such a program is, then, reproduced in Fig. 5.3. In that program N is the number of service departments and the D array holds the total cost of each service department. The S array holds

```
20  INPUT "NO. OF SERVICE DEPTS.";N: PRINT
25  DIM D(N),S(N),C(N),A(N,N): PRINT "TOTAL PERIOD COSTS TO BE ALLOCATED:"
26  FOR J=1 TO N: PRINT "DEPT."J;: INPUT D(J): NEXT: PRINT
40  PRINT "% APPORTIONMENT OF COSTS:":FOR J=1 TO N: FOR K=1 TO N: IF J=K THEN 49
42  PRINT "DEPT."J"TO DEPT."K;: INPUT Z: A(J,K)=Z/100
49  NEXT K,J: PRINT: FOR J=1 TO N
50  PRINT "DEPT."J;D(J);: FOR K=1 TO N: PRINT A(J,K)*100;: NEXT: PRINT: NEXT
55  FOR J=1 TO N: S(J)=D(J): NEXT
60  F=0: FOR J=1 TO N: FOR K=1 TO N: T=S(J)*A(J,K): IF T<.0001 THEN 68
62  C(K)=C(K)+T: F=1
68  NEXT K,J
69  FOR J=1 TO N: D(J)=D(J)+C(J): S(J)=C(J): C(J)=0: NEXT: IF F=1 THEN 60
70  PRINT: PRINT "APPORTIONMENTS TO PRODUCTION DEPTS.": PRINT
71  PRINT "PRODUCTION DEPT.": FOR J=1 TO N: PRINT
72  PRINT "% CHARGE OF SERVICE DEPT."J;: INPUT Z: PRINT
73  PRINT "APPORTIONED CHARGE"D(J)*Z/100: PRINT: NEXT: GOTO 71
```

Figure 5.3 *Computer program for reciprocal services computations*

the step amounts since after each allotment step of all the departments there will, of course, be new amounts which have been apportioned to departments and require re-apportioning. And the C array holds the cumulative re-apportioned costs for each department as the step proceeds (the final C amounts of one step being the S amounts of the next step).

Briefly, the data is entered in instructions 20–50 (the table of costs and apportioned percentages being printed out in 50 so that the user can check that the data has been entered correctly). In 60, F, a flag which signals if any apportionments have been made during the allotment step, is set at 0 (F = 0 signalling no apportionments made; F = 1 signalling at least one apportionment made) and, in respect of each department from which an apportionment is to be made and each department to which an apportionment is to be made, the apportionment figure T is computed. If this figure is less than 1/100th of a penny the apportionment is ignored (without this the computer would stay in the 60–68 loop for ever). If it is more, the apportionment is made to the receiving department and F is set at 1 (62). At the end of this step (69) the departments' costs are increased by the C amounts, the new amounts for re-apportionment entered in the S array, the C array initialized and, if F is 1, a new step taken. When the whole step has been completed with no apportionments made the computer moves to the 70s, where entering for each production centre involved the share of the costs that centre receives from each service department, results in the total apportionment cost of that department for that centre being displayed – and this repeats

('GOTO 71' in 73) until the accountant has the figures for as many production centres as are required.

Absorption of overheads

20. Overhead absorption. Once overheads have been analyzed to production cost centres they can be charged to cost units. In essence, the procedure is to take each centre and *share its overheads among all the cost units passing through that centre*. This procedure is clearly akin to apportionment, only in this case cost units are charged and not cost centres. The technical term for this is *absorption*, and can be defined as the *charging of overheads to cost units*.

As we saw in **4**(*c*), there are two steps to be taken: first, computing an overhead absorption rate, and second, the application of this rate to cost units.

21. Computation of overhead absorption rate. To compute the overhead rate some basis of absorption is first selected in a similar manner to the selection of an apportionment base (*see* **9**, **10**). The overhead rate is then found by means of the following formula:

$$\text{Overhead absorption rate} = \frac{\text{Total cost centre overheads}}{\text{Total units of base used}}$$

Since there are a number of different bases that can be selected for absorption, in practice one comes across a number of different kinds of rates. The six most common rates have been listed below, together with their individual formulae and an illustrative example of the computation of the rates for a typical cost centre, 101, which, it is assumed, has been allotted £4,000 overheads.

	Overhead rate	*Cost centre 101*	
Title	*Formula*	*Statistics*	*Rate*
Units of output	$\dfrac{\text{TCCO}^\star}{\text{Units of output}}$	200 units	$\dfrac{£4,000}{200} =$ £20 per unit
Direct labour hr	$\dfrac{\text{TCCO}}{\substack{\text{Total direct labour} \\ \text{hours worked o.a.p.} \dagger}}$	500 direct labour hrs	$\dfrac{£4,000}{500} =$ £8 per hr

	Overhead rate	*Cost centre 101*	
Title	*Formula*	*Statistics*	*Rate*
Machine hr	$\dfrac{\text{TCCO}}{\text{Total machine hours engaged o.a.p.}}$	1,600 machine hrs	$\dfrac{£4,000}{1,600} =$ £2.5 per hr
Wages percentage	$\dfrac{\text{TCCO}}{\text{Total direct wages paid o.a.p.}}$	£4,000 direct wages	$\dfrac{£4,000}{£4,000} =$ 100 %
Materials cost percentage	$\dfrac{\text{TCCO}}{\text{Total direct material used o.a.p.}}$	£12,000 direct materials	$\dfrac{£4,000}{£12,000} = 33\frac{1}{3}\%$
Prime cost percentage	$\dfrac{\text{TCCO}}{\text{Total prime cost incurred o.a.p.}}$	£16,000 prime cost	$\dfrac{£4,000}{£16,000} = 25\%$

*TCCO = Total cost centre overhead. (TCCO charged to cost centre 101 in overhead analysis = £4,000.)

†o.a.p. = on all production, i.e. in cost centre 101 production.

It is important to appreciate that only *one* rate will be computed for any single group of overheads. The table above shows the rates from which a selection can be made; it is not meant to suggest that all the rates given are to be computed simultaneously.

22. Applications of rate to cost units. Overheads are charged to individual cost units by simply multiplying the overhead rate by the units of the base that apply to each cost unit, i.e. the formula is:

Cost unit overheads = Overhead rate × Units of base in cost unit.

EXAMPLE:

Apply the different, overhead rates computed in **21** to a cost unit, Job X, passing through 101 and having the following bookings:

		£
Direct labour hours (which included 3 hrs' work on a machine)	4 hrs at £3.00 per hr	12.00
	1 hr at £4.80 per hr	4.80
	5 hrs	16.80
Direct materials		24.00
	Prime cost	£40.80

Solution:

OVERHEAD RATE   JOB X

Title	Rate	Units of base	Overhead charged £
Units of output	£20 per unit	1 unit*	20.00
Direct labour hour	£8 per hr	5 hours	40.00
Machine hour	£2.50 per hr	3 hours	7.50
Wages percentage	100%	£16.80 wages	16.80
Materials cost percentage	$33\frac{1}{3}$%	£24.00 materials	8.00
Prime cost percentage	25%	£40.80 prime cost	10.20

*In the case of this particular rate it must be assumed that all the cost units are identical units.

23. Choice of overhead rate. As with apportionment, sound absorption hinges on finding an appropriate basis for sharing the overheads. In the case of most overheads, *time* is the factor associated with cost units that is most closely related to overhead costs. It is logical, therefore, to charge those products that utilize factory facilities for the longest time with the largest share of the overheads, and so overheads are best absorbed on a time basis, i.e. using a direct labour hour, machine hour or wages percentage rate.

The following points should be noted in connection with the six methods of absorption.

(*a*) *Units of output.* This is the best of the rates, but unfortunately can be used only when all the cost units passing through the cost centre are identical.

(*b*) *Direct labour hour.* This is a good all-round rate. Students should use this rate in their answers unless there is a good reason for selecting a different one.

(*c*) *Machine hour.* When production is carried out on machines this rate is appropriate. Beware, however, of using this rate simply because most of the production is put on machines; using a machine hour rate in such circumstances would mean that any *non-*

machine production would be charged no overheads at all. Indeed, where this rate is adopted it should be used to absorb what are essentially the machine overheads – a second rate being applied in parallel to absorb all the other production overheads.

(*d*) *Wages percentage rate.* This rate will give identical results to the direct labour hour rate if there is only one rate of pay in the cost centre. If otherwise, then when times are the same overheads charged to cost units worked on by highly-paid employees will exceed those charged to units worked on by lower-rated employees. This is not strictly logical (since the overheads incurred per hour are the same whether the employee is highly paid or otherwise), but as this method is clerically simpler than the direct labour hour method (for which direct labour hours must be separately recorded and added on job cards), it is a good practical rate.

(*e*) *Materials cost percentage rate.* Overheads are in no way related to the cost of material used. A large, expensive piece of material could be on the factory floor for only a few minutes, utilizing virtually nothing of the factory facilities, and yet it would be given an overhead charge proportional to its material cost. This is clearly unsatisfactory, and students should almost always avoid its use.

(*f*) *Prime cost percentage rate.* Again overheads are not often related to prime cost, and so usually this rate is quite unsuitable. One notable exception to this, however, arises with certain kinds of contract work where the rate is acceptable (*see* 6: **10**(*d*)).

24. Predetermined overhead rates. In order to enable costings to be made from the first day of operations, overhead rates are almost invariably calculated on a basis of future overheads and production. Such rates are called *predetermined overhead rates*, and the use of such rates gives rise to the following points:

(*a*) *Calculation of predetermined overhead rates.* These rates are calculated from the following formula:

$$\text{Predetermined overhead rate} = \frac{\text{Budgeted overheads for the next year}}{\text{Budgeted units of base for the next year}}$$

(b) *Under- and over-absorption of overheads.* It is most unlikely that the actual overheads and units of base will exactly equal the budgeted amounts. Consequently, using predetermined overhead rates will result in actual production being charged somewhat more or less than the actual overheads incurred. The difference between the overheads charged and the overheads incurred is called the *under-* (or *over-*) *absorption of overheads.*

For example, assume:

Budgeted overheads	£15,000
Actual overheads	£15,160
Budgeted direct labour hours	10,000
Actual direct labour hours	9,820

$$\text{Predetermined overhead rate} = \frac{£15,000}{10,000} = £1.50 \text{ per hour.}$$

Therefore, since 9,820 hours were worked, a total of £1.50 × 9,820 = £14,730 would be charged to production. However, actual overheads were £15,160.

∴   Under-absorption of overheads = £15,160 − £14,730 = £430.

In other words, £430 of the overheads incurred were not charged to production.

(c) *Disposal of under- and over-absorbed overheads.* Monthly under- or over-absorption can be disposed of in one of two ways, as follows.

(i) If seasonal, transfer to a suspense account since the under-absorption in the slack months should in all fairness be carried by the over-absorption in the busy months. Over the year under- and over-absorptions should, of course, virtually cancel out. At the year end any balance should be transferred to the annual profit and loss account.

(ii) If not seasonal, transfer at once to monthly profit and loss account.

In *no* circumstances should any under- (or over-) absorption be included in the overheads of following periods (a basic costing principle, *see* 1: **16**(*e*)).

NOTE: Sometimes 'u/o' is used as an abbreviation for 'under or over'.

(d) *SSAP 9.* SSAP 9 lays down that overhead rates used to value stocks should be based on the enterprise's normal level of activity and not on exceptional short-term activity levels.

25. Blanket overhead rate. This is a single overhead rate computed for the entire factory, i.e. total factory overheads divided by total units of base throughout the factory.

Blanket overhead rates should never be used (other than in output costing, *see* 6: 5), since cost units passing through centres with high overhead costs (e.g. machine shops) will be undercosted and those passing through low overhead centres (e.g. an assembly department) will be overcosted.

26. Absorption of non-production overheads. Traditionally non-production overheads have been treated in a very cursory manner – indeed early cost accountants would probably have included them among the production overheads were it not for the fact that this would have resulted in cost units being charged with selling and distribution overheads *before* the units had incurred any such costs. This, of course, would be a serious breach of one of the fundamental costing principles (*see* 1: **16**(*b*)). In the event the following absorption methods were usually adopted.

(*a*) *Selling overheads.* Since the benefit received by a cost unit in respect of selling overheads is usually in proportion to the value of the unit, these overheads were usually absorbed as a percentage of the cost unit value, the overhead rate formula being:

$$\text{Selling overhead rate (factory cost percentage)} = \frac{\text{Total selling overheads}}{\text{Total factory cost of all sales}} \times 100$$

By applying this percentage to the factory cost of individual cost units, the selling overheads applicable to each unit were found.

(*b*) *Distribution overheads.* A distribution department is very similar to a production department from the point of view of costs. Thus there are direct materials (packing cases, wood-wool), direct labour (packers, van drivers), direct expenses (freight), departmental overheads (supervision, heat and light) and 'machines' (vans, lorries, packing machines). It followed therefore that it could be treated in a similar way to a production department, with materials requisitions, time sheets and overheads absorbed by means of overhead absorption rates. The overhead rates for vans and lorries would be based on miles, tonnes, or hours, or a combination of these (*see* 6: **6**).

(*c*) *Administration overheads.* These overheads are so divorced from both production and selling that any basis of absorption must necessarily be very artificial. In practice the overheads were often apportioned between production, selling and distribution prior to preparing any other overhead analyses on a basis of common sense – and in the overhead analyses further apportioned on the basis of the number of employees.

27. Objections to overhead absorption. Students should be warned that nowadays many cost accountants regard overhead absorption as a discredited technique. Their objections are based on the fact that many overheads, such as rent and audit fees, are completely independent of whether an individual cost unit (or even a product line) is made or not. The sharing out of such overheads among cost units does not therefore provide any useful information to management. Moreover, since such apportionments are very often arbitrary, different cost accountants often arrive at different cost unit costs. Such procedures hardly form satisfactory bases for making intelligent management decisions.

Progress test 5

Principles
1. What are overheads? (**1**)
2. What are notional charges and why are they made? (**3**)
3. Distinguish between allocation and apportionment. (**7, 8**)
4. Which overheads would usually be apportioned on the basis of the number of employees? (**9, 26**(*c*))
5. Name three ways of apportioning service costs to reciprocal services. (**16–18**)
6. What are the main absorption rates and which are the most satisfactory? (**21, 23**)
7. How should under- and over-absorbed overheads be disposed of? (**24**(*c*))
8. What is a blanket overhead rate? (**25**)

Practice
9. XY Ltd. operates a factory whose quarterly budget is given below:

	£	£	£	£
Selling value of goods produced				6,800,000
Production cost:				
Direct wages		1,200,000		
Direct material cost		4,200,000	5,400,000	
Indirect wages and supervision:				
Machine department X	38,000			
Machine department Y	43,500			
Assembly department	41,250			
Packing department	23,000			
Maintenance department	22,500			
Stores	11,500			
General department	24,250			
		204,000		
Maintenance wages:				
Machine department X	10,000			
Machine department Y	20,000			
Assembly department	5,000			
Packing department	5,000			
Maintenance department	5,000			
Stores	2,500			
General department	4,500			
		52,000		
Indirect materials:				
Machine department X	27,000			
Machine department Y	36,000			
Assembly department	18,000			
Packing department	27,000			
Maintenance department	9,000			
Stores	6,750			
General department	4,000			
		127,750		
Power		60,000		
Rent and rates		80,000		
Lighting and heating		20,000		
Insurance		10,000		
Depreciation (5%)		200,000		
			753,750	
				6,153,750
Budgeted factory profit				646,250

The following operating information is also available:

Department	Effective HP	Area occupied (sq. ft.)	Book value: machinery and equipment £	Productive capacity (Quarterly) Direct labour Hours	Cost £	Machine hours
Productive:						
Machine X	40	10,000	1,200,000	100,000	409,000	50,000
Machine Y	40	7,500	1,600,000	75,000	321,000	60,000
Assembly	—	15,000	200,000	75,000	293,000	
Packing	10	7,500	200,000	50,000	177,000	
Service:						
Maintenance	10	3,000	600,000			
Stores	—	5,000	100,000			
General	—	2,000	100,000			
		50,000	4,000,000			

The general department consists of the factory manager, and general clerical and wages personnel.

(a) Prepare a quarterly overhead analysis sheet for the departments of the factory. (Show clearly the bases of apportionment.)

(b) Calculate hourly cost rates of overhead absorption for each productive department. Ignore the apportionment of service department costs among service departments.

(CIMA, adapted)

6

Absorption costing: costing methods

1. Costing methods. Although the *principles* of cost ascertainment remain unchanged in the various production circumstances, the actual application does depend very much upon these circumstances. The various applications can be said to constitute different costing *methods* (*see* also Fig. 6.1).

2. Specific order costing. Specific order costing is the application of the principles of cost ascertainment in situations where *all the cost units are separately identified and costed individually* (or 'where the work consists of separate contracts, jobs or batches each of which is authorized by a special order or contract', CIMA Terminology). The basic formula for this method is:

Specific order cost = Direct costs of specific order + Overheads absorbed by specific order cost unit.

The direct costs in this formula are charged from the documents recording the direct materials, wages and expenses used on the order, and the overhead absorbed is computed under one of the absorption methods given in Chapter 5.

3. Job costing. This is used where the *cost units are relatively small* (e.g. making furniture to customers' specifications). Being small units the work is normally carried out within the walls of the factory. This, however, need not always be the case. Plumbing repairs in private households will, for example, be costed using the factory job costing method. The method involves the following procedure (*see* Fig. 6.2).

Costing methods:	Specific order			Unit				Batch
Features:	Cost units separately identifiable			Cost units all identical				Identifiable batches each containing identical units
Formulae:	Order cost = (Direct costs + overheads absorbed) of order			Cost centre unit cost = $\dfrac{\text{(Direct costs + overheads charged) of cost centre}}{\text{No. of units produced in cost centre}}$ Total unit cost = Total of all cost centre unit costs				Cost per unit = $\dfrac{\text{Batch cost}}{\text{No. of units in batch}}$
Sub-methods:	Job	Contract		Operating	Output	Process		
						Discrete unit	Continuous unit	
Features:	Small	Large		Service	Single cost unit and single process	Discrete units (i.e. counted)	Continuous units (i.e. measured)	
	Cost units							
Examples:	Furniture made to customer's specification; Plumbing repairs	Dams; Civil engineering projects; Research projects		Railway; Hospital; School; Telecommunications	Quarry; Dairy	Light bulbs; Tennis balls	Refinery; Steelworks	Bakery; Pottery

Figure 6.1 *Tabular summary of the main costing methods*

Job 707:	Usage	Price	£	£
		£		
Direct materials: X 312	32 m[(a)]	0.75 m[(b)]	24.00	
P 99/8	44 kg[(a)]	0.62 kg[(b)]	27.28	51.28
Direct labour: Dept. 1	3 hr[(c)]	2.90 hr[(d)]	8.70	
	6 hr[(c)]	2.10 hr[(d)]	12.60	
Dept. 4	$1\frac{1}{2}$ hr[(c)]	3.00 hr[(d)]	4.50	
Dept. 6	8 hr[(c)]	2.50 hr[(d)]	20.00	45.80
Direct expenses:				
Royalty (units)		5.00[(e)]	5.00	
Plating charge (sub-contract)	As invoice 913[(f)] 14.14		14.14	19.14
Factory overheads:				
Dept. 1	9 Direct labour hr[(c)]	2.20 hr[(g)]	19.80	
Dept. 4	3 Machine hr[(h)]	6.50 hr[(i)]	19.50	
Dept. 6	£20 Direct Wages[(j)]	150 %[(k)]	30.00	69.30
	Factory cost			185.52
Selling overheads:				
20% factory cost			37.10	
Distribution costs:				
job 707D[(l)]			18.20	55.30
	Total cost*			240.82
	Profit			59.18
	Selling price[(m)]			£300.00

Figure 6.2 *Example of a job cost preparation*

*Administration overheads have already been apportioned to production, selling and distribution (*see* 5: **26**). Therefore no separate charge is shown here.

Sources of data:

(a) Materials requisition.
(b) Stores records card.
(c) Time sheets.
(d) Employee record card.
(e) Royalty agreement.
(f) Subcontractor's invoice.
(g) Direct labour hour overhead rate.
(h) Machine time sheet.
(i) Machine hour overhead rate.
(j) Department 6 direct labour cost entry on this cost card.
(k) Wages percentage overhead rate.
(l) Subsidiary job card prepared in distribution department.
(m) Original sales quotation.

(*a*) Each job:

(*i*) is given a *job number* (or works order number) that identifies it from every other job, and

(*ii*) has a *job card* prepared for it that bears the job number and which is used to collect all the cost data relating to the job.

Job cards must be carefully designed so that they effectively and logically collect all the cost data involved.

(*b*) During production:

(*i*) direct costs are charged to the job;

(*ii*) a share of the overheads of each cost centre that the job passes through is charged by means of overhead absorption rates.

(*c*) When the job is completed and put in the finished goods store it will not be valued at more than the sum of the two charges specified in (*b*) above. This sum is the *factory, production* or *works cost.*

(*d*) Later, when the job is sold and delivered:

(*i*) a share of the selling overheads is charged;

(*ii*) the cost of delivery is charged.

This now brings the cost up to the *total cost*. The difference between this and the selling price is the profit (or loss).

4. Unit costing. This is the application of the principles of cost ascertainment in situations where *all the cost units are identical.* The basic formulae for this method are:

Cost centre unit cost =

$$\frac{\text{Direct costs of cost centre} + \text{Overheads charged to cost centre}}{\text{No. of units produced in cost centre}};$$

Total unit cost = Total of all cost centre unit costs.

Unit costing divides into three sub-methods: output, operation and process costing.

5. Output costing. This is used where the enterprise essentially produces only *one product in a single process* (e.g. a quarry). It is a very simple method of costing. Since there is only one product and one cost centre there is no point in making complex calculations.

Cost ascertainment will involve, therefore, little more than collecting and analyzing all the costs and then dividing each cost by the total production to find the unit cost. Figures for the previous period may also be given for comparison.

6. Operation costing. This is used where the cost unit is a unit of service (e.g. railways). The units of service may be sold by the enterprise (as railways sell transport) or used within the enterprise (as in the case of a factory canteen or boiler-house). It is a common form of costing in local government offices.

The method of costing is similar to output costing. All the costs incurred during a period are collected and analyzed and then expressed in terms of a cost per unit of service.

Probably the most important aspect of operation costing is the selection of the unit of service, for it is frequently difficult to find any wholly satisfactory form of cost unit. In practice the following are some of the units used:

Enterprise	Unit
Bus companies	Passenger-kilometres; seat-kilometres
Hospitals	Patient-days; operations
Electricity boards	Kilowatt-hours
Boiler-houses	Kilograms of steam raised
Canteens	Meals served; cups of tea sold
Road maintenance	Kilometres of road maintained
Transport departments	Tonne-kilometres; kilometres travelled

In operation costing, two-part units such as the passenger-kilometres and tonne-kilometres mentioned above are very useful measures. A tonne-kilometre, for example, represents 1 tonne carried for 1 kilometre. Thus, if 5 tonnes were carried 3 kilometres this would represent $5 \times 3 = 15$ tonne-kilometres. (Note that if a second similar load were carried there would be a total of $15 + 15 = 30$ tonne-kilometres, *not* $(5 + 5) \times (3 + 3) = 60$ tonne-kilometres.)

Frequently, too, costings are improved if two or more cost units are used simultaneously, and two or more sets of costs-per-unit figures computed. For example, in the field of higher education, costs can be expressed in terms of cost per student, cost per student-hour, cost per course, cost per lecture-room, and cost per class-hour.

7. Process costing. This is used when identical cost units *pass through two or more cost centres*. It is the commonest form of unit costing.

Although conventional theory recognizes only the one sub-method it pays to distinguish a division of this method between the situation when the units are discrete and when the units are continuous. We can say, then, that we have:

(*a*) *discrete units process costing* which is used where the *cost units are physically separate* and the production measured by counting (e.g. light bulbs);

(*b*) *continuous units process costing* which is used where the *cost units are units of measurement* such as tonnes, litres, or square metres (e.g. a refinery).

Although these methods certainly have much in common, they also have points of difference which warrant rather separate treatment. In this book, then, each method is given a chapter to itself (8 and 9), further discussion being reserved until these chapters are reached.

8. Batch costing. This is the application of the principles of cost ascertainment in situations where a batch of identical units is initially treated as a single identifiable job cost unit (e.g. book production). It is no more, in fact, than the application of job and unit costing methods in sequence. As long as a batch remains unbroken it is treated as a job cost unit and costed by the job costing method. On break-up of the batch, the cost per unit is found from the formula:

$$\text{Cost per unit} = \frac{\text{Total batch cost}}{\text{No. of units in batch}}$$

If the units are subsequently rebatched, the new batch cost card commences with the batch cost found by multiplying the number of units rebatched by the cost per unit.

9. Uniform costing. Finally a mention must be made of uniform costing, which is not a costing method but merely the name given to a system which *standardizes costing methods and procedures over a group of factories, regional service centres or enterprises,* the object being to make all costings comparable. Installing such a system involves specifying carefully the way in which all the participating units must treat their costings, and in particular standardizing stores issue pricing, depreciation methods, cost classifications, overhead apportionment bases, overhead absorption rates, costing periods and the format of costing statements.

Contract costing

Contract costing is really nothing other than ordinary job costing except that it is applied to relatively large cost units, particularly units that take a considerable length of time to complete and are constructed away from the enterprise's premises (e.g. buildings, road construction and other civil engineering works). However, because there are a number of factors that are unique to this kind of situation the method warrants a complete section to itself.

10. Features of contract costing. Where contract work is carried out away from the enterprise's premises it generally shows the following features:

(a) Most of the materials ordered are specifically for contracts. They will, therefore, be charged direct from the supplier's invoices. Any materials drawn from a main store will be drawn on materials requisitions in the normal way.

(b) Nearly all labour will be direct, even though it is a type of labour not usually regarded as direct, e.g. night-watchmen and site clerks.

(c) Most expenses are direct, e.g. electricity (meters will be installed on the site), insurance, telephone (the site will have its own telephones and, therefore, telephone invoices), postage, sub-contracts, architects' fees, etc.

(d) Nearly all overheads are head office costs. These obviously form only a small proportion of the total costs and so, since errors of overhead absorption are not likely to be as serious as in other costing methods, only simple absorption methods are called for.

NOTE: Many head office costs will arise in preparing tenders and material procurement as well as labour administration. This means head office costs will tend to vary with the *prime cost* of contracts, and therefore the prime cost percentage absorption rate may well be the most appropriate.

(*e*) Plant and machinery may be charged to contracts in one of two ways:

(*i*) An hourly rate for each item of plant is calculated in a similar way to a machine hour rate (*see* 5:21) and contracts charged on a basis of hours of use.

(*ii*) If plant is at the contract sites for long periods of time contracts are charged with the full plant value on arrival and credited with the depreciated value on departure.

11. Architects' certificates. In the building trade progress payments are often made. Periodically the architect inspects the work and issues certificates to the contractor detailing work satisfactorily completed. It is important to note that these architects' certificates show the value of the work completed at *contract* price (i.e. 'selling' price), not cost price. The contractor then submits to his customer invoices claiming these amounts as progress payments and encloses the certificates as evidence of work done.

12. Retention moneys. There is frequently a contract clause that entitles the customer to withhold payment of a proportion of the contract value (e.g. 10%) for a specified period after the end of the contract. During this period and before these retained moneys are paid the contractor must make good all constructional defects that appear. The prudent contractor will therefore hold in suspense part of the contract profit until all the retention moneys have been received. Any costs of remedying defects during the retention period would then be debited against this profit-in-suspense.

13. Contract cost accounting: basic procedure. The basic procedure for costing contracts is to open a separate account for each contract, debit it with all contract costs and credit it with the contract price. This means each contract account becomes a small profit and loss account, the profit or loss being transferred to a Profits and Losses on Contracts Account.

A summary of the procedure for an individual contract is as follows:

(*a*) Open an account for the contract.
(*b*) Debit all contract direct costs (including cost of plant transferred to site if this method of charging plant is being used).

(c) Credit materials, plant and other items transferred *from* the contract.

(d) Debit head office overheads charged to the contract.

(e) Credit contract price.

(f) Transfer balance, profit or loss, to the Profits and Losses on Contracts Account.

14. Uncompleted contracts. When a contract is uncompleted at the year end the simple procedure given in **13** is, unfortunately, complicated somewhat since the profit earned during the year is not really known. We are faced with the problem, then, of subjectively estimating the appropriate figure.

Now, cost accounting aims to measure performance as accurately as possible and it is as unacceptable to err, on grounds of prudence, on one side of the best measurement as it is to err on the other side. However, running parallel to this is the fact that the cost accountant must be able to provide year-end values for the final accounts and this work is controlled by the accounting requirements in respect of published figures. This means that when it comes to valuing year-end uncompleted contracts and contract profits it is necessary to make the computation in line with accepted accounting conventions – though for *management* a set of alternative informal computations can, of course, be prepared. As it happens, there are two slightly different approaches to this problem of contract profit estimations.

15. SSAP 9 profit on an uncompleted contract. The most important of these approaches is the one embedded in SSAP 9. The crucial points in this standard can be summarized as follows:

(a) A key term is *attributable profit* which the standard defines as 'that part of the total profit currently estimated to arise over the duration of the contract (after allowing for likely increases in costs so far as not recoverable under the terms of the contract) which fairly reflects the profit attributable to that part of the work performed at the accounting date.' The standard also lays down that there can be no attributable profit until the outcome of the contract can be assessed with reasonable certainty.

(b) The *total contract cost* comprises:

(i) total costs incurred to date;

(ii) total estimated costs to complete;

(iii) future costs of rectification and guarantee work.

(c) The *total foreseen* contract profit should be calculated by deducting the total contract cost from the contract sales value.

(d) The *attributable* contract profit is the same proportion of the total profit as the work done is to the total contract work. In effect:

$$\text{Attributable profit} = \text{Total foreseen profit} \times \frac{\text{Cost of work done}}{\text{Total contract cost}}$$

(e) The profit *for the year* is the attributable profit less any profits already taken in previous years.

(f) If any *loss* is anticipated, then the entire loss should be taken.

As may be appreciated, SSAP 9 lays down a valuation procedure which accords closely to the one that a cost accountant applying normal costing principles would adopt.

The actual calculations which follow from the above procedure can be illustrated from the following figures:

Contract value £1M; total contract costs to date £720,000; estimated cost to complete £80,000; anticipated rectification costs (based on past experience) 10% contract value. Total profit taken in previous years £45,000.

Profit computations:

Total contract cost = 720,000 + 80,000 + 10% of 1M = £900,000.
Total foreseen contract profit = 1M − 900,000 = £100,000.

$$\text{Attributable profit} = 100,000 \times \frac{720,000}{900,000} = £80,000.$$

Profit for year = 80,000 − 45,000 = £35,000.

And if the contract is completed for a total cost of £800,000 at the very end of the following year, the profit for that year will be:

Total contract cost = 800,000 + 10% of 1M = £900,000.

$$\text{Profit for year} = (1M - 900,000) \times \frac{800,000}{900,000} - 80,000 = £8,889.$$

16. Traditional profit on uncompleted contracts. While the SSAP 9 approach to profit assessment will normally be followed, the student should also know the traditional approach. This can be summarized as follows:

(a) The *contract profit* to date is computed by subtracting the cost of the work certified from the value of the work certified (*see* **11**).

(*b*) The *attributable* profit is computed from the formula:

$$\tfrac{2}{3} \times \text{contract profit} \times \frac{\text{cash received}}{\text{value of work certified}}$$

And again the profit for the year is the attributable profit less any profits taken in earlier years (though, if applicable, the loss for the year is the *entire* foreseeable loss).

This approach, in effect, regards each section of the contract as a job which can earn profit in its own right rather than viewing the contract as being a single indivisible profit-earning job (albeit that profit is apportionable between time periods).

It is easy to be critical of this traditional method. As will be appreciated, step (*b*) uses arbitrary reducing ratios – indeed, an unusual ratio in the second part for in no other book-keeping context do we reduce profit on sales by a cash receipts to sales turnover ratio. But it must be admitted that the method does avoid an over-optimistic assessment of the contract profit.

17. Contract accounts – uncompleted contract. Where a contract is incomplete the procedure given in **13** needs some amendment. First, steps (*e*) and (*f*) become inappropriate and the following steps should be inserted in lieu:

(*e*) Mark off two blank spaces in the Contract Account. (For reference purposes the first of these will be termed the P/L section and the second the Future section. The part of the account already containing the period costs will be referred to as the Current section.)

(*f*) Debit the Current section and credit the Future section with any accruals.

(*g*) Credit the Current section and debit the Future section with:

(*i*) prepayments;
(*ii*) stock on hand at site;
(*iii*) plant remaining on site at written-down values.

(*h*) Credit and close off the Current section with the balance now remaining (which must be the cost of work done) and *split this figure* into:

(*i*) cost of work done *and certified*, which is debited to the P/L section;

(*ii*) cost of work done and not yet certified, which is debited to the Future section.

(*i*) Credit P/L section with the sales value of the work certified as shown on the certificates (the customer's personal account being debited).

(*j*) Complete the book-keeping as follows:

(*i*) Balance the P/L section to find profit to date.

(*ii*) Determine the profit to be taken (*see* **15, 16**) and debit the P/L section with this figure, the Profits and Losses on Contracts Account being credited.

(*iii*) Debit the P/L section and credit the Future section with the remaining balance which is profit-in-suspense.

The P/L section is now closed and the Future section contains the opening figures for the new period.

18. Contract cost accounting – illustration. The book-keeping procedure applicable to a contract can be illustrated using the following data:

Basic data:

(*i*) Details of Contract 158, for Customer AZA, begun during the year and having a total contract value of £9.5M:

Item	*£000s*
Materials purchased and delivered to site	4,421
Materials issued from store	374
Materials returned to store	86
Site wages	1,440
Site direct expenses	195
Plant sent to site	480
Plant returned from site	130
Architect's fees	200
Sub-contract work	680
Head office overheads to be charged at 12½% of site wages	

(*ii*) At the year end valuations were:

Item	
Materials on site	124
Plant on site	205
Cost of work done but not yet certified (work in progress)	371
Prepayments	11
Accruals	37
Estimate to complete	$£\frac{1}{2}$M
Estimated rectification costs	£0.8M

(*iii*) During the year architects' certificates to the value of £8,100,000 were issued and AZA made progress payments to this amount, less 10% retention monies (*see* **11** and **12**).

Account entries:

The letters in brackets in the accounts below refer to the steps detailed in **13**(*a*) – (*d*) and **17**(*e*) – (*f*).

x and *y* in the P/L section are the period attributable and non-attributable profits. See Note 1 at the end for their determination.

CONTRACT 158 A/C[a] (CLIENT AZA)

[*Current section*]

	£000s		£000s
Materials purchased[b]	4,421	Materials returned[c]	86
Materials ex store[b]	374	Plant returned[c]	130
Site wages[b]	1,440	Prepayment c/d[g]	11
Site direct expenses[b]	195	Stock at site c/d[g]	124
Plant sent to site[b]	480	Plant at side c/d[g]	205
Architect's fees[b]	200	Cost of work certified c/d[h]	7,080*
Sub-contract work[b]	680	Work in progress c/d[h]	371
Head office overheads[d]	180		
Accruals c/d[f]	37		
	£8,007		£8,007

*After all the entries (*b*) to (*g*) have been made there is a debit balance of £7,451,000 on this part of the account. This balance represents the total cost of work done. Since the cost of work done and *not* certified is £371,000, then the cost of work certified is £7,451,000 less £371,000 = £7,080,000.

[*Profit and loss section*]

	£000s		£000s
Cost of work certified b/d[h]	7,080	Work certified, AZA A/c[i]	8,100
P/L on Contracts[j]	x		
Profit in suspense c/d[j]	y		
	£8,100		£8,100

[*Future section*]

	£000s		£000s
Prepayment b/d[g]	11	Accruals b/d[f]	37
Stock at site b/d[g]	124	Profit in suspense b/d[j]	y
Plant at site b/d[g]	205		
Work in progress b/d[h]	371		

CUSTOMER AZA A/C (CONTRACT 158)

Invoices and certificates, Contract 158 A/c[i]	£8,100,000	Cash, progress payment (less 10% retention)	£7,290,000

NOTES: 1. The values of x and y depend upon the method of determining the period attributable profit. In this instance we have the following two sets of values:

(a) SSAP 9 profit assessment (**15**)

Total contract cost
$$= 7,451,000 + 500,000 + 800,000 = £8,751,000$$
Period attributable profit
$$= (9,500,000 - 8,751,000) \times 7,451,000/8,751,000 = \underline{£637,733}.$$

So x is £637,733 and y, therefore, must be the balancing figure in the P/L section, i.e. $8,100,000 - (7,080,000 + 637,733)$ $= \underline{£382,267}.$

(b) Traditional method (**16**)

Total profit in P/L section
$$= 8,100,000 - 7,080,000 = £1,020,000$$
Period attributable profit $= (1,020,000 \times \frac{2}{3})$
$$\times 7,290,000/8,100,000 = \underline{£612,000}.$$

So x is £612,000 and again y is the balancing figure, i.e. $1,020,000 - 612,000 = \underline{£408,000}.$

2. Since the contract began during the year, no previous profit attributions enter the computations.

19. Uncompleted contracts and the balance sheet format. A further unusual feature of the SSAP 9 requirements for contract book-keeping is the manner in which an uncompleted contract is to be shown on the balance sheet. Such a contract must be shown as the cumulative contract cost plus any attributable profits (or less any foreseeable losses) and less progress payments received and receivable – and on this latter point it should be borne in mind that there may well be uncertainty as to whether a particular receivable has the same legal status as a normal trade debt. In effect the contract value is shown as akin to a debtor – i.e. at the cost-of-sales plus mark-up less receipts to date – and a work-in-progress figure combined, the overall amount being declared as 'Work-in-progress'. In the case of the illustration just given (and adopting, of course, the SSAP 9 method of ascertaining the attributable profit) the balance sheet will, therefore, show the following:

Work-in-progress:	Cost to date	£7,451,000
	Plus attributable profit	637,733
		8,088,733
	Less cash received and receivable	7,290,000*
		£798,733

*Work certified less 10% retention monies = 90% of £8.1M

Progress test 6

1. Distinguish between the following: (*a*) specific order costing; (**2**) (*b*) job costing; (**3**) (*c*) unit costing; (**4**) (*d*) Output costing; (**5**) (*e*) Operating costing; (**6**) (*f*) Process costing: (*i*) discrete units; (*ii*) continuous units; (**7**) (*g*) Batch costing; (**8**) (*h*) Uniform costing; (**9**) (*i*) Contract costing. (**10**)

2. Outline the procedure followed when preparing a job cost. (**3**)

3. (*a*) What has SSAP 9 to say about profit on an uncompleted contract? (**15**)

(*b*) Distinguish between an SSAP 9 profit and a traditional profit. (**15, 16**)

4. State two methods of charging plant to contracts. (**10**(*e*))

5. What are: (*a*) architects' certificates; (**11**) (*b*) retention monies? (**12**)

6. Distinguish carefully between the three sections into which an uncompleted contract account divides at the end of a trading period. (**17**)

Practice

7. From the following data prepare the job cost for job 111 and find the profit earned:

Job 111 details:

(*a*) On 3 May 20 units of PQ were issued.

(*b*) An extract from the wages analysis for week ending 12 May showed the following:

Dept.	Employee	Total hours	Hourly rate	Hours booked to job 111
X	A. Able	48	£4.00	9
Y	B. Baker	52	£4.50	5 + 2*

*2 hours 'special' overtime.

(*c*) On 15 May a subcontractor's invoice showed a charge of £3 for a storage box into which job 111 was to be packed.

(*d*) The finished job was collected by the customer who paid £200.

Accounting details:

(*a*) The stores record card for PQ showed that the first purchase of PQ was on 1 April when 100 units were bought for £200, a further purchase of 100 units at £2.40 each being made on 24 April. The only issues were 40 units on 15 April to job 94 and the issue of 20 units to job 111 on 3 May. The company uses the weighted average method of pricing.

(*b*) The company operates a 40-hour week, overtime being paid at double time. Each employee's overtime premium for 'normal' overtime work is spread over all the hours (excluding 'special' overtime) worked by the employee during the week. The premium on 'special' overtime is, however, charged direct to the job worked upon since it represents overtime at the customer's request. The only 'special' overtime worked during the week was the two hours on job 111.

(c) The company's budget contains the following figures:

Dept. X: £40,000 overheads and 20,000 direct labour hours
Dept. Y: £100,000 overheads and 100,000 direct labour hours

Sales Dept.: £150,000
Factory cost of sales: £3,000,000

8. In the second year of the AZA contract described in **18** the client requested a slow-down in the work. In consequence the contract was not completed as expected though some work was done, including some early rectification work. During the year the following transactions took place:

Materials purchased and delivered to site	£92,000
Site wages	16,000
Site expenses	2,000
Sub-contract work paid for	3,000

And at the year-end the following valuations were made:

Materials on site	61,000
Plant on site	195,000
Cost of work done but not certified	112,000
Accruals	1,000

During the year architects' certificates to the value of £500,000 were issued but AZA made no payments on these. The end of year estimate to complete and the estimated rectification costs were £300,000 and £700,000 respectively.

Show the Current, Profit & Loss and the Future sections of the contract account as at the end of the second year as it would appear:

(a) Adopting SSAP 9 for ascertaining the profit to be taken;

(b) Adopting the traditional method of ascertaining the profit to be taken.

Show how the contract would appear on the Balance Sheet under SSAP 9 and say which method of profit-taking you prefer in this particular case.

9. The Thorough Garage finds that the conventional way of job costing small repair and service work on job cards is far too costly. Outline an alternative system.

7

Cost accounts

There are two basic types of cost accounting: *integral accounts* and *interlocking accounts*. They exist separately for purely historical reasons and not because their use depends upon different circumstances. Integral accounts evolved after and from interlocking accounts and is the better and more efficient system. However, interlocking accounts are still used in industry, and are still examined upon, and therefore both types are outlined here.

It should, perhaps, be appreciated that the current level of computer technology does, in fact, render the traditional form of double-entry book-keeping obsolete. Today the most effective accounting technique is data-base accounting which incorporates set theory mathematics. However, it will no doubt be some time before accountants accept this newer form of computer accounting and probably even longer before double-entry is abandoned in examinations. This chapter, then, concerns itself only with the older traditional form of cost book-keeping.

Cost accounts

The cost accounts are those accounts which relate to all the transactions involving enterprise costs and are physically held in the cost ledger. And whichever system is adopted, integral or interlocking accounts, those *cost accounts* are essentially the same – it is only the way they relate to the financial accounts that is different.

1. **Basic cost ledger data flow.** There is a fundamental difference between the structure of financial accounts and that of cost accounts in that whereas the financial accounts aim to classify

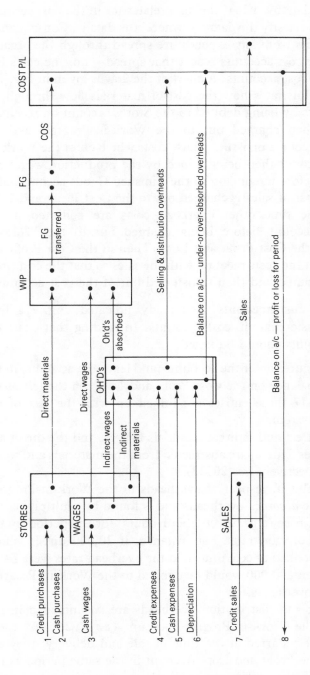

Figure 7.1 *Chart of accounts in the cost ledger*

Note that in this and the following two figures accounts having a double line at the bottom are those which are in principle closed off at the end of each accounting period

transaction data by 'what' the data relates to, in the cost accounts the aim is to classify the data by 'where' the data is. Consequently, as the benefits from any expenditure spread through the organization, so the cost accounts reflect that spread – i.e. the costs flow through the cost accounts. A chart of the flow is given in Fig. 7.1. This chart illustrates how the cost of materials flow through the cost accounts by being debited to the Stores account on receipt of materials, then charged out to the Work-in-Progress and the Overhead accounts on issue – those costs which enter the Work-in-Progress account then being joined by the production wages and overheads before moving on to the Finished Goods account, after which the cost-of-sales is charged out to the Cost Profit and Loss. At the same time other overhead costs are collected in the Overhead account before being charged out to the Work-in-Progress or the Cost Profit and Loss. Then in the Cost Profit and Loss account the costs meet up with the sales so that the cost profit can be computed and then transferred out of the cost accounts.

2. Chart of cost accounts. As already indicated, Fig. 7.1 illustrates the basic chart in cost accounts. In reading that chart the following points should be noted:

(*a*) Cost figures enter the accounts (and leave the accounts in the case of the balance on the Cost Profit and Loss) on the left of the chart. In **7–17** these entries are linked up with the rest of the accounting system.

(*b*) The direct and indirect materials figures, and the direct and indirect wages figures, are abstracted from the materials and wages analyses respectively (*see* **20, 23**).

(*c*) The debit in respect of overheads to the Work-in-Progress account is the *absorbed* overheads and is found by multiplying the total units of base (e.g. direct labour hours) for the period by the overhead absorption rate. For instance, if 20,000 direct labour hours were booked to cost units and the overhead rates were £4.50 per hour, then £90,000 would be debited to the Work-in-Progress account for overheads.

(*d*) Selling and distribution overheads are *not* included in the charges to the Work-in-Progress account (*see* 5:**26**). As these overheads are incurred at the time of sale and delivery, they are charged to the Profit and Loss Account in the same period as the sales to which they relate are credited.

(*e*) The final balance on the Overhead account must be the under- or over-absorbed overhead (*see* 5 : 24(*b*)), and this, of course, is transferred to the Cost Profit and Loss account (unless the business is seasonal, *see* 5 : 24(*c*)).

(*f*) The balances on the Stores account, Work-in-Progress account and Finished Goods account are all closing stock values. An analysis of these figures can always be found in the subsidiary records (*see* **19**).

(*g*) Since the cost-of-sales transferred into the Cost Profit and Loss account is the total production cost of sales, it only remains to set this off against the sales and deduct the selling and distribution costs (either the actual costs or the absorbed costs) for a profit figure to be found (although this profit is often adjusted by under- or over-absorbed overheads).

3. Further analysis of chart. Our chart is inevitably a highly simplified version of a full set of cost accounts in practice. In a more practical context the following account sub-divisions will normally be found:

(*a*) The Stores account may well comprise an account for each physical store or class of store held.

(*b*) There will be a Work-in-Progress account for each department (and even perhaps classes of work within each of the departments) and as work is physically transferred from department to department, so the associated Work-in-Progress accounts are debited and credited to reflect the movement of the corresponding values.

(*c*) The Overheads account is made up of a number of sub-accounts. Firstly, there may be a group of Overhead accounts which collate the expenses under a 'nature' or 'what' classification (e.g. heating, rent and rates, security). The costs accumulated in these accounts would then be transferred to a set of Overhead accounts relating to locations, i.e. cost centres or departments. In the case of service departments, the overall costs of these departments would in turn be transferred to the Overhead accounts of the locations which benefit from those services. And, finally, the costs incurred by these latter locations would be transferred to the work-in-progress accounts using one of the methods of absorption. (For details of the mathematics of these cost apportionments, *see* Chapter 5.)

(d) Although in the chart the Overhead account is shown as being closed off at the period end, nevertheless in practice there is often a small residue of expense accruals and prepayments which will be carried down on this account into the next period.

4. Cost account sub-systems. Within the accounts as a whole there are often sub-systems – particularly in respect of materials, labour and scrap (*see* **18–26**).

5. Cost accounting trading periods. Because of the role costing plays in providing day-to-day management with vital cost data, in cost accounting a one-month trading period is adopted far more often than it is in financial accounting. Indeed, it is difficult to conceive of a worthwhile cost accounting system which adopted a trading period longer than one month.

6. Cost audits. As will be appreciated, just as financial accounts can be audited so can cost accounts – and a *cost audit* is, of course, simply the verification of the correctness of the cost accounts and of the adherence to proper cost accounting procedures. Clearly, this will involve checking that:

(a) the figures themselves are correct;

(b) the cost accounts, cost centres and cost units are correctly charged.

It should be appreciated that the purpose of a cost audit is essentially to check that the various systems can be relied upon to operate in the intended manner rather than to locate and correct individual errors.

Cost audits generally follow the same procedural approach as normal financial audits.

Interlocking accounts

7. Interlocking accounts. This is a system of cost accounting in which the cost accounts have no double-entry connection with the financial accounts, but use the same basic data. With interlocking accounts, therefore, the cost ledger is kept quite independently from the financial ledger, but since the basic data is the same, the two ledgers should be essentially in accord with each other.

8. Chart of interlocking accounts. Since under interlocking accounts the actual ledger accounts have no connection with each other, the financial accounts in the financial ledger are in no way affected by the existence of the cost accounts and so, in principle, can be ignored. However, since both sets of accounts use the same *data* there is a link between the financial and cost data figures. This link is illustrated in Fig. 7.2 where it can be seen that, as regards the *financial accounts:*

(*a*) There is a total block on any double entry crossing from the financial ledger to the cost ledger, and vice versa.

(*b*) The financial accounts are essentially the accounts of any normal book-keeping system.

(*c*) The financial ledger account entries which use the interlocking data have been shown aligned against those same entries in the cost accounts – i.e. the left hand side of Fig. 7.1 – so that the link beween the two sets of ledger accounts can be seen.

(*d*) The financial ledger sometimes records data which is not incorporated into the cost accounts – and the Financial Expenses account illustrates this point in Fig. 7.2.

(*e*) The Financial Profit and Loss account is identical to the normal book-keeping Profit and Loss account.

9. Cost Control account – interlocking accounts. Looking at the cost ledger side of Fig. 7.2 it will be seen that a new account appears in this ledger – the Cost Control account – and that apart from this account the cost accounts are simply those shown in Fig. 7.1. This new Cost Control account has only one function – to accept the second part of the double-entry of all the otherwise uncompleted cost ledger entries. It acts, in fact, rather like a dustbin – if, on introducing cost data into the ledger, one has to find some account where the second half of the double-entry can be dumped, then the Cost Control account is the place.

As will be quickly appreciated, the sole reason for the Cost Control account is to enable the cost ledger to be self-balancing. The figures within it are rarely revealing and the end-of-period balance is a rather uninformative amalgam of stock values, cumulative profits and losses, notional costs (*see* **10**), accruals and pre-payments (i.e. a total of all the cost account balances, and displayed on the 'wrong' side of the account).

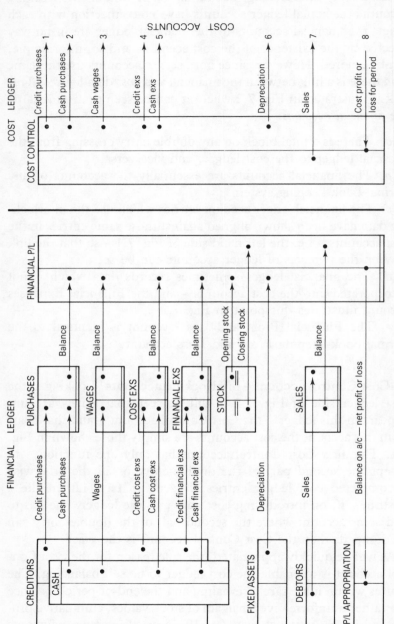

Figure 7.2 *Chart of interlocking accounts*

10. Notional accounts. Just as it is possible to have financial data that appears only in the financial ledger (*see* **8**(*d*)), so it is possible to have cost data that appears only in the cost ledger. Typically notional costs record such data. Where accounts for notional costs exist the double-entry is quite straightforward – the cost account bearing the cost is debited and the Cost Control account is credited.

11. Reconciliation of financial and cost profits. If all the data in the overall system is both the same and treated the same then the cost and financial profits will inevitably be identical. However, values and treatment are often not the same. Sometimes, as we have seen, there are accounts in one ledger which are not in the other. Also stock is frequently valued more conservatively in the financial accounts than in the cost accounts, and on occasion the two sets of accounts use different depreciation figures. As a result of all this the financial and cost profits do *not* agree. This being so it is a worthwhile exercise to reconcile the two both so that the differences in the data treatment can be highlighted and, more importantly, so that the correctness of the system is checked (e.g. such a reconciliation may reveal that certain data is improperly being included in, or excluded from, one or the other set of accounts). To reconcile the financial and cost profits, the following procedure should be adopted:

(*a*) Start with the cost profit.
(*b*) Adjust for differing views.
   (*i*) Ascertain all the points where the financial accountant viewed a transaction or value differently from the cost accountant.
   (*ii*) Compute for each point the money difference between the two views.
   (*iii*) Ask yourself, 'If the cost accountant had adopted the financial accountant's view, would the *cost* profit have been increased or decreased?' If increased, add the money difference, and vice versa.
(*c*) After taking into consideration all the points the resulting figure should be identical to the financial profit. If it is not, the two profits have not been reconciled and further differences must be sought.

EXAMPLE:

Data:

Cost P/L account	£12,800 profit
Financial P/L account	£11,300 profit

In the cost ledger: a £5,000 charge was made for depreciation, and the closing stock of raw materials was valued at £23,600.

In the Financial Ledger: depreciation was £4,400 and closing raw materials stock was valued at £21,500.

Method of reconciliation:

	£
Profit as per cost P/L account	12,800
Change if cost accountant had adopted financial accountant's depreciation charge	+600
	13,400
Change if cost accountant had adopted financial accountant's raw materials stock value	−2,100
Profit as per financial P/L account	£11,300

NOTE: 1. The narrative for change entries can be abbreviated to the name of the difference, e.g. 'depreciation', 'raw materials stock value'. 2. Where there are more than two differences the layout is improved if all the additions are collected together and subtotalled, and similarly the subtractions.

12. Interlocking account – illustration. An illustration of the workings of an interlocking system of accounts is given in **17** where a single set of data is used to illustrate the accounts formed under both interlocking and integral account techniques.

13. Reconciliations in general. It should be appreciated that the technique of reconciling profits can be extended to any other book-keeping reconciliation (or 'analysis of differences' as it is sometimes referred to in examination questions). If we designate the figures to be reconciled in the two sets of accounts A and Z respectively, the general procedure is as follows.

(*a*) Start with A.

(*b*) Adjust for each item that shows different amounts in the two sets of accounts by considering how A would have altered if the figure in the Z set of accounts had been used in lieu of the figure actually used in the A set of accounts.

(c) At the end, check that Z is the resulting figure.

EXAMPLE:

The estimated cost of job 1001 was £3,500 but the actual cost was £3,850. Using the information below reconcile (analyze the differences between) these costs.

(a) The estimate specified among other things 100 units of material at £10 each less a quantity discount of 4 per cent, labour of 500 hours at £1.90 per hour and an overhead absorption rate of £2.50 per direct labour hour.

(b) The actual cost included a material cost of 100 units at £10 less a quantity discount of 10 per cent and a labour charge of 580 hours at £2 per hour.

SOLUTION:

			£
(a) Estimated cost			3,500
(b) Effect of extra quantity discount: (10–4)% of 100 × £10			−60
			3,440
Effect of extra labour time: 80 hrs labour at £1.90 per hr	£152		
80 hrs overhead at £2.50 per hr	200	+352	
			3,792
Effect of higher wage rate: 580 hrs at 10p			+58
(c) Actual cost			£3,850

Integrated accounts

14. Integrated accounts. This term relates to a single accounting system which contains both financial and cost accounts and which uses a common input of data for all accounting purposes. In theory, all accounts are in a single ledger, though for practical purposes the accounts are usually kept in two physically separate ledgers.

15. Chart of integrated accounts. Figure 7.3 illustrates the essential accounting flow in the system of integrated accounts. The chart shows a dotted Cost Control account. Since such an account is purely optional the chart should initially be looked at as if the account did not exist, and on this basis the following points should be observed:

(a) The double-entry flows from the financial accounts to the cost accounts (it will be seen that the double-entries for the accounts in Fig. 7.3 are to be found in Fig. 7.1). In the pure book-keeping theory there is no distinction between the accounts in the two ledgers and so the demarcation line between them is shown in the chart as a dashed line.

(b) All the old nominal accounts and the Stock account disappear entirely from the financial accounts with the exception possibly of the occasional account relating to expenses or income which it is not intended should be entered in the cost accounts (represented in the chart by the Financial Expenses account).

(c) The assets and liability accounts (other than the Stock account which disappears) are in no way affected by the adoption of an integrated accounts system.

(d) The Financial Profit and Loss account comprises the profit transferred from the Cost Profit and Loss in the cost accounts together with the occasional nominal account balance relating to data excluded from the cost accounts. Since this profit and loss account incorporates the cost profit there is *no need to reconcile the cost and financial profits*.

(e) Stock values, accruals and pre-payments are all to be found in the balances on the various cost accounts.

16. Cost Control account – integrated accounts. As has been mentioned, in practice it is generally found to be physically inconvenient to keep all the accounts in a single ledger. The ledger is, therefore, physically divided into two, the financial ledger under the responsibility of the financial accountant, the cost ledger under the responsibility of the cost accountant. This does *not* affect the

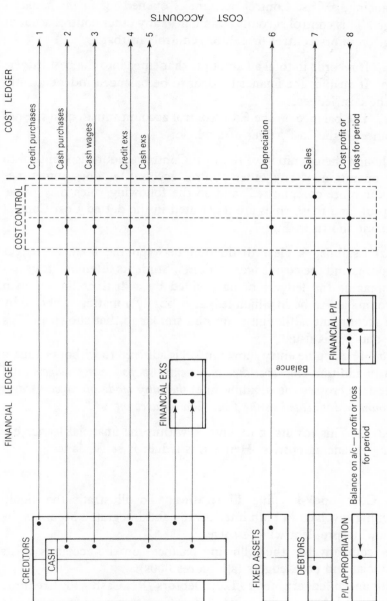

Figure 7.3 *Chart of integrated accounts*

double entry given in Figs 7.1 and 7.3 but, in order to assist balancing, a Cost Control account is opened up *in the financial ledger*. This control account is similar to any other control account (e.g. creditors control or debtors control) in that:

(*a*) It records in total all amounts that enter into the cost ledger;

(*b*) It enables the financial ledger to be balanced independently of the cost ledger;

(*c*) The balance on the Cost Control account must equal the net balance in the cost ledger as a whole.

Although the operation of the Cost Control account is identical to the operation of any other control account, it does sometimes appear more complicated, and so the following rules may prove helpful (and these rules are illustrated in the dotted Cost Control account shown in Fig. 7.3).

(*a*) Establish a clear distinction between the financial ledger accounts and the cost ledger accounts. Students often find it useful to imagine the ledgers being divided by a distinct line. Which accounts are to be in which ledger is purely a matter of choice by the accountant, although a division similar to that shown in Figs 7.1 and 7.3 is usual.

(*b*) The double entry shown in 7.3 is adhered to without change, but in addition *whenever the double-entry spans the two ledgers* (and therefore crosses the dividing line) *the entry made in the cost ledger account is duplicated in the Cost Control account.*

NOTE: This results in *all* entries within the financial ledger being balancing entries. Hence this ledger is self-balancing.

17. Cost book-keeping illustration. To illustrate the book-keeping involved in both interlocking and integrated accounts the following problem will be solved:

A company has the following balances on the accounts in its financial and cost ledgers (all figures 000s):

Financial ledger: Stock £120; Debtors £91; Cash £30; Creditors £40; Fixed Assets (w/d value) £100; Cost Expenses (accrual) £1; Capital & Reserves £300.

Cost ledger: Stores £38; Work-in-Progress £40; Finished Goods £62.

During the trading period the following transactions took place (000s):

Credit trading: Purchases £62; Sales £145; Cost expenses £24.
Cash payments: Purchases £8; Wages £35; Cost expenses £12; Financial expenses £3; Creditors £80.
Cash receipts: Debtors £132.
Stores issues: Direct materials £75; Indirect materials £4.
Transfers: Work-in progress to finished goods £151; Cost of sales from finished goods £115

You also have the following information:

Production overheads are absorbed at 200% direct wages.
£10,000 of the overheads related to selling and distribution.
The wage analysis disclosed that there were £26,000 direct wages and £9,000 indirect wages.
Depreciation: Financial accounts – 10% w/d asset value; Cost accounts – £8,000
Closing stocks: All classes were conservatively valued in the financial accounts at £153,000.
Financial expenses are never incorporated into the cost accounts.
A notional charge of £3,000 was made for rent in the cost accounts.
At the period end there was a cost expense prepayment of £5,000 which was carried forward in the financial accounts but not in the cost accounts.

(*a*) On the basis of an interlocking accounts system prepare all the financial and cost accounts and reconcile the financial and cost profits.
(*b*) Re-write all the financial and cost accounts on the basis of an integrated accounts system, given the following changed circumstances:

(*i*) The stock values and depreciation are those to be found in the cost accounts, but a Stock Provision account, which adjusts the total stock valuation to that previously recorded in the financial accounts, is kept in the financial ledger.
(*ii*) The accruals and pre-payments are now incorporated in the cost accounts (although the financial expenses continue to remain outside the cost accounts).

FINANCIAL LEDGER

CREDITORS
Dr		Cr	
Cash	80	Bal b/d	40
Bal c/d	46	Purchases	62
		Cost exs	24
	46		46
		Bal b/d	46

PURCHASES
Dr		Cr	
Creditors	62	P/L	70
Cash	8		
	70		

WAGES
Dr		Cr	
Cash	35	P/L	35

FINANCIAL P/L
Dr		Cr	
Purchases	70	Sales	145
Wages	35		
Cost exs	30	Close stock	30
Fin exs	3		
Deprec.	10		
Open stock	120		
Profit c/d	30		

COST EXS
Dr		Cr	
Creditors	24	Bal b/d	1
Cash	12	P/L	30
		Bal c/d	5
			5
Bal b/d	5		

FINANCIAL EXS
Dr		Cr	
Cash	3	P/L	3

STOCK
Dr		Cr	
Bal b/d	120	P/L	120
P/L	153		

SALES
Dr		Cr	
P/L	145	Debtors	145

APPROPRIATION
Dr		Cr	
		P/L	30
Approp.	30	Profit b/d	30

DEBTORS
Dr		Cr	
Bal b/d	91	Cash	132
Sales	145	Bal c/d	104
			104
Bal b/d	104		

CASH
Dr		Cr	
Bal b/d	30	Purchases	8
Debtors	132	Wages	35
		Cost exs	12
		Fin exs	3
		Creditors	80
		Bal c/d	24
Bal b/d	24		

FIXED ASSETS
Dr		Cr	
Bal b/d	100	P/L	10
		Bal c/d	90
Bal b/d	90		

CAPITAL
Dr		Cr	
		Bal	300
Bal	300		

COST LEDGER

COST CONTROL
Dr		Cr	
Sales	145	Bal b/d	140
		Cr. pur	62
		Cash pur	8
		Wages	35
		Cr. ohds	24
		Cash ohds	12
		Deprec.	8
		Not. rent	3
Bal c/d	169	Profit	22
	169		
		Bal b/d	169

NOTIONAL RENT
Dr		Cr	
C.C.	3	Ohds	3

WAGES
Dr		Cr	
C.C.	35	WIP	26
		Ohds	9

SALES
Dr		Cr	
P/L	145	C.C.	145

OH'D'S
Dr		Cr	
C.C.	24	WIP	52
C.C.	12	P/L	10
Stores	4		
Wages	9		
Deprec.	8		
Rent	3		
P/L	2		

STORES
Dr		Cr	
Bal b/d	38	WIP	75
C.C.	62	Ohds	4
C.C.	8	Bal c/d	29
	29		
Bal b/d	29		

WIP
Dr		Cr	
Bal b/d	40	FG	151
Stores	75	Bal c/d	42
Wages	26		
Ohds	52		
Bal b/d	42		

F.G.
Dr		Cr	
Bal b/d	62	P/L	115
WIP	151	Bal c/d	98
Bal b/d	98		

COST P/L
Dr		Cr	
FG	115	Sales	145
S & D	10	Ohds	
		O-absorb	2
Profit c/d	22		
C.C.	22	Profit b/d	22

Note: C.C. = Cost Control

Figure 7.4(a) Solution (a) Interlocking accounts (all figures in £000s)

FINANCIAL LEDGER

CREDITORS

Cash	80	Bal b/d	40
Bal c/d	46	Stores	62
		Ohds	24
		Bal b/d	46

CASH

Bal b/d	30	Stores	8
Debtors	132	Wages	35
		Ohds	12
		Fin exs	3
		Creditors	80
		Bal c/d	24
Bal b/d	24		

FIXED ASSETS

Bal b/d	100	Ohds	8
		Bal c/d	92
Bal b/d	92		

DEBTORS

Bal b/d	91	Cash	132
Sales	145	Bal c/d	104
Bal b/d	104		

FINANCIAL EXS

Cash	3	P/L	3

NOTIONAL RENT

Fin P/L	3	Ohds	3

COST CONTROL

Sales	145	Bal b/d	139
Bal c/d	174	Creditors	62
		Creditors	24
		Cash	8
		Cash	35
		Cash	12
		FA	8
		Rent	3
		P/L	28
			174
		Bal b/d	174

STOCK PROVISION

P/L	20	Bal	20
		P/L	16

FINANCIAL P/L

Fin exs	3	Cost P/L	28
Close stock prov.	16	Not. rent	3
Approp.	32	Open stock prov.	20

APPROPRIATION

		P/L	32

CAPITAL

		Bal	300

COST LEDGER

STORES

Bal b/d	38	WIP	75
Creditors	62	Ohds	4
Cash	8	Bal c/d	29
Bal b/d	29		

WAGES

Cash	35	WIP	26
		Ohds	9

SALES

P/L	145	Debtors	145

WIP

Bal b/d	40	FG	151
Stores	75	Bal c/d	42
Wages	26		
Ohds	52		
Bal b/d	42		

OH'D'S

Creditors	24	Bal b/d	1
Cash	12	WIP	52
Stores	4	P/L	10
Wages	9	Bal c/d	5
Deprec.	8		
Rent	3		
P/L	8		
		Bal b/d	5

F.G.

Bal b/d	62	P/L	115
WIP	151	Bal c/d	98
Bal b/d	98		

COST P/L

FG	115	Sales	145
S & D	10	Ohds	10
Profit c/d	28	O-absorb	8
Fin P/L	28	Profit b/d	28

Notes:

1. Treatment of Notional Rent:
   (a) Amount credited to Notional Rent a/c in the Financial Ledger and debited to Overheads (and Cost Control).
   (b) Amount released to profit via credit to the Financial P/L.

2. Stock Provision a/c: If desired (and as called for in this question), a Stock Provision a/c can be held in the Financial Ledger and a provision equal to the difference between the cost stock value and the more conservative financial stock value can be made by adjustments to the Financial P/L.

Figure 7.4(b) Solution (b) Integrated accounts (all figures in £000s)

SOLUTION:

(a) For the accounts – see Fig. 7.4(a)

Reconciliation:

		£
COST PROFIT		22,000
Depreciation: Difference £10,000 and £8,000		−2,000
Stocks: Value change:		

Financial a/cs:	120,000 to 153,000 = £+33,000
Cost a/cs:	140,000 to 169,000 = £+29,000

		£
Difference	£4,000	+4,000
Accruals: Opening £1,000 in financial accounts only		+1,000
Prepayments: Closing £5,000 in financial accounts only		+5,000
Financial expenses: £3,000 in financial accounts only		−3,000
Notional rent: £3,000 in cost accounts only		+3,000
FINANCIAL PROFIT		£30,000

(b) See Fig. 7.4(b).

Accounting for material costs

With the financial and cost accounting framework now in place we can look in this and the following two sections at how the specific and more detailed routines for accounting for materials, labour and scrap may be handled. To the extent that it is relevant an integrated accounting system will be assumed.

18. Chart of material accounts. Figure 7.5 shows the accounting flow chart for materials. The lower half shows in slightly more detail than Fig. 7.1 the ledger accounts involved, while the top half shows the parallel subsidiary records and accounting procedure required for individual transactions.

19. Subsidiary records. Study of Fig. 7.5 shows that each of the three main ledger accounts acts as a control account for a particular set of subsidiary records – the Creditors Control account controlling the Creditors ledger (as in normal book-keeping practice), the Stores account controlling the stores records cards, and the Work-in-progress account controlling the job cards. This results in the

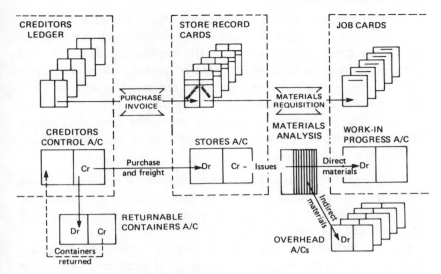

Figure 7.5 *Material accounting flow chart*
This chart shows the flow of data and the pattern of record-keeping
necessary in materials cost book-keeping

following.

(*a*) All details relating to figures in the main accounts can be
obtained by referring to the subsidiary records.

(*b*) The overall balance on any set of subsidiary records *will
equal the balance on the control account*. Thus the balance on the
Stores account will equal the total of all the value balances on the
stores records cards, and the balance on the Work-in-progress
account will equal the total of the costs shown on all the job cards.
(It should be appreciated that once a job is complete the job card
is removed from the job card file, the total of all such jobs removed
during a period being *credited to the Work-in-progress account.*)

20. Material accounting documents.

(*a*) *Materials requisition.* This document is used to draw the
materials from the store (*see* 2: **2**(*b*)), the original copy passing
through the following procedures:

   (*i*) The requisition is initiated by the foreman who states the
material, quantity, job number or overhead account, and other
minor details.

(*ii*) The requisition is exchanged for the material at the store.

(*iii*) It is then passed to the Stores Records office where the clerk prices the requisition from the appropriate stores record card, computes the value of the material drawn and enters this on the requisition while at the same time entering the quantity and value on the stores record card.

(*iv*) The requisition is finally passed to the Cost office where the cost clerk enters the value onto the materials analysis sheet (*see* (*b*) below).

(*b*) *Materials analysis.* This is an analysis of materials drawn from stores to job numbers and overhead accounts. It ensures that all materials issued are charged to some part or other of the cost accounts and are not overlooked.

It is important that the analysis does not omit any materials requisitions. To guard against this the serial numbers of all requisitions analyzed should be checked to make certain none are missing. To ensure that all requisitions for the period have been received and none are still in the procedure 'pipeline', the foremen's books of requisitions should be examined and the serial numbers of the last requisitions issued by them in the period noted. The materials analysis should not be completed until all requisitions up to and including these final requisitions have been received and entered.

21. Finished goods account. Though not part of the material accounting system, the similarity of the Finished Goods account to the Stores account warrants a mention here. Like the Stores account, the Finished Goods account is a control account controlling, in this case, the *stock* records cards, the balances on these cards collectively equalling the balance on the account.

Accounting for labour costs

22. Chart of labour accounts. Figure 7.6 shows the accounting flow chart for labour and wages. It can be seen that the first step is the computation of gross wages and subsequent deductions. The total gross wage is then analyzed and debited to the appropriate work-in-progress and overhead accounts, while credits to the appropriate financial accounts complete the double entry.

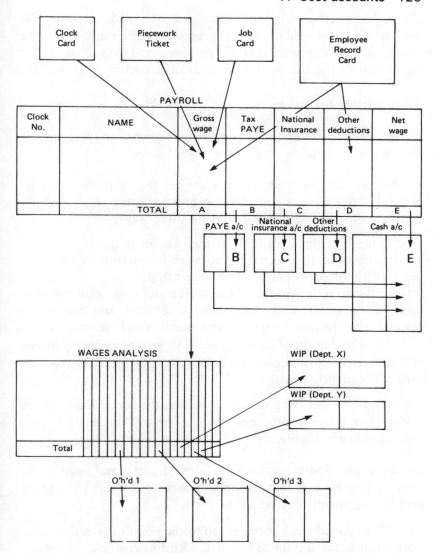

Figure 7.6 *Wage accounting flow chart*
This chart shows the accounting entries involved in accounting for labour costs

23. Wages analysis. A wages analysis is similar to a materials analysis and analyzes the total gross wage to the various cost activities, i.e. jobs and overheads. Essentially the object is to examine each employee's gross wage and compute how much is chargeable to the individual jobs and overhead activities the employee was engaged upon. It is prepared by consulting the same sources of data that were used for preparing the payroll (*see* 3:28), together with the labour time records discussed in 3 : 25 and **26**.

Accounting for scrap

A cost closely associated with material and labour but lying outside the normal accounting flow is the cost of scrap.

24. Scrap. Scrap is material that can no longer be used for its original purpose, e.g. off-cuts or broken parts. It is usually accounted for in one of the following three ways.

(*a*) Sales of scrap are simply treated as 'other income'.

(*b*) Sales of scrap are credited to work-in-progress or the overheads of the department incurring the scrap.

(*c*) If the scrap is kept for an alternative use, then again work-in-progress or department overheads is credited and the stores debited with the *re-use price*, i.e. the worth of the scrap in its new capacity. The deposit of the scrap in the store is recorded by means of a materials returned note (*see* 2:2(*c*)), and a scrap stores records card subsequently raised.

NOTE: If the job (or product) on which the scrap arose can be identified, work-in-progress and the job are credited. If not, overheads are credited.

25. Spoilage. Spoiled work is a form of scrap and may be so treated. However, if circumstances warrant, the following more detailed treatment may be used.

(*a*) The spoiled work is costed up to the point of rejection. The work-in-progress account is credited with this cost and a Spoilage account debited.

(*b*) The Spoilage account is credited with any sales of spoiled materials.

(*c*) The balance on the Spoilage account is transferred to overheads, or alternatively, written off to profit and loss.

26. Rectification. If the spoiled work is to be rectified its cost is transferred to a Rectification account instead of a Spoilage account.

This Rectification account is then debited with all costs of rectification and credited with the normal cost value of the rectified work. Any balance is then transferred to overheads or written off to profit and loss.

Alternatively, rectification costs can simply be regarded as normal costs of production and debited directly to the appropriate work-in-progress account.

Progress test 7

Principles
1. Distinguish between integrated and interlocking accounts. (**7, 14**)

2. What is a cost audit? (**6**)

3. What are the rules for operating a cost control account? (**9, 16**)

4. Explain why the cost and financial profit and loss accounts in integrated accounts do not need to be reconciled. (**15(*d*)**)

5. What detailed records (subsidiary ledgers) do the following accounts control: (*a*) stores; (*b*) work-in-progress; (*c*) finished goods? (**19**)

6. How is scrap accounted for? (**24–6**)

Practice
7. The stock checker's report for the week ended 4th May 19–2 showed the following items and explanations:

Part no.	Physical stock	Stores ledger	Explanation
1234	510	540	Requisition for Job 819 not recorded
2317	486	492	Breaking bulk
4186	295	300	Requisition for factory consumable stores not recorded
1982	309	289	Materials returned from Job 312 not documented
3123	623	423	Supplier's invoice not recorded
5028	210	220	Issue of components for servicing salesman's car not documented

Assuming that all parts are valued at £2 a unit, write up the materials control account (pre-adjustment balance £9,834) indicating the double entry in each case. (*ACCA adapted*)

8. Tiny Ltd. started the year with the following trial balance:

	£	£
Capital: authorized and issued:		
10,000 £1 ord. shares		10,000
Fixed assets	3,000	
Debtors	1,000	
Cost control: stores	£2,000	
work-in-progress	£2,000	
finished goods	£3,000	7,000
Creditors		2,000
Bank	1,000	
	12,000	12,000

During January the following transactions took place:

	£
Stores purchases on credit	2,000
Sales on credit	2,500
Creditors paid (cash)	1,500
Wages	1,000
General operating expenses (cash)	1,000
Discounts allowed	150
Discounts received	100
Payments by debtors (cash)	2,000
Issues from raw materials store	3,000
Issues from finished goods store	2,000
Finished production transferred to finished goods store	4,000
Finished production kept in factory as an addition to fixed assets	500

In the cost accounts £100 was charged to overheads for notional rent and depreciation was taken at 1 per cent for the month on fixed assets (no depreciation on the addition). The company operates an integrated accounting system that incorporates a cost control account.

Prepare:

(a) all ledger accounts;
(b) cost profit and loss account;

(c) financial profit and loss account;
(d) the company trial balance as at the month end.

NOTE: The capital expenditure should be transferred to the financial accounts.

9. A company's trading and profit and loss account for January 19–2 was as follows:

	£		£
Purchases	25,210	Sales: 50,000 units at	
Less Closing stock	4,080	£1.50 each	75,000
		Discounts received	260
	21,130	Profit on sale of land	2,340
Direct wages	10,500		
Works expenses	12,130		
Selling expenses	7,100		
Administration			
expenses	5,340		
Depreciation	1,100		
Net profit	20,300		
	77,600		77,600

The cost profit, however, was only £19,770. Reconcile the financial and cost profits, using the following information.

(a) Cost accounts value of closing stock: £4,280.

(b) The works expenses in the cost accounts were taken as 100 per cent of direct wages.

(c) Selling and administration expenses were charged in the cost accounts at 10 per cent of sales and £0.10 per unit respectively.

(d) Depreciation in the cost accounts was £800.

(e) Purely financial transactions were excluded from the cost accounts.

10. In the absence of the accountant you have been asked to prepare a month's cost accounts for a company which operates a batch costing system fully integrated with the financial accounts. The cost clerk has provided you with the following information, which he thinks is relevant.

Balances at beginning of month:	£
Stores Ledger Control Account	24,175
Work in Progress Control Account	19,210
Finished Goods Control Account	34,164
Prepayments of production overheads brought forward from previous month	2,100

Transactions during the month:	£
Materials purchased	76,150
Materials issued: to production	26,350
for factory maintenance	3,280
Materials transferred between batches	1,450

	Direct Workers	Indirect Workers
	£	£
Total wages paid—Net	17,646	3,342
Employees deductions	4,364	890

	£
Direct wages charged to batches from work tickets	15,236
Recorded non-productive time of direct workers	5,230
Direct wages incurred on production of capital equipment, for use in the factory	2,670
Selling and distribution overheads incurred	5,240
Other production overheads incurred	12,200
Sales	75,400
Cost of finished goods sold	59,830
Cost of goods completed and transferred into finished goods store during the month	62,130
Physical stock value of work in progress at end of month	24,360

The production overhead absorption rate is 150% of direct wages and it is the policy of the company to include a share of production overheads in the cost of capital equipment constructed in the factory.

Required:

(*a*) Prepare the following accounts for the month:

Stores Ledger Control Account

Work in Progress Control Account

Finished Goods Control Account

Production Overhead Control Account

Profit/Loss Account

(*b*) Identify any aspects of the accounts which you consider should be investigated.

(*ACCA*)

8

Process costing: discrete units

Basic process costing

1. Basic principles.

(a) *All* costs, direct and indirect, incurred during the period are charged to each process so that a total process cost for each is obtained.

(b) The total process cost of each process is then shared equally among all the cost units processed in that process. The basic process costing formula, therefore, is:

$$\text{Cost per unit (CPU)} = \frac{\text{Total process cost incurred during period}}{\text{Total units processed during period}}$$

For instance, if the total process cost incurred in processing 1,000 units were £5,000, the CPU would be £5,000/1,000 = £5.

(c) The cost unit cost is built up cumulatively as the cost units pass through the different processes.

2. Discrete and continuous units.
As was indicated in 6:7, the process cost units are either discrete (i.e. physically separate such as light bulbs) or continuous (when units are expressed in measurement terms, e.g. a liquid where the cost unit is a litre). For the rest of this chapter all cost units considered will be discrete units.

3. Equivalent units.
Where discrete units are involved it is rare for every unit in a process to be fully processed by the end of the period. Frequently some units are still in-process and so the figure for the number of units processed in the basic formula must include an allowance for these as some of the process costs were

incurred in their partial processing. This allowance is made by adding to the units fully processed an *equivalent units* figure which is computed by the formula:

Equivalent units = No. of units in progress × % complete.

This is logical, since a cost that enables, say, two units to be each half completed may be regarded as the cost needed to complete fully one unit.

The basic formula now becomes:

$$\text{CPU} = \frac{\text{Cost incurred during period}}{\text{Units completed} + \text{Equivalent units in-progress}}$$

Using the data given in 1, assume that of the 1,000 units, 600 are complete and 400 are in-progress and 50 per cent complete.

COMPUTATIONS:

Equivalent units in-progress = 400 × 50% = 200.

∴ Total equivalent production = 600 + 200 = 800 units.

∴ $\text{CPU} = \dfrac{5,000}{800} = £6.25.$

It should be appreciated that this CPU figure gives the cost incurred for a *fully completed unit*.

4. Cost elements. When we consider the degree of completion of any units in-progress we may well find that the degree differs according to the cost element. To take a domestic example, if one is making a cake, then just before it is put in the oven the cake may well be complete as regards all materials, nearly complete as regards labour, but only just started as regards overheads since the oven heating costs will be the largest part of this element. In order to allow for this, it is necessary to treat cost elements separately and calculate a cost-per-unit figure for each element. Again note that the resulting calculation gives the cost-per-unit for each element for a *complete* unit. This means that the *total* cost of a complete unit can be found by simply adding the separate element costs-per-unit.

For example, assume that our £5,000 illustrative cost was made up of: materials £1,000; labour £2,500; overheads £1,500. 600 units are complete and the 400 in-progress are 75 per cent complete in materials; 50 per cent in labour and 25 per cent in overheads. The CPU for each element can be computed as follows, using the formula in **3** above:

Cost element	£	WIP equivalent units	Total equivalent units produced	CPU £
Materials	1,000	$400 \times 75\% = 300 + 600 = 900$		1.111
Labour	2,500	$400 \times 50\% = 200 + 600 = 800$		3.125
Overheads	1,500	$400 \times 25\% = 100 + 600 = 700$		2.143
Total	£5,000		Total cost per unit	£6.379

5. Valuation of completed units and work-in-progress. The value of completed units is simply:

Number of completed units × Total CPU.

From the figures given in **4** it can be seen that the value of the completed units = $600 \times £6.379 = £3,827$ (to nearest £).

On the other hand, work-in-progress is valued by multiplying *each element cost-per-unit* by the number of *equivalent units* and then adding the products as follows:

Materials: 300 equivalent units at £1.111 =   333.3
Labour: 200 equivalent units at £3.125 =   625.0
Overheads: 100 equivalent units at £2.143 =   214.3

   Total WIP value   £1,173 (to nearest £)

6. Input-output cross-check. Note that since the output value of production must account for all the input costs, the combined values of the completed units and the work-in-progress must equal the total process cost, i.e. in this case our £3,827 + £1,173 must equal the total cost of £5,000 – which it does.

This is clearly a valuable cross-check on the accuracy of the calculations.

7. Units transferred from a previous process. In process costing, units pass through a number of processes in sequence. Consequently, many processes start with units from a previous process.

Now it is a basic costing principle that cost units are transferred to later stages at their cumulative cost, and therefore these costs must be brought into the figures of the new process. It is convenient to treat such a cost as a separate cost element termed 'previous process' and restrict the term 'materials' to material added to production during processing.

'Previous process' is treated no differently from any other cost element. However, its degree of completion is always 100 per cent, since it is that part of the unit cost relating to the cost of previous operations which, clearly, must be fully complete.

Assume now that our 1,000 units were transferred from a previous process at a cost of £5 a unit. This element will appear in the computations as follows:

			Work-in-progress					
1 *Cost element*	2 *Costs*	3 *Completed units*	4 *Units*	5 *% complete*	6 *Equivalent units*	7 *Total equivalent units*	8 *CPU*	9 *WIP value*
	£						£	£
Previous process	5,000	600	400	100	400	1,000	5.000	2,000
Materials	1,000	600	400	75	300	900	1.111	333
Labour	2,500	600	400	50	200	800	3.125	625
Overheads	1,500	600	400	25	100	700	2.143	214
Total	£10,000						£11.379	£3,172

Input-output check:

Value of completed units
= 600 × £11.379 = £6,827
Value of work-in-progress = £3,172
£9,999 total costs

NOTE: The £1 difference in the total costs is due to rounding. It is usual to adjust one of the valuations slightly to bring the output total into line with the total costs. This aids subsequent double entry.

8. The 9-by-4 layout. The layout of nine columns and four rows used above (7) has been devised for the solution of unit costing problems, and the student is advised to learn it thoroughly. Columns 2–5 reproduce the given data (the previous process cost will, of course, always be 100 per cent complete as regards work-in-progress). Columns 6–9 are computed as follows:

$$\text{Column } 6 = \text{column } 4 \times \text{column } 5$$
$$\text{Column } 7 = \text{column } 3 + \text{column } 6$$
$$\text{Column } 8 = \text{column } 2 \div \text{column } 7$$
$$\text{Column } 9 = \text{column } 6 \times \text{column } 8$$

Note that column 3 records the total *completed* units, i.e. it will include units transferred to the next process and also any units completed but lost at the end of the process (*see* **12**).

The layout should, of course, always be balanced using the input-output check described in **6**, i.e. by ensuring that:

Total value of completed units + WIP value =
Total cost of all elements (column 2)

9. Work-in-progress at beginning of period. Where there is work-in-progress at the beginning of the period, two different methods of treatment are open to the accountant, depending upon whether the processed units are to be valued on a FIFO basis or an average price basis. The two methods of treatment are as follows.

(*a*) *FIFO.* The overall object under the FIFO method is to find the CPU of processing all units during the period, use this CPU to determine the cost of completing the in-progress units and then assume that the first units transferred from the process are the old in-progress units which will be valued at their opening value plus the cost of completion. This is done by taking the following steps (*see also* example below).

(*i*) Insert three more 'work-in-progress' columns in the 9-by-4 layout to accommodate the opening WIP data (be careful to distinguish opening WIP and closing WIP).

(*ii*) Head the middle column '% to complete' (in lieu of '% complete'), i.e. if the units are already 70 per cent complete at the beginning of the period then a further 30 per cent is needed to complete and this is the figure that should be entered in this column.

(*iii*) The last of the three columns, then, will show the units processed during the periods in respect of the opening in-progress units.

(*iv*) Amend the heading of column 3 of the 9-by-4 layout to 'Units started and completed' and insert the total units completed in the period less the number of units in the opening work-in-progress.

(*v*) Complete the 9-by-4 layout, by adding the opening WIP equivalent units as found in (*iii*) to the other equivalent units and finding the CPU in the normal manner.

(*vi*) To value the units transferred, follow the steps outlined below.

(1) Take each element of cost and multiply the element CPU by the equivalent units in the opening work-in-progress column. Then add these products. This gives, of course, the total cost of completing the opening work-in-progress.

(2) Add the figure in (1) to the opening work-in-progress value to give the total value of the completed opening work-in-progress units.

(3) Apply the following formula:

Value transferred units =
[(Total units transferred − No. opening WIP units) × Total CPU]
+ Value in 2 above.

In other words, the value of the units transferred is the value of the completed in-progress units together with the balance of units transferred valued in the normal way.

(*b*) *Average price method*. Under the average price method all costs, i.e. period and opening work-in-progress, are averaged. All that is necessary, therefore, is the addition of the opening work-in-progress element values to the period element costs to give a combined column 2 'Costs' figure. All other computations then proceed as usual.

EXAMPLE:
Find the value of the transferred units from the following process data:

	Opening WIP			Period costs (£)
	Units	% Complete	Value (£)	
Previous process	30	100	400	750*
Materials	30	80	100	300
Labour	30	50	150	800
Overheads	30	$33\frac{1}{3}$	80	700
Total			£730	£2,550

*Cost of 70 units transferred during period from the previous process.

100 units were completed and 55 of these transferred to the next process. There was no closing work-in-progress.

FIFO method of valuation.

Cost element	Costs (£)	Units started and completed	Opening work-in-progress			Total equivalent units	CPU (£)
			Units	% to complete	Equivalent units		
Previous process	750	70	30	0	0	70	10.714
Materials	300	70	30	20	6	76	3.947
Labour	800	70	30	50	15	85	9.412
Overheads	700	70	30	$66\frac{2}{3}$	20	90	7.778
Total	£2,550						31.851

		£
Value transferred units:		
30 units opening WIP – cost to complete:	6×3.947	23.682
	15×9.412	141.180
	20×7.778	155.560
		320.422
Opening value		730.000
Total cost of opening WIP units		1,050.422
25 units started and completed: 25×31.851		796.275
55 units transferred		£1,846.697

Check:

Total input = Opening WIP + Period costs
= £730 + £2,550 = £3,280

Total output = Units transferred + Closing stock
= £1,846.697 + (45 × £31.851)
= £3,280 (rounded).

Average price method.

| | Costs (£) | | | Units | CPU |
Cost element	Opening WIP	Period	Total	completed	(£)
Previous process	400	750	1,150	100	11.50
Materials	100	300	400	100	4.00
Labour	150	800	950	100	9.50
Overheads	80	700	780	100	7.80
Total	£730	2,550	3,280		32.80

Value of units transferred = 55 × £32.80 = £1,804

Check:

Total input, as before £3,280.

Total output = Units transferred + Closing stock =
£1,804 + 45 × 32.80 = £3,280.

Normal losses in process

So far it has been assumed that no units have been lost during the processing. In practice this would be extremely rare.

10. Costing principle regarding normal losses. It is a fundamental costing principle that the cost of normal losses should be borne by the good production. The logic of this lies in the fact that such losses are one of the normal costs of production and therefore chargeable to whatever production emerges. Where discrete units are involved the large majority of losses arise, of course, from rejection on inspection.

11. Units lost at the beginning. If units are lost right at the beginning before any materials, labour or overheads have been incurred, then the 9-by-4 layout can be used as it stands without any adjustments.

For example, assume that in the illustration given in **7**, 100 units are lost at the very beginning of the process, resulting in only 500 good units being completed. This will produce the following computations:

Cost element	Costs	Completed units	Work-in-progress Units	Work-in-progress % complete	Equivalent units	Total equivalent units	CPU	WIP value
	£						£	£
Previous process	5,000	500	400	100	400	900	5.556	2,222
Materials	1,000	500	400	75	300	800	1.250	375
Labour	2,500	500	400	50	200	700	3.571	714
Overheads	1,500	500	400	25	100	600	2.500	250
Total	£10,000						£12.877	£3,561

Check:

	£
Value of 500 completed units = 500 × £12.877 =	6,439
Value of work-in-progress =	3,561
	£10,000

12. Units lost at the end. In unit costing it is vital to remember that costs must not be charged until they are incurred (*see* **1:16**(*b*)). This means that if units are lost at the end the cost of such losses can be charged only *to units which have reached the end*, i.e. completed units, and *not to any units still in process*. The procedure then is as follows.

(*a*) Complete 9-by-4 layout as normal remembering that column 3 shows completed units, i.e. total units completed, good and bad.

(*b*) Using the total cost-per-unit figure, find the cost value of the lost units.

(c) Divide this cost by the number of good, completed units. This gives the charge per good unit for the losses. Add this charge to the original cost-per-unit figure to give the final cost-per-unit of good production.

If, then, the 100 units were lost at the end the 9-by-4 layout would show the computations given below:

Cost element	Costs £	Completed units	Work-in-progress		Equivalent units	Total equivalent units	CPU £	WIP value £
			Units	% complete				
Previous process	5,000	600	400	100	400	1,000	5.000	2,000
Materials	1,000	600	400	75	300	900	1.111	333
Labour	2,500	600	400	50	200	800	3.125	625
Overheads	1,500	600	400	25	100	700	2.143	214
Total	£10,000						£11.379	£3,172

The 600 completed units comprise 500 good and 100 lost but completed units.

Cost value of 100 lost units = $100 \times £11.379 = £1,138$

This cost shared between 500 good units $= \dfrac{£1,138}{500} = £2.276$

Final CPU £13.655

Check:

£

Value of 500 completed good units = $500 \times £13.655 = 6,828$

Value of work-in-progress $= 3,172^{\star}$

£10,000

[star]Note that this is the same WIP value as in 7. This is logical. The WIP units have not reached the point of rejection and so cannot incur any costs of rejection arising at this point.

13. Scrap: normal losses. If any units classed as 'normal loss' have scrap value, it is necessary that the value of such scrap is deducted from both:

(a) the costs of the process; and

(b) the valuation of the lost units before dividing that valuation by the number of good units.

EXAMPLE:

The 100 units lost in **12** above were sold for a scrap value of £128. This sale of scrap means that the cost of the 100 lost units now becomes £1,138 − 128 = £1,010. This cost shared between 500 good units results in a unit cost of £1,010/500 = £2.020. So the final CPU in this case would become £11.379 + 2.020 = £13.399, say £13.4.

New check figures:

$$\text{Input} = £10,000 - 128 = \underline{\underline{£9,872}}$$

Output:

Value of 500 completed good units = 500 × £13.4 =	£6,700
Value of work-in-progress (unchanged) =	3,172
	£9,872

Abnormal losses in process

A further principle to be carefully observed in process costing asserts that only *normal* costs are to be charged to production (*see* 1:**16**(*d*)). Consequently any abnormal losses must be written off against the profit and not included in the CPU figure for the good production.

14. Ascertaining units lost that are to be classified as abnormal. The following steps outline the method for ascertaining how many lost units are to be classified as abnormal losses.

(*a*) Predetermine a normal loss rate to be applied at *a given point in the process.*

(*b*) Compute the normal loss for any given production.

(*c*) Then Abnormal loss = Actual loss − Normal loss.

(Note that if the actual loss is *less* than the normal loss an 'abnormal gain' is made.)

It is absolutely essential in this calculation to be quite clear as to where the physical point of rejection is, since *normal loss can only be computed on a basis of the number of units that pass that point.* For instance, if the normal loss rate is 10 per cent, units are lost at the *end*, and a total of 500 units, good and bad, have reached the end, then the normal loss is 50 units. This figure is quite independent of the input, whether it was 1,000 or 10,000. Similarly, if the loss occurs in the *middle* of the process and 800 units have reached this point, then the normal loss would be 80, regardless of how many entered, completed or remained in the process.

15. Valuing abnormal losses. When pricing abnormal losses it is important to remember that such losses must carry a share of the cost of *normal losses*.

To appreciate this, consider the following extreme example: 100 total units are completed; the actual loss is 99; the normal loss is 20 per cent. The total good production, then, is only 1 unit, and the normal loss 20 units. Now if the abnormally lost units do not carry a share of the normal loss, then the 1 good unit will have to carry the whole cost of the 20 units normal loss, a cost 'normally' shared between 80 units. This great burden is, then, clearly a non-normal charge arising on account of the abnormal loss. To keep the charge normal it is necessary to share the 20 units normal loss among all 80 other units so that the one good unit takes an eightieth part of the cost of the normal loss and the 79 abnormally lost units the remainder of the cost. In other words, abnormal losses must carry a share of the normal loss.

We can now give the procedure for valuing abnormal losses where such losses occur *at the end of the process*.

(*a*) Complete the 9-by-4 layout, remembering that column 3 includes *all* completed units: good units, normal loss and abnormal loss.

(*b*) Having done this, complete the following steps to obtain the final cost-per-unit.

(*i*) Compute the units of normal loss on the basis of this column 3 figure, i.e. col. 3 × normal loss rate.

(*ii*) Value the normal loss by multiplying these units by the initial total cost-per-unit figure.

(*iii*) Divide this value by the total number of good and abnormal loss units to give a cost-of-normal-loss-per-unit figure (but *see* **16**(*b*)(*i*) *re* scrap value).

(*iv*) Add this figure to the initial total cost-per-unit figure to obtain the final cost-per-unit.

(*c*) Multiply the final cost-per-unit figure by the number of units of abnormal loss to obtain the value of the abnormal loss.

NOTE: (1) The value of the good production is simply good units × final CPU. (2) The value of the work-in-progress is unaffected, since the lost unit costs are incurred at the end of the process, i.e. they have not yet been incurred by work-in-progress units, and therefore such units must carry no charge for such losses. (3) The abnormal loss value is transferred to an abnormal loss account. (4) The overall formula for finding the final cost-per-unit figure to be applied to both good and abnormal loss units can be written:

Final CPU = Initial CPU +

$$\frac{\text{No. of completed units} \times \text{Normal loss rate} \times \text{Initial CPU}}{\text{Good units completed} + \text{Abnormal loss units}}$$

EXAMPLE: Using the computations given above (*see* 12), where the actual loss is 100 units, assume that we now have a predetermined normal loss rate of 6 per cent. Since the total units completed of all kinds is still 600, and since the work-in-progress is unaffected by the losses, the 9-by-4 layout in 12 remains unaltered down to the initial total CPU of £11.379. The abnormal loss value is computed as follows:

The normal loss of 6 per cent must relate to the total units passing the loss point (in this case the end), i.e. 600 units.

∴   Normal loss = 6% of 600 = 36 units.
The actual loss is 100 units.
∴   Abnormal loss = 100 − 36 = 64 units.
Cost of the normal loss is 36 × £11.379 = £410.
This loss shared between remaining 564 units

$$(\text{i.e. good units} + \text{abnormal loss}) = \frac{410}{564} = £0.727.$$

∴   Final CPU = £11.379 + £0.727 = £12.106.
∴   Value of abnormal loss = 64 units × £12.106 = £775.

Check: £
Value of 500 completed good units = 500 × £12.106   = 6,053
Value of abnormal loss charged to abnormal loss a/c   =   775
Value of work-in-progress   = 3,172
                                                       £10,000

16. Scrap: abnormal losses. Where scrap arises in a process experiencing abnormal losses then deduct:

(*a*) the total scrap value from the cost of the process;

(*b*) (*i*) the scrap value of the normal loss units from the cost of these normal loss units before dividing by the total good and abnormal loss units;

(*ii*) the scrap value of the abnormal loss units from the cost of these abnormal loss units.

NOTE: If there is in fact an abnormal gain, the scrap value of the units *not* scrapped must be deducted from the abnormal gain figure. This is necessary, since the initial apparent gain must be reduced to allow for the loss of scrap income that would otherwise have been received if the full normal loss had been suffered.

17. Units lost part-way through the process (*see* layout in Fig. 8.1). If units are lost part-way through a process, the costs incurred relate only to partial completion. This means that two complete sets of three columns need to be added to the 9-by-4 layout. These sets record normal and abnormal units lost and are both similar to the three work-in-progress columns (units lost; % complete; equivalent units lost). The equivalent units lost are added to the completed units (note that the lost units are *not* completed units, so must not be included in this figure) and the equivalent work-in-progress units to obtain the total equivalent units figure (column 7 of 9-by-4 layout (*see* 7)). The layout is then completed, and after this the procedure continues as follows.

(*a*) The work-in-progress and lost units degrees of completion are compared to ascertain whether the work-in-progress units lie before or beyond the point of loss.

(*b*) The value of the normal loss is found by multiplying normal equivalent units lost by the relevant element cost-per-unit (column 8 of 9-by-4 layout) and totalling products.

(*c*) This loss value is divided equally between all good completed units, abnormal loss units and if, but only if, the work in progress lies beyond the point of loss, the work-in-progress units. (All actual units, not just equivalent units, are counted, since each unit passing the point of loss shares equally in this loss regardless of the degree of completion.) The resulting 'cost-per-unit loss' figure is added to the total cost-per-unit (column 8) to give the final cost-

Cost element	Complete units*	Cost	Work-in-progress Units	WIP % complete	WIP Equivalent units	Normal loss Units	NL % complete	NL Equivalent units	Abnormal loss Units	AL % complete	AL Equivalent units	Total equivalent units	CPU	Values Normal loss	Values Abnormal loss	Values WIP
		£											£	£	£	£
Previous process	500	5,000	400	100	400	60	100	60	40	100	40	1,000	5.000	300	200	2,000
Materials	500	1,000	400	75	300	60	50	30	40	50	20	850	1.176	35	23	353
Labour	500	2,500	400	50	200	60	25	15	40	25	10	725	3.448	52	34	690
Overheads	500	1,500	400	25	100	60	25	15	40	25	10	625	2.400	36	24	240
		10,000											12.024	423	281	3,283
Scrap: 100 units at £1		–100												–60	–40	
Total		£9,900											12.024	363	241	3,283
CPU loss													0.386			
Final CPU £													12.410	363	241 / 15 = £256	154 / 3,437

Normal loss of £363 shared equally between all units that passed the loss point, i.e. all units except normal loss units.

$$\therefore \text{CPU loss} = \frac{363}{1,000 - 60} = £0.386.$$

Charge for lost units: Abnormal loss of 40 units at £0.386
WIP: 400 units at £0.386

Final CPU £12.410

Check:
	£
Value of completed units = 500 × £12.410	= 6,205
Value of abnormal units transferred to Abnormal Loss a/c	= 256
Value of work-in-progress	= 3,437
	9,898
	9,900

(Difference due solely to rounding)

Total cost was £9,900

*If units are lost before completion, the costs incurred relate only to partial completion, so this column records *fully* completed units only.

Figure 8.1 Process cost computations: units lost part-way through the process

per-unit figure. This figure is then used to value the completed good units.

(*d*) The value of the abnormal loss is found by multiplying the equivalent abnormal loss units by the relevant element cost-per-unit (column 8), totalling the products and adding a full 'cost-per-unit loss' charge for each abnormal unit lost.

(*e*) Work-in-progress is valued as usual, but if it lies beyond the point of loss, then in addition each unit is given a full 'cost-per-unit loss' charge.

For example, keeping the data used in previous computations above (e.g. in **12** and **15**), assume also that the lost units completion was: materials 50 per cent, labour 25 per cent, overheads 25 per cent and the scrap value of lost units was £1 each.

A comparison of the completion figures of work-in-progress and lost units clearly indicates that the units in-progress lie *beyond* the loss point.

∴   Normal loss = 6 per cent of all units beyond loss point
      = 6 per cent of 1,000 = 60 units.
∴   Abnormal loss = 100 − 60 = 40 units.

The layout and computations in this instance are shown in Fig. 8.1.

18. Abnormal gains. When an abnormal gain arises the easiest way of handling the computations is to enter the units' abnormal gain in the 'Abnormal loss – Units' column as *negative numbers*. Do not forget, though, that where there is an abnormal gain more units are completed. To ensure that all the unit columns have been filled in correctly the following cross-check should be made:

Previous process: Total equivalent units
      = Completed units + WIP units + Normal loss units
        − Abnormal gain units.

It should also be appreciated that having negative numbers in the abnormal gain column means that all subsequent mathematical computations must be carried out with due regard to the minuses. Thus, the first four figures in the 'Values – Abnormal gain' column will all be negative and the 'Scrap' figure will be positive (since all the income which could have been expected from the sale of lost units will not now be received). So if the loss in our illustration had actually been only 40 units, the total scrap sales would be £40 – which would be apportioned £60 for the normal loss of 60 units and £–20 for the abnormal gain units. Note, too, that the charge to the abnormal gain for the lost units will also be negative, as will be the value of the abnormal gain units transferred to the Abnormal Loss account.

Whilst the adoption of this procedure will give a correct answer, students should nevertheless try and see for themselves the logic of the various values that arise in the course of the computations.

Process cost book-keeping

Process cost book-keeping follows the chart shown in Fig. 7.1 except that the Work-in-progress account takes the name 'Process Account'. In practice there are, of course, a number of processes and each has its own process account. Despite this close adherence to the chart there are a few book-keeping points special to process costing.

19. Units columns. It is a feature of process accounts that they have columns for units as well as values. Where discrete units are involved the debit and credit units columns in a process account must balance.

20. Scrap. Scrap sales are usually credited to the process account. If, however, abnormal losses are computed, *only the sales of normal scrap are credited*, the scrap sales of the abnormal loss being credited to the Abnormal Loss account. This is a logical requirement for it is clear that if the normal loss is a legitimate charge to the process then the income from the normal loss should be a credit to the process, while if the abnormal loss is *not* to be charged then neither should the income from that loss be credited.

21. Abnormal Loss account. Operating the Abnormal Loss account simply involves:

(a) debiting the cost of the abnormal loss (prior to deducting the abnormal loss sales);

(b) crediting the abnormal loss sales;

(c) writing off the balance on the account to profit and loss as an abnormal loss.

22. Process cost accounts illustrated. To illustrate process accounts, the process costs detailed in **17** and in Fig. 8.1 are shown as book-keeping entries below. It should be appreciated that the data in Fig. 8.1 appears in the form of practical working sheets, and the accounting entries given in the following example would be picked up from such sheets.

Process Account

	Units	£		Units	£
Transferred from previous process	1,000	5,000	Transferred to next process	500	6,205
Materials	—	1,000	Abnormal loss to Abnormal Loss a/c	40	*298
Labour	—	2,500	Scrap sales, normal loss	60	60
Overheads	—	1,500	Work-in-progress c/d	400	3,437
	1,000	£10,000		1,000	£10,000
WIP b/d	400	£3,437			

*This figure is the value of the abnormal units lost (£256) with their scrap sales value (£40) written back, since this amount is credited in the accounts to the Abnormal Loss account and not the process account (*see* **20**). In addition, the £2 adjustment to allow for the rounding error in the working sheet (Fig. 8.1) has been made to this figure.

Abnormal Loss Account

	Units	£		Units	£
Process account, abnormal loss	40	298	Scrap sales, abnormal units	40	40
			Net loss to P/L a/c	—	258
	40	298		40	298

23. Abnormal gain. It should be appreciated that in the case of abnormal gains the scrap value of the full normal loss is *still* credited to the process account, the difference between this and the actual scrap sales received being debited to the Abnormal Loss account (which should now take the name Abnormal Gain account).

For example, if the actual loss in the process account above (**22**) had only been 40 units, i.e. an abnormal gain of 20 units, the book-keeping entries would have been:

(a) Dr. Cash account 40 units at £1   £40
     Dr. Abnormal Gain account 20 units at £1   £20
     (i.e. scrap value of the 20 units which were *not*
       scrapped)
     Cr. Process account 60 units at £1   £60
     (i.e. scrap value of the normal loss)
(b) Dr. Process account 10 units   £146*
     Cr. Abnormal Gain account   £146
     Transfer of gain to Abnormal Gain account

The Abnormal Gain account would, therefore, ultimately appear as follows:

Abnormal Gain Account

	Units	£		Units	£

Process a/c,
  units not lost
	20	20	Process a/c,
			  cost of units
			  gained*
				20	146

Net gain to P/L a/c		126			
	20	£146		20	£146

*As will be appreciated, changing the abnormal units in Fig. 8.1 changes a large number of other figures. If you were to re-write Fig. 8.1 on the basis of an abnormal gain of 20 units you would find that the 'Abnormal gain' column totalled £ – 126. So writing back the £20 scrap sales lost gives £ – 146.

Progress test 8

Principles

1. What are the basic principles of process costing? (1)
2. How is scrap handled in process costing? (13, 16, 20)
3. What entries are found in an abnormal gain account? (23)

Practice

4. The following figures relate to a single industrial process:

Quantity of work-in-process at commencement: 8,000 units
Costs of work-in-process at commencement:

Material:	£29,600
Wages:	£6,600
Overhead:	£5,800

During the period under review, a further 32,000 units were introduced, and the additional costs were:

material: £112,400; wages: £33,400; overhead: £30,200

At the end of the period, 28,000 units were fully processed, and 12,000 units remained in-process. This closing stock was complete as regards material cost, and one-third complete as regards wages and overhead.

Using the average method of valuation, tabulate these production and cost figures to give quantities, unit values, and total values for completed output, and for each of the three elements comprising the closing work-in-process.

Attention should be paid to the form of presentation. (*CIMA*)

5. Using the information given in question 4 above, recompute the cost per unit of the completed units and the value of the closing work-in-process if 8,000 units are lost at the end of the process.

9

Process costing: continuous units

So far we have examined process costing only in the context of discrete units which are all physically separate. Now we must look at the method of costing adopted where the product is often an unending flow, production being only measurable in terms of tonnes or litres or (as in the case of a gas) cubic metres.

To a large extent costing such units follows much the same line as costing discrete units. However, there are some important differences.

Principles of continuous unit costing

1. Discrete unit v. continuous unit costing. The difference between discrete unit costing and continuous unit costing arises from the differences between the product and its production (as do all method differences). It is the following features of continuous units and their production which create these differences.

(*a*) *By-products and joint products.* Continuous unit production almost invariably gives rise to by-products and joint products. So significantly do these products affect the costs that they are given a complete section to themselves (*see* **5–11**).

(*b*) *Changes in units of measurements.* A process can often start with units of one measurement and end with units of another. Indeed, it is possible to have three different kinds of units in a single process as, for instance, where an acid (measured in litres) reacts with a solid (measured in kilograms) to give a gas (measured in cubic metres). This means that the units input will not always balance the units output – such a balance is an almost invariable feature of discrete units accounting (although it should be noted that units can occasionally change in discrete units production, as, for example, when two or more separate units are assembled to make a larger unit).

(c) *Unobserved losses.* Where continuous units are processed, often the losses may be unobserved, at least in terms of direct measurement. For example, there can be losses from evaporation or spillage which can only be detected by the difference between the input and the output (and only then if the input and output units are the same).

(d) *Work-in-progress.* Where continuous units are being processed, more often than not work-in-progress can be ignored, since production is usually on a flow basis and the quantity actually in-process at any moment between the input and output points is both very small relative to throughput and also constant from period to period. Only where the product is processed in separate containers, each of which undergoes treatment for a number of days, does work-in-progress become a significant factor. On those occasions when work-in-progress does arise the computations involved (e.g. ascertainment of equivalent units) follow the principles discussed in Chapter 8.

2. Normal and abnormal losses. The principle put forward in Chapter 8 that normal losses are charged to the process and abnormal losses to profit and loss still holds where there are continuous units, although the calculations usually prove simpler since normally losses are measured at the end of a process. This means, of course, that the valuation of in-process losses is avoided and a simple division of the actual process cost by the expected output gives the CPU figure required for valuing transferred and untransferred units and abnormal losses (*see* **3**).

NOTE: Do not forget that the disposal value (if any) of the normal loss is credited to the Process account, while the disposal value of the abnormal loss is credited to the Abnormal Loss account.

3. Illustrative example. The following example illustrates a typical continuous unit process costing in which no by-products or joint products arise.

Data: Material from a previous process is heated with A and B to give product Z. The normal loss is 30 per cent of input, this loss being sold at £7 per tonne. During a given month there was an input of 300 tonnes costing £5,000 from the previous process, 200 tonnes of A at £5 per tonne and 100 tonnes of B at £10 per tonne. The process direct labour amounted to £2,000, the process direct expenses to £600 and the process overheads to £3,000. The actual output was 380 tonnes of which 350 tonnes were transferred to the next process.

Method: The following layout adequately caters for a costing exercise of this nature:

	Tonnes	Price (£)	£
Previous process cost	300	–	5,000
Materials: A	200	5	1,000
B	100	10	1,000
Process labour			2,000
Process direct expenses			600
Process overheads			3,000
Total input	600		12,600
Normal loss: 30% input	– 180	7	– 1,260
Expected output of Z	420		11,340

$$\therefore \; \text{CPU} = \frac{£11,340}{420} = £27 \text{ per tonne}$$

	Tonnes	Price	£
Abnormal loss	– 40	27	– 1,080*
Actual output of Z	380		10,260
Transferred to next process	– 350	27	9,450
Held in stock	30	27	£810

*The 40 × £7 sales value of this loss is credited to the Abnormal Loss account.

From these figures the Z process account is quickly drawn up as follows:

Z Process Account

	Tonnes	£		Tonnes	£
Previous process	300	5,000	Next process	350	9,450
Materials: A	200	1,000	Losses: Normal	180	1,260
B	100	1,000	Abnormal	40	1,080
Labour		2,000	Closing stock c/d	30	810
Direct expenses		600			
Overheads		3,000			
	600	12,600		600	12,600
Stock b/d	30	810			

NOTE: In the following period the treatment of the stock held would depend upon whether the FIFO or average price method were adopted. In either case it is advisable to regard the account entry as being equivalent to a purchase entry on a stores record card (*see* Fig. 2.1), the next period's costed output as being a second purchase, and the transfer to the next process at the end of that period as a subsequent issue. This should ensure a valid transfer price.

4. Process costing and standards. Although it has so far been assumed that all process unit costs will be computed from the actual figures for the period (other than the normal loss percentage), it is doubtful if this is the best approach to process costing. After all, if identical units are being produced then identical unit costs should be incurred over the year (inflationary effects excepted) and any differences between the costs of one period and another should arise from random or abnormal events and not from any real differences between the units. For this reason it is better to base the unit costs on standards and regard any deviations from the standards as being untypical and so to be written off against the profit for the period. Moreover, such an approach simplifies the computations since once the initial standards are set the CPU figures will hold for a year or so and will no longer need to be recomputed each period. The significance of this will not be lost on any student who has worked through this and the previous chapter.

By-products and joint products

5. By-products. A by-product is any product of value that is produced *incidentally* to the main product. For example, basic slag, a useful fertiliser, is obtained in the process of converting iron into steel. The following are the four basic cost treatments of by-products.

(a) *By-product sales regarded as 'other income'*. This method is convenient if the value is small.

(b) *By-product sales value deducted from joint cost*. Here the sales value of the by-product is deducted from the joint cost of producing both main and by-product. The resulting figure is then termed the 'main product cost'.

(c) *By-product sales added to the main product sales*. In this method the combined sales figure for all products is computed and the total costs then deducted, the difference being the combined profit or loss on operation. This approach is based on the view that since it is physically impossible to produce one product without the other, accounting statements must reflect this by producing *combined* figures.

(d) *By-product treated as if it were a joint product*.

6. Joint products and joint costs. *Joint products* are 'two or more products separated in the course of processing, each having a sufficiently high saleable value to merit recognition as a main product', and *joint costs* are 'the costs of providing two or more products or services whose production cannot, for physical reasons, be segregated' (CIMA Terminology). Joint products and costs are a particular feature of the butchery trade.

In any situation where joint costs are incurred the problem arises as to how to charge those costs to the joint products. The following two solutions have been put forward to solve this:

(a) *Apportionment on a physical units basis*. In this method the output relating to all the joint products is measured in some common physical unit (e.g. tonnes, litres) and the joint costs apportioned in proportion to these outputs.

(b) *Apportionment on a sales value basis*. Here the *sales values* of the joint products are used to apportion joint costs. Note that the basis is sales value, *not* selling prices. Use of selling prices results in completely invalid apportionments.

EXAMPLE:

Data: 100 tonnes of Z is processed to give 70 tonnes of A and

30 tonnes of B. Total joint cost (i.e. process costs and cost of 100 tonnes of Z) = £900.

Selling prices: A, £12 per tonne; B, £8 per tonne.

Method of apportionment (physical units basis):

	Total	A		B	
Sales	£1,080	70 tonnes at £12	= £840	30 tonnes at £8	= £240
Joint cost	£900	$\frac{70}{100} \times £900$	= £630	$\frac{30}{100} \times £900$	= £270
Profit	£180		£210	Loss	£30

Method of apportionment (sales value basis):

	Total	A		B	
Sales	£1,080	70 tonnes at £12	= £840	30 tonnes at £8	= £240
Joint cost	£900	$£\frac{840}{1,080} \times 900$	= £700	$£\frac{240}{1,080} \times 900$	= £200
Profit	£180		£140		£40

7. Assessment of methods. As can be seen, these two methods give quite different results and the question arises as to which is the better.

The short answer to such a question is, neither. The fact is that joint costs are in reality wholly indivisible. Since one product cannot be produced without the other it is not possible to determine what it costs to produce just that one. Certainly such an exercise provides no help to management – it is clearly ridiculous to stop producing B in the example above on the grounds that apportionment on a physical units basis shows that it is making a loss since stopping B means also stopping A which is making a good profit.

Careful thought can lead to only one conclusion – that joint costs must be set against joint income and no attempt made to carry the analysis further. In our example A and B together give a profit of £180. If this is satisfactory, production should be continued. If not, an alternative should be sought. Nothing is gained by trying to apportion the profit.

This said, however, it must be pointed out that year-end stocks of A and B would need to be *valued*. In this context it may be that the apportionment of joint costs is acceptable, though very probably a net realizable sales value (*see* **10**) less a judiciously chosen profit margin would be a better basis of valuation.

8. Split-off point and subsequent processes and costs. It is important to appreciate that the methods discussed relating to by-products and joint products relate only to that production where the products are being processed jointly. Once a product separates out and becomes independent, it is treated by the usual cost methods. The point of separation is called the *split-off point* and all events that come after the split-off point are termed *subsequent* events. Thus the terms *subsequent processes* and *subsequent costs* relate to processes and costs that come after the split-off point. Events prior to split-off are termed 'joint'.

These definitions are illustrated in Fig. 9.1.

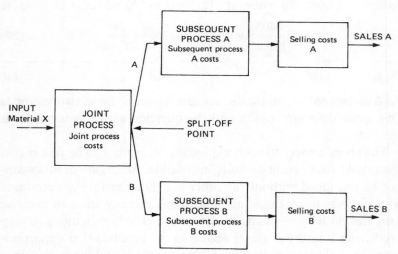

Figure 9.1 *Joint and subsequent processes and costs*

9. Treatment of subsequent costs. It is very necessary when preparing by-product and joint-product cost statements to ensure that all subsequent costs are charged only to *the appropriate product, and are not regarded as joint*. For example, where the by-product value is to be deducted from the joint cost (*see* **5**(*b*) above) the subsequent costs of the by-product must first be deducted from the by-product sales value before attempting to deduct the sales value from the joint cost, e.g.:

	£	£
Joint cost		5,000
Less By-product value, i.e.:		
By-product sales	1,000	
Less By-product subsequent costs	−200	800
Main product cost		£4,200

It should be noted and remembered that selling and distribution costs are virtually always subsequent costs.

10. Net realizable value. When subsequent costs are deducted from the sales value of a product, the resulting figure is called the *net realizable value*. In the above example, therefore, the £800 is the net realizable value of the by-product.

Net realizable values are particularly relevant if a joint-costs apportionment on the basis of sales value is required, for in such a case it is essential that the apportionment is made on the basis of the *net realizable values of the joint products at the split-off point* and not on the full sales value. As a moment's thought will indicate, using full sales value would bias the apportionment illogically against any product having a relatively high subsequent cost, since much of the sales value would arise as a result of the economic value of the subsequent processes, which, of course, is wholly unconnected with the other now separate joint products.

11. Illustrative example. To illustrate the points made above the following example is worked.

Data: Assume that in the example given in **3** there was, in fact, no normal loss at all, but instead 180 tonnes of J was jointly produced with 400 tonnes of Z. From this production 100 tonnes of J and 360 tonnes of Z were processed in subsequent processes, the process costs being £200 and £4,860 respectively. By the period end 80 tonnes of the fully processed J and 300 tonnes of the fully processed Z had been sold at prices per tonne of £30 and £40 respectively. Selling costs amounted to 10 per cent of the sales values and the joint costs were apportioned on a sales value basis. Prepare the profit and loss account.

Method:

Step 1. Computation of the net realizable value (NRV):

	J			Z		
	Tonnes	*Price (£)*	*£*	*Tonnes*	*Price (£)*	*£*
Sales	80	30	2,400	300	40	12,000
Selling costs (10% sales)	—	−3	−240	—	−4	−1,200
NRV: Cost of sales	80	27	2,160	300	36	10,800
NRV: Completed production	100	27	2,700	360	36	12,960
Subsequent costs*	—		−200	—		−4,860
NRV: Completed production at split-off point	100	25	2,500	360	$22\frac{1}{2}$	8,100
NRV: Joint process production	180	25	4,500	400	$22\frac{1}{2}$	9,000

*Note that the subsequent process unit costs are £200/100 = £2 and £4,860/360 = £13.50 respectively.

Step 2. Joint costs:

	Tonnes	*Price (£)*	*£*
Total joint process costs (as before, *see* 3)	600	—	12,600
Normal loss: Nil	—		
Expected output	600		12,600
∴ CPU = $\dfrac{£12,600}{600}$ = £21 per tonne			
Abnormal loss	20	21	−420
Actual output	580*	21	12,180

*180 tonnes of J and 400 tonnes of Z.

Step 3. Apportionment of joint costs on sales value basis:

	Total	*J*	*Z*
NRV: As above	£13,500	£4,500	£9,000
Joint costs (as in step 2)	12,180	$\dfrac{4,500}{13,500} \times 12,180 = £4,060$	$\dfrac{9,000}{13,500} \times 12,180 = 8,120$
Cost per unit		£4,060 ÷ 180 = £22.56	£8,120 ÷ 400 = £20.30

Step 4. Closing stock valuations (at cost):

	J			*Z*		
	Tonnes	Price (£)	£	Tonnes	Price (£)	£
Stocks at split-off point	80	22.56	1,805	40	20.30	812
Finished goods stocks*	20	24.56	491	60	33.80	2,028
Total			£2,296			£2,840

*Note that the finished goods unit costs are £22.56 + £2 = £24.56 and £20.30 + £13.50 = £33.80 respectively.

Step 5. Profit and loss account:

	J		*Z*		Total	
	£	£	£	£	£	£
Sales		2,400		12,000		14,400
Costs: Joint (excluding abnormal loss)	4,060		8,120		12,180	
Subsequent	200		4,860		5,060	
Selling	240		1,200		1,440	
	4,500		14,180		18,680	
Less Closing stocks	2,296	2,204	2,840	11,340	5,136	13,544
Product profits		£196		£660		£856
			Less abnormal loss			420
			Net profit			£436

Progress test 9

Principles

1. Distinguish between by-products and joint products. (**5, 6**)

2. What are the four methods of cost treatment for by-products? (**5**)

3. Which is the best way of apportioning joint costs to joint products? (**7**)

4. Define: (*a*) split-off point; (*b*) subsequent process; (*c*) subsequent cost. (**8**)

5. What is meant by 'net realizable value' in the context of joint products? (**10**)

Practice

6. From the following information, find the profit made by each

product, apportioning joint costs on a sales value basis:

	A	B
Sales	£38,000	£42,000
Selling costs	£5,000	£20,000

Joint costs: Materials £31,200, Process costs £13,800.

7. Product P63 is made by three sequential processes, I, II and III. In process III a by-product arises and after further processing in process BP, at a cost of £2 per unit, by-product BP9 is produced. Selling and distribution expenses of £1 per unit are incurred in marketing BP9 at a selling price of £9 per unit.

	Process		
	I	II	III
Standards provide for:			
Normal loss in process, of input, of	10%	5%	10%
Loss in process, having a scrap value, per unit, of	£1	£3	£5

For the month of April 19–8 the following data is given:

	Process			
	I	II	III	BP
Output, in units	8,800	8,400	7,000 of P63	420 of BP9

Costs:				Total
	£	£	£	£
Direct materials introduced (10,000) units	20,000			20,000
Direct materials added	6,000	12,640	23,200	41,840
Direct wages	5,000	6,000	10,000	21,000
Direct expenses	4,000	6,200	4,080	14,280

Budgeted production overhead for the month was £84,000. Absorption is based on a percentage of direct wages.

There were no stocks at the beginning or end of the month.

You are required, using the information given, to prepare

accounts for:

- (*a*) each of processes I, II and III;
- (*b*) process BP;
- (*c*) (*i*) abnormal losses;
     (*ii*) abnormal gains;

showing the balances to be transferred to the profit and loss statement.   (*CIMA*)

Part two

Cost analysis

10

Cost behaviour

Behaviour classification

We have already seen that there is more than one way of classifying costs. When cost behaviour is being considered a further type of classification is required, this time based on the pattern of behaviour of the cost in respect of changes in the activity level.

1. Costs and activity. Costs are dependent upon, and change with, activity – the greater the activity the greater, usually, the cost. Making an accurate prediction of a cost involves both:

(*a*) a realistic identification of the activity upon which the cost is primarily dependent, and

(*b*) an accurate assessment of the mathematical relationship between the cost amount and the level of activity.

For explanatory purposes the problem of identifying the appropriate activity will be left until the section on measuring activity (*see* **17**). For the present any activity element will merely be either asserted without question or assumed to be physical units of production.

2. Relevant activity range. To know only that a cost is dependent upon a particular activity is not in itself of very much help. More useful is knowing just how a cost behaves in relation to that activity. Now, not only will the cost amount differ at different levels of activity, but if the difference between these levels is large the behaviour *pattern* will differ as well. It was this phenomenon which, of course, underlay the extensive fall in the cost of microprocessors, the cost patterns prevailing when just a few were being produced being very different from those prevailing when thousands were being produced. To predict costs in practice within a specific organization it is necessary therefore to limit consideration solely to the range of activity anticipated. This range is called the *relevant activity range* and can be defined as the *range of activity over which predictions are required in practice*.

3. Fixed costs. There are some costs that remain the same whatever the level of activity. These include rent, local government rates, debenture interest, audit fees, etc. Such costs are called fixed costs. Another typical fixed cost is the cost of top management salaries. Note, however, that this particular cost is very dependent upon the scale of operations, any large increase or, conversely, decrease down to shut-down level almost certainly affecting this cost significantly. So the concept of the relevant activity range is sometimes very important in the case of a fixed cost.

A *fixed cost*, then, can be defined as a cost which *remains unchanged regardless of the level of activity within the relevant range*.

Note that this does not mean that a fixed cost within this range cannot alter. It most certainly can – local government rates alter every year. All the definition lays down is that the cost is unaffected by *changes in activity*. Other factors can, and do, change a fixed cost.

4. Time and specific project costs. The student should note that other definitions of fixed cost often include a reference to a period of time (e.g. CIMA *Terminology*), and, indeed, the term *period cost* is often used as an alternative to 'fixed cost'. In other words, such a cost is defined as being incurred on a time basis. While in the majority of contexts this is factually correct, there are still occasions when no time basis is involved. For instance, in predicting the cost of a specific project such as printing a book the term 'fixed cost' can relate to any cost that will be incurred regardless of the number of copies to be printed and without reference to any time period (e.g. set-up costs). This use of the term in respect of a specific project is too convenient for it to be excluded by the narrower, though more common, definition.

5. Variable cost. The opposite of a fixed cost is a *variable cost* which is a cost which *varies in direct proportion to the level of activity*. A good example of a variable cost is the raw materials cost since a 10 per cent increase in production usually results in a 10 per cent increase in this cost. Again, strictly speaking, a reference to the relevant activity range should be included in the definition since the greater this range the less it may be true to say that the cost is in direct proportion to the activity (e.g. quantity discounts on materials above a given level can lower the cost per unit so that the cost of producing five times as many units is not five times as much). However, in practice this point is much less important in the case of the variable costs than it is in the case of the fixed costs.

6. Semi-variable costs. Unfortunately there are a good many costs which neither remain unchanged nor vary in direct proportion to activity. These costs change with changes in activity but not in direct proportion.

Careful examination of a cost of this nature often shows that it is a combination of a fixed cost element and a variable cost element. Thus, the cost of a telephone expense comprises a fixed rental charge plus a variable charge for calls. Similarly, the cost of maintenance is often made up of the costs of regular maintenance (e.g. weekly servicing) which tend to be fixed and the costs of breakdown maintenance which tend to vary with machine running time. A cost having this dual nature is called a *semi-variable cost* and can be defined as *a cost which is partly fixed and partly variable*. The total semi-variable cost is, of course, the sum of these two parts.

In practice it will generally be found that most indirect labour costs are semi-variable.

7. Unit costs. It is important to appreciate that the definitions of costs being developed relate to the total of a cost and not the unit cost. So if material costing £1 per kg was used and 5,000 and 6,000 kg respectively were processed we would say that the variable cost was £5,000 and £6,000 respectively. A variable cost, therefore, increases as activity increases although the variable cost *per unit* remains unchanged. Conversely, if the fixed cost of the process were £30,000 the fixed cost *per unit* would fall from £6 to £5 as the activity changed from the lower to the higher level.

8. Policy costs. Most costs are incurred as a result of engaging in an activity and are quite inescapable. Thus, if you wished to process 5,000 kg of material, you would be obliged to pay for the 5,000 kg required (such a cost sometimes being referred to as an *engineered variable cost*). However, some costs are not obligatory. You do not *have* to incur advertising costs or research costs or public relations costs, though it may be unwise not to spend money on these activities. In other words, the amount of such costs depends solely upon your *policy* and not upon your product. Such a cost is called, therefore, a *policy cost* (or, sometimes, a *discretionary fixed cost*) and is a *cost incurred as a matter of policy*.

There is no sharp division between policy costs and other costs, one shading gradually into the other. Sick pay is, by definition, a policy cost, yet such a cost is to some extent like any other variable cost since the greater the activity the greater the work-force and, therefore, the greater the payments made. Where such a cost can be analyzed it should be; otherwise, since policy costs are not the direct consequence of the activity of the enterprise, they should, strictly speaking, be excluded from most cost analyses. If they are included then they are probably best regarded as fixed costs, though it should be noted that they differ from a normal fixed cost in so far as this latter cost *is* a direct consequence of the activity of the enterprise even though it remains unaffected by the level of that activity.

Finally, note that where an escapable fixed cost is referred to as a discretionary fixed cost its converse, an inescapable fixed cost, is referred to as a *committed fixed cost*.

9. Costs in the long and short term. Finally it should be noted that the classification of a cost into fixed or variable sometimes depends upon the time-span involved. For instance, with a time-span of a day even direct wages must often be classified as a fixed cost since staff cannot be discharged (or engaged) at such short notice. Conversely, a twenty-year time-span means that even debenture interest may become a variable cost (since increased activity over this period may result in further debentures being issued). It is this feature of cost behaviour that underlies the saying: 'In the long run all costs are variable'.

Behaviour patterns

One of the best ways of understanding the behaviour pattern of a cost is by means of a graph showing the effect of activity on the cost.

10. The economist's total cost curve. (*See* Fig. 10.1.) If the total cost of running an organization is plotted against activity, it is usually found that at the lowest activity levels the cost rises sharply (though progressively less sharply) as the initial activity calls into being necessary but grossly under-employed facilities (curve of increasing returns). The curve then straightens out and rises steadily and consistently (curve of constant returns). Ultimately, at the higher activity levels the curve begins to rise more and more steeply as facilities are progressively more and more overloaded (curve of diminishing returns).

This is the traditional cost curve of the economist. However, since an enterprise normally operates between the extremes of under-employment and over-employment of facilities, the relevant activity range usually includes only the straight part of the curve. So in practice many of the accountant's cost curves are straight lines and, provided these curves are not read outside the relevant range, the oversimplification that depicts them as straight *across the*

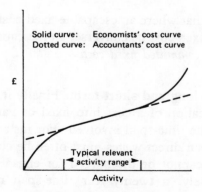

Solid curve: Economists' cost curve
Dotted curve: Accountants' cost curve

£

Typical relevant
◄ activity range ►

Activity

Figure 10.1 *Total cost curve*

whole graph can be employed – and will be employed in the rest of this chapter.

11. Fixed, variable and semi-variable cost curves. (*See* Fig. 10.2.) The three fundamental and commonest patterns of cost behaviour are as follows.

(*a*) *The fixed cost curve* (Fig. 10.2(*a*)). Since a fixed cost does not change with activity a fixed cost curve is no more than a horizontal straight line across the graph.

(*b*) *The variable cost curve* (Fig. 10.2(*b*)). Since a variable cost varies in direct proportion to the activity, the variable cost at zero activity must be zero and the cost must rise at a constant slope reflecting the constant cost increase per unit of activity.

(*c*) *The semi-variable cost curve* (Fig. 10.2(*c*)). At zero activity only the fixed cost element of the semi-variable cost has any value

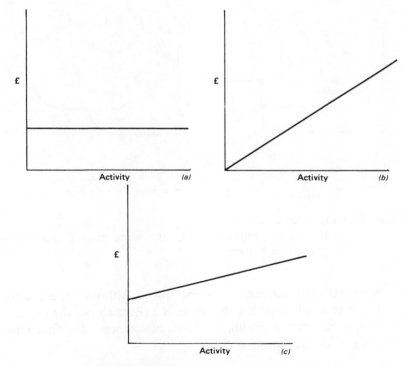

Figure 10.2 (*a*) *Fixed cost curve*
(*b*) *Variable cost curve*
(*c*) *Semi-variable cost curve*

and so the cost curve starts from the cost axis at a point equal to the fixed cost element, and then rises at a constant slope which reflects the variable cost increase per unit of activity.

12. Stepped fixed costs. (*See* Fig. 10.3(*a*).) It is a feature of fixed cost curves that in practice they often produce a step pattern. This arises because usually a fixed cost can only increase in jumps. For example, up to a certain level of activity it may be that three people can service that activity (e.g. storekeepers) but above that level a fourth person is required. Engaging this fourth person results in the fixed cost rising at once by the whole of that person's salary, and so the fixed cost curve rises vertically at this activity level. At a yet higher activity level the process may well repeat itself.

Note that if the engagement of a new employee can be postponed by paying overtime or other diminishing returns costs, the kind of pattern shown in Fig. 10.3(*b*) results.

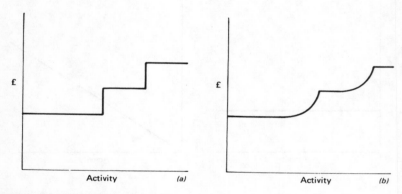

Figure 10.3 (*a*) *Stepped fixed cost*
(*b*) *Stepped fixed cost with diminishing returns expenditure incurred between steps*

13. Variable cost patterns. (*See* Fig. 10.4.) Although the underlying feature of all variable cost curves is a rising slope, the pattern of the slope can vary according to the circumstances. The following are some of the variations.

(*a*) *The variable cost per unit increases at different activity levels* (Fig. 10.4(*a*)). This situation can arise where, for example, the work for the first eight hours is paid for at, say, £5 per hour, the

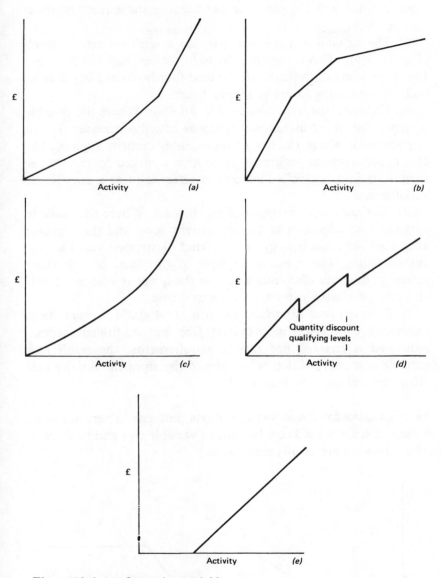

Figure 10.4 (a) *Increasing variable cost*
       (b) *Decreasing variable cost*
       (c) *Curvilinear variable cost*
       (d) *Stepped variable cost, e.g. quantity discount curve*
       (e) *Penalty variable cost*

next four hours at £10 per hour and the four subsequent hours at £20 per hour.

(b) *The variable cost per unit decreases at different activity levels* (Fig. 10.4(b)). This is the opposite to (a), when, say, the first four hours are paid at £20 per hour, the next four hours at £10 per hour and the remaining hours at £5 per hour.

(c) *The cost curve is curvilinear* (Fig. 10.4(c)). Where the variable cost per unit itself increases steadily as activity increases (i.e. in any situation where the law of diminishing returns applies), the cost curve steepens progressively to give a curved 'curve' rather than a straight 'curve'. This cost is referred to as a curvilinear variable cost.

(d) *The cost curve is stepped* (Fig. 10.4(d)). Where the variable cost per unit decreases at a given activity level and the decrease affects *all the lower activity costs*, a kind of stepped variable cost curve results. The classical example of this kind of behaviour relates to quantity discounts when, at the quantity discount level, all units purchased carry the lower unit cost.

(e) *There is a penalty variable cost* (Fig. 10.4(e)). If a certain basic minimum of service is provided free but additional service requested is charged pro rata to requirements, the result is a variable cost curve which only starts to rise from the activity axis at the critical basic activity level.

14. Changing fixed and variable costs patterns. There are often occasions when a fixed cost becomes a variable cost and vice versa. The following are two typical cases.

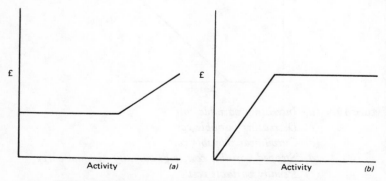

Figure 10.5 (a) *Fixed cost changing to variable cost*
(b) *Variable cost changing to fixed cost*

(a) *Fixed cost changes to variable cost (see* Fig. 10.5(a)). This arises when, for example, an indirect worker (e.g. storekeeper) is required to work overtime once a given level of activity is exceeded.

(b) *Variable cost changes to fixed cost (see* Fig. 10.5(b)). This arises when there is a charge per unit up to a given activity level after which no additional charge is made. For example, some car hire agreements incorporate a daily or weekly charge per mile up to a stipulated mileage after which all additional miles are 'free'.

Analyzing cost behaviour

Knowing the potential patterns of costs is, of course, quite different from knowing the particular pattern of a specific cost in a specific organization. This pattern can only be discovered by means of a careful analysis of the immediate past costs incurred.

In this section the approach to analyzing costs is outlined, though it must be emphasized that only the simplest situation, albeit the commonest, will be considered, i.e. where a semi-variable cost can be broken down into a non-stepped fixed element and an unchanging linear variable element.

15. Individual costs analyzed. Different costs behave in different ways. To try and analyze the total cost of a combination of individual costs risks unsolvable complications. Sometimes a total cost includes only costs which all respond in the same way to activity (e.g. the costs of milk bottle tops and of washing bottles both vary directly with the number of bottles handled), but this is often far from the case. Consequently when analyzing cost behaviour it is important to *analyze each individual cost separately.*

16. Steps in a behaviour analysis. The following steps are taken in order to analyze the behaviour pattern of an individual cost.

(a) A measure of activity is selected.

(b) The appropriate time period and the relevant activity range are determined.

(c) The cost is analyzed graphically or mathematically.

(d) The results of the analysis are used to predict future costs.

These steps are considered in more detail in **17–23**.

17. Measuring activity. In analyzing cost behaviour the first step is to decide on the measure of activity. Where factory production is closely associated with the cost this is usually the obvious candidate.

However, it should be noted that whereas production is often an excellent measure when dealing with the usual direct costs, this is not necessarily so in the case of overheads. Most overheads that vary at all vary more with *hours worked*. For instance, power, light, heat, shop-floor administration costs (including supervision) and many indirect labour costs, such as canteen wages, all tend to vary far more in relation to actual working hours than to actual production. For this reason hours worked are often employed as the measure of activity when dealing with variable overheads.

In the case of non-production costs factory production is not usually appropriate. It is therefore necessary to find some activity having a major influence on the cost to be analyzed and itself capable of being accurately predicted. Thus vehicle costs will be very much affected by distances travelled and so distance travelled may well prove an effective activity measure. For the costs of some offices, numbers of invoices or some other suitable document produced may prove an equally effective measure.

It could be that in some situations there is no natural activity measure; for instance, where there is a despatch department that packs various types of parcels. In this situation the creation of an artificial *activity unit* made up of the essential cost determinants may be warranted. Thus, a carefully determined number of units could be assigned to each kilogram despatched and each type of parcel as well. The activity in the department would then be measured by the total activity units 'earned' during the period.

EXAMPLE: A despatch department assigns 4 units of activity to each kilogram despatched, 3 units to each A-type parcel and 7 units to each B-type parcel packed. During the month 2,000 A-type parcels and 1,000 B-type parcels weighing respectively 1,200 and 1,800 kg were despatched. What was the activity of the department for the month?

SOLUTION:	*Activity units*
A-type parcels: $2,000 \times 3$ units	6,000
B-type parcels: $1,000 \times 7$ units	7,000
Weight: $(1,200 + 1,800) \times 4$ units	12,000
Total activity for month	25,000 units

When deciding upon an activity measure never forget that the object of the exercise is to predict costs. The measure that gives the best prediction should therefore be selected. The quality of a measure for this task can be judged by how closely actual results come to a mathematically determined line (in this section, a straight line). In other words, the closer the fit of the actual points to the analyzed cost curve, the better the measure.

18. Time periods and the analysis. It was pointed out that cost behaviour is to some extent dependent on the time-span involved. It is, then, necessary to select an appropriate time period for any analysis. Ideally, this should be as short as possible since the value of an analysis increases not only with the number of past observations but also the extent to which cost observations are up to date. Unfortunately, however, a very short time period often results in slightly abnormal events (and no time period ever comprises typical events only) while unmatched costs and activity can also seriously bias the figures.

The time period selection must, therefore, be something of a compromise. Under normal circumstances monthly time periods are found to be both the best compromise and the most convenient.

19. Determining the relevant range. Having decided upon the activity measure and the time period the next step is to determine the relevant activity range. This essentially is the range over which predictions are required, though it is also necessary that the organization should have some not too distant experience at both ends of this range if the analysis is to prove satisfactory.

Note that the actual range taken as relevant may well have a profound effect on the resulting curve (*see* Fig. 10.6 where the selection of two differing ranges from a single comprehensive curve results in wholly different cost curves, both equally valid within their ranges). This is immaterial so long as it is never forgotten that the curve must only be read inside the relevant range.

20. Analysis of cost by scattergraph. Given that the cost to be analyzed broadly involves no more than a non-stepped fixed cost combined with an unchanging linear variable cost, an analysis of the cost into its fixed and variable components can be made by

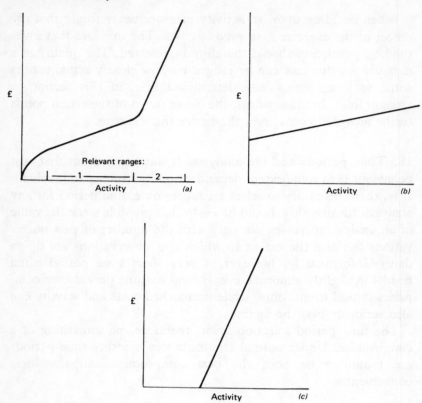

Figure 10.6 (a) *Total cost curve*
(b) *Relevant range 1 cost curve*
(c) *Relevant range 2 cost curve*

employing a scattergraph technique in the following way (*see also* Fig. 10.7).

(a) From past records abstract previous costs and statistics of the selected activity measure. This data should not extend too far back into the past (remember, it is a prediction of future behaviour that is needed and not an estimate of ancient behaviour) and should not include data:

(i) relating to activity outside the relevant range;
(ii) reflecting an unusual situation (e.g. a strike).

(b) Prepare a graph with activity on the horizontal axis and cost on the vertical axis (both axes should start at zero).

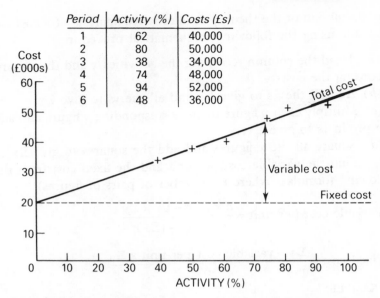

Period	Activity (%)	Costs (£s)
1	62	40,000
2	80	50,000
3	38	34,000
4	74	48,000
5	94	52,000
6	48	36,000

Figure 10.7 *Segregation of fixed and variable costs by scattergraph*
Activity and costs for each period are plotted as single points. The 'line of best fit' is the total cost curve. The point where it cuts the cost axis gives the fixed cost. This graph shows that the fixed cost is approximately £20,000 and the variable cost is £360 per 1 per cent of activity

(*c*) Plot the past cost against the corresponding activity.

(*d*) Draw the 'line of best fit' through the points and extend this to the cost axis. This is the total cost curve for the cost being analyzed.

(*e*) The component fixed and variable cost elements can now be read from the graph as follows.

(*i*) The fixed cost is the amount shown at the point where the curve cuts the cost axis.

(*ii*) The variable cost per unit of activity is the rise in the curve between any chosen activity level and the level one unit greater. In practice this can be found by measuring the rise in the curve between the cost axis and any chosen activity level and then dividing this cost rise by units of activity at this level.

21. Analysis of cost by regression line. Without entering into any discussion of the theory, an alternative analysis of a cost can be made using the following mathematical procedure:

(a) Head the column recording the activities x and the column recording the costs y.

(b) Add all the xs to give Σx and all the ys to give Σy.

(c) Multiply each x figure by its corresponding y figure and add the products to give Σxy.

(d) Square all the x figures and add the squares to give Σx^2.

(e) Find the variable cost per unit and the fixed cost from the following formulae (where $n =$ number of pairs of figures):

$$\text{Variable cost per unit} = \frac{n \times \Sigma xy - \Sigma x \times \Sigma y}{n \times \Sigma x^2 - (\Sigma x)^2}$$

$$\text{Fixed cost} = \frac{\Sigma y - \text{variable cost per unit} \times \Sigma x}{n}$$

EXAMPLE:

Using the figures in Fig. 10.7 the cost analysis is:

	ACTIVITY	COST		
(a)	x	y	xy	x^2
	62	40,000	2,480,000	3,844
	80	50,000	4,000,000	6,400
	38	34,000	1,292,000	1,444
	74	48,000	3,552,000	5,476
	94	52,000	4,888,000	8,836
	48	36,000	1,728,000	2,304

(b) $\Sigma x = 396$. $\Sigma y = 260,000$.   (c) $\Sigma xy = 17,940,000$.   (d) $\Sigma x = 28,304$.

(e) Variable cost per unit $= \dfrac{6 \times 17,940,000 - 396 \times 260,000}{6 \times 28,304 - 396^2}$

$$= \frac{4,680,000}{13,008} = £360$$

$$\text{Fixed cost} = \frac{260,000 - 360 \times 396}{6} = £196,000$$

NOTES:

1. The figures are rounded since at best they can only be approximate estimates.

2. In view of the large numbers that arise the procedure assumes that a calculator is used.

3. The cost curve that results from using this procedure is called a regression line. See *Statistics*, M&E Handbook, for the theory behind this form of analysis.

22. Other factors determining cost. Sometimes other factors besides activity affect a cost, e.g. heating costs are also affected by the season of the year. As far as possible such factors must be allowed for in the analysis and also in the prediction subsequently made from the analysis.

23. Use of analysis in predictions. Knowing the fixed cost and the variable cost per unit of activity elements of a given cost, prediction simply involves multiplying this variable cost by the predicted units of activity and adding the fixed cost (or even, more simply, by reading the cost directly from the graph). However, when making such a prediction the following points should be borne in mind.

(*a*) The prediction must be adjusted to allow for other factors (e.g. season of the year, inflation, etc.).

(*b*) The prediction will be valid only to the extent that:

(*i*) the future behaviour of a cost is consistent with its past behaviour – this whole analysis does assume a stable and continuing relationship between cost and activity;

(*ii*) it is made within the relevant activity range.

Progress test 10

Principles

1. Define: (*a*) relevant activity range; (2) (*b*) fixed cost; (3) (*c*) variable cost; (5) (*d*) semi-variable cost; (6) (*e*) policy cost. (8)

2. Why is it important to know the relevant activity range and on what basis is this range selected? (2, 19)

3. How does the economist's total cost curve differ from a cost curve produced by an accountant? (10)

4. What are the steps taken when making a cost behaviour analysis? (16)

5. What is an artificial activity unit? (17)

6. What two techniques can be employed to analyze a cost into its fixed and variable components? (20, 21)

Practice

7. It is necessary to predict a crucial future cost in a market research department. Two measures of activity have been suggested for this department: interviews conducted and pages of analyses prepared. The following are the figures for the eight most recent periods:

Period	Interviews conducted (no.)	Analyses prepared (pages)	Cost (£)
1	6,290	310	23,200
2	4,550	200	19,500
3	6,200	600	23,600
4	4,630	480	20,220
5	6,200	400	23,600
6	3,800	440	18,480
7	3,560	440	16,200
8	4,770	330	20,200

The relevant activity range is considered to be 25 per cent either side of the mean activity of these eight periods.

The first cost prediction required is in respect of period 9 when it is estimated that there will be 4,000 interviews conducted and 480 pages of analyses prepared.

Predict the departmental cost for period 9.

8. The graphs below depict the behaviour of certain costs of an enterprise in the course of a period. The vertical axis represents the cost and the horizontal axis the activity. The zero of all scales is at the intersection of the axes, though the scales of the different graphs are not necessarily the same.

Which graphs specifically relate to the following costs?

NOTE: one graph fits two costs and one cost is not graphed.

(a) Depreciation incurred on a straight line basis.

(b) A variable cost of £1 per unit throughout plus a fixed cost of £100 up to 100 units and then an additional fixed cost increase of £100 at this point and at every additional 100 units thereafter.

(c) An overhead made up of a variable cost of £5 per unit and a fixed cost of £1,000.

(d) A fixed cost of £1,000 up to 40 per cent capacity and then

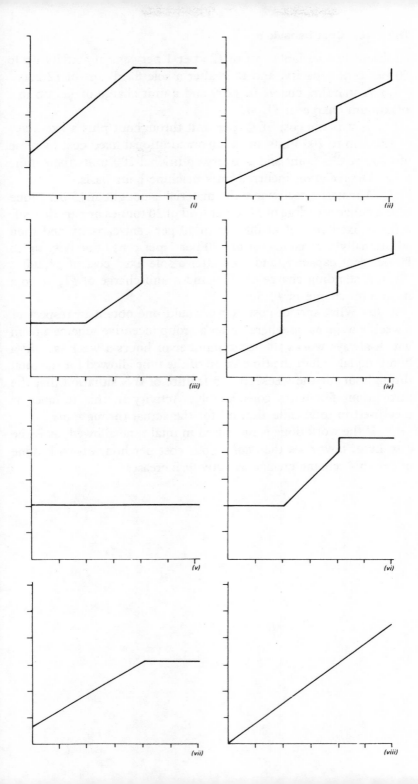

(i)

(ii)

(iii)

(iv)

(v)

(vi)

(vii)

(viii)

additionally a variable cost of £25 per 1 per cent of activity up to 80 per cent capacity, and thereafter a sole fixed cost of £2,200.

(e) A standing charge of £200 and a unit charge of £2, up to a maximum charge of £1,000.

(f) A variable cost of £2 per unit throughout plus a fixed cost of £200 up to 200 units and then an additional fixed cost increase of £200 at this point and at every additional 200 units thereafter.

(g) Depreciation incurred on a machine hour basis.

(h) A material cost where the material is bought at £5 per tonne plus a delivery charge of £100 per load of 20 tonnes or part thereof.

(i) A fixed cost of £1,000 up to 40 per cent capacity and then additionally a variable cost of £20 per 1 per cent of activity up to 80 per cent capacity, and thereafter a sole fixed cost of £2,200.

(j) A standing charge of £500 and a unit charge of £1, up to a maximum charge of £1,500.

9. (a) What sort of cost curve would one obtain in respect of a weekly wage *bonus* where under a group incentive scheme a team which always works the same number of hours a week is paid a bonus equal to half the time saved of the time allowed for the total throughput for the week? It is a feature of this situation that the throughput fluctuates considerably. Activity in this instance is measured in total time allowed for the actual throughput.

(b) If the work done is measured in total time allowed, as is the case here, how does the *total* labour cost per hour of work done under this scheme change as activity increases?

11

Introduction to decision-making

To make a right decision a manager must make a correct judgement as to how the people affected will react to the decision, make a correct prediction as to the future values of the economic figures involved in the decision, and make a correct analysis of these figures. The latter task is usually delegated in its entirety to the management accountant.

Although most of the principles below are explained as they are introduced, one or two rely for their full appreciation upon aspects that have not so far been discussed. For completeness these principles are included in this section, though you may need to wait until you read later chapters before you fully grasp all their implications. This also applies to some of the terminology. Ideally, having read this introduction so as to have some appreciation as to what you will study in the next four chapters, you should, at the end of those chapters, re-read this section in order to bring together all the principles you have learnt.

1. **All alternatives must be identified.** The first thing that must be appreciated is that decision-making involves *choice between alternatives* – even if these solely comprise doing what is proposed or not. Indeed, to do or not to do is, perhaps, the most common of all decision-making exercises. But whatever the circumstances all the alternatives must be identified for it is quite impossible to select the best alternative if that alternative is not included in the analysis. The first task of any decision-maker, therefore, is to identify all the viable alternatives. In the majority of decisions this is often the hardest part of the whole decision-making exercise. Although analysing the figures may not be easy, it is rarely as dif-

ficult as marshalling the viable alternatives. All too often the full range is not considered because of either ignorance of the existence of an alternative, e.g. of unadvertised equipment, or lack of forethought, or even because the selection of some alternatives is outside the authority of the decision maker, e.g. when purchasing materials a buyer is rarely allowed to amend the design of the product even slightly. Nevertheless, in principle *all* alternatives must be formally identified.

2. Relevant costs. In most decision-making situations costs abound. It is, however, a fundamental principle that only the *relevant* costs should be considered.

In itself this statement is something of a tautology since the test of relevance is the need for consideration. However, emphasizing the very need to identify which costs are relevant and which are not is itself very useful in decision making. Note, for instance, that an associated cost is not necessarily a relevant cost. Thus, it may cost £50 to transport a unit to a customer. This cost is a cost associated with the unit, but if the decision lies between painting the unit black or white it is not a relevant cost since it has no bearing on the decision.

It should, perhaps, be made clear that to include an irrelevant cost will not of itself give rise to an error in the decision analysis. An irrelevant cost is, in effect, neutral and in no way alters the analysis. However, what often happens in practice is that the analyst incorporates an irrelevant cost incorrectly simply because he feels it *should* have some influence on the result. By first carefully identifying which costs are relevant and which are not, the danger of wrongly incorporating an irrelevant cost is considerably reduced.

Virtually all the other decision-making principles relate to determining the relevance of a cost.

3. Future costs only are relevant. Since the past cannot be changed, then all decisions relate to future events. This means that *all past and sunk costs are irrelevant* and the use of such costs in decision making must be wholly restricted to their value in making predictions. Indeed, were it not that cost-behaviour patterns analysed from past costs often prove the soundest basis for predicting future costs, they would be totally excluded from decision making.

Ignoring past costs is often psychologically difficult. After all, if you had just paid £100,000 for some equipment this amount would appear to be a very relevant cost should you be faced with the choice of retaining it or replacing it with more efficient equipment. Yet retain or replace, the £100,000 remains spent and is, therefore, wholly irrelevant. For the purpose of any retain-or-replace decision the only relevant value is the net realizable value, i.e. the *future* 'cost'.

4. The differential principle. Of all the decision-making principles perhaps the most important is the differential principle. This asserts that when deciding between alternatives *only those factors which differ between alternatives should be considered.* From this it follows that the only relevant costs are those which differ between alternatives.

To apply this principle in an analysis it is necessary to look at each factor that has a bearing on the overall profit of the enterprise, and decide if selecting one alternative rather than another would alter that factor's effect on the profit. If it would, it is relevant – if not, it isn't.

Close adherence to this principle will not only guide the student towards the correct solution of a problem but also often lessen the work load. In many decision-making examination questions there are a number of irrelevant figures and being able to ignore these almost invariably simplifies the whole problem.

A frequent difficulty in applying the differential principle lies in selecting a base from which differences can be measured. If, for example, only four out of five products can be manufactured, which do you compare with which? To break this deadlock it often pays to select arbitrarily any alternative as a base and test the other alternatives against it. When another alternative proves better, the first is discarded and this other becomes the new base (*see* question 9 in progress test 14).

5. Common costs and common incomes are irrelevant. It follows from the differential principle that any costs or incomes which are shared in total between the alternatives and will remain unchanged regardless of which alternative is selected are irrelevant and should not be included in the analysis. However, if it is desired to give additional background material such costs and incomes may be added at the end of the analysis, providing that their irrelevance to the decision is made very clear.

6. Interest as a relevant cost. Interest is only a relevant cost where the alternatives have cash-flow differences involving significant amounts and, in addition, significant timing differences, i.e. when the interest payable by the enterprise will differ significantly depending upon the alternative selected. Note that if interest *is* a relevant cost in a decision the decision is called a 'long-term decision' and as such falls outside the scope of this book.

7. Tax as a relevant cost. It should not be forgotten that tax also becomes a relevant cost if the tax payable by the enterprise differs significantly depending on the alternative selected.

8. Existing conditions. If one of the alternatives being considered involves the use of existing equipment or any loss of an existing advantage, then:

(*a*) if an asset, charge its opportunity cost, i.e. net realizable value (*see* **12**(*b*)), to the alternative requiring the use of the asset;

(*b*) if an advantage, charge the cash loss which would be sustained by giving up the advantage. (For example, assume adopting alternative X will result in the loss of bulk discounts. Charge X with value of lost discounts for purpose of making the decision.) It is under this heading that consideration should be given to the contribution per unit of key factor (*see* **13** : **19**).

9. Principles of data presentation. Analyzing the data correctly is only part of the management accountant's responsibility in decision-making. Equally important is the presentation of the data in an appropriate manner.

(*a*) Always comply with the general principles of data presentation. (These principles are essentially statistical in origin and the student is advised to refer to any of the appropriate texts on this subject, e.g. *Statistics*, W. M. Harper, M & E Handbook series.)

(*b*) Always bear in mind *the use to which the figures will be put.* (This, of course, is a fundamental cost accounting rule.) Do not include any figures which may mislead, e.g. a cost-per-unit figure based on full capacity when full capacity cannot be attained.

(c) Always present figures in a comparative form. This enables managers to see how, why and where differences between alternatives arise and gives them insight into, and confidence in, the final conclusions.

(d) Always present the conclusion clearly. State the obvious – to the uninitiated in management accounting it could well be the most perfectly camouflaged data in the whole presentation.

10. Decision-making advice.

(a) *Irrelevance of book values.* Don't forget that book values, being past costs, are *never* relevant in decision making (and even if the book value is an up-to-date replacement value it is still rarely the value required in decision-making – see **12**).

(b) *Time span.* It is often advisable to calculate all figures in an analysis in respect of the total time-span involved. Although this may result in large figures, this is preferable to combining figures computed for shorter terms when errors of principle may arise in the combination process, e.g. to take a trivial case, if 300 and 100 units are produced in the first and second halves of the time span at costs of £6 and £4 a unit respectively, the overall cost per unit is *not* £5.

(c) *Fixed and variable costs.* Do not assume that fixed costs are always irrelevant nor that variable costs are always relevant. As will be seen, it is always possible that some fixed costs will differ between alternatives and sometimes these are variable costs which do not differ, e.g. if the decision lies between buying the raw material at £5 a ton from one supplier or £4 a ton from another, the other unit variable costs are clearly all irrelevant.

(d) *Standing alternatives.* It should be remembered that there are almost always two standing alternatives with which any new plan can be compared. These are:

(i) doing nothing, i.e. carrying on as currently engaged;

(ii) straight investment of funds required for the plan in an outside investment.

This means in the case of (i) a comparison of the consequences following from the operation of the plan with continued current operations, and in the case of (ii) a comparison of the return on capital with outside investment possibilities.

It should be noted that *at any time* a comparison can be initiated between (*i*) and (*ii*) for *any project*, i.e. between carrying on as currently engaged, as against the liquidation of current operations, and the subsequent investment of the funds released elsewhere.

(*e*) *Inflation*. Where inflation is likely to complicate the figures, then it is advisable to edit out its effects. This, however, requires a statistical technique and so the student is again referred to the texts that illustrate such a technique.

(*f*) *Decisions involving multi-alternatives*. When the number of alternatives to be considered is large, it is often advisable to split the alternatives into small groups (sometimes even pairs). Each group is then considered in turn, and the best alternative singled out. Subsequent comparisons between these preferred alternatives will indicate the best one to adopt, i.e. in effect, run a knock-out competition between the alternatives.

Such a course is advisable because the relevance of a factor often depends upon which alternatives are being compared. To try to compare all alternatives simultaneously will involve so many factors that the comparison will be very complicated. Initial rejection of inferior alternatives within given groups very much lessens the complexity of the final analysis.

(*g*) *Applying the differential principle*. Finally, remember that in a decision-making analysis it is necessary to:

(*i*) introduce any and every factor that will differ between alternatives and which will have an effect on the profit of the enterprise, e.g. changes in incomes, changes in fixed costs, interest;

(*ii*) ignore every factor that will remain the same whichever alternative is selected.

This can, perhaps, be summarized by saying that the costs that are relevant to decision making are *the future costs that differ*.

11. Historical, net realizable and replacement values. At this point the student may be uncertain as to the role in decision making of the different ways of valuing existing assets.

(*a*) *Historical values*. These should *never* be used (although historical *cost* figures may, of course, be used as a basis for predicting costs).

(*b*) *Net realizable values*. The net realizable value (i.e. what would be received on disposal of an asset less the costs of the disposal) should always be taken as the true measure of the worth of an asset. It follows, therefore, that the depreciation cost of using such an asset over the decision period is the difference between its net realizable value at the beginning and its net realizable value at the end of that period.

(c) *Replacement values*. The function of a replacement value is to provide a measure of the economic worth of an existing asset outside the particular circumstances of the enterprise, and in these kind of circumstances it should be used to reach a decision. For instance, in setting a price a manager may not be so much concerned with the minimum level that follows from using net realizable value as the average economic price that the market would regard as reasonable. For this replacement value serves best.

12. Full cost v. differential cost. It is here advocated that only differential costs should be used in decision making and never full costs (i.e. costs resulting from common costs being apportioned between alternatives). However, where there is a disturbing element of uncertainty about the behaviour of future costs – particularly where there has previously been experience of so-called 'fixed' costs creeping upwards with increasing activity – many managers feel it is safer to use a full cost approach. While the accountant may, and should, try to allay the manager's fears, he must nevertheless respect his feelings. After all, if the accountant's evidence fails to convince then it is probable that some valid doubt does exist.

Progress test 11

Principles

1. What is a relevant cost? (2)
2. How are the following to be classified in terms of relevance for decision-making: (a) future costs; (3) (b) common costs; (5) (c) common income; (5) (d) interest; (6) (e) tax. (7)
3. What is the differential principle? (4)
4. What are the principles of data presentation? (9)
5. When do you use historical, net realizable and replacement values in a decision-making situation? (11)

12

Short-term decision-making

There is really only one decision-making technique and that is differential costing. However, in different circumstances some kinds of cost differences are more significant than others. As a result there are a number of different decision-making techniques, although since all do no more than emphasize different aspects there is inevitably no clear distinction between one technique and another. In selecting a technique, therefore, it is not so much a matter of selecting the correct technique as selecting the most convenient technique. Correctness relates only to the application of the decision-making principles given in Chapter 11.

The decision-making techniques can initially be divided into short- and long-term techniques, again with no hard-and-fast dividing line. The criteria for the division is no more than the relevance of interest – if interest is a significant cost then a long-term technique is needed while if it is not significant a short-term technique can be used. These latter techniques include marginal costing (*see* Chapter 13), cash flow and opportunity costing and conventionally fall within the ambit of costing – long-term decision-making being regarded as an essentially management accounting topic.

Differential costing

1. Scope of differential costing. This technique identifies the most profitable of a group of alternatives by *identifying the cost differences between the alternatives and ignoring those costs that remain unaffected by the decision* (cost here includes income). While variations in this technique give rise to techniques that exist in their own right, e.g. marginal costing (*see* Chapter 13), there are occasions when none of these specialist techniques are wholly suitable. Analyses that use a direct application of the differential principle are frequently termed *differential cost analyses*.

2. Common differential costing circumstances. Differential costing is most commonly used where two alternatives are, in cost differential terms, nearly identical. Thus selecting which out of a number of suppliers should be given an order rarely involves more than comparing prices – nothing more complicated is needed. Similarly, if two schemes will result in identical variable costs and incomes and only certain fixed costs will be different, then a direct comparison of these fixed costs will at once identify the more profitable alternative.

It should be appreciated that there are occasions when alternatives appear more at variance than they really are. Thus, if there is a decision involving a critical resource then the cost of this resource will remain unchanged whichever alternative is selected (if it won't, then the resource is not being fully exploited). Consequently in a differential cost analysis this cost will be ignored. For example, if the critical resource were labour hours, of which there were only 1,000, to be paid at £5 an hour, then, since the full number available will inevitably be used, the total labour cost will always be £5,000 whichever alternative is selected. Since such costs do not alter they will be excluded from the differential cost analysis.

EXAMPLE

	Product A	Product B
Selling price	£30	£70
Material	£4	£20
Labour (at £5 hr)	5 hr	10 hr

Labour is the critical resource. Should A or B be produced?

Solution

Relevant figures:	A	B
Production per 10 hours:	*2 units*	*1 unit*
Sales	£60	£70
Materials	£8	£20
Net differential income per 10 hours	£52	£50

A should be selected since £2 more profit will be earned every 10 hours of the crucial resource than would be earned if B were selected.

NOTE:

(1) Labour costs, being the same for both alternatives, are excluded.

(2) The figures show only the *differences* between the alternatives and in no way measure actual profit, only profitability.

3. Unchanged income decisions. There are sometimes occasions when the total income remains unaffected by the decision. This is particularly the case where a decision has to be made as to which products should be sub-contracted where demand exceeds capacity. On these occasions the income can be ignored and the decision based on a cost minimization analysis.

4. Absolute and relative costs. When a comparison is required between two alternatives only, then the presentation of differential costs can be made using either absolute costs or relative costs.

(*a*) *Absolute costs.* Using this approach the full costs and incomes that differ are listed for each alternative so that the two net differential figures can be compared and the more profitable alternative identified, as in 2 above.

(*b*) *Relative costs.* Using this approach one alternative is taken as 'base' and the gain or loss in respect of each item of income and cost that would result if the *other* alternative were selected instead is detailed. This results in a final figure that indicates the net total gain or loss that would follow if the second alternative were substituted for the 'base' alternative, and so indicates whether or not such a substitution is profitable. If this method had been adopted for the problem in 2 above the presentation would have been as follows.

EXAMPLE: Taking the production of A as base, the substitution of B would have the following consequences:

Extra sales every 10 labour hours: £70 − £60	£10
Extra costs producing B: £20 − £8	£12
Net difference	£2 loss

Producing B will lose £2 per 10 hours of labour. Therefore A should be produced.

Cash flow technique

The differential approach in decision-making can be applied to cash alone in many situations – which needless to say simplifies much of the work involved in assessing the alternatives.

5. Definition of cash flow. *Cash flow* is the actual movement of cash in and out of an enterprise. Cash flow in (or *positive cash flow*) is cash received, and cash flow out (*negative cash flow*) is cash paid out. The difference between these two flows is termed the *net cash flow*.

6. When to use the cash flow technique. The circumstances in which a cash flow decision-making technique can be applied are those in which the prime differences can be measured in terms of the future cash flows of the alternatives. In essence the underlying principle of the technique can be stated as follows: *the most profitable alternative is the one that will, over the period for which a solution is required, most favourably affect the bank balance of the enterprise, other things being equal.* In other words, the most profitable alternative is that alternative which makes one richest.

7. Application of the cash flow technique.

(*a*) For each alternative compute:

(*i*) the *future* cash flows both in and out that would result from the selection of the alternative;
(*ii*) the overall net cash flow.

(*b*) Select the alternative having the most favourable net cash flow.

EXAMPLE: A finished goods stock item that cost £200 to make is in danger of becoming completely obsolete. There are two alternative ways of disposing of it: sell it to X for £200 or to Y for £216. Y is situated twice as far away as X (although owing to road conditions the delivery time will be the same) and the cost accountant has supplied the following cost estimates for delivery:

X – petrol and oil £10; wages £12; share of licence, insurance and depreciation (based on mileage) £14;

Y – petrol and oil £20; wages £12; share of licence, insurance and depreciation £28.

Should the item be sold to X or Y?

Solution

	X	Y
Case flow in: Sales	£ + 200	£ + 216
Cash flow out: Petrol, oil and wages	– 22	– 32
Net cash flow	£ + 178	£ + 184

Since Y has the most favourable net cash flow the correct decision is to sell to Y.

NOTE:

(1) The £14 and £28 share of the licence, insurance and depreciation are not included as there is no actual future outflow of *cash* in respect of these costs. This exclusion is, of course, as it should be since the actual amounts incurred by the business remains unchanged whichever delivery is undertaken – or even if neither is undertaken.

(2) The net cash flow does not measure the profit (there is a loss whichever alternative is selected) but only indicates which alternative is the more profitable.

8. Qualification to the cash flow principle. Despite the unarguable logic of the cash flow principle, students are often concerned at the total disregard of those costs which are not represented by actual future cash flows. In one respect their concern is justified, for the principle does contain a vital qualification, *other things being equal.* In other words it is necessary that, whichever alternative is selected, at the very end the enterprise will be in exactly the same position except as regards its bank balance. Sometimes this is not so: under one alternative the enterprise may be left with goods in stock, or a plot of land, or an old machine. In such cases the net cash flow figures emerging as a result of employing the pure cash flow technique must be adjusted to allow for such left-over items.

9. Past flows irrelevant. In another respect – that involving past flows – the concern of students is unfounded. If an enterprise had earlier paid out a sum of money for some item, then this amount does *not* enter the calculations, for no matter which alternative is selected the payment cannot be eliminated and, therefore, under the decision-making principles it fails to be relevant. It may be difficult to accept that a sum of £1m paid last week for a piece of equipment has absolutely no bearing on the decision to dispose of that piece of equipment this week, but it is nevertheless a correct statement of principle.

10. Depreciation and cash flow. It was noted in the example in 7 above that since depreciation does not involve a flow of cash it does not appear in a cash flow analysis. This does not mean that it will be overlooked completely. For instance, where one alternative calls for the purchase of an asset the purchase price of the asset will enter the analysis as a negative cash flow while the anticipated receipt for the final residual value will enter as a positive cash flow. Since the difference between these amounts is, in fact, the asset depreciation, the depreciation is taken into account, though not as a single specified sum.

This inclusion of depreciation also occurs in respect of an existing asset in a replacement decision (*see* Progress test, q. 9) albeit in a somewhat roundabout way. Careful study of the cash flow analysis made in such a case will show this depreciation to be allowed for by the combined effects of:

(*a*) recording the positive flow that would arise from the *ultimate* sale of the asset as part of the case for retaining the asset; and

(*b*) recording the higher positive flow that would arise from the *immediate* sale of the asset as part of the case for replacing the asset.

Again, the difference between these two figures is the asset depreciation.

11. Absolute and relative cash flows. Cash flows can be presented as absolute flows or relative flows in exactly the same way as costs (*see* **4**).

In **7** above a statement using absolute flows was given. The same problem can be reworked using relative flows as follows.

EXAMPLE: Taking the sale to X as base, the substitution of the sale to Y gives the following relative cash flows:

Sales – extra cash flow (in)	£ + 16
Costs – extra cash flow (out)	– 10
Net relative flow	£ + 6

Selling to Y will improve the overall cash flow by £6. Therefore the sale should be to Y.

12. Advantages of using the cash flow technique. The advantages of using the cash flow technique are as follows.

(*a*) It is a relatively simple technique – only actual cash flows in and out have to be considered. There are no complications involving the matching of costs and revenue, no temptations to apportion fixed costs to alternatives, and no problems of depreciation.

(*b*) By concentrating on future cash flows it automatically prevents past costs being unnecessarily included in the calculations and so avoids the possibility of erroneous treatment of such past costs.

(*c*) It avoids misguided attempts to saddle particular alternatives with unrecovered past costs. For example, some managements believe they cannot discontinue a specific product until it has 'recovered' its tooling costs. They fail to appreciate that continued production of an inferior product often makes less profit than the introduction of a better product, despite heavy unrecovered costs.

(*d*) It is needed if a discounted cash flow analysis is required (although the analysis then becomes a long-term one and as such falls outside the scope of this book).

Opportunity costing

In many ways the concept of opportunity costs is the hardest of all the costing concepts to apply, both in practice and in theory. It is difficult in practice because the opportunity costs are all too often not known and not accessible, and it is difficult in theory because opportunity costs are not absolute – as will be shown, they depend very much on the probability that the opportunity can be taken.

13. Opportunity cost. An *opportunity cost* is an economic concept that can perhaps be most simply defined as *the value of a benefit sacrificed in favour of* (or as a result of) *taking an alternative course of action.* For instance, if you have a material that you can sell at £1 a kilo, then the opportunity cost of using that material in your own production is £1 a kilo, *regardless of how much you paid for it.* Again, if you could earn a net income of £200 by travelling to London, then the opportunity cost of your travelling to Manchester instead is £200.

As can be seen, the concept of an opportunity cost is not difficult. Problems do begin to arise, however, when there are doubts about the validity of the opportunity, e.g. if it is only possible, and not certain, that you can sell your material at £1 a kilo or that you would earn £200 by travelling to London.

14. Opportunity costing. In opportunity costing all the costs involved in an analysis are opportunity costs. In principle opportunity costs should always be used in decision-making since decision-making aims at maximizing profit and such profit maximization depends upon the up-to-date economic valuation of all resources and capacity used. Thus if you bought a gallon of solvent for £1.10 and then sold it for £1.20 when the market price was £1.30 it could be argued that as far as the book-keeping went you had made a profit of 10p, but as far as the decision-making went you had made a loss of 10p. In other words, since the cost objective in decision-making is to find the relative profit of one alternative over another, all competing resources and activities must be valued on the basis of their own maximum profit potential rather than on any other basis.

15. Resources and activities. Although there is no theoretical distinction between the opportunity cost of a resource and an activity it probably pays in practice to be aware of the difference between these two factors. They can be defined roughly as follows.

(*a*) An *activity* is anything that the enterprise *will* 'produce' (or process), be it a product or a service.

(*b*) A *resource* is anything that the enterprise holds that can be disposed of without further processing. Timber and screws are obvious examples, but contracted labour, too, is a resource, as is land. Plant and equipment are resources which must not be overlooked.

The crucial distinction is that an activity, as against a resource, will make a future demand on the capacity of an enterprise. Whereas resources can be sold in whatever quantities the enterprise happens to possess without affecting other aspects of the enterprise's work, selling an activity does affect those aspects and these must be assessed.

16. Zero and negative opportunity costs. It is a feature of opportunity costs that in many instances they are zero. This can arise, for instance, when an employee is engaged for 40 hours at an inescapable £150 but there is only 30 hours work for him to do. Here the remaining 10 hours are free as regards valuing his time for any other work. Even if a net income of only £5 (excluding any charge for labour) is earned, that is £5 more profit than would otherwise be made. Thus the opportunity cost of the 10 hours is zero (though note that once this £5 net income work exists the opportunity cost to any other alternative now rises to £5).

Although labour is probably the commonest example of a zero opportunity cost, instances also arise where, through obsolescence, a machine is completely worthless. Clearly, in using such a machine an enterprise suffers no sacrifice and the opportunity cost, therefore, is zero.

There are also, though rarely, cases where the opportunity cost is negative, e.g. where an obsolete machine not only has no residual value but would even incur costs in its disposal. Regrettably, in such a case the opportunity cost of the 'depreciation' would not be negative since disposal would be no cheaper after use than before. However, if a project actually resulted in the disposal of the machine as a spin-off then the opportunity cost could be included in the project analysis as a negative figure.

17. Complications in determining a resource opportunity cost. Strictly speaking, it could perhaps be argued that to find the value of a resource opportunity cost it is necessary to ascertain the highest net receipt that could be obtained if the resource were sold on the same day as it was to be used in the proposed alternative. However, this runs contrary to the spirit of the definition, for if it were known that the disposal value of the resource would be doubled a week later then this doubled value should really be adopted as the opportunity cost – it is certainly the opportunity cost of disposing of the resource now as against holding it for a little longer. But if *future* disposal values are valid opportunity costs, where does the process of looking to the future end? And how sure must one be that the value will rise for a future value to be a valid opportunity cost?

This is not all, for it can also be queried as to whether an opportunity cost has to be based on a disposal value. For example, if, because of transport complications, a resource would cost an enterprise twice as much to buy as it would to sell, is the disposal value or the replacement value the correct opportunity cost? The answer seems to depend upon whether the resource would in fact be replaced. If it would, then the replacement value should be taken. If not, the disposal value is used. But if the replacement value is to be used, should that be the current replacement value or the known future value, or even the suspected future value?

18. Opportunity costs and uncertainty. As is becoming clear, an opportunity cost is by no means a certain cost, even where the problems of future values and replacement costs do not arise, for it depends very much on making an economic valuation in a world that is notoriously lacking in economic certainty. So it is often very difficult to say just what you would receive if you sold some of a given material held in stock. You may get the ruling market price or you may not. Indeed, you may get above the market price if you were to sell to a financially insecure customer, but would the higher price really be the opportunity cost? These problems can become even bigger if the resource is your own product, and your product is unique. You *may* be awarded a contract for £200,000 if you really made the effort but if you decide to select a different alternative you will never know if you would have succeeded or not. So how can you value the sacrifice made by not making the attempt to win the contract at £200,000? And if you don't value it at £200,000 what *do* you value it at?

19. Conclusion. From all this it can be seen that determining an opportunity cost is not always a straightforward exercise. In practice it may also be difficult even to find disposal values on the day in question, let alone future replacement values in what is possibly a very imperfect market. An opportunity cost, therefore, is often far more of a subjective than an objective valuation. How, then, should one proceed?

Unfortunately, no firm criteria can be laid down. Given the concept that the opportunity cost to be charged to a given alternative is the maximum sacrifice that an enterprise would suffer in giving up some other alternative, then all the practitioner can do is to test each item against that concept. When your figures are certain you can proceed with confidence. When uncertainty and doubt begin to enter you must be more cautious of the interpretation of your results.

Progress test 12

Principles

1. What is: (*a*) differential costing?   (**1**) (*b*) cash-flow technique for decision making?   (**7**) (*c*) opportunity costing?   (**14**)

2. Distinguish between: (*a*) absolute and relative costs;   (**4**) (*b*) absolute and relative cash flows.   (**11**)

3. How does depreciation enter into a cash flow analysis?   (**10**)

4. What is an opportunity cost?   (**13**)

5. Explain when an opportunity cost can be: (*a*) zero? (*b*) negative?   (**16**)

6. What problems arise in using opportunity costs?   (**17–19**)

Practice

7. A company is considering replacing a sound but somewhat old-fashioned machine by a more up-to-date special purpose one. Unfortunately, in five years' time the work done on these types of machine will end. The facts are as below and you are to determine whether or not to replace the existing machine.

	Existing machine	*New machine*
Book value	£24,000	—
Resale value now	10,000	—
Purchase price	40,000	£30,000
Residual value in 5 years	4,000	2,000
Annual cash running costs	9,000	6,000
Annual receipts from production	10,000	12,000

8. The Mix Chemical Company Ltd produces joint products A, B and C from input material X. From 150 lb of X, which costs $33\frac{1}{3}$p per lb, 50 lb of A, 45 lb of B and 45 lb of C can be produced. The 10 lb of process scrap is sold at 10p per lb, as can be any of the finished products which cannot be disposed of on the open market. The standard costs and revenues of A, B and C are as follows.

Joint Products A, B and C – Standard Cost and Revenue Table

	A		B		C	
Quantity	50 lb		45 lb		45 lb	
Standard revenue		£50.0		£55.0		£35.0
Less Joint costs:						
Material	£17.5		£19.25		£12.25	
Labour	12.5	30.0	11.25	30.5	11.25	23.5
		20.0		24.5		11.5
Less Direct costs:						
Finishing	5.0		5.0		1.0	
Packing	5.0		4.5		4.5	
Distributing	5.0	15.0	4.5	14.0	4.5	10.0
Standard direct profit		£5.0		£10.5		£1.5
Standard cost per lb		£0.90		£0.99		£0.74

NOTE: Joint cost basis of allocation – materials allocated on standard revenue; labour allocated on standard weight.

The company has received, from its biggest customer, an additional order of 10,000 lb per annum of product A at a price of 95p per lb. You have been asked to advise as to whether this order should be accepted, and if so what will be the additional profit, and what is the minimum price the company could accept so that a loss would not be made? The answers to these questions have to be made under each of the following assumptions.

(a) At present because of the demand for B and C, 12,000 lb per annum of product A has to be sold as scrap because it cannot be sold on the open market.

(b) The present demand for product A is such that all of production of B and C cannot be sold on the open market and has to be scrapped.

(c) The whole of the present production is being sold on the open market, and there is an unlimited demand, at standard selling price, for product C, but it is estimated that only an additional 6,750 lb of B can be sold annually on the open market.

Interest charges can be ignored. (*ACCA* adapted)

NOTE: There is an ambiguity in this question. It says that 'finished products' have a rock-bottom value of 10p per lb. However, the subsequent costs of finishing, packing and distributing the three products are all greater than this – so it is more profitable to throw away any excess production than sell it. To avoid this interpretation the suggested answer assumes that, like the process scrap, the 10p selling price is for the products that exist immediately after the split-off point, i.e. prior to incurring any subsequent costs.

9. The company of which you are the management accountant has obtained a contract to supply 200,000 metal fittings at £5 each.

To undertake this work a special purpose machine has been purchased for £22,000 which at the end of the contract will have a residual value of £2,000.

Estimated production costs are:

Direct material, per unit	£1.50
Direct labour, per unit	£1.00
Variable production overhead, of direct labour costs	60%
Fixed production overhead, excluding depreciation, for the contract	£40,000
Variable selling overhead, per unit	£0.30
Fixed selling overhead, for the contract	£80,000

Although the contract has not yet started a second machine of more advanced design has been offered to the company for £36,000. This machine will produce 25 per cent more units per operator hour but will use 5 per cent more material. The machine will have no residual value at the end of the contract. The makers are prepared to buy back the first machine for £5,000.

The works manager has in the circumstances asked if the second machine should be purchased. You are required to advise the works manager of the action to be taken.   (*CIMA* adapted)

10. A company incurred a tooling cost of £200,000 for a product whose manufacture and sales were planned to be 5,000 units a year for five years. The total cost build-up per unit is as follows:

Direct materials		£4
Direct labour (2 hr at £4 hr)		8
Share of tooling cost		8
Fixed overheads (at £8 hr)		16
		36
	Profit	4
	Selling Price	£40

After only six months' production the company learns there is a good market (lasting at least $4\frac{1}{2}$ years) for another type of product which has a direct material cost of £6, a selling price of £16 and requires $\frac{1}{2}$ hour's labour to make. Unfortunately labour is in short supply and to make this product would mean permanently abandoning the first product, scrapping the tools, and switching all labour over to the second product. This second product would, in addition, require an extra expenditure of £12,000 p.a. on fixed costs.

Which product should the company manufacture?

11. A foundry sells for £200 a unit a product which is essentially two halves assembled together, a right-hand half and a left-hand half. The casting requirements to make either half are:

> Material, 1 tonne at £40 a tonne;
> Labour, £10

The assembly cost for joining the two halves together is £20 per finished unit, i.e. per pair of halves.

Unfortunately material is in scarce supply and the foundry has only 200 tonnes available for the forthcoming period. It has, however, been offered a supply of completed right-hand halves. What is the maximum price the foundry would be prepared to pay to buy these halves if all units made could be sold and if a total cost of £400 would be incurred in transporting the load of purchased halves to the foundry?

12. A furniture company manufactures one type of lounge suite

exclusively. This suite contains the following seven components: one settee, two armchairs, four armless chairs. These components can either be manufactured by the company or sub-contracted, and the relevant data relating to the components is as follows:

	Settee	Armchair	Armless chair
Direct material cost per component	£80	£40	£44
Direct labour hours per component	10	5	1
Sub-contract price per component	£200	£80	£60

Suite sales are currently running at 8,000 per period, each suite selling for £600. Though the company would like to manufacture all its own components, a capacity limit of 50,000 direct labour hours obliges the company to sub-contract some components.

Cost studies have shown that variable overheads vary with direct labour hours worked and are incurred at a rate of £1.60 per hour. Fixed costs are £140,000 per period and labour costs £4.40 per hour.

(a) Which components, and how many, should be manufactured by the company?

(b) What is the maximum profit that could be earned:

(i) at current sales?
(ii) if sales were unlimited?

(c) If the selling price has to be reduced to £560 per suite, what is the maximum profit the company can obtain?

13. AB Limited has just completed production of an item of special equipment for a customer, ST Limited, only to be notified that the customer has gone into liquidation.

After much effort, the sales manager has managed to locate one potential buyer, VW Limited, which has indicated that it might be prepared to buy the machine if certain conversion work could be carried out.

The selling price of the machine to the original buyer had been fixed at £101,200 and had included an estimated normal profit mark-up of 10 per cent on total costs. The costs incurred in the manufacture of the machine were:

Direct materials	£38,000
Direct wages	24,000
Overheads:	
variable	6,000
fixed, production	20,000
fixed, selling and administration	4,000
	£92,000

If the machine is converted, production management assesses that the following extra work would be needed.

Direct materials, at cost, £6,400
Direct wages:
Department L: 3 men for 4 weeks at £300 per man/week
Department M: 1 man for 4 weeks at £240 per man/week
Variable overhead:
20 per cent of direct wages
Fixed production overhead:
Department L: $83\frac{1}{3}$ per cent of direct wages
Department M: 25 per cent of direct wages.

The following additional information is available.

(a) In the original machine there are three types of basic materials:

(i) type P could now be sold to a scrap merchant for £6,000;
(ii) type Q could be sold to the scrap merchant for £4,000, but it would take 120 hours of labour paid at £3 per hour to put it into a suitable condition for sale;
(iii) type R would need to be scrapped at a cost to AB Limited of £1,200.

(b) The materials for the conversion are at present in stock. If not needed for the conversion, they could be used in the production of another machine in place of materials that would currently cost £7,600.

(c) The conversion would be carried out in two departments. Department L is currently extremely busy and it is estimated that its contribution to overhead and profits is £2.50 per £1 of labour.

Department M is very short of work. For organizational reasons its labour force cannot be reduced below its present level of four employees, all of whom are paid at the standard wage of £240 per week. The load of work on these employees is, however, only 40 per cent of their standard capacity.

(*d*) The designs and specifications of the original machine could be sold overseas for a sum of £3,000 if the machine is scrapped.

(*e*) An additional temporary supervisor would have to be engaged for the conversion work at a cost of £1,800. It is the company's normal practice to charge supervision to fixed overhead.

(*f*) Customer ST Limited paid a non-returnable deposit to the company of 12 per cent of the selling price.

You are required to:

(*a*) calculate the minimum price that AB Limited should accept from VW Limited for the converted machine, explaining clearly how you have arrived at your figure;

(*b*) state briefly any assumptions that you have made in arriving at your conclusions.   *CIMA* (adapted)

13

Marginal costing

In Chapter 5 total absorption costing was shown to adopt the principle of *sharing* each cost between cost units and cost centres on the basis of benefit received. The underlying objective of that technique was to obtain an overall average economic cost of carrying out whatever activity was being costed. However, overall averages are of only limited use where day-to-day management is involved – as many people paying income tax will confirm for if they are given the chance of overtime it is their marginal rate of tax that is of significance and not their average rate. In this chapter, therefore, a more immediately useful technique of ascertaining costs will be outlined.

1. Marginal cost ascertainment. This is based on the view that in many practical short-term situations the cost of any given activity is the cost that that activity specifically generates – and no more. Put another way, it is the difference in cost between carrying out and not carrying out that activity. To achieve this the following principle is adopted in respect of all cost data:

In *marginal cost ascertainment* each cost unit and each cost centre is charged with only those costs that are generated as a consequence of that cost unit and that cost centre being a part of the enterprise's activities.

2. Marginal costs. The costs which are generated solely by a given *cost unit* are the variable costs associated with that unit (the variable cost here including the variable cost element of any associated semi-variable cost). Ascertaining these costs simply involves ascertaining:

(a) all the unit direct costs;
(b) the variable overhead cost per unit incurred by the cost unit.

Costs ascertained on this basis are termed *marginal costs,* and the marginal cost of a cost unit can be defined as the *additional cost of producing one such unit.* It follows as a matter of course that the marginal cost of a number of units (similar or otherwise) is the sum of all the unit marginal costs.

NOTE: The difference between the terms 'variable cost' and 'marginal cost' is primarily one of context. We normally talk of the marginal cost of a cost unit, but the variable cost of a cost centre.

3. Preparation of a unit marginal cost. To prepare a unit marginal cost, therefore, involves ascertaining the unit direct costs and the variable overhead costs per unit. Finding the unit direct costs in marginal costing is no different from finding these costs in absorption costing. Finding the variable overhead cost per unit for each overhead cost, however, calls for the following steps.

(a) The variable cost per unit of activity (e.g. direct labour hours) is found from a cost behaviour analysis.
(b) The number of units of activity per cost unit are ascertained.
(c) The variable overhead cost per cost unit is found by multiplying (a) by (b).

EXAMPLE: If a cost behaviour analysis showed that the variable cost element of a certain overhead was £2 per direct labour hour and that a cost unit required 4 hours of direct labour, the cost unit variable overhead would be $4 \times £2 = £8$.

Once all the individual variable costs per unit, direct and variable overhead, have been found they are added together to give the marginal cost of the cost unit.

EXAMPLE: *Odds and Ends.* The Odds 'n' Ends Department manufactures Odds and Ends. Each Odd requires £15 of direct material and 3 direct labour hours while each End requires £10 of direct material and 5 direct labour hours. Direct labour is paid at £3 per hour and an analysis of the overheads shows there is a variable overhead cost of £2 per direct labour hour. Ascertain the marginal cost per unit of each product.

		Odd	*End*
SOLUTION:		£	£
Marginal cost:	Direct material	15	10
	Direct labour	3 × £3 = 9	5 × £3 = 15
	Variable overhead	3 × £2 = 6	5 × £2 = 10
Marginal cost per unit		£30	£35

4. Marginal costing. This is the name given to any system of costing which is based upon the preparation and use of the marginal cost of cost units. Formally it has been defined as 'A principle whereby variable costs are charged to cost units and the fixed cost attributable to the relevant period is written off in full against the contribution for that period' (CIMA Terminology). For contribution, *see* **9**.

5. Identifiable fixed costs. A fixed cost has been defined as a cost which remains unchanged regardless of the level of activity within the relevant activity range. The word 'activity', however, can refer not only to *how much* is being done but also to *what* is being done. So if an employee made screws one day and washers the next we could say that the *nature* of the activity had changed. Now, as a little thought will indicate, there will be some fixed costs which will still stay unchanged in this situation regardless of changes in the nature of the activity (e.g. audit fees) and there are some which will not stay unchanged (e.g. the hire charge per day for a tool that can only be used to make screws). A fixed cost that *changes with the nature of the activity* is called an *identifiable fixed cost*. To identify such a cost it is only necessary to ask oneself if the cost would disappear if the activity were different. If it would, then the cost is identifiable.

In marginal cost ascertainment the cost of any identifiable fixed cost is added to the *total* marginal cost of the activity with which it is identified.

EXAMPLE: *Odds and Ends* (continued). In the Odds 'n' Ends Department the production of Odds requires an Odd Moulding machine, which is hired at £100 a week, while the production of Ends requires an End Moulding machine at a hire charge of £60 a week. Ascertain the weekly costs of Odds and Ends for a week in which 30 Odds and 20 Ends were produced.

SOLUTION:	*Odds*	*Ends*
	£	£
Marginal costs for the week	$30 \times £30 = 900$	$20 \times £35 = 700$
Identifiable fixed costs:		
Moulding machine hire	100	60
Product costs for week	£1,000	£760

It should be appreciated that fixed costs may not only be identifiable with products. They can also be identifiable with cost centres. Thus the salary of the Odds 'n' Ends foreman would be an identifiable fixed cost in respect of that department.

6. Unidentifiable fixed costs. Fixed costs that cannot be identified with either a product or a cost centre are called *unidentifiable fixed costs*. Such costs must never be charged out to products or centres.

The student should carefully note that fixed costs which are unidentifiable at one level may well be identifiable at another. Thus while the Odds 'n' Ends foreman's salary is unidentifiable as regards the products it is identifiable as regards the Odds 'n' Ends Department. On the other hand, the managing director's salary is not identifiable with any of the departments but only with the company as a whole.

EXAMPLE: *Odds and Ends* (continued). Further analysis of the costs in the Odds 'n' Ends Department reveals that the departmental fixed cost element amounts to £600 per week. Ascertain the departmental cost for the week specified in **5**.

SOLUTION:	£
Costs for week: Odds	1,000
Ends	760
Fixed cost unidentifiable with products but identifiable with department	600
Departmental cost for week	£2,360

7. Contribution per unit. Having seen how costs are ascertained under the marginal costing technique we can now turn to see how sales enter the marginal cost statements.

First of all it should be realized that there is a very direct link between unit marginal cost and selling price since the selling price is a price per unit. On the one hand, therefore, the unit marginal cost will show the *additional cost* of producing one more unit, while on the other hand the selling price will show the *additional income* from selling one more unit. Clearly the difference will be the *additional profit* to the enterprise that will result if just one more unit is made and sold. This direct linkage is the most important consequence that flows from using a marginal cost technique, and this additional profit figure is so important that it is given its own name: the *unit contribution*.

In view of the importance of this concept it is worth reiterating the logic behind it. This asserts that since all fixed costs remain unchanged by the production of one more unit, the only cost increase resulting from the production of one more unit is the increase in the variable cost. This variable cost increase is measured by the marginal cost of the unit and so the difference between the selling price and this marginal cost, the unit contribution, must measure the increase in the profit of the enterprise that arises from the production and sale of that one unit.

EXAMPLE:

Odds and Ends (continued). The selling prices of Odds and Ends are £50 and £75 respectively. What are the unit contributions?

SOLUTION:	Odds	Ends
	£	£
Selling price	50	75
Unit marginal cost	30	35
Unit contribution	£20	£40

8. Net contribution. Where more than one unit is made and sold the total contribution is obviously the sum of all the unit contributions. Where the units are all identical this is equal to the number of units multiplied by the unit contribution. However, if the number of units is the total units of the product then any product identifiable fixed costs can be deducted to give the additional profit that arises from the production and sale of the product itself. This figure, which is obtained by deducting the identifiable fixed costs from the total contribution, can be called the *net contribution*.

Note that the net contributions at one level can be added together and then the identifiable fixed costs at a higher level can be deducted to give the net contribution at that higher level (e.g. product net contributions can be added and then the departmental identifiable fixed cost deducted to give the departmental net contribution, and this procedure repeated at a higher level so that a yet more wide-ranging contribution is found).

EXAMPLE:

Odds and Ends (continued). From the earlier figures find the weekly product net contributions and the departmental net contribution.

SOLUTION:

	Odds		*Ends*	
	£		£	
Product contributions:				
Total cost unit contributions $30 \times £20 =$	600		$20 \times £40 =$	800
Less Product identifiable fixed costs	100			60
Product net contribution	£500			£740

	£
Departmental contributions:	
Product net contributions: Odds	500
Ends	740
Total product net contribution	1,240
Less Departmental identifiable fixed costs	600
Departmental net contribution	£640

9. Interpreting contributions. Contributions must be interpreted correctly if the cost information is to prove useful. Though such interpretation is essentially a matter of common sense, the contributions so far discussed will be briefly reinterpreted as follows:

(*a*) The unit contribution shows how much additional profit will be earned if just one more unit is made and sold, e.g. if one more Odd were made and sold the profit would increase by £20. This profit increase repeats for each additional unit up to the point where there is a change in the pattern of the cost behaviour –

usually when fixed costs increase as a result of additional facilities being required.

(b) The product net contribution shows how much additional profit is earned as a result of the product being made and sold in its entirety, e.g. in the case of Odds, £500 per week. To put it the other way round, discontinuing a product would result in the enterprise profit falling by the product net contribution.

(c) The departmental (or cost centre) net contribution shows how much additional profit is earned as a result of the activities of the department, e.g. in the case of the Odds 'n' Ends Department, £640 per week. Again, putting it the other way round, if the department closed down the enterprise profit would fall by the departmental net contribution.

From these interpretations it can be seen that the term *contribution* can be defined generally as *the additional profit resulting from carrying out a specified activity*. More formally it can be defined as 'The difference between the sales value and the variable cost of those sales, expressed either in absolute terms or as a contribution per unit' (CIMA terminology).

10. The irrelevance of the enterprise overall profit position. When interpreting contributions the interpretation is usually made in terms of increasing or decreasing the enterprise profit. Note, however, that the interpretation is essentially unaffected if the enterprise, is, in fact, making a loss. In such a case any contribution lessens the enterprise loss by the amount of the contribution. Phrasing the interpretation more generally still it can be said that a *contribution directly measures the effect of an activity on the overall profit and loss position of the enterprise*.

11. Worked example. A processing plant, producing 30- and 50-litre drums of solvent, has the following costs and sales:

	30-litre drums	50-litre drums
Direct costs per drum	£5	£8
Selling price per drum	£26	£40
Activity: Drums processed and sold:		
Period 1	200	100
Period 2	150	150

Overheads (semi-variable): Period 1 – £6,200; Period 2 – £6,600. Litres are an excellent measure of activity.

(*a*) How much profit would the plant earn if 100 30-litre and 200 50-litre drums of solvent were processed and sold?

(*b*) How much more profit would be earned if the output in (*a*) were increased by 10 per cent?

SOLUTION:

(*a*) (*i*) If the overhead is a semi-variable, the difference in cost between the two periods must represent the variable cost change (since the fixed cost element does not change at all) as a result of the activity change. Therefore:

	Period 1		*Period 2*	
	Litres		*Litres*	*Difference*
Activity: 30-litre drums	$30 \times 200 =$	6,000	$30 \times 150 =$ 4,500	
50-litre drums	$50 \times 100 =$	5,000	$50 \times 150 =$ 7,500	
		11,000	12,000	1,000
Overheads		£6,200	£6,600	£400

∴ 1,000 litres have a variable cost of £400.

∴ Variable cost per unit of activity (litre) = $\dfrac{£400}{1,000}$ = £0.40

In addition, if the variable cost is £0.40 per litre, the variable cost element in period 1 would be $11,000 \times £0.40 = £4,400$. Since the total cost was £6,200, the fixed cost element must be £6,200 – £4,400 = £1,800.

(*ii*) Knowing the variable overhead cost per litre, the unit contributions can be found:

	30-litre drum	*50-litre drum*
	£	£
Direct costs	5	8
Variable overheads	$30 \times £0.40 =$ 12	$50 \times £0.40 =$ 20
Unit marginal cost	17	28
Selling price	26	40
Unit contribution	£9	£12

(*iii*) Knowing the unit contribution, the profit can be found:

Product contributions:		£
30-litre drums	100 × £9	900
50-litre drums	200 × £12	2,400
Total contribution from products		3,300
Less total fixed costs		1,800
Profit		£1,500

(*b*) If output were increased by 10 per cent the total contribution from products would increase by 10 per cent. Moreover, this whole increase would be additional profit.

∴ Additional profit = 10 per cent of £3,300 = £330.

12. Marginal cost accounting. While marginal costing is often employed outside the formal book-keeping system, it is possible to keep all the accounts on a marginal costing basis. When marginal cost book-keeping is practised the system differs from the accounting systems discussed in Chapter 7 only as regards the fixed costs. Since in marginal cost accounting it is argued that fixed costs are time and not activity based, they should be charged only against time and not activities, i.e. written off to profit and loss in the period they are incurred, and never charged to cost units. Application of this principle has the following effects.

(*a*) Fixed costs are charged to a fixed overhead control account, and then *written off* to the profit and loss account at the period end (accruals and prepayments being carried down in the overhead account in the normal way, of course).

(*b*) No cost units carry any fixed overhead and so *all stocks are valued at marginal cost only.*

The essential distinguishing features of marginal cost accounting are shown diagrammatically in Fig. 13.1.

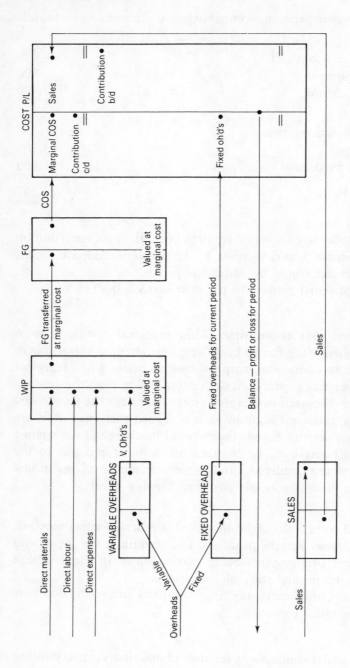

Figure 13.1 *Chart of marginal cost accounting*

This chart indicates how the Overheads, Work-in-Progress, Finished Goods and Profit and Loss accounts differ in a marginal costing system from the same accounts in a normal absorption accounting system (see Fig. 7.1)

Marginal cost decision-making

13. Marginal costing and decision-making. As we saw in 11 : 3, in decision-making it is only future costs that are relevant. And to prepare an analysis that uses future costs means that it is necessary to be able to predict costs, and this, as has been seen, requires a knowledge of the behaviour of costs. A costing technique that is based on cost behaviour, as marginal costing is, is therefore a logical technique to adopt for decision-making. Moreover, the fact that marginal costing is also based on the view that only costs *specifically* generated by a cost unit or centre should be charged to that unit or centre gives it a particularly valuable decision-making feature.

14. Testing product economic viability. A commonly recurring decision involves testing to see if an existing product should be discontinued or, alternatively, a new product initiated. As this is achieved by ascertaining whether the existence of the product increases the profit of the enterprise or not, marginal costing is the logical technique. For instance, assume three products, A, B and C, are made in a department having identifiable fixed costs of £60,000. The sales of these products are expected to be £50,000, £100,000 and £150,000 respectively and the marginal costs £20,000, £70,000 and £130,000. Setting out the figures in a marginal cost format results in the following:

Product	Predicted sales (£)	Marginal costs (£)	Contribution (£)
A	50,000	20,000	30,000
B	100,000	70,000	30,000
C	150,000	130,000	20,000
Total product contributions			80,000
Less Departmental identifiable fixed costs			60,000
Departmental net contribution			£20,000

Clearly, if any product is discontinued the whole of its contribution will be lost, and the enterprise profit will be reduced by the amount of that contribution. A, B and C, then, are all economically viable.

Note, however, how the apportionment of the departmental fixed costs can lead to possible decision mistakes. If in the above example departmental fixed costs were apportioned on the basis of sales turnover (i.e. initially in the ratio of 1 : 2 : 3 respectively) and if it were a rigid policy rule that any product that failed to make a profit on its total cost must be discontinued, the following decisions would result:

		A £		B £		C £
Departmental fixed costs: £60,000						
Predicted sales		50,000		100,000		150,000
1st analysis: All three products:						
Contribution		30,000		30,000		20,000
Fixed cost apportionment	$\frac{1}{6}$	10,000	$\frac{2}{6}$	20,000	$\frac{3}{6}$	30,000
Profit		20,000		10,000		(10,000)
Decision: Discontinue C						
2nd analysis: C discontinued:						
Contribution		30,000		30,000		—
Fixed cost apportionment	$\frac{1}{3}$	20,000	$\frac{2}{3}$	40,000		—
Profit		10,000		(10,000)		—
Decision: Discontinue B						
3rd analysis: B and C discontinued:						
Contribution		30,000		—		—
Fixed cost		60,000		—		—
Profit		(30,000)		—		—
Decision: Discontinue A						

As can be seen, the final decision is that all the products will be discontinued and even if this resulted in all the departmental fixed costs ceasing there would still be an overall loss to the enterprise of £20,000 (the departmental net contribution computed earlier).

Naturally, where the situation is as simple as this the absurdity of discontinuing any of the three products is clear. However, in a more complex case, and particularly where the fixed and marginal costs are not segregated so that only a single total cost figure is set against product sales, it would not be surprising if an economically wrong decision resulted from such an analysis.

Finally, the student is reminded that should a product have an identifiable fixed cost (which was not the case in the above example), then since discontinuing the product would bring the cost to an end such a cost must be deducted from the product contribution (to give the product *net* contribution) before deciding upon the viability of the product.

15. Testing departmental viability. The economic viability of a department can be tested in the same way as product viability, the only difference being that, whereas product identifiable fixed costs are uncommon, there will almost always be departmental identifiable fixed costs to be deducted from the sum of the product net contributions. As can be seen, in the example above the department is economically viable – and this is so regardless of any share of the unidentifiable fixed costs that the accountant may decide to apportion to the department.

16. The relevance of substitution. Underlying the analysis just made has been the assumption that nothing could be substituted for the products under review. Where substitution is possible (as it usually is) and some new product could replace an existing product or, alternatively, production of one of the remaining products could be expanded to fill the capacity left by the discontinued product, a more complex analysis needs to be made. Such an analysis often adopts the differential costing technique which was discussed in the previous chapter.

17. Acceptance of a special contract. Another type of decision often relates to the acceptance or otherwise of a special contract under which units are sold below normal selling prices. In such circumstances the contribution is the relevant figure to be considered, since the whole of any contribution must be extra profit. From this it follows in principle that it is always better to take a special contract if there is some contribution, no matter how small, than to reject the contract and have no contribution.

Note, however, the following two qualifications to this.

(*a*) It is assumed that the fulfilment of the contract will not affect normal sales. Nothing is gained by selling units at £4 which otherwise would have been sold at £5.

(b) It is also assumed that nothing better is likely to come along. A business that fills its workshops with many low-contribution contracts and then has to turn away high-contribution work is not making the best decisions. Judging whether or not anything better may come along is, of course, the responsibility of management.

18. Key factors. There is always something that limits an enterprise from achieving an unlimited profit. Usually this is sales, i.e. the enterprise cannot sell as much as it would like. Sometimes, however, an enterprise can sell all that it can produce, but output is limited by the scarcity of some economic factor of production, e.g. materials, labour, machine capacity or cash. Such a factor is called a *key factor* – although the term *constraint* is now becoming increasingly used instead.

19. Contribution per unit of key factor. If a key factor is operating, then it is important that the enterprise makes as much profit as it can each time it uses up one of its scarce units of key factor. Since fixed costs do not alter, this means *maximizing the contribution per unit of key factor.*

EXAMPLE:

Data: Materials are limited to 1,000 tonnes. A choice must be made between two jobs requiring such materials, A and B. Job details are as follows:

	Job A	*Job B*
Selling price	£3,000	£2,000
Marginal cost	£1,000	£1,200
Contribution	£2,000	£800
Tonnes required	4	1

Method: On the face of it A is in all respects the more profitable; it has a higher selling price, lower marginal cost and contribution over twice that of B. But in using 4 tonnes of materials it earns a contribution of only £500 a tonne, i.e. if all jobs were of this type our 1,000 tonnes would allow us to earn only £500,000 contribution. B, on the other hand, earns a contribution of £800 a tonne, so jobs of this type would allow us to earn £800,000 contribution. Type B jobs are therefore more profitable in these circumstances, and so should be selected in preference to type A jobs.

Where a key factor is involved, then, the work giving the highest contribution per unit of key factor used should be selected.

20. Make-or-buy decisions. This type of decision arises when the product being manufactured has a component part that can either be made within the factory or bought from an outside supplier. On the face of it, since the only extra cost to make the part is the marginal cost, the amount by which this falls below the supplier's price is the saving that arises on making. However, this may not be so, as it is also important to consider what work would otherwise be carried out using the relevant facilities if the part were not made. Clearly, if other work has to be displaced so as to make the part, the business will *lose the contribution this work would otherwise have earned.* Such a contribution loss must be added to the marginal cost of the part.

So, in a make-or-buy decision there are two factors which must be compared, namely:

(*a*) the supplier's price;
(*b*) the marginal cost of making, plus the loss of contribution of displaced work.

This loss of contribution is usually best found by use of the contribution per unit of key factor (*see* **19** above). You may well also appreciate that this lost contribution is an opportunity cost of the kind previously discussed in 12:**13–19**.

EXAMPLE:
Data: An X takes 20 hours to process on machine A6. It has a selling price of £300 and a marginal cost of £180. A Y (a component part used in production) could be made on machine A6 in 3 hours for a marginal costs of £15. The supplier's price is £30. Should one make or buy Ys?

Method: Contribution per X = 300 − 180 = £120.

$\therefore$ Contribution earned per hour on machine A6 is $\dfrac{120}{20} = £6$.

If then a Y is made in 3 hours, £18 contribution is lost.

∴ Real cost to make Y = £15 + £18 = £33.

This is more than the supplier's price of £30, and so it is better to buy than make.

Note that this decision assumes that machine A6 is working to full capacity. If this were not so and the machine were frequently idle, no loss of contribution would result from using it to make the component. In such circumstances the sole cost of making would be the marginal cost of the component – in this example £15 – which, being less than the supplier's price of £30, would indicate that the component should be made rather than bought.

21. Profit planning. Very often an enterprise first decides its sales, costs and activity and then computes what profit will emerge. In profit planning this is reversed; the enterprise first decides what profit it wants and then works *backwards* to see what sales, costs and activity are needed to produce that profit.

In practice, certain factors are usually determined before planning begins (e.g. capacity may be limited, or selling prices determined by competitors' activities) and then profit planning indicates the value that the remaining factors must take to achieve the profit target.

EXAMPLE:

Data: A company manufactures a single product having a marginal cost of £3 a unit. Fixed costs are £48,000. The market is such that up to 40,000 units can be sold at £6 a unit, but any additional sales must be made at £4 a unit. There is a planned profit of £80,000. How many units must be made and sold?

Method: Contribution from first 40,000 units = 40,000 × (6 − 3) = £120,000.

Deducting the fixed costs from this contribution shows that these units would generate a profit of £120,000 − 48,000 = £72,000. However, this is £80,000 − 72,000 = £8,000 shortfall on the required profit. So enough extra units have to be sold at a unit contribution of £4 − £3 = £1 to generate an additional £8,000 contribution.

∴ Additional units = $\dfrac{£8,000}{£1}$ = 8,000.

∴ Total number of units to be made and sold = 40,000 + 8,000 = 48,000 units.

Marginal versus absorption costing

22. Advantages of marginal costing. The following advantages are claimed for marginal costing over absorption costing.

(a) No attempt is made to relate fixed costs, which are incurred on a time basis, with products, since such costs are independent of production. This avoids complicated and misleading statements (*see* **14**).

(b) Under- or over-absorption of overheads cannot arise.

(c) Fictitious profits cannot arise due to fixed costs being absorbed and capitalized in unsaleable stock. (For example, assume 100 units are produced for a cost, all fixed, of £1,000, i.e. £10 a unit. Twenty only are saleable and are sold for £15 each. If the remainder are valued in stock at £10 each the profit and loss account will show a profit of £100, whereas a loss of £700 would be a truer figure.)

(d) Marginal costing avoids the false sense of security that absorption costing can give when all products show a satisfactory profit, but owing to the activity level being lower than that planned, such profits are unknowingly being more than offset by under-absorbed overheads.

(e) Contribution is a more correct measure of the effect of making and selling a product than the product profit figure obtained from absorption costing, which is not only incorrect when the activity level is different from that planned but may even indicate quite the reverse of the true situation.

(f) Marginal costing is simpler and less ambiguous than absorption costing, and avoids the complexities of apportionments which are really only arbitrary divisions of indivisible fixed costs.

(g) If a variety of products is offered to customers, marginal costing enables the planned profit to be made (assuming the activity is as planned) regardless of sales mix (e.g. if a contribution of £1 per hour is obtained in respect of all products, then if the planned number of hours are worked, the contribution and hence the profit obtained will be that planned, no matter which products are actually produced).

(*h*) Pricing can be done more intelligently since the contribution to be added onto any cost unit will:

(*i*) be based on the total contribution required from all production (i.e. planned profit and fixed costs);

(*ii*) take account of the use made by the unit of any relevant key factor.

23. Advantages of absorption costing. The following advantages are claimed for absorption costing over marginal costing.

(*a*) Since production cannot be achieved without incurring fixed costs, such costs *are* related to production, and absorption costing attempts to make an allowance for this relationship. This avoids the danger inherent in marginal costing of creating the illusion that fixed costs have nothing to do with production.

(*b*) Fictitious losses cannot arise as they can in marginal costing owing to fixed costs being written off in a period when merchantable goods are produced and stocked for sale in a later season (e.g. fireworks).

(*c*) Use of absorption costing avoids the stock valuation anomalies associated with marginal costing. For example, a manufacturer may pay a fixed monthly rental for a machine. Under marginal costing such a charge would not be included in the stock value. If, though, he renegotiates to pay a rental based on his *production*, this charge will be included in the stock value. Thus, although an article remains exactly the same, and is made in exactly the same way, nevertheless under marginal costing its stock value increases.

(*d*) When pricing, finding the marginal cost alone is not sufficient, since it is essential that the added contribution should relate to fixed costs; otherwise an enterprise with a high fixed cost could set prices that gave too small a contribution and so resulted in an inadvertent loss. In absorption costing an addition is automatically made based on the utilization of the fixed cost facilities by the different products.

NOTE: This claim is valid only if the cost accountant is not setting prices as outlined in **22**(*h*) but is simply adding an arbitrary contribution to the marginal cost.

(*e*) Use of marginal costing in pricing tends to lead to low prices being quoted at a time of slack demand. Customers may then expect the business to maintain such prices on future occasions.

(*f*) If a wide range of goods involving differing fixed cost requirements are offered to customers and no pre-knowledge of likely demand is available, then absorption costing enables a more consistent profit to be earned.

(*g*) In a situation where the enterprise has a monopoly and wishes to charge its customers for its different products on a basis of average economic cost, absorption costing enables the enterprise to achieve this object better than marginal costing.

24. Choice of technique. The paragraphs above indicate that the choice of technique is not easy to make. Unfortunately, no rules can be given; all that can be said is that the technique which is most appropriate to the circumstances should be chosen.

At the heart of the controversy lies the implication that since fixed costs are incurred on a time basis and are irrespective of the volume of production, they cannot form part of the individual costs of units produced. This is not so. Without the fixed costs the units could not be produced at all. The relationship between fixed costs and cost units may be tenuous and changing, but the problem cannot be solved by denying the relationship entirely.

In the ultimate analysis the two techniques are not really contradictory; they simply represent the extremes of this elusive relationship, and cost accountants serve management best by ensuring that their statements reflect the appropriate relationship existing in any given circumstances.

25. Differential costing and marginal costing. In marginal costing one looks at the difference between the costs and incomes that would result if an activity were carried out and the costs and incomes that would result if the activity were not carried out. It employs, then, the differential costing principle and so is a differential costing technique. However, marginal costing is a narrower technique since it does not concentrate solely upon differences. For instance, if two kinds of material could be used to make a product, the choice in no way affecting the conversion cost, then under marginal costing one should in theory compare the product marginal costs whereas only the material cost difference is really relevant.

EXAMPLE:

Data: A product uses 2 kg of material and 5 hours of direct labour at £3 per hour. Variable overheads are £2 per direct labour hour. 1,000 units of product are to be made. Currently material at £5 per kg is being used but a substitute material at £4 per kg may become available. What would the saving be if this new material were used? (This is a very trivial example and is intended to do no more than illustrate the difference between marginal costing and differential costing.)

Method:
Marginal cost analysis:

		Current material	*New material*
		£	£
Unit cost:	Material	2 × £5 = 10	2 × £4 = 8
	Direct labour	5 × £3 = 15	5 × £3 = 15
	Variable overheads	5 × £2 = 10	5 × £2 = 10
	Unit marginal cost	35	33
Marginal cost of 1,000 units		£35,000	£33,000

∴ Saving using new material = £35,000 – £33,000 = £2,000.

Differential cost analysis:
Difference in material price = 5 – 4 = £1 per kg.
Material usage = 1,000 units × 2 kg = 2,000 kg.
∴ Saving using new material = 2,000 × £1 = £2,000.

26. Incremental costing. A form of differential costing which is very similar to marginal costing is *incremental costing*. This is a cost technique which shows the cost change associated with each incremental change in activity, i.e. a change in either the level or the nature of the activity. The similarity to marginal costing follows from the logical consequence that a marginal cost is, in fact, the incremental cost of producing one more unit.

In most circumstances the terms marginal cost and incremental cost tend to be used interchangeably.

Progress test 13

Principles

1. What is the principle of marginal cost ascertainment? (**1**)
2. What is: (*a*) a marginal cost; (**2**) (*b*) an identifiable fixed cost; (**5**) (*c*) a net contribution; (**8**) (*d*) a key factor; (**18**) (*e*) profit planning? (**21**)
3. How is a contribution figure to be interpreted? (**9**)
4. How does marginal cost accounting differ from absorption cost accounting? (**12**)
5. What is the relevance of key factors to decision-making? (**19**)
6. What factors enter a make-or-buy decision? (**20**)
7. Compare and contrast marginal costing and absorption costing. Are these techniques wholly contradictory? (**22–24**)
8. How does differential costing differ from marginal costing? (**25**)

Practice

NOTE: Although the principles of marginal costing are essentially simple, the permutations and combinations of these principles are so numerous that the technique provides a rich mine of questions for examiners. The student, therefore, is advised to work through all of this and the next Progress test since more will probably be learnt in this way than by any detailed study of the chapter text.

9. The following information is available for XY Ltd. which manufactures a standard product:

Quarterly budget for each of quarters 3 and 4:

		Total		*Per unit*
		£		£
Sales (30,000 units)		30,000		1.00
Production cost of sales:				
Variable	£19,500		£0.65	
Fixed overhead	£6,000	25,500	£0.20	0.85
		4,500		0.15
Selling and administration cost				
(fixed)		2,100		0.07
Profit		£2,400		£0.08

Actual production, sales and stocks in units for quarters 3 and 4:

	Quarter 3	Quarter 4
Opening stock	—	6,000
Production	34,000	28,000
Sales	28,000	32,000
Closing stock	6,000	2,000

You are required to show in tabular form trading and profit and loss accounts for each of the quarters:

(a) when fixed production overhead is absorbed into the cost of the product at the normal level shown in the quarterly budget;

(b) when fixed production overhead is not absorbed into the cost of the product, but is treated as a cost of the period and charged against sales.

NOTE: The bases of calculations should be shown.   (CIMA)

10. A company produces a standard product, each unit of which has a direct material cost of £24, requires 2 hours' labour and sells for £60. The company has no variable overheads, only fixed overheads of £64,000 a month. Labour, which is paid at £3 per hour, is currently very scarce, while demand for the company's product is heavy.

A contract worth £5,400 has just been offered to the company, and the estimating department has ascertained the following facts in respect of the work.

(a) The labour time for the contract would be 200 hours.

(b) The material cost would be £1,140 plus the cost of a special component.

(c) The special component could be purchased from an outside supplier for £300 or alternatively could be made by the company for a material cost of £120 and an additional labour time of 12 hours.

Advise management regarding the action it should take.

11. As cost consultant to a Mexican farmer who grows summer vegetables and exports them to USA, you are required, using the information given below, to:

(a) calculate the profit or loss per box of each type of vegetable that your client will obtain from operating the farm on the present basis;

(b) advise your client of:

(i) the area to be cultivated with each line to produce the largest total profit; and

(ii) the amount of the largest total profit.

The farmer owns 240 acres of land on which he grows: staked tomatoes, ground tomatoes, cucumbers and green beans. Of the land 70 acres are unsuitable for staked tomatoes or green beans but are suitable for cucumbers or ground tomatoes. On the remainder of the land any of the four crops may be grown. There is an adequate supply of labour for all kinds of farm work.

Marketing policy requires that each season there is produced:

(i) all four types of vegetable; and

(ii) not less than 5,000 boxes of any one line.

It is decided that the area devoted to any one line should be in terms of complete acres and not in fractions of an acre. You may assume there are no other physical or marketing limitations.

Details relating to production, market price and direct and fixed costs are given below.

	Staked tomatoes	Ground tomatoes	Cucumbers	Green beans
Acreage at present devoted to each line	105	50	60	25
Summer season's yield, in boxes per acre	700	200	150	300
Weight, in lbs per box	60	60	80	36
	$	$	$	$
Market price per box	3.86	3.86	4.56	5.68
Costs:				
Direct:				
Materials per acre	189	74	63	108
Labour:				
Growing, per acre	224	152	93	132
Harvesting and packing, per box	0.80	0.72	1.00	1.20
Transport and export, per box	1.30	1.30	1.00	2.40

Fixed overhead, incurred each season:

	$	Basis of apportionment to products
Cultivation:		
Growing	36,000	Direct labour costs incurred
Harvesting	12,000	Direct labour costs incurred
Transport and export	12,000	Weight produced
General administration	40,000	Number of boxes produced
Notional rent	12,000	Number of acres cultivated

(*CIMA*)

NOTE: Suggested answer given in respect of Question (*b*) only.

14

Break-even analysis

One of the spin-offs from marginal cost theory is our ability to determine the level of activity at which neither a profit nor a loss is made.

Break-even theory

1. Definitions.

(a) *Break-even.* This is the term given to any situation in which neither a profit nor a loss is made.

(b) *Break-even point.* This is the level of activity at which a break-even situation exists.

(c) *Break-even chart.* This is a graph depicting the break-even point with the income and costs that determine the point.

NOTE: (1) It should be appreciated that break-even situations can arise in respect of enterprises, divisions, cost centres and specific projects. At a further level the concept of break-even can also be used when comparing two alternatives (*see* **20**). (2) Frequently 'break-even' is abbreviated to 'B/E'. (3) In break-even theory it is an *activity* which is being costed and valued. It is not merely an analysis of how a cost behaves relative to activity.

2. Fundamental break-even principles. The basic principle which underlies the whole of break-even theory is that at the very lowest level of activity costs exceed income but that as activity increases income rises faster than costs and eventually the two amounts are equal, after which income exceeds costs until diminishing returns bring costs above income once again.

This very general statement on the relationship between costs, income and activity merely states the obvious. To be of practical value break-even theory must incorporate information relating to cost behaviour and sales policy. So as to enable a theory having practical value to be developed the following simplifying assumptions are usually made.

(*a*) That within the relevant activity range the *total* cost of whatever *activity* is being costed behaves as a simple straight-line semi-variable cost.

(*b*) That the unit selling price remains constant throughout the relevant activity range.

(*c*) That costs and income are matched, i.e. there is no build-up or run-down of stocks.

Although rather sweeping, these assumptions are valid in the majority of cases. Even where they are not, in most instances the error resulting is either of small practical importance or can be allowed for in a short subsidiary analysis (e.g. where there is a stock build-up the cost of the build-up can, for analytical purposes, be excluded from the total cost).

3. The traditional break-even chart. (*See* Fig. 14.1.) Given these assumptions it is quite easy to show the total cost curve on a cost-activity graph. Such a curve shows as a semi-variable having a fixed cost equal to the point where the curve cuts the cost axis and a straight curve rising at an angle reflecting the variable cost per unit of activity. This, of course, is a normal cost behaviour curve, albeit for the total cost of the activity. However, it is now possible to add the income curve. Since at zero activity there will be zero income this curve starts at the origin of the graph and is a straight line rising at an angle reflecting the constant unit selling price. Where cost and income curves cross, cost and income must be the same and the crossing must, therefore, mark the break-even point.

EXAMPLE: A total cost has a fixed cost element of £90,000 and a variable cost element of £500 per 1 per cent activity. Sales are made at a price equal to £2,000 per 1 per cent activity. These figures give the break-even chart shown in Fig. 14.1 where it can be seen that the total cost curve starts at £90,000 and by 100 per cent activity rises to $90,000 + 100 \times 500 = £140,000$ while the income curve starts at zero and by 100 per cent activity rises to

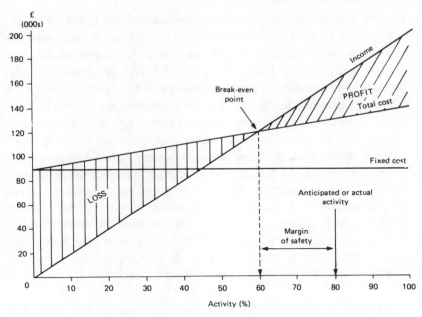

Figure 14.1 *Traditional break-even chart*

The break-even point is measured in terms of activity. This chart shows that if the anticipated activity is 80 per cent, then:

Expected income   = £160,000;
Expected total cost = £130,000;
Expected profit   = £30,000;
Margin of safety   = 20 per cent.

The following data is used in Figs. 14.1–14.5:
At 100 per cent activity:

Sales   = £200,000;
Fixed costs   = £90,000 (includes £30,000 depreciation);
Variable costs = £50,000.

$100 \times 2,000 = £200,000$. Since the curves cross at 60 per cent activity, the break-even point is 60 per cent activity (when cost and income are both £120,000).

It should be noted that the *vertical* distance between the cost and income curves at any given level of activity measures the profit or loss (depending upon which curve is the higher) at that activity level.

4. The significance of the enterprise break-even point. A break-even point is always of importance in so far as it indicates the lowest activity level at which the activity under analysis is economically viable. The point has, however, even greater importance when it relates to a whole enterprise for then it is virtually a life-and-death measure. This arises because if an enterprise continually operates below its break-even point (i.e. makes losses), no matter how fractionally, then without question its life is limited. On the other hand, if it continually operates above its break-even point (i.e. makes profits), again no matter how fractionally, then it may live indefinitely. The break-even point, therefore, marks very clearly for the management of an enterprise the very lowest level to which activity can fall without putting the continued life of the enterprise in jeopardy. Working occasionally below the break-even point is not necessarily fatal, of course, but on the whole the enterprise must operate above this level.

5. Margin of safety. This term is often given to the difference between the break-even point and an anticipated or existing level of activity above that point. In other words, the margin of safety measures the extent to which anticipated or existing activity can fall before a profitable operation turns into a loss-making one. If desired, this safety margin can also be expressed as a ratio of the absolute margin to the contemplated activity level, i.e.:

Margin of safety ratio =

$$\frac{\text{Contemplated turnover} - \text{B/E turnover}}{\text{Contemplated turnover}} \times 100$$

NOTE: The CIMA defines margin of safety a little more narrowly as 'the excess of normal or actual sales over sales at break-even point'. The definition given earlier allows the term to be used additionally in connection with budgeted or other predicted activities. Note, too, that '100 per cent activity' can also be defined as the level of normal or actual sales.

Break-even chart variants

6. Break-even chart: variable costs at base. (*See* Fig. 14.2.) Break-even charts can be drawn showing the variable cost and its

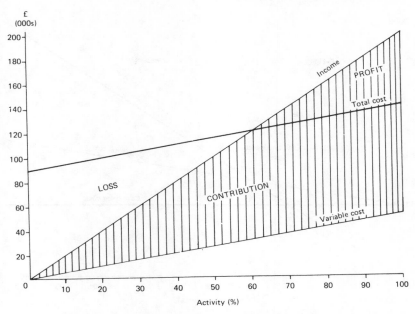

Figure 14.2 *Break-even chart with variable costs at base*

relation to activity first, and then adding the fixed cost to give the total cost curve. This really is a better form of chart, since it shows as much as the traditional form, and in addition the gap between the variable cost and income curves is a direct measure of contribution.

7. Cash break-even chart. (*See* Fig. 14.3.) Here only *cash* costs and income are graphed; book charges are ignored. The major effect of this is to eliminate depreciation, which results in a reduction of the fixed (and therefore total) costs. On such a chart the cash break-even point measures the level of activity required to ensure that the cash received from income is sufficient to cover all costs requiring cash payments.

Note, however, that the chart cannot be used as a cash forecasting device since it does not incorporate the payment and receipt timings (payments are almost certain to precede receipts from sales) but only the overall net cash results.

8. Break-even chart with profit appropriation. (*See* Fig. 14.4.) This is a normal break-even chart in which the profit wedge is split

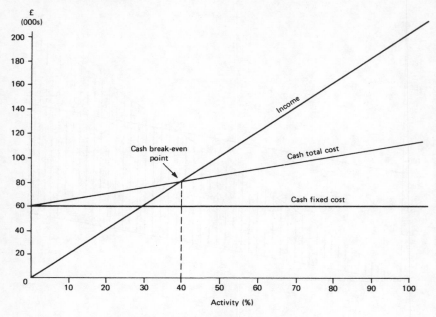

Figure 14.3 *Cash break-even chart*
This chart shows that if activity reaches 40 per cent, enough cash
will be received from income to cover all *cash* costs; this excludes
timing considerations, however

into the different profit appropriations. This enables the activity
required to attain any selected appropriation result to be read off
the chart directly (e.g. in Fig. 14.4 increases in reserves of £4,500
after payment of 20 per cent ordinary dividend requires an activity
level of 90 per cent).

9. Profit graph. (*See* Fig. 14.5.) Profit cannot be read *directly* off
a break-even chart – it is necessary to deduct the total cost reading
from the income reading. A profit graph overcomes this by plotting the profit directly against activity. This means that at nil
activity a loss equal to the fixed cost will be suffered (£90,000 in
Fig. 14.5), and at break-even (i.e. nil profit) the profit curve will
cut the activity axis (in Fig. 14.5 at 60 per cent).

10. Multi-product break-even chart. Where there is more than
one product near-insurmountable problems arise in attempting to
prepare a break-even chart. These stem from the difficulty of find-

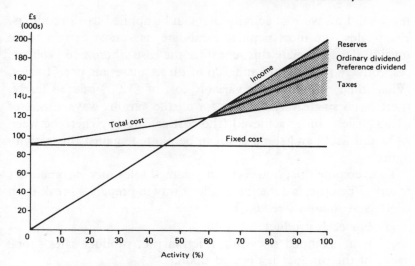

Figure 14.4 *Break-even chart with profit appropriations*
It is assumed that taxes are £0.50 in the £ (average); preference
shares are £75,000 at 8 per cent; and ordinary dividend is 20 per
cent maximum on £60,000 issued capital

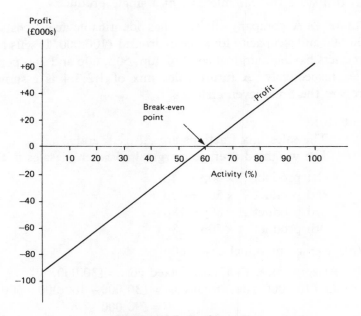

Figure 14.5 *Profit graph*

ing a valid measure of activity that can be applied to all products. Even sales, the most popular candidate, is almost certain to be invalid. To appreciate this, consider the case where two products respectively require 40p and 50p of direct materials per £1 sales. What, then, would be the variable cost of £1,000 sales? Clearly, there is no single variable cost for all the various ways a total of £1,000 sales can be achieved (the cost can lie anywhere between £400 and £500) and so no cost can be plotted against this activity figure.

To overcome this, however, an assumed sales mix is sometimes taken. When this is done the quickest way to prepare a break-even chart is as follows (*see also* Fig. 14.6).

(*a*) For each product:

(*i*) the assumed sales mix fraction (i.e. product sales ÷ total sales) of the product is decided upon;

(*ii*) the marginal cost per £1 sales is multiplied by this fraction.

(*b*) All the answers from (*a*)(*ii*) are added. This gives the weighted average variable cost for £1 sales.

(*c*) A break-even chart is prepared using the variable cost from (*b*) as if it were the variable cost of a single product.

EXAMPLE: A company division has identifiable fixed costs of £30,000 and a capacity for sales of around £100,000. It sells four products having marginal costs of 40p, 50p, 60p and 70p per £1 sales respectively. A future sales mix of 1:2:3:4 is assumed. Prepare the break-even chart.

SOLUTION:

(*a*)(*i*) The sales mix fractions are $\frac{1}{10}$, $\frac{2}{10}$, $\frac{3}{10}$ and $\frac{4}{10}$.

(*ii*) The weighted average marginal cost per £1 sales is:

$$\begin{aligned}
\text{1st product } \tfrac{1}{10} \times 40p &= 4p \\
\text{2nd product } \tfrac{2}{10} \times 50p &= 10p \\
\text{3rd product } \tfrac{3}{10} \times 60p &= 18p \\
\text{4th product } \tfrac{4}{10} \times 70p &= \underline{28p}
\end{aligned}$$

(*b*) Average marginal cost = $\underline{60p}$

(*c*) At zero sales, total cost = fixed cost = £30,000.

At £100,000 sales, total cost = £30,000 + 100,000 × 60p
$$= £90,000.$$

From these figures the break-even chart in Fig. 14.6 can be prepared.

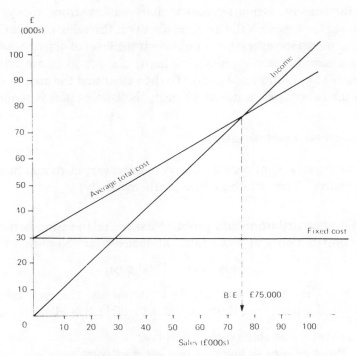

Figure 14.6 *Multi-product break-even chart*

Given: Fixed cost of £30,000;
Marginal costs of 40p, 50p, 60p and 70p respectively
per £ sales;
Sales mix of 1:2:3:4

Then: Average marginal cost = 60p;
Break-even = £75,000 sales.

(*Check:* £75,000 in ratios of 1:2:3:4 = £7,500; £15,000; £22,500;
£30,000;
∴ contributions:

$$7,500 \times 60p = £4,500$$
$$15,000 \times 50p = 7,500$$
$$22,500 \times 40p = 9,000$$
$$30,000 \times 30p = 9,000$$
$$£30,000.)$$

Unfortunately a multi-product chart suffers from the grave disadvantage that its validity depends upon the sales mix remaining constant. However, this is unlikely if the level of activity (sales) changes significantly – unless, perhaps, the products are linked naturally (e.g. lamps and bulbs). To the extent that the assumption of an unchanging sales mix is suspect, the whole chart is suspect.

Break-even mathematics

It is not necessary, of course, always to draw graphs to find break-even figures. They can be found mathematically.

11. Total contribution and profit. First the relationship between total contribution and profit must be made clear. Note that:

$$\text{Profit} = \text{Sales} - \text{Total cost.}$$

Now according to our simplifying assumptions, the total cost is made up of a fixed cost element and a variable cost element, i.e.:

Total cost = Variable cost + Fixed cost.
∴ Profit = Sales – (Variable cost + Fixed cost)
       = Sales – Variable cost – Fixed cost.
But Sales – Variable cost = Total contribution.
∴ Profit = Total contribution – Fixed cost.

Note that in a break-even situation, Profit = 0.
∴ 0 = Total contribution – Fixed cost.
∴ Fixed cost = Total contribution.

Or, in words, at the break-even point the total contribution is equal to the fixed cost.

12. Unit contribution is a constant. It was explained earlier (*see* 13: 7) that the difference between the marginal cost of a unit and its selling price gives the unit contribution. Given the simplifying assumption that the marginal cost (i.e. the variable cost element of the total cost) and the selling price are unchanged with changing activity, then the difference, too, must remain unchanged, i.e. the unit contribution is the same at all levels of activity (within the relevant activity range, of course). From this a number of logical consequences flow.

13. Unit contribution and profit. First, assume that we have a product with a selling price of £12 and a marginal cost of £8. It has, therefore, a unit contribution of £12 – £8 = £4. This means that every time we make and sell a unit we receive £12 from the customer, pay £8 for the marginal cost and have £4 over. This £4 is not, of course, profit, since the fixed costs still remain to be paid. Indeed, until we have sufficient lots of £4 to pay all these fixed costs there can be no profit. For instance, if the fixed costs are £400, then we need to make and sell 100 units before we have enough £4 lots to pay the fixed costs. Note that:

(*a*) at this level we break even and this, then, must be the break-even point;

(*b*) if we make and sell one unit more the £4 contribution received is no longer required for the fixed costs, and is therefore all profit.

This means that *above the break-even point all earned contribution is profit.*

14. P/V ratio. Next it should be appreciated that sales and total contribution are in direct proportion to each other, i.e. if the sales increased by 20 per cent, the total contribution increases by 20 per cent, etc. For instance, if we sell 10 of the units discussed above our sales are £120 and our contribution is £40. Increase sales by 20 per cent (i.e. 2 units) and the contribution rises to £48, i.e. by 20 per cent.

Since sales and total contribution are always in direct proportion, dividing one by the other will always give the same figure, e.g. contribution divided by sales in the above examples gives:

$$\frac{4}{12}; \frac{40}{120}; \frac{48}{144}; \text{ all of which cancel down to } \tfrac{1}{3}$$

This fraction is called the *P/V ratio* and can always be calculated as follows:

$$\text{P/V ratio} = \frac{\text{Total contribution}}{\text{Sales}}$$

This ratio is useful in as much as it enables the contribution to be quickly calculated from any given level of sales (or vice versa), since the formula can be turned round to:

$$\text{Total contribution} = \text{Sales} \times \text{P/V ratio}$$

(e.g. given a sales figure of £180, the contribution will be £180 × $\frac{1}{3}$ = £60).

15. Break-even formulae. Next, the constant value of the unit contribution, together with the earlier defined cost and income relationships, enable a series of formulae to be developed which can be applied in marginal costing and break-even circumstances. The most useful of these formulae are the following:

(*a*) Sales – Marginal cost of sales = Total contribution.

(*b*) Profit (Loss) = Total contribution – Fixed cost.

(*c*) P/V ratio = $\dfrac{\text{Total contribution}}{\text{Sales}}$.

(*d*) Break-even point:

(*i*) measured in units = $\dfrac{\text{Fixed cost}}{\text{Unit contribution}}$.

(*ii*) measured in £ sales = Fixed cost $\times \dfrac{\text{Sales}}{\text{Total contribution}}$

$$= \dfrac{\text{Fixed cost}}{\text{P/V ratio}}.$$

Given sufficient initial data, use of the above formulae will enable any missing figures to be found.

EXAMPLE 1:
Data:

$$\text{B/E} = 1,000 \text{ units}$$
$$\text{Sales} = 1,500 \text{ units at £6 each}$$
$$\text{Fixed cost} = £2,000$$

Find the marginal cost per unit and the profit (using formulae (*d*)(*i*) and (*b*) above).

Method:

$$\text{B/E (units)} = \frac{\text{Fixed cost}}{\text{Unit contribution}}$$

$$\therefore \quad 1{,}000 = \frac{2{,}000}{\text{Unit contribution}}$$

$$\therefore \quad \text{Unit contribution} = \frac{2{,}000}{1{,}000} = £2.$$

And since selling price is £6, the marginal cost per unit must be:

$$£6 - £2 = \underline{\underline{£4}}.$$

In addition, total contribution must be $1{,}500 \times £2 = £3{,}000$.

$$\therefore \quad \text{Profit} = \text{Total contribution} - \text{Fixed cost}$$
$$= £3{,}000 - £2{,}000 = \underline{\underline{£1{,}000}}.$$

EXAMPLE 2:
Data:

$$\text{Fixed cost} = £4{,}000$$
$$\text{Profit} = £1{,}000$$
$$\text{Break-even is at } £20{,}000$$

Find the sales and marginal cost of sales (using formulae (b), $(d)(ii)$ and (a) above).

Method:

$$\text{Profit} = \text{Total contribution} - \text{Fixed cost}$$
$$\therefore \quad £1{,}000 = \text{Total contribution} - £4{,}000$$
$$\therefore \quad \text{Total contribution} = £5{,}000$$

$$\text{And B/E} = \text{Fixed cost} \times \frac{\text{Sales}}{\text{Total contribution}}$$

$$\therefore \quad 20{,}000 = 4{,}000 \times \frac{\text{Sales}}{5{,}000} = \tfrac{4}{5} \text{ Sales}$$

$$\therefore \quad \text{Sales} = \tfrac{5}{4} \times £20{,}000 = \underline{\underline{£25{,}000}}.$$

In addition, Sales − Marginal cost of sales = Total contribution
$$\therefore \quad 25{,}000 - \text{Marginal cost of sales} = 5{,}000$$
$$\therefore \quad \text{Marginal cost of sales} = \underline{\underline{£20{,}000}}.$$

16. Break-even logic. The formulae given help to provide insight into the various marginal cost and break-even relationships. However, you are strongly advised always to try and reach your answer in practice by logical argument. Not only is one's memory fallible but frequently slightly more sophisticated questions cannot be solved by the simple application of these formulae.

NOTE: When using logical argument, one can often use the fact that the contribution at break-even exactly equals the fixed cost.

EXAMPLE: Reworking Examples 1 and 2 in **15** using logical argument.

1. Contribution at break-even = fixed cost (i.e. contribution exactly covers fixed cost), and since break-even is 1,000 units and fixed costs £2,000, then £2,000 is the contribution from 1,000 units.

$$\therefore \quad \text{Unit contribution} = \frac{2,000}{1,000} = £2.$$

∴ Since selling price is £6, marginal cost must be £6 – £2 = £4 per unit.

In addition the total contribution from 1,500 units at £2 per unit is £3,000.

Out of this, £2,000 fixed costs must be paid leaving profit of £1,000.

2. Since the total contribution is made up of fixed cost and profit, a total contribution of £4,000 + £1,000 = £5,000 is obtained here from the level of sales attained.

Now since contribution at break-even equals the fixed cost, then at break-even a contribution of £4,000 is obtained from the given break-even sales of £20,000.

In addition, sales and contributions are in proportion to each other, and so to have increased the contribution from £4,000 to £5,000 (i.e. a quarter) sales must have increased by a quarter – that is, from £20,000 to £25,000.

(Alternatively, contribution of £4,000 from £20,000 sales gives a P/V ratio of $4,000/20,000 = \frac{1}{5}$. Therefore sales required to give contribution of £5,000 is £5,000 × 5 = £25,000.)

Finally, since £5,000 of this £25,000 sales is contribution, the remainder, £20,000, must be the marginal cost of sales.

The practical use of break-even theory

17. The validity of break-even charts. Although break-even charts are very useful in giving visual insight into the relationship between fixed costs, variable costs, sales, contribution and profit when looked at in terms of activity, they must always be used with caution in any real-life situation. In such practical circumstances the validity of these charts should always be assessed in the light of the following possibilities.

(a) *That the total cost may not be a simple semi-variable cost* because:

(i) the fixed cost element may, in fact, contain stepped fixed costs;

(ii) the variable cost element may not be made up only of unchanging linear variable costs.

(b) *That the income curve itself may not be linear* (e.g. as sales increase discounts may need to be given in order to bring in yet further sales).

(c) *That a required graphical reading may fall outside the relevant activity range.* Reading outside this range (or, in statistical terminology, extrapolating) can lead to serious errors.

(d) *That a required estimate may fall outside the selected time-span.* Remember, a change of time-span can affect the behaviour classification of a cost (*see* 10: **9**).

(e) *That changed conditions may have altered the cost behaviour pattern.*

(f) *That managerial decisions may have interchanged fixed and variable elements.* Management can often interchange fixed and variable costs. For instance, it can replace a small labour team on piecework, a variable cost, by an automatic machine having mainly fixed costs. This means that a break-even chart can be completely outdated by a management decision. It is, then, usually necessary to prepare a new chart every time break-even data is required.

Possibly the greatest shortcomings of break-even charts lie in their inability to handle multi-product situations and also the difficulty at times of finding a valid measure of activity of the behaviour of all the costs involved, even when there is only a single product. This is particularly the case in the service industries. How, for example, would you measure activity in a dock which handles many varieties of ships and cargoes and uses a number of different freight-handling facilities? In such cases the use of break-even charts may well be extremely limited.

All this being said, however, it must be appreciated that there are a great many situations where break-even charts can be validly used – more, perhaps, than might be thought from the above list of potential disqualifying possibilities. Where they can be validly used such charts are without question of real value.

18. Break-even theory applied to proposed projects. Break-even theory does not only apply to enterprises or parts of enterprises. It applies also to projects. For instance, a project may have a fixed set-up cost of £5,000, a unit variable cost of £5 and a unit selling price of £7. Here it can quickly be seen that for the project to break even, sales of $5,000 \div (7-5) = 2,500$ units (£17,500) are required. All the other break-even mathematics can similarly be applied of course. Indeed, one is on firmer ground when applying break-even theory to projects since the fewer the costs and the more homogeneous the product the more likely it is that the theory assumptions will actually hold.

Note one trap that must be avoided for yet again no *apportioned* fixed overheads must ever be used in the analysis. Only the project identifiable fixed costs must be considered.

19. Break-even theory applied to profit planning. In simple circumstances break-even theory can be applied to profit planning. To apply it in this context all that is necessary is that the planned profit is regarded as a fixed cost and added to the fixed costs total. Finding the break-even point on this basis gives the required activity level needed for the desired profit.

EXAMPLE: A company sells for £20 a product having a unit variable cost of £12. The company has a fixed cost of £30,000 and plans to make a profit of £10,000. How many units must be made and sold?

SOLUTION: Fixed cost and planned profit = £30,000 + £10,000 = £40,000. To break even at the equivalent of a £40,000 fixed cost (i.e. to obtain a contribution of £40,000) when selling a product having a unit contribution of £20 − £12 = £8 calls for sales of £40,000 ÷ £8 = <u>5,000 units</u>.

20. The break-even point as a point of indifference. If the anticipated activity level of a proposed project proved to be the break-even point, it would be a matter of economic indifference whether the project was carried out or not since the enterprise profit would be unaffected. This concept is a useful one. For example, assume that a department can carry out a required task by incurring either a fixed cost of £10,000 and a unit variable cost of £10 or a fixed cost of £14,000 and a unit variable cost of £8. In this case the chosen method will depend upon the anticipated level of activity – the higher the level the more the choice will tend towards the high-fixed/low-variable cost alternative. If, however, there is considerable doubt as to just what level of activity can be anticipated it may be more acceptable to find first the point of indifference. In this case, since an extra £4,000 fixed costs must be spent to reduce the variable cost (i.e. increase the contribution) by £2 per unit, the point of indifference is the same as the break-even point in a parallel situation, i.e. it is £4,000 ÷ £2 = 2,000 units. At 2,000 units, then, it is a matter of indifference which alternative is selected since the overall cost will be the same. (*Check:* first alternative cost = £10,000 + 2,000 × £10 = £30,000; second alternative cost = £14,000 + 2,000 × £8 = £30,000.) Now the final decision may be made much more easily since even though there may be considerable doubt as to the actual future activity, it may be possible to predict with reasonable certainty *which side* of 2,000 units that activity will lie.

Progress test 14

Principles

1. What are the assumptions that underlie break-even theory? (**2**)

2. What is: (*a*) the margin of safety; (**5**) (*b*) a cash break-even chart; (**7**) (*c*) a profit graph? (**9**)

3. Why are multi-product break-even charts rarely practical? (**10**)

4. How is a P/V ratio calculated and why is it useful? (**14**)

5. A well-known writer commenting on the break-even chart said: 'It (the break-even chart) must be applied with an intelligent discrimination, with an adequate grasp of the assumptions underlying the technique and of the limitations surrounding its

practical application.' Expand on this statement giving illus-
trations of the points which the writer had in mind. (*ACCA*) (**17**)

Practice

6. (*a*) Find the break-even point and the profit from sales of
£40,000 when: selling price is £5; marginal cost £3; fixed cost
£10,000.

(*b*) Find the profit when: sales are £80,000; marginal cost of
sales £60,000; break-even point £60,000 sales.

(*c*) A company makes £5,000 profit from £60,000 sales. Its fixed
costs are £15,000. What is its break-even point?

(*d*) A company has sales of £100,000, fixed costs of £20,000 and
a break-even point of £80,000. What profit has it made?

(*e*) A company has a profit of £5,000, fixed costs of £10,000 and
a break-even point of £20,000. What were its sales?

7. A company has abstracted the following data for the past two
successive periods:

	Period 1	*Period* 2
Material costs	£30,000	£36,000
Labour costs	£21,200	£24,700
Overhead costs	£41,800	£45,300
Production	10,000 units	12,000 units

Sales throughout were made at £10 per unit.

(*a*) Use a break-even chart to find:

(*i*) the company fixed costs;
(*ii*) the current break-even point.

(*b*) A plan is proposed whereby variable costs will be reduced
by £1 per unit; fixed costs will rise by £11,600. Find:

(*i*) the new break-even point;
(*ii*) the minimum sales level that will justify changing from
the current position to the proposed plan.

8. During 19–2 the Even Brake Company obtained sales of
£336,000. Their total variable costs for the year amounted to
£340,000 and their fixed costs were £140,000. They had no finished
goods at the beginning of 19–2, but they did have a finished goods
stock at the end of the year which they valued at marginal cost.

If their volume of sales had been 25 per cent higher (i.e. if they had sold 25 per cent more units with no change in their selling prices) they would have broken even.

(a) Construct a break-even chart for the Even Brake Company.
(b) Find the value of their finished goods stock at the end of 19–2.

(You may assume there are no raw material or work-in progress stocks involved.)

9. Your enterprise wishes to subcontract a job involving a number of identical units. You have received the following quotes from four subcontractors, A, B, C and D:

> A: £20 per unit;
> B: £1,000 + £15 per unit;
> C: £3,000 + £10 per unit;
> D: £5,000 + £5 per unit.

Which quote do you accept?

10. The Chairman of a company faces a difficult board meeting. Last period the company lost £2,000 and the Chairman's four colleagues on the Board are far from happy. Each has a pet proposal he would like to see adopted, at the expense, if need be, of those of his colleagues'. The only thing on which they are all agreed is that they should have a profit target of £4,000 per period.

To assist in evaluating each director's proposal the Chairman has invited you to the meeting, so as to be able to give figures implied by the different proposals. You know that the company has a fixed cost of £20,000 per period, and a variable cost per unit of £5 up to 12,000 units, and £6 for units in excess of 12,000. Last period 9,000 units were sold.

Director	Proposal	Chairman requests:
A	Improved package of product at a cost of £0.50 a unit and so increase sales.	Percentage increase in sales required.
B	Spend £2,000 on advertising.	Percentage increase in sales required.
C	Drop the selling price by £0.50 a unit.	Percentage increase in sales required.

D   Buy more efficient machinery. This   Maximum increase
will cut the variable cost per unit   in fixed machine
by £1 at all levels. Sales to remain   cost per period
at 9,000 units.   to justify the
proposal.

11. Earlier this year our company launched a new product – a special kind of 4-wheeled vehicle. Our selling price is £900 excluding tyres which can be bought from us for £9 and have a life of 6,000 miles.

We have just heard that our competitor has launched a similar vehicle, though his is 6-wheeled. His selling price is £999, exluding tyres which he sells at £8 each and which have a life of 10,000 miles. Despite the extra tyres required for his vehicle, he claims that in the long run his vehicle is the cheaper to run.

(a) What life would the vehicles need to have to make customers indifferent as to which one they bought?

(b) If the actual lives of both vehicles were 120,000 miles, what life must our tyres have in order to enable us to compete in respect of cost to the customer? What effect would an offer by the sales manager to sell our vehicle at £900 *inclusive* of a set of tyres have on the tyre-life figure?

15

Decision-making: conclusion

We have now looked at various decision-making techniques. However, students may wonder how they are to decide on which technique to use.

1. General principles of selection. First it must again be emphasized that the fundamental principle in decision-making work is to examine *differences* between alternatives – or between undertaking a project and not undertaking it.

Applying this principle to short-term decisions, the following points become clear.

(*a*) If the alternatives under consideration *have no effect on the fixed costs*, then the break-even or marginal cost technique is indicated. Generally speaking, the *break-even technique* is limited to single-product situations and the *marginal cost technique* to decisions involving the selection of different products or projects.

(*b*) If *fixed costs are affected* then either the *differential cost* or the *cash flow technique* should be used. The actual choice between the two is often only a matter of preference, though probably cash flow will be somewhat easier to apply as long as the essential qualification of the technique, that all other things are equal, holds good in the given situation.

Finally, remember that the only costs relevant in decision-making are *future opportunity* costs. Though these will often be the same as the expected actual costs there will be times when they are not and it is important to always be alert for this possibility.

2. Solution independent of technique. Note that it makes no difference which technique is selected. If the technique is used correctly then the correct solution will emerge.

To demonstrate the validity of this last point the following very simple problem will be solved using the marginal cost, differential cost and cash flow techniques.

EXAMPLE: A factory has the choice of producing A, B or C. It has a total fixed cost of £150,000 per year, a total capacity of 40,000 hours and can always sell whatever it produces. Product details are as follows:

	A	B	C
Selling price per unit	£20	£50	£120
Marginal cost per unit	£12	£26	£70
Hours per unit	2	4	10

(a) Using marginal cost technique:

	A	B	C
Selling price	£20	£50	£120
Marginal cost	£12	£26	£70
Contribution	£8	£24	£50
Contribution per unit of key factor (hr)	£4	£6	£5

Decision: produce B.

(b) Using differential cost technique:

	A	B	C
Potential production (units)	20,000	10,000	4,000
Sales	£400,000	£500,000	£480,000
Total marginal cost	£240,000	£260,000	£280,000
Net differential income*	£160,000	£240,000	£200,000

Decision: produce B.

*As the fixed costs do not alter they are not entered into the differential cost analysis. As a result in this particular problem the net differential income is the same as the contribution.

(c) Using cash flow technique:

	A	B	C
Cash in: Sales	£ + 400,000	£ + 500,000	£ + 480,000
Cash out:			
Marginal costs	− 240,000	− 260,000	− 280,000
Fixed costs	− 150,000	− 150,000	− 150,000
Net cash flow	£ + 10,000	£ + 90,000	£ + 50,000

Decision: produce B.

Note that if absorption costing (which is not, of course, a decision-making technique) is used without reference to the production capacity there is a danger that the higher unit profit earned from C will induce management to accept C rather than B (*see* below).

(*d*) *Using absorption costing technique:*
Overhead absorption rate = £150,000/40,000 = £3.75 per hour.

	A	B	C
Marginal cost per unit	£12	£26	£70
Fixed overheads at £3.75 per hour	$7\frac{1}{2}$	15	$37\frac{1}{2}$
Total absorption cost	$19\frac{1}{2}$	41	$107\frac{1}{2}$
Selling price	20	50	120
Profit	£ $\frac{1}{2}$	£ 9	£ $12\frac{1}{2}$

Possible (wrong) decision: produce C.

3. Combining techniques. Techniques are essentially tools for solving problems and just as skilled tradespeople will often combine tools to make a product, so skilled cost accountants will combine techniques. For example, when employing the cash flow technique they may well ignore flows common to all alternatives, e.g. fixed cash flows, so that 'net cash flow' is in effect a differential net cash flow. The same solution emerges, of course, as would if a 'pure' technique were used, but time and effort is saved.

4. Conclusion. Applying decision-making principles is admittedly not always easy. However, if you bear in mind the fundamental differential principle then your own common sense should enable you to pick a way through the figures successfully. Never forget that the object of presenting decision-making data to management is to enable managers to determine which is the best course to set for the business. Under some circumstances all courses are unwelcome but it is still management's task to find the least unwelcome, and the cost accountant must assist in this task.

This may be stated in another way by saying that in decision making the cost accountant is concerned with *profitability*, not profit. It is essential that this distinction is absolutely clear to the modern accountant.

Above all, the emphasis on the future must never be forgotten. Today's decisions must be based on tomorrow's opportunities, not yesterday's errors.

Part three

Planning and variance analysis

16

Budgets

Introduction

Budgets are prepared for a variety of reasons and understanding the reason behind the preparation of any budget is essential to understanding the mechanics of that budget.

1. Definition. A budget is a *quantitative economic plan in respect of a period of time*. Because this is an important definition it will pay us to look at each key word in turn.

(a) *Quantitative*. A budget must comprise quantities. An enterprise may plan to build up a reputation for fair trading but it is not possible to budget for such a reputation since this is an intangible that cannot be quantified.

(b) *Economic*. To be a budget a plan must be in economic terms. An enterprise may plan to make the strongest steel in the world but such a plan cannot be properly referred to as a budget.

(c) *Plan.* A budget is a plan. It is not a hope or a forecast (*see* **3**) but an authoritative intention.

(d) *Time.* A budget is always in respect of a period of time (*see* **4**). Budgets are five-yearly, yearly, quarterly, monthly, weekly, daily or other time period. Note that while quantitative economic plans can also relate to cost units such plans are *not* budgets (they are, in fact, termed standard costs, *see* 17: **21**).

Budgets can be divided into a number of different categories. These are shown diagrammatically in Fig. 16.1 and discussed in **5–8** below.

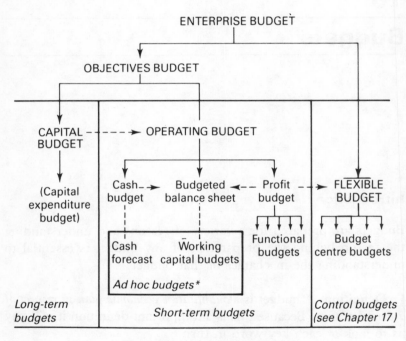

Figure 16.1 *Categories of budget*

Note that in this chapter only operating budgets are explained in detail, flexible budgets being left until later more appropriate chapters. This necessary spread of the topic indicates the extent to which the technique extends into all fields of management accounting.

*These are budgets prepared for special periods or projects and rarely incorporated into the overall enterprise budget.

2. Economic v. monetary plans. An economic plan is not one that is primarily prepared in narrow monetary terms. More fundamental than money are the *quantities* of economic resources and utilities involved, and it is these that must form the bedrock of all budgets. All that the monetary figures do is to express those quantities in a common economic measure.

3. Forecasts v. budgets. As was stated above, a budget is a plan and not a forecast. The difference may be put as follows.

(*a*) A *forecast* is a prediction of what will happen as a result of a given set of circumstances.

(*b*) A *budget* is a planned result that an enterprise aims to attain.

From this it follows that a *forecast* is a judgment that can be made by anybody (provided they are competent to make judgments), whereas a *budget* is an enterprise objective that may be specified only by the authorized management. (Moreover, note that the announcement of a plan is an implicit instruction to employees to work to achieve that objective.)

4. Budget period. This is the period of time for which a budget is prepared and used. Such periods depend very much on the type of budget involved and also on the circumstances. The following are typical periods.

(*a*) Operating budget: one year.
(*b*) Capital budget: many years.
(*c*) Research and development budget: some years.

5. Objectives and flexible budgets. There are two forms of planning and they are fundamentally different. One form is based on determining the best way to achieve one's objectives and the other on identifying divergences from planned performances. On the face of it, it would appear that one planning exercise can result in a plan that will cover both functions, since it would seem reasonable to argue that comparison of actual performance with the plan would reveal the required divergences. However, for the reason explained in 17: **10**, this argument is invalid.

As there are two different forms of planning there needs to be two different kinds of budget.

(a) *Objectives budget.* This lays down the manner by which the enterprise's objectives are to be achieved. It specifies in detail the planned quantities and values of each economic factor and also all the activity levels involved in the achievement of those objectives.

(b) *Flexible budget.* This lays down what should have happened in respect of each budget factor in view of the *actual* activity levels achieved.

This chapter will only be concerned with objectives budgets, flexible budgets being discussed in the next.

6. Capital and operating budgets. An enterprise has both long-term and short-term objectives, though naturally the short-term objectives are no more than the intermediate steps towards the enterprise's long-term objectives. In theory, planning for long-term objectives should be no different from planning for short-term ones. However, in practice there is a difference of emphasis. In long-term planning it is the viability of the capital structure that is management's primary concern while in short-term planning it is the day-to-day management of resources. Consequently two different kinds of objectives budgets have been developed.

(a) *Capital budget.* This plans the capital structure and liquidity of the enterprise over a long period of time. It is concerned, therefore, particularly with equity, liabilities and fixed and current assets, especially the year-end cash balances. A major sub-budget of the capital budget is the *capital expenditure budget* which plans the capital expenditure, especially expenditure on new plant and facilities.

(b) *Operating budget.* This plans the day-to-day use of resources and creation of utilities. It is particularly concerned, therefore, with materials, labour, overhead resources, sales and cash. An operating budget usually runs for a year.

Capital and operating budgets are clearly interconnected since capital budgets can only be developed on the basis of planned operations over the years. However, at the end of the planning process the capital budget in effect lays down the objectives for each of the sequential operating budgets and Fig. 16.1 therefore shows the connection in this form.

Since capital budgets relate more to long-term financing than costing, their preparation is not covered in this book.

7. Types of operating budgets.

(a) *Profit budget.* This budget plans the resources (excluding cash) to be used and the utilities to be created and sold during the budget period. Planned prices are then placed on the resources and utilities so as to convert the budgeted quantities into costs and income, from which figures a budgeted profit can be found. In addition, the budget often shows the planned closing stocks. This budget is closely connected with the flexible budget for the period since if all actual activity levels accord with those planned the flexible budget will be identical to the objectives budget, though this event is rare in practice. On this point note that in order to distinguish the profit budget from its superficially similar flexible counterpart, the former is described as a *fixed budget*, i.e. a budget that employs a fixed level of activity. Note, too, that the profit budget divides into sub-budgets referred to as 'functional budgets' (which are further discussed in 16).

(b) *Cash budget.* This budget simply plans the receipts and payments. The majority of the required figures can be abstracted from the profit budget but some important (and usually very large) amounts relating to capital expenditure and income are taken from that part of the capital budget that relates to the cash budget period. The prime function of a cash budget is to show the budgeted cash balances at various points of time throughout the budget period.

(c) *Budgeted balance sheet.* This budget plans the balance sheet for the end of the budget period. It embodies the budgeted profit from the profit budget, the budgeted closing cash balance from the cash budget and the planned changes in the other asset and liability values, in particular those relating to the working capital.

8. Ad hoc operating budgets.
In addition to those budgets which form the overall enterprise operating budget there are two classes of budget which are normally prepared on an *ad hoc* basis for a selected period of time (rarely the normal operating budget period).

(a) *Working capital budget.* A working capital budget is a budget that is usually prepared in respect of a project, and plans the working capital requirements of the project.

(b) *Cash forecast.* Despite the term a cash forecast is usually a cash budget prepared in respect of the whole enterprise for a particular period of time with the object of enabling the enterprise's cash to be effectively managed over especially crucial moments arising during that period.

9. Steps in the preparation of a budget. Preparing a budget almost always involves taking the following steps.

(*a*) Selecting the budget period.

(*b*) Setting objectives to be reached by the end of the budget period or, where relevant, at points during the budget period.

(*c*) Either or both:

　(*i*) preparing forecasts for the period;

　(*ii*) abstracting relevant figures from budgets already prepared.

(*d*) Determining enterprise policies (e.g. product range; normal hours of work per week; channels of distribution, stocks; research and development appropriation; credit policy; investments).

(*e*) Computing from the forecasts or budgets already prepared the requirements in terms of the economic quantities needed to meet the objectives while complying with the policies – and subsequently converting these quantities into monetary values. This results in an initial provisional budget.

(*f*) Reviewing this initial budget with regard to the planned objectives and amending the objectives or policies or both repeatedly until an acceptable budget emerges.

(*g*) Formally accepting the budget which then becomes an executive order.

10. Functions of a budget. At first glance it does seem that a budget is no more than an accounting statement relating to future rather than past performance. However, the shift from the past (where events are known and cannot be changed) to the future (where events are uncertain and subject to manipulation) is crucial and the provision of accounting statements forms only a minor function of a budget – almost, in fact, no more than a spin-off. To view budgets realistically the student should fully understand that budgeting is primarily a *management* and not an accounting technique. However, in this chapter only the mechanics of budgeting will be discussed.

11. Other forms of budget.

(a) *Continuous (rolling) budget.* This is a budget having an end-point in time always the same distance ahead in the future. Thus a five-year capital budget which is continually extended a year at a time as each year passes (so that the enterprise is always looking five years ahead) would be a continuous capital budget. Similarly an operating budget with a one-year budget period which at the end of each month incorporated a further month so that there was always a budget for the twelve immediate future months would be a continuous operating budget.

There are two reasons why a continuous budget is recommended. Firstly, it provides an opportunity to reassess in the light of up-to-date information the viability of the remainder of the budget. Secondly, since enterprises do not progress in a series of kangaroo hops but progress continuously, continuous budgeting is more closely aligned to business reality than budgeting intermittently only as and when the end of the current budget period approaches.

(b) *Summary budget.* This is a budget that merely brings together all the summary data from a group of sub-budgets so as to provide management with all overall appreciation of the consequences that would follow the achievement of their more detailed plans.

(c) *Master budget.* 'Master budget' is, perhaps, a term to be avoided. The CIMA regards a master budget as being synonymous with a summary budget. It has also been defined both as a comprehensive planning model and as the budget after its formal adoption by the management of an enterprise (to distinguish it from the provisional budgets which alone exist before such formal adoption).

12. Zero-base budgeting. In practice budgeting is often done on the basis of taking existing costs as the starting point of the budget and adjusting these costs for changed circumstances and future planned activities. Under *zero-base budgeting* this approach is dismissed as being ineffective and instead all aspects of operations are looked at in critical detail and with a fresh eye. For each type of operation a case has to be made for its budgeted expenditure which will include a careful analysis of alternative ways of achieving the objectives of the operation. As in all forms of sound budgeting, budgets are first expressed in terms of resources needed and only subsequently converted into monetary terms.

An essential aspect of zero-base budgeting is an initial preparation of a 'minimum' budget which details the resources and costs needed to meet the minimum basic level of achievement and then the preparation of separate 'incremental' budgets that detail the resources and costs needed to reach higher levels of achievement. Subsequently, all budgets are ranked so that a final decision can be made as to which are to be accepted.

Zero-base budgeting is a budgetary method that adopts a thoroughly organized approach to preparing a comprehensive and exhaustive set of budget documents, themselves carefully designed, which detail the case for each individual budget proposal together with supporting figures and which ultimately enable a soundly-based final budget to be set by the organization. The technique is particularly suitable for non-profit-making bodies since its use of incremental budgets enables management – or government authorities – to compare the different levels of services and costs that are available to them and so be able to provide the best value for the money on hand in terms of a mix of services and efficiency standards.

Operating budgets

13. General principle of budget preparation. An operating budget is essentially a budget that lays down the planned requirements for the day-to-day operations of an enterprise over the budget period.

Apart from the straightforward application of ordinary costing and receipts and payments procedures to future figures instead of past figures, the preparation of an operating budget requires two essentials: clear thinking and common sense. Unfortunately no book can help students with these, and so this kind of budgeting is the easiest technique to learn and the hardest to apply. In this section a few useful words will be defined and a logical approach suggested. In the majority of budget situations, however, you must use your own initiative.

14. Profit budget. The first operating budget is the *profit budget.* This specifies, both in quantities and in values, all the economic resources to be used (apart from cash) and utilities to be created and sold during the budget period. From these budgeted figures a budgeted profit statement can be prepared and the budgeted profit computed.

In the next three paragraphs some key points relating to the preparation of this budget are discussed.

15. Principal budget factor. Before any detailed planning for the profit budget can start it is necessary to identify the *principal budget factor,* i.e. that factor which prevents an enterprise from immediately expanding to infinity. The principal budget factor is usually sales, the enterprise being unable to sell all it can produce. However, there are other possible factors which may limit enterprise activity, such as shortage of machinery, cash, labour, space, materials and managerial ability.

Clearly, the principal budget factor dictates the whole course of planning short-term operations. Indeed, part of the art of management is to make plans so that this factor is fully exploited. We have already discussed in connection with key factors this aspect of maximizing return from the use of a limiting factor (*see* 13: **19**).

The principal budget factor does not remain constant. If the limitations imposed by one factor are removed, another takes its place and becomes the principal budget factor. In practice, it is important that one is aware when this type of switch-over is imminent.

16. Functional budgets. The considerable detail and large number of managers usually involved in the preparation of a profit budget make it near-impossible for this to be prepared in the form of a single document. Instead the budget preparation task is divided up between the various functions and the sub-budgets prepared by these functions are called *functional budgets.* Each function is budgeted on the basis of the objectives of the enterprise and any relevant data from the other functional budgets. The inevitable dependence of one budget on another requires these budgets to be prepared in a hierarchical manner and Fig. 16.2 indicates a common form of budget hierarchy together with the necessary data flow between budgets.

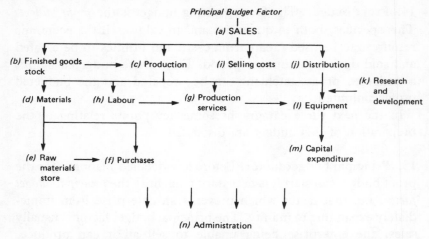

Figure 16.2 *Interrelationships of functional budgets*
It is assumed here that the principal budget factor is sales. The
letters in brackets refer to sub-paragraphs of **16**

Essentially, preparing a functional budget involves providing
answers to relevant questions relating to the role of the function
within the enterprise and in respect of other budget objectives.
Thus, on the assumption that sales is the principal budget factor,
the basic information required for each functional budget would be
given by the answers to the following questions.

(*a*) *Sales.* In view of this being the principal budget factor, what
quantities can be sold and at what prices?

(*b*) *Finished goods stock.* What finished goods stock will be
required to support the budgeted sales?

(*c*) *Production.* What production must be achieved to meet
budgeted sales and secure the budgeted finished goods stock?

(*d*) *Materials.* What materials will be required to meet the
budgeted production?

(*e*) *Raw material stores.* What raw material stocks will be
required in view of the materials budget?

(*f*) *Purchases.* What purchases must be made to obtain the
budgeted materials and raw material stocks, and at what prices?

(*g*) *Production services.* What production services will be required
to support the budgeted production, and at what cost?

(*h*) *Labour.* What labour must be employed to achieve the

budgeted production and staff the budgeted services, and at what remuneration rates?

(*i*) *Selling costs.* What selling services will be required to achieve the budgeted sales, and at what cost?

(*j*) *Distribution.* What distribution services will be required to distribute the budgeted sales, and at what cost?

NOTE: Students often make the error of basing these last two budgets on production instead of *sales*.

(*k*) *Research and development.* What research and development will be needed and at what cost?

(*l*) *Equipment.* What equipment will be needed to enable budgeted production to be achieved, budgeted research and development to be supported, and budgeted services to be set up?

(*m*) *Capital expenditure.* What capital expenditure will be needed in the budget period to acquire the budgeted equipment?

(*n*) *Administration.* What administration will be required, and at what cost, to administer effectively an enterprise engaged in achieving all the foregoing budgets?

17. Summary profit budget. Once the functional budgets have been prepared it only remains to collate the summary figures from these budgets so as to produce the summary profit budget and ascertain the budgeted profit figure that emerges as a result. If this profit is acceptable then the budget holds, but if not then some or all of the functional budgets have to be revised – this revision continuing until an acceptable profit does finally emerge.

18. Cash budget. In addition to the budgeted profit figure the profit budget provides much of the data needed for the cash budget. Once, then, the profit budget is set the cash budget can be started.

In principle the cash budget involves no more than listing the planned receipts and payments. Though conceptually simple, care must be taken when preparing a cash budget. Note particularly that the cash pattern may differ considerably from the income and expenditure pattern, especially as regards timing. It is necessary to watch out carefully for such factors as credit trading (this will 'shift' the cash flow into a later period than the date of the sales or purchases), capital payments and receipts, tax and dividend payments, and non-trading income and expenditure. It should be appreciated, too, that cash fluctuations can be very rapid and involve large sums, and for this reason the cash budget should be prepared on the basis of a budget period of not more than one month at the longest. The preparation is essentially as follows.

(*a*) Begin with the cash balance at the start of the budget period.
(*b*) Add receipts and deduct payments for the period.
(*c*) Finish with the cash balance at the end of the period.

19. Cash budget illustration. To illustrate the layout of a typical cash budget the following very simple problem is solved.

QUESTION: A company has been experiencing a £20,000 increase in sales each month for the past half year or so and it anticipates that this monthly increase will continue for the immediately foreseeable future. Its profit statement for last month was as follows:

		£	£
Sales			200,000
Costs:	Direct materials	100,000	
	Direct labour	40,000	
	Variable overheads	20,000	
	Fixed overheads (excluding rent)	20,000	
	Rent	5,000	
			185,000
Profit			£15,000

The company's sales are on credit, the debtors paying two months after the sale while the creditors for materials and overheads are paid after the company has taken one month's credit. Labour costs are, of course, paid as they are incurred and the rent is paid quarterly. Last month the rent was paid and the month-end cash balance was £10,000. £10,000 capital expenditure is planned for month 2. There are no stocks at any time.

Prepare the cash budget for the next four months.

SOLUTION:
NOTES:
(1) From the profit statement it can be seen that the marginal

costs are: materials, 50 per cent of sales; labour, 20 per cent of sales; variable overheads, 10 per cent of sales.

(2) Since the fixed overheads are the same each month, the one month's credit does not affect the cash budget over the four months.

(3) Sales for the month before last must be £200,000 – 20,000 = £180,000.

(4) Since the rent is £5,000 a month the quarterly rent payable must be £15,000, and since this was paid last month it must be due again in month 3.

	Cash Budget (£000s)				
	Last month	Month 1	Month 2	Month 3	Month 4
Operating Data (Note 1):					
Sales	200	220	240	260	280
Materials, 50% sales	100	110	120	130	140
Labour, 20% sales	N/a	44	48	52	56
Variable overheads, 10% sales	20	22	24	26	28
Budgeted receipts:					
Debtors (2 months) (Note 3)	N/a	180	200	220	240
Budgeted payments:					
Materials (1 month)	N/a	100	110	120	130
Labour	N/a	44	48	52	56
Variable overheads (1 month)	N/a	20	22	24	26
Fixed overheads (Note 2)	N/a	20	20	20	20
Rent (Note 4)	15	0	0	15	0
Capital expenditure	—	—	10	—	—
TOTAL	N/a	184	210	231	232
Budgeted excess cash receipts over payments	N/a	(4)	(10)	(11)	8
Month end cash balance	10	6	(4)	(15)	(7)

N/a = Not applicable.

20. Budgeted balance sheet. Finally, with the profit and cash budgets completed it is possible to turn to the budgeted balance sheet which plans the assets and liabilities at the end of the budget period. Of all the operating budgets this is usually the simplest to prepare and, with the opening balance sheet at hand, involves no more than the following.

(*a*) Taking the budgeted profit from the profit budget and, after deducting the forecast tax and any intended dividends, adding the retained profit to the opening equity.

(*b*) Changing the opening long-term liabilities and fixed assets to reflect any changes in these items (the cash budget will often be of help in identifying these, though events such as revaluations will need to be specifically noted). The asset depreciation for the year will, of course, be abstracted from the profit budget.

(*c*) Ascertaining the working capital items as follows.

(*i*) Current liabilities other than tax can normally be picked up from the cash budget (operating data section) though reference to the purchases and sales budgets may be necessary to ascertain the full values of the creditors and debtors.

(*ii*) Stock values will be taken from the profit budget (though if this only indicates the stock *changes* reference will also need to be made to the opening stock values).

(*iii*) The cash amount is the closing cash balance in the cash budget.

In preparing a budgeted balance sheet it is unwise to find any missing figure by merely computing the amount needed to make the balance sheet balance. Since all the balance sheet figures must be ascertainable from the other operating data or must be implicit in management's plans (e.g. policy of reducing goodwill yearly), it is much better to utilize the balancing feature of balance sheets to confirm that all the balance sheet figures are both included and correct in amount.

Budget administration

Finally, a few brief observations on the administration of budgets, although many aspects of this topic more appropriately arise under the heading of management accounting.

21. Budget committee. Budgets are set by managers. Only managers can decide what utilities will sell, what resources will be necessary to create those utilities, and what prices should obtain throughout the budget period. In addition budgeting involves considerable management coordination. For these reasons, and also because budgeting involves managers in all parts of the enterprise, it is essential that a budget committee is set up with representatives from all functions and that this committee is charged with the preparation and the administration of the enterprise budgets.

22. Budget officer. In addition to the committee, a budget officer should be appointed. His work is essentially that of secretary to the committee, and entails:

(a) ensuring that the committee secretarial work is carried out (e.g. agendas, minutes, notice of meetings);

(b) ensuring that committee instructions are passed to the appropriate people;

(c) collecting data and opinions for consideration by the committee;

(d) keeping managers to the budget time-table (*see* **23** below);

(e) coordinating and briefing the members of the committee.

Clearly, the management accountant is well suited for, and is often appointed to, this post.

23. Budget time-table. When preparing major budgets it is first necessary to prepare many of the smaller, but key, budgets. If these smaller budgets are not completed quickly, the preparation of the major budgets will be held up, which in turn will hold up the summary budget and therefore the ultimate budget approval. Delay in approving the budget is clearly serious, for a budget issued after the start of a period has very much reduced value, and may even result in the delay of vital projects. In order, then, that the budget can be approved before the period begins, it is necessary to prepare a carefully thought-out time-table for all budget activities. Such a time-table must be rigidly adhered to, since delays in this type of work tend to snowball and quickly assume serious proportions.

24. Budget manual. To assist everyone engaged in budgeting and budget administration, a budget manual should be issued. This sets out such matters as the responsibilities of the people engaged in, the routine of, and the forms and records required for, budgeting (together with the control procedures that will subsequently follow any comparison of actual performance relative to the budget).

More generally, the budget manual will set out all information needed by all persons involved in budgeting and budgetary control to enable them to maximize both:

(a) their contribution to the budget compilation; and

(b) their benefit from the control data ultimately reported back to them.

Progress test 16

Principles

1. What is a budget? (**1**)
2. Distinguish between a budget and a forecast. (**3**)
3. What is a budget period? (**4**)
4. Define: (a) capital budget; (**6**(a)) (b) operating budget; (**6**(b)) (c) working capital budget; (**8**(a)) (d) continuous budgeting; (**11**(a)) (e) zero-base budgeting. (**12**)
5. What is a principal budget factor and why is it important in budgeting? (**15**)
6. What are the steps to be taken in the preparation of a budgeted balance sheet? (**20**)
7. What is the purpose of each of the following: (a) budget committee; (**21**) (b) budget officer; (**22**) (c) budget time-table; (**23**) (d) budget manual? (**24**)

Practice

8. You are given the following data regarding the operation of a company for a 4-week period at two forecast levels of activity:

	Forecast A	Forecast B
Sales (at £5 per unit)	50,000 units	100,000 units
Variable and semi-variable overheads:		
Indirect labour	20 men	35 men
Power	£5,000	£10,000
Maintenance	£15,000	£25,000
Distribution	£10,400	£14,800

In addition, the following information applies to both forecasts:

Direct materials	50% sales value
Direct labour	1 man produces 200 units a week
Depreciation	£5,000
Other fixed costs	£15,000
Selling costs	$2\frac{1}{2}$% sales
Labour costs	£100 per man per week

Prepare comparative profit budgets.

9. (This question is an extensive budgeting exercise. However if you work through it you will find that in all probability you will have covered most aspects met in examination questions on operating budgets.) Untrue, a branch of Proverbs Ltd., makes silcpercys from sowzeers. Last year's accounts were as follows.

Profit and Loss

		£	£
Sales: 80,000 barrels of silcpercys at £50			4,000,000
Less: discounts			140,000
			3,860,000
Costs of sales: Production: 320,000 barrels of			
	sowzeers at £5	1,600,000	
	Direct labour	800,000	
	Variable overheads	400,000	
	Fixed overheads*	700,000	
Marketing:	Contract total	100,000	3,600,000
	Profit		£260,000

*Includes £90,000 depreciation and £110,000 rent.

Balance Sheet

		£	£
Plant and equipment (at cost)			900,000
Less depreciation: 4 years at 10%			−360,000
			540,000
Stocks: Raw materials, 100,000 barrels			
	sowzeers at £5	500,000	
	Finished goods, 15,000 barrels		
	silcpercys at £45	675,000	1,175,000
Debtors: Entitled to 5% discount		200,000	
	Other		30,000
			230,000

Less Provision for discount	−7,000	223,000
Prepayments: Rent	27,500	
Marketing	11,000	38,500
Cash		500,000
		£2,476,500
Head office account		2,014,833
Creditors: Purchases for month 2 production		400,000
Accruals: Fixed overheads		41,667
Variable overheads		20,000
		£2,476,500

From the following additional data prepare all the operating budgets for the first four months of the current year.

(*a*) The sales quantity for the current year is planned to be 25 per cent up on last year.

(*b*) Planned sales for the first five months are 10 per cent, 15 per cent, 20 per cent, 25 per cent and 5 per cent respectively of the planned annual sales.

(*c*) All prices and rates (excluding rent but including selling prices) are expected to be 20 per cent more than last year.

(*d*) To allow for settling, sowzeers have to be purchased two months before processing (which can be regarded as being instantaneous).

(*e*) Creditors allow one month credit. Debtors who pay one month after delivery receive a 5 per cent cash discount and 70 per cent of the debtors avail themselves of this discount. The remainder pay after two months.

(*f*) For policy reasons the settled stock of sowzeers at the end of month 5 must be sufficient for sales for the rest of the year. Apart from this, raw material stocks are to be kept to a minimum.

(*g*) Finished goods stocks at month end are to be equal to the month's sales, except at the end of month 4 when the planned stock is zero.

(*h*) Fixed overheads are incurred equally throughout the year but are absorbed into production on a direct wages basis.

(*i*) Apart from rent, which is paid at the end of month 3 for the whole year in advance, the fixed overhead payments are the same each month and these costs together with the variable overheads are paid one month in arrear.

(*j*) Most of the direct labour is casual (and hence variable).

(*k*) Marketing is undertaken by a different branch of Proverbs. Under a new contract this branch will charge monthly £5,000 plus 1 per cent sales, the amount due being payable one month in advance (budgeted sales being used initially and amounts subsequently adjusted in the light of actual sales).

(*l*) Plant and equipment worth £100,000 will be purchased for cash at the end of month 4.

(*m*) The company prices stores issues on a FIFO basis.

17

Flexible budgets and standard costs

It is one thing to make a plan, quite another to achieve it. If the plan is to be achieved it is essential that progress should be monitored, and monitoring calls for performance measurement in terms of the plan.

In the remaining chapters of this book the accounting aspects of performance measurement are outlined. In this particular chapter the method of formulating plans so that such measurement can be carried out is discussed.

Introduction

1. Control. The purpose of performance measurement in the context now being considered is to assist management to achieve the plans made when preparing the operating budgets, in particular the profit budget. On the basis of such measurement managers will take steps to counter any falling away from the plans. They will, in other words, attempt to *control* costs and sales. The touchstone, then, of the success of the techniques employed is their ability to assist managers in maintaining such control.

2. A plethora of names. Although from now on we will be primarily concerned with the technique of controlling profit the student should be warned that this technique has many names. Historically it developed through the integration of the previously separate techniques of *standard costing and budgetary control*, and it is often still referred to by this composite title. It is also often loosely referred to as *cost control*, even though the control of income is an important facet of the technique. Sometimes the term *responsibility*

accounting is used in recognition of the fact that control and responsibility are inseparably linked. More recently the term *variance
accounting* has arisen, this title recognizing the importance of the
measurement of the divergence of actual from plan.

Yet it is questionable if any of these terms are a good description
of the technique as a whole. The latter two betray the dominance
of an accounting approach over what is a management technique
(*see* 19 : 5(*b*)), while 'cost control' implies that only costs are subject to control. But since at the end of the day the technique aims
at enabling management to control profit, the term *profit control*
does seem the more appropriate one to adopt.

3. Control and the cost accountant. As we have said, control is
primarily a management, not an accounting, technique. The cost
accountant can, however, assist management in the operation of
the technique by:

(*a*) drafting management proposals in the form of monetary
statements that indicate the profitability of management plans;
and

(*b*) making a comparison of actual with planned costs and
preparing clear and meaningful statements detailing any
divergences and their effects on the profit.

The accountant is in no way responsible for determining the
necessary action to be taken to correct the divergences. This is
wholly a line management responsibility.

4. The influence of tradition. In the development of any technique it frequently happens that the early stages are to a greater
or lesser extent misdirected because of initial misconceptions, with
the result that the later development is burdened with out-of-date
attitudes having their roots in history. This is so in the case of the
current subject for historically the techniques involved were
developed primarily as accounting techniques rather than control
techniques. This early wrong emphasis is with us still so that today
the accounting aspects are often stressed at the expense of the control aspects. Yet the fundamental objective of all work in this area
is to help managers to control costs and sales. A modern approach,
therefore, will reverse the priorities and subordinate the accounting aspect to the control aspect.

Regrettably it may be some time before this view is fully accepted. Until then examination papers will naturally tend towards questions reflecting the traditional view rather than the modern. It is necessary, then, for the student to learn both approaches to the subject. But it must be pointed out that, apart from emphasis, the two techniques have many more similarities than differences. Indeed, the modern technique leaves the bulk of the traditional one basically unchanged and differs primarily in the method by which it handles the fixed cost. And this difference, in turn, arises because the traditional method employs absorption costing and the modern method marginal costing.

5. Features of the traditional (standard costing and budgetary control) technique.

(*a*) An emphasis on accounting as against control.

(*b*) The adoption of the absorption cost technique.

(*c*) Statement formats which reproduce the conventional historical cost statements with planned figures substituted for past figures.

(*d*) Performance analysis more in terms of products than economic factors and management responsibilities.

(*e*) The cost accounts prepared by grafting the new figures onto the traditional book-keeping pattern.

6. Features of the modern (profit control) technique.

(*a*) An emphasis on profit control as against accounting conventions.

(*b*) The adoption of the marginal costing technique (and for the student this is the most distinctive feature of the modern technique).

(*c*) Statement formats specifically designed to aid management control (e.g. product cost statements will rarely be prepared since control is achieved by monitoring individual production activities, not the costs of individual cost units).

(*d*) Performance analysis in terms of economic factors and management responsibilities.

(*e*) The cost accounts relegated to a very minor role in the technique and then used primarily only to incorporate the overall result into the enterprise's monthly final accounts.

7. Budget centre. Traditionally a budget centre has been defined as 'a section of the organization for which separate budgets can be prepared and control exercised' (CIMA terminology). However, it is now considered that because a crucial principle of control involves holding managers responsible for their decisions, control data should be based on managers rather than sections. Although the two are, in practice, all too often the same thing it is perhaps advisable to bear in mind a definition which reflects this principle. Under such a definition a *budget centre* can be regarded as *a part of the organization for which a given manager has responsibility and authority and to which profit control data can be assigned.*

Note, now, the distinction between a cost centre (which is used for cost ascertainment) and a budget centre, for what is chargeable to a cost centre isn't necessarily chargeable to a budget centre. For instance, under cost ascertainment an inspector's salary would be chargeable to the cost centre in which he worked but in a control system it would be chargeable to the budget centre of the manager to whom he was responsible.

8. Budgetary control. This can be defined as 'the establishment of budgets relating the responsibilities of executives to the requirements of a policy, and the continuous comparison of actual with budgeted results, either to secure by individual action the objective of that policy or to provide a basis for its revision' (CIMA terminology).

Note that from now on the word 'standard' will be increasingly employed. You should be aware that the word 'planned' can be substituted for 'standard' at all times.

9. The planning sequence. Like the functional budgets described in 16 : 16 the planning statements now to be considered are prepared in sequence, and, indeed, they follow on directly from the budgets looked at in Chapter 16. This planning sequence is shown diagrammatically and in its entirety in Fig. 17.1.

The sequence can be briefly described as follows.

(*a*) All the *operating plans* for the operating budget period are formulated by management.

(*b*) The operating plans are incorporated into an *operating profit budget* (*see* 16 : 14). This can be regarded as comprising a costs budget and a sales budget.

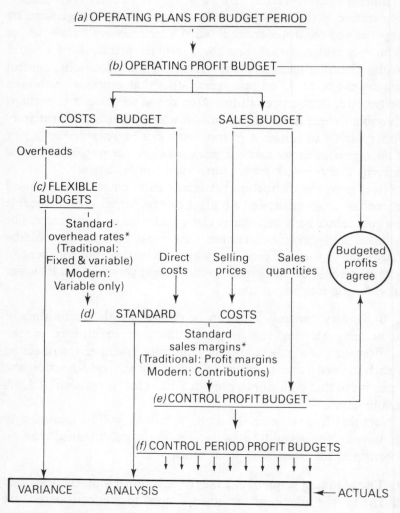

Figure 17.1 *Standard cost and budgetary (profit) control planning sequence* (Letters in brackets refer to subsections of the example in **29.**) This sequence is appropriate for both the traditional and the modern techniques except where marked with *. At those points the sequence is appropriate for the traditional technique. In the modern technique the fixed overheads are taken direct from the flexible budgets to the control profit budget

(c) The overheads in the costs budget are re-analyzed through the medium of *flexible budgets* so that standard overhead rates for both fixed and variable overheads are found.

(d) The direct costs in the costs budget are re-analyzed to give the *cost unit* direct costs and these are combined with the standard overhead rates and the cost unit selling prices detailed in the sales budget to give the *standard cost* for each cost unit. From this, the unit *standard profit* is found.

(e) By combining the unit standard profits and the budgeted unit sales quantities detailed in the sales budget a *control profit budget* can be prepared and the total budgeted profit found. This budgeted profit must be identical to that shown in the operating profit budget and the agreement of the two profits proves the accuracy of the overall re-analysis.

(f) The control profit budget is itself analyzed into shorter *control period profit budgets*.

Although this last analysis brings the planning sequence to an end, Fig. 17.1 shows that when the control period plans and the actual results are brought together, a *variance analysis* can be prepared. This is the performance measurement device that the flexible budget and standard costs technique aims to provide (*see* Chapter 18).

10. The failings of a fixed budget. Chapter 16 showed that a profit budget calls for a quite thorough analysis of all the needed economic resources and at first glance it may appear that performance measurement involves no more than a comparison of the actual results with this budget. Unfortunately nothing is further from the truth. The profit budget discussed earlier is a *fixed* budget and fixed budgets have serious failings when it comes to using them for performance measurement. For instance, assume that a fixed budget laid down that a department was to make 1,000 units for a cost of £2,000. In the event, because of poor sales, the departmental manager was subsequently instructed to make only 500 units. This was done for a cost of £1,400. To what extent was the *cost* performance good or bad?

From the data given it is impossible to say. If all the budgeted £2,000 costs were variable costs then the manager has done badly since producing half the budgeted production should have resulted in a cost one-half of budget, i.e. £1,000. Conversely, if the £2,000 had represented fixed costs the manager has done well since the reduced activity should have left these costs unaffected. (Do not fall into the trap of assuming a fixed cost is an *unchangeable* cost. It is not. Local government rates are a fixed cost but change yearly. Remember, what makes a cost a fixed cost is the fact that it does not change simply because *activity* changes.)

So a fixed budget is quite useless for performance measurement and should never be used for that. Indeed, it is in respect of this sort of budget that the old saying 'the budget is out of date before the period even begins' is often perfectly true. However, this is irrelevant since such a budget should never be used after the period begins anyway.

11. Allowances. Since a fixed budget is an inappropriate device for performance measurement the question arises as to what method is appropriate. This question can be answered by looking again at the example. Clearly, planning that there shall be a budgeted cost of £2,000 for 1,000 units is, as it stands, insufficient. In addition, the division of costs between fixed and variable must be known. Assume that of the total £2,000, £1,000 relates to fixed costs and £1,000 to variable costs. There is, then, a planned fixed cost of £1,000 for the period and a planned variable cost of £1 per unit. Since the manager produced 500 units we would, if he kept to his cost plan, expect him to incur a total cost of £1,000 + 500 × £1 = £1,500. Since he has spent only £1,400 he saved £100, and this, of course, means the profit will be £100 more than it would have been if he had merely achieved his planned cost performance. He has therefore performed well.

In order, then, to measure a manager's cost performance it proves necessary to compute how much he should be allowed to spend in view of the actual circumstances surrounding his performance. Such a figure is called an *allowance* and is defined as the *figure one would expect to see achieved if the manager or factor being controlled had performed as planned after allowing for the actual performance on the part of other managers or factors.*

NOTE: Traditionally an allowance as defined above is referred to as a standard cost, so that the £1,500 allowance above would be called the standard cost of 500 units. This means that in the traditional terminology 'standard cost' refers to a planned cost set for a single cost unit for an indefinite period and also the expected cost of a particular number of units for a single particular period. This can lead to confusion and so the use of two different terms is strongly advised. Students are, however, warned that in examinations the expression 'standard cost' may well be used where they would expect the word 'allowance'.

12. The comparison rule. Clearly, measuring the performance of a manager (or factor) will be based on the manager's (or factor's) performance in relation to the allowance. It is no use looking at the original fixed budget figure, for such a figure relates almost certainly to a quite different set of circumstances from those which appertain at the time of the actual performance. It follows, then, that it is a fundamental rule in performance measurement that actuals must only be compared with allowances – never with budgets.

13. Control plans. Obviously, in order to be able to compute allowances it is necessary to analyze the fixed budget in terms of fixed and variable costs. Furthermore, such an analysis must also be in terms of detailed economic factors, and prepared in such a way that allowances can be easily and unambiguously computed. As the ultimate objective is to help managers to control their performances the resulting statements can be called *control plans*.

Although in theory one single control plan should be possible, in practice this work is more effectively carried out by using two kinds of plans, as follows.

(*a*) *Flexible budgets*. These are plans that relate specifically to periods of time, overheads and budget centres.

(*b*) *Standard costs*. These are plans that relate specifically to single cost units.

When preparing control plans it is necessary to prepare the flexible budgets first since these provide the standard overhead rates which are needed to prepare the standard costs of the cost units.

14. Control periods. Fixed budgets are generally made for a relatively long period of time – normally one year. This, of course, is far too long a period for effective performance measurement where comparisons must be made at intervals of no more than a month at most. In consequence the final control plans must relate to such shorter control periods.

Flexible budgets

These budgets are prepared with the aim of providing both standard overhead rates for inclusion into the standard costs and also overhead allowances which can be compared with the actual overheads so that performance is respect of these overheads can be measured.

15. Flexible budget. This is 'a budget which, by recognizing the difference in behaviour between fixed and variable costs in relation to fluctuations in output, turnover, or other variable factors such as number of employees, is designed to change appropriately with such fluctuations' (CIMA terminology) – in other words, one that changes (flexes) in accordance with the level of activity actually attained. As a by-product it also enables standard overhead rates to be calculated.

Preparing a flexible budget in effect is simply a matter of analyzing the overheads into fixed and variable elements and determining the extent to which the variable overheads will vary within the relevant range of activity. There are two methods of preparing such a budget.

16. Preparation of a flexible budget: formula method.

(a) *Before* the period begins:

(i) budget for a normal level of activity;
(ii) segregate the fixed and variable overheads;
(iii) compute the variable overhead per unit of activity.

(b) At the *end* of the period:

(i) ascertain the actual activity;
(ii) compute the variable overheads allowed for this level and add the fixed overheads to give the budget overhead allowance (this is known as 'flexing the budget').

This is expressed in the formula:

Allowed overhead =

$$\text{Fixed} \atop \text{overhead} \quad + \quad \left(\begin{array}{c} \text{Actual units of activity} \\ \text{for period} \end{array} \times \begin{array}{c} \text{Variable overhead per} \\ \text{unit of activity} \end{array} \right)$$

EXAMPLE:

	Preparation of flexible budget before period begins:				Application of flexible budget at end of period: Actual activity attained: 900 hours	
	Budgeted activity: 800 hours					
Overhead	Budget *	Fixed o'h'ds *	Var. o'h'ds *	Var. o'h'd per hr. of activity	Var. o'h'ds allowed	Total budget o'h'd allowance
	£	£	£	£	£	£
Power	400	—	400	0.5	450	450
Rent	800	800	—	—	—	800
Indirect labour	2,300	700	1,600	2.0	1,800	2,500
Maintenance	900	100	800	1.0	900	1,000
Heat and light	200	40	160	0.2	180	220
Supervision	1,000	760	240	0.3	270	1,030
Total £	5,600	2,400	3,200	4.0	3,600	6,000

*The figures in these columns are assumed in this example. In practice, they would be found by first preparing a fixed budget and then segregating the fixed and variable overheads by the analysis detailed in 10: **20–21**.

The figures in the overhead allowance column are then ready for comparing with the actual overhead costs for the period.

17. Preparation of a flexible budget: multi-activity method. The alternative method of preparing a flexible budget involves preparing a budget for every major level of activity. When the actual level of activity is known the allowed overhead is found by interpolating between the budgeted overheads for the activity levels on either side.

EXAMPLE:

Overhead	Activity level: % capacity					
	50%	60%	70%	80%	90%	100%
	£	£	£	£	£	£
Rent	500	500	500	500	500	500
Depreciation	400	400	400	450	500	500
Indirect labour	2,000	2,400	2,800	3,200	3,600	4,000
Indirect materials	100	100	120	140	150	160
Power	100	120	140	160	180	200
Supervision	1,000	1,000	1,000	1,100	1,400	1,500
Maintenance	300	300	350	450	600	900
Storekeeping	200	200	250	250	300	300
Administration	1,300	1,400	1,500	1,700	2,000	2,000
Total £	5,900	6,420	7,060	7,950	9,230	10,060

If the actual activity level were, say, 72 per cent, the allowed overheads would be computed by interpolating between the 70 per cent and 80 per cent budget levels (i.e. adding two-tenths of the difference to the 70 per cent figures) as follows:

	£
Rent	500
Depreciation	410
Indirect labour	2,880
Indirect materials	124
Power	144
Supervision	1,020
Maintenance	370
Storekeeping	250
Administration	1,540
Total	£7,238

Again, the allowances are ready for comparing with the actual overheads.

18. Choice of method of preparation. The choice of method depends primarily upon how 'fixed' the fixed overheads are. If they are likely to change significantly over the relevant range of activity (due to large stepped fixed costs *see* 10: **12**), the second method should be employed. If, on the other hand, fixed overheads remain relatively unchanged over this range, the first method is perfectly satisfactory and requires less work in preparation.

19. Measuring activity. The problem of measuring activity arises very much when flexible budgets are being prepared (see 10: **17**).

20. Flexible budgeting chart. Finally a chart summarizing the main steps taken in flexible budgeting is given in Fig. 17.2. The last step, the comparison of the actual overhead costs with the allowances, will be discussed in the next chapter.

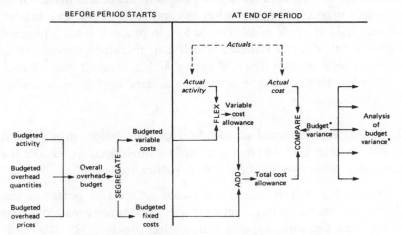

Figure 17.2 *Main steps in flexible budgeting*

Before the period begins budgeted fixed and variable overheads must be segregated. At the end of the period the actual figures are compared with the budget allowances (*not* with the original budgeted figures). Determining the variable overhead allowances is called 'flexing the budget'.

See **16.**

Standard costs

The second stage in planning for control involves planning the unit direct costs and incorporating the unit overheads, i.e. preparing the standard costs.

21. Standard cost. This is a *cost plan relating to a single cost unit.*

It covers all aspects of the cost plan including the planned sales margin and the selling price.

Note that traditionally a standard cost is defined as 'a pre-determined calculation of how much costs should be under specified working conditions' (CIMA terminology). Clearly, under this definition a flexed flexible budget is a standard cost (*see*, too, Note to **11**). For reasons of clarity the modern definition given above will be used in explaining the various control procedures and calculations in this book.

22. Cost standards. As was explained in 1 : **10**, every cost consists of a usage component and a price component. Consequently, when planning a cost, it is necessary to plan both usage and price. Often it is also necessary to plan other factors, such as the specification of material, or grade of labour, or loss in process. Such a planned figure is called a *cost standard* which can, therefore, be defined as *a usage, price or other standard upon which a standard cost is based*.

Clearly, the first step in setting a standard cost is to determine the cost standards.

23. Ideal and expected standards. However, before management begins to determine the cost standards it must decide which of the following two types of standards it wishes to use.

(*a*) *Ideal standards* which are based on perfect performance. These assume no wastage, inefficiencies, idle time, breakdowns or other imperfections in the manufacturing process. The standards reflect only what would be necessary if everything went perfectly.

(*b*) *Expected standards* which are based on expected performance (albeit that the expected performance is assumed to be at high efficiency). Thus unavoidable wastage is allowed for, and a reasonable allowance made for breakdowns and other inevitable lapses from perfect efficiency.

Ideal standards are used to measure the loss resulting from imperfection and indicate the points where a close investigation may result in large savings. Unfortunately it is very difficult to reconcile the resulting ideal costs with the more realistic costs given by the fixed budget. In addition, since such standards can never be achieved in practice, they tend to dishearten managers. This is not true, however, of expected standards. Managers can hope to achieve and even better expected standards and, indeed, they pose a definite challenge. For both these reasons virtually all standards today are expected standards.

It should be noted, however, that such standards as a result fulfil two separate functions, that of a *criterion* and that of a *target*. These functions are occasionally opposed to each other, and so sometimes lead to awkward dilemmas (*see* **26** below).

24. Setting a standard cost. Setting a standard cost for a cost unit follows much the same procedure as preparing a job cost, except that planned figures are used in lieu of actuals. For any given cost unit the following standards must be set.

(*a*) *Standard direct material costs.* This calls for setting standard material specifications, the standard usage per unit of each kind of material used, the standard price of these materials and the standard material mix ratios and losses expected (*standard yield*) if process work is involved.

(*b*) *Standard direct wages costs.* This calls for setting the standard labour grades (i.e. the grades of labour to be employed on making the units), the standard labour times per unit of each grade of labour employed and the standard wage rates of those grades. Note that the standard labour times are traditionally referred to as the *unit standard hours*.

(*c*) *Standard direct expenses.* This calls for setting the unit cost of any direct expenses incurred in producing (or selling) the units.

(*d*) *Standard factory overhead costs.* This calls for setting predetermined rates (*see* 5:24) in respect of the variable and fixed overheads and then using these rates to compute the variable and fixed overhead costs per unit of production.

(*i*) *Standard factory variable overhead cost.* Setting this cost simply involves ascertaining how many units of activity the cost unit uses and multiplying this figure by the variable overhead rate per unit of activity (standard variable overhead rate) as given by the flexible budget. Thus, in the example in **16** it can be seen that the variable overhead rate is £4 per hour. If, then, a given cost unit were planned to take 12 hours, activity the standard variable overhead cost would be $12 \times £4 = £48$.

(*ii*) *Standard factory fixed overhead cost.* Setting this cost calls for a standard fixed overhead rate, which is determined by dividing the budgeted units of activity into the budgeted fixed overhead cost as given by the flexible budget. This rate is then multiplied by the units of activity used by the cost unit in the normal way to give the standard factory fixed overhead cost. Thus, in the example in **16** a budgeted activity of 800 hours and fixed overheads of £2,400 gives a standard fixed overhead rate of £2,400/800 = £3 per hour. If the planned activity units used by the cost unit were again 12 hours the standard factory fixed overhead cost would be £3 × 12 hours = £36.

Note that the procedure in (*ii*) only relates to the traditional method of standard costing since the modern method employs marginal costing.

(*e*) *Standard selling and distribution overhead costs.* The standard selling and distribution overhead costs of the unit are set in the same way as the unit standard manufacturing overhead costs.

(*f*) *Standard selling price and standard margin.* Finally the planned, standard, unit selling price is set, and by deducting from this the total unit standard cost the unit standard sales margin is found. Under the traditional technique this margin is the *standard profit* and under the modern technique it is the *standard contribution*.

25. Standard cost cards. All the above standards should be recorded on a *standard cost card*. Such a card, which is very similar to a job card, is made out for each cost unit manufactured and forms a complete record of all the cost standards and standard costs relating to that unit. In practice it should be laid out in such a way that the standard cost of the unit when only partly completed can be quickly found. This is important for valuing work in progress.

NOTE: When solving standard cost problems the standard cost card is an invaluable source of data. If an examination question does not give a standard cost card, students are strongly advised to prepare their own before attempting to calculate any of the variances discussed in Chapter 18.

26. Revision of standards. If some economic factor alters permanently (e.g. if the unions negotiate an increased wages rate), the question arises as to whether or not the standard cost should be amended. This problem can be considered both theoretically and practically as follows.

(*a*) In theory, this is one of the difficulties that arise from using a standard as both a plan and a target, because of the following factors.

(*i*) As a *plan*, standards should rarely be altered. A plan that was always changing would be quickly discredited. A relatively un-changing standard also enables comparisons to be made between different periods. Revise it too frequently and this advantage is lost.

(*ii*) As a *target*, standards must be revised. Out-of-date targets provide no incentive. There is no challenge in attempting to keep wages rates down to impossible levels.

(*b*) In practice, revising a standard cost involves considerable work and sometimes leads to serious confusion. For instance, the revision of one single minor raw material cost standard means a careful revision of:

(*i*) all standard cost cards of cost units using the material;

(*ii*) all price lists detailing standard prices of the material *and* products;

(*iii*) all valuations of stores, work-in-progress and finished goods stocks.

For all these reasons standard cost revisions are usually made only at year-ends. Where factors alter during the year, then in order to maintain the 'target' appeal of standards, the *effect* of the revision is allowed for in management statements, although the revision is not taken into the standard costs themselves.

Control profit budget

Once the flexible budgets and standard costs have been prepared all the planning is essentially complete. However, if only to prove the arithmetical accuracy of the analysis, it is useful to make a sum-mary of these control plans showing that adherence to them will in fact result in the budget profit given in the original fixed budget. Such a summary is called a *control profit budget*.

27. Preparation of a control profit budget.

(*a*) The budgeted units sales quantities as detailed in the operating profit budget are listed.

(b) Each budgeted quantity is multiplied by the unit margin as shown in the standard cost of the unit to give the budgeted product margin.

(c) The budgeted product margins are totalled to give the total budgeted margin. In the traditional method this is the total budgeted profit. In the modern method, however, it is the total budgeted contribution – and to obtain the budgeted profit all the budgeted fixed overheads in the flexible budgets must be added together and the total subtracted from the total budgeted margin.

If the analysis of the figures in the operating profit budget to the flexible budgets and the standard costs has been accurately made, the budgeted profit in (c) will be the same as the budgeted profit in the operating budget.

28. Subdivision of control plans into control periods. Since control budget periods are always very much shorter than operating budget periods it is necessary to subdivide the control plans accordingly. Fortunately this merely involves appropriately subdividing the sales in the operating sales budget and the fixed costs in the flexible budgets and then preparing short-term control profit budgets so that a control profit budget is obtained for each control period.

Often in examinations these short-term budgets are prepared on the assumption that the organization concerned has twelve identical control periods. Note, however, that identical control periods are neither necessary nor usual, for often seasonal factors result in sales differing from period to period. This means, of course, that the budgeted sales quantities heading the control profit budgets will be the quantities planned for *that specific budget period*. Fixed overheads can naturally also be treated in the same way if necessary. In this manner seasonality can be eliminated from the analysis of the subsequent performance data.

29. Example of the preparation of control plans. This example illustrates the full planning sequence from a set of original management plans. For simplicity the example involves an organization manufacturing only one product and, since flexible budgets have already been illustrated, only two very sparse flexible budgets are shown. The figures will be prepared in accordance with the traditional technique but **30** shows the changes that would follow a marginal cost form of analysis.

(a) *Management operating plans – one year.*
 (i) Planned production operations:
  (1) output for the year – 120,000 cwt of Z;
  (2) Z produced by mixing X and Y in the ratio of 3 : 2;
  (3) normal loss of 20 per cent input.
  (4) 75 employees working a 1,600 hour year.
 (ii) Planned sales: 120,000 cwt of Z.
 (iii) Planned prices and rates:
  X – £4 per cwt; Y – £10 per cwt; Z – £20 per cwt;
  Direct labour – £3 per hour;
  Production royalty – 20p per cwt.
 (iv) Planned overheads:
  (1) Factory: Variable overheads – £120,000;
          Fixed overheads – £480,000;
          Measure of activity – direct labour hours.
  (2) Marketing: Variable overheads – £96,000;
          Fixed overheads – £240,000;
          Measure of activity – cwt sold.
 (v) Planned control periods: management plan to have twelve identical control periods during the year.
 (b) *Operating profit (fixed) budget.* From the management operating plans the following operating budget can be prepared:

			£	£
Sales:	120,000 cwt Z at £20 cwt			2,400,000
Costs:	Factory: Direct materials:			
		X, 90,000 cwt at £4 cwt	360,000	
		Y, 60,000 cwt at £10 cwt	600,000	
		Direct wages:		
		120,000 hrs* at £3 hr	360,000	
		Direct expenses:		
		Production royalty at 20p cwt	24,000	
		Overheads: Fixed	480,000	
		Variable (with direct labour hrs)	120,000	
	Marketing: Overheads: Fixed		240,000	
		Variable (with cwt sold)	96,000	2,280,000
	Budgeted profit			£120,000

*75 employees × 1,600 hrs.

(c) *Flexible budgets.* From the management operating plans and the operating profit budget the following flexible budgets can be prepared:

(i) Factory: Budgeted activity 120,000 direct labour hrs.

Overheads	Fixed	Variable	Standard Variable per D.L. hr
	£	£	£
All	480,000	120,000	1

Standard fixed overhead rate per direct labour hour = £480,000/120,000 = £4 hr.

(ii) Marketing: Budgeted activity 120,000 cwt.

Overheads	Fixed	Variable	Standard Variable per cwt
	£	£	£
All	240,000	96,000	0.80

Standard fixed overhead rate per cwt = £240,000/120,000 = £2 cwt.

NOTE: Since there are twelve identical control periods during the year the fixed factory and marketing overheads per period will be £40,000 and £20,000 respectively.

(d) *Standard cost.* From the management operating plans, the operating profit budget and the flexible budgets, the following standard cost can be prepared:

		£
Standard Cost Card–1 cwt Z		
Standard direct materials: X, ($\frac{3}{5}$), 0.75 cwt at £4 cwt		3.00
Y, ($\frac{2}{5}$), 0.50 cwt at £10 cwt		5.00
	1.25 cwt	8.00
Standard loss (20%)	−0.25 cwt	–
Standard yield (80%) Z,	1.00 cwt	8.00
Standard direct wages: 1 D. labour hrs at £3 hr		3.00
Standard direct expenses: Production royalty per cwt		0.20
Standard factory variable o'h'ds: 1 D. labour hr at £1 hr		1.00
Standard factory fixed o'h'ds: 1 D. labour hr at £4 hr		4.00
Standard factory cost		16.20

Standard marketing variable o'h'ds: 1 cwt at £0.80 cwt	0.80
Standard marketing fixed o'h'ds: 1 cwt at £2 cwt	2.00
Standard total cost	19.00
Standard profit	1.00
Standard selling price	£20.00

(e) *Control profit budget.* From the operating profit budget (sales) and the standard cost the following control profit budget can be prepared:

	£
Budgeted profit: 120,000 cwt Z at £1 cwt	120,000

This budgeted profit agrees with that in the operating profit budget so confirming the mathematical accuracy of the analysis.

(f) *Control profit budget – first control period.* The management operating plans show that management planned to have twelve identical control periods during the year. As a result of this the control profit budget for each control period is easily prepared by dividing the overall control profit budget by twelve:

	£
Budgeted profit: 10,000 cwt Z at £1 cwt	10,000

NOTE: £10,000 per control period for twelve periods gives the £120,000 year's profit as laid down in the overall control profit budget.

30. Control plans under marginal costing technique. If the control plans above were prepared on the basis of the modern, marginal costing, technique the only differences would be as follows:

(a) The standard factory and marketing fixed overheads of £4 and £2 would be excluded from the standard cost in **29** (d) with the result that the standard total cost would be £13 and the standard margin (contribution) £7 cwt.

(b) The control profit budget in **29** (e) would be prepared as follows:

		£
Budgeted contribution: 120,000 cwt Z @ £7		840,000
Less budgeted fixed overheads: Factory	480,000	
Marketing	240,000	720,000
Budgeted profit		£120,000

And, of course, the first control period budget would need to be similarly amended.

Progress test 17

Principles

1. What are the main differences between the traditional and the modern techniques of profit control?   (**5, 6**)

2. What is a budget centre?   (**7**)

3. Why is a fixed budget inappropriate for performance measurement?   (**10**)

4. What is an allowance?   (**11**)

5. Distinguish between: (*a*) standard cost and flexible budget; (**13**(*b*)) standard cost and cost standard.   (**21, 22**)

6. What is the formula for calculating an overhead allowance? (**16**)

7. What cost standards are involved in setting: (*a*) a standard direct materials cost;   (**24**(*a*)) (*b*) a standard direct wages cost? (**24**(*b*))

8. How are standard overhead costs set?   (**24**(*d*))

9. What is: (*a*) a standard sales margin;   (**24**(*f*)) (*b*) a standard cost card?   (**25**)

10. Should standards be revised?   (**26**)

11. How is a control profit budget prepared?   (**27**)

12. How do control plans prepared on the basis of the modern marginal costing technique differ from those prepared on the basis of the traditional technique?   (**30**)

Practice

13. (*a*) From the information given in the following fixed budget prepare on an absorption cost basis all the necessary control

plans:

Budgeted Profit and Loss Account for Year

	£	£
Sales: 1,000 15-gal containers of Z at £600 each		600,000
Costs:		
Dept. 1: 20,000 gal A at £3 gal	60,000	
30,000 hrs Grade I direct labour at £3 hr	90,000	
20,000 hrs Grade II direct labour at £1.50 hr	30,000	
Variable overheads (variable with process hrs)	125,000	
Fixed overheads	55,000	
Dept. 2: 1,000 empty containers at £8 each	8,000	
12,000 direct labour hrs at £2 hr	24,000	
Variable overheads (variable with indirect labour hrs)	8,000	
Fixed overheads	14,000	
Marketing: Variable overheads (variable with units sold)	50,000	
Fixed overheads	60,000	524,000
Budgeted profit		£76,000

NOTE: Department 1 produces Z and has 25,000 budgeted process hours. Department 2 fills the containers with Z and has 4,000 budgeted indirect labour hours.

(*b*) Given that there are ten control periods of equal activity in each year, prepare the control profit budget for the first control period.

18

Variance analysis

Once the control plans have been completed the next step in the performance measurement routine is to await the end of the first control period. Once this moment has passed all the *actual* operating figures should be collected as quickly as possible. As soon as this is done the actuals should be compared with their allowances and an analysis of the differences made. Such an analysis is called a *variance analysis*.

Mathematical principles of variance analysis

Differences between actuals and allowances should not be computed in a disorganized manner for the dangers of differences overlapping or failing to be analyzed at all are too great to risk. So before looking at the various differences that can arise it is necessary to outline in this section a theoretical basis on which an analysis can be constructed.

1. **Profit variances.** When comparing an actual and an allowed figure a difference is usually found to exist. If this difference is valued so that the effect on the profit is measured then the valuation is referred to as a profit variance. For instance, in the example earlier (*see* 17: 11) the departmental manager's actual expenditure was £1,400 and his allowance was £1,500. Since the difference of £100 directly measured the effect on profit, the £100 is a profit variance. A *profit variance*, then, can be defined as a measure of the effect on profit of a given manager's performance or factor diverging from plan (note that this is not the same as *the* profit variance – *see* 7). Since in computing an allowance we adjust for all the

actual circumstances except those in relation to the manager or factor under consideration, the difference between actual and allowance must measure the effect of that manager or factor, *and no other*, diverging from plan.

To take a further illustration, assume we plan to use 5 kg of A at 10p per kg per cost unit produced and actually use 10,240 kg producing 2,000 units. Our allowed usage for 2,000 units is clearly $2,000 \times 5 = 10,000$ kg and so we used 240 kg of A too much. And 240 kg at 10p per kg means the profit would be reduced by £24 as a result of our performance. We would, therefore, have a variance of £24.

The following points should be noted:

(*a*) A profit variance measures the effect on *profit*, not anything else. Thus if sales were planned to be £5,000 and actually amounted to £4,000 the divergence of £1,000 would not be a profit variance since the profit would not be affected to the extent of £1,000 (in fact the £1,000 is known as a *sales* variance).

(*b*) A profit variance is a *monetary* figure. If sales were planned to be 300 units and only 200 were actually sold, the 100 units deficit would not be a profit variance. Not until this 100 deficit is valued in terms of the effect on profit is a profit variance produced.

Profit variances are not the only kind of variances (e.g. the difference between an actual and planned cash receipt would be a *cash* variance). These, however, are virtually the only variances examined upon and so the only ones discussed in this book.

2. Variance computation. As already indicated, the computation of a profit variance essentially involves no more than the valuation of the difference between an actual and an allowance. However, to state it more explicitly, it can be said that to compute a profit variance for any given factor it is necessary to:

(*a*) compute the allowance for that factor on the basis of the planned factor details given in the operating plans;

(*b*) ascertain the actual figure;

(*c*) find the divergence between actual and allowance;

(*d*) value the divergence in terms of the effect on profit.

3. Direction and name of variance. All profit variances must meet the following criteria.

(*a*) *They must state the direction of the profit effect*, i.e. state if the divergence affects the profit favourably or adversely. Note that:

(*i*) a *favourable variance* (denoted by an F) is one which on its own would result in the ultimate profit being higher than planned;

(*ii*) an *adverse variance* (denoted by an A) is one which on its own would result in the ultimate profit being lower than planned.

The two variances illustrated earlier, then, would be reported as £100F and £24A respectively.

(*b*) *They must be named.* Naming a profit variance is simply a matter of identifying it to the people involved in the profit control system. The name can, then, be whatever people choose. Some variances have fairly obvious names – those that measure the effect on profit of material price divergences are commonly called material price variances. Others, such as the variance that measures the effect on profit of a particularly cold spell coinciding with a fuel shortage, do not have such obvious names. In general, however, an individual variance can be defined as follows:

An X variance (where X is the factor under analysis) *is the variance arising due to the actual X diverging from the planned X* (e.g. a *materials price* variance is the variance arising due to the actual *materials price* diverging from the planned *materials price*).

Since all variances can be defined in this general form no variances will be specifically defined in the text.

4. All valuations to be at standard. It can be regarded as an absolute rule that valuations in a standard cost and budgetary control system *must be made at standard* (i.e. standard price or standard cost). This rule includes both the valuations of divergences which are initially in physical units and also valuations of stock in the 'actual profit' statement. Proving the validity of this rule would lead into deep water but essentially it arises from the fact that isolating variances adjusts for the difference between actual and standard values and to use actual values for valuing would therefore result in double counting. So failure to observe this rule will result in a non-balancing analysis and also in variances appearing in the wrong control periods.

It will be appreciated that this rule also meets the need of providing performance measurement data in logical management terms since a manager responsible for the *usage* of a resource will expect any divergence between the allowance and actual usage to be valued at the price he agreed to when the plans were made (i.e. at standard) rather than some subsequent actual price over which he had no control.

5. **'And every plan shall have its variance.'** Every planned factor will have its associated variance since each factor plan will enable a factor allowance to be computed – and comparison of this with the factor actual will reveal the factor divergence. It must, however, be admitted that finding every factor variance does depend upon the actuals being reported in parallel with the control plans. This is not always possible, though an effective standard cost and budgetary control system will be designed with this need in mind.

6. **Segregating an actual semi-variable.** One instance in which it is often impossible to ascertain an actual factor in parallel with a planned factor relates to the semi-variable overheads. A semi-variable overhead plan sets both a budgeted fixed overhead and a variable overhead per unit of activity. It is, however, usually impossible to segregate an *actual* semi-variable into its fixed and variable components. As can be seen in Fig. 10.7, the segregation technique depends upon the existence of a number of points on a graph. Just one point is not sufficient. Of course, if the semi-variable is made up of two distinct costs (e.g. an electricity standing charge and a unit charge) its segregation is possible, but usually there is no way of breaking down the actual semi-variable into its two components (do *not* fall into the trap of arguing that the actual fixed component must, by definition, be the same as the budgeted fixed component). This means that the two semi-variable allowances – the fixed allowance and the variable allowance – cannot be compared with separate actuals but can only be added together and compared in total with the total actual semi-variable overhead.

It should be appreciated that in examinations this limitation on the provision of actual figures does not, of course, apply, and separate actuals may in fact be given in any of the questions.

7. **The profit variance.** Of all the variances, the most important is the one that measures the divergence of the actual profit from

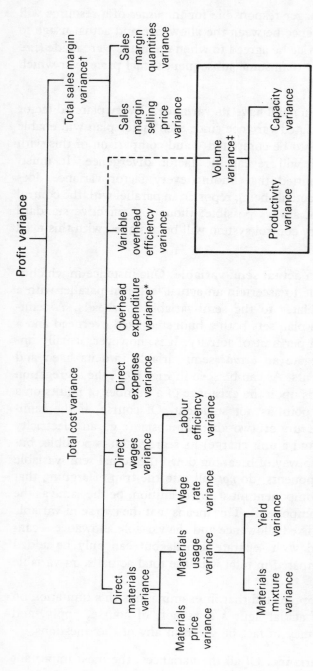

*If an examination question gives the actual fixed and variable overheads as separate figures, this variance can be analyzed into a fixed overhead expenditure variance and a variable overhead expenditure variance.

†In standard absorption costing the sales margin is the profit margin, whereas in standard marginal costing it is the contribution.

‡This variance, and its sub-variances, only arises if standard absorption costing is employed.

Figure 18.1 *Chart of common cost variances*

the allowed profit – the *profit variance*. If the variance is favourable there is much good cheer. If adverse, then there is gloom in proportion to the size of the variance.

8. Variance analysis. Good cheer or gloom, once the profit variance is known, management will quickly wish to know in detail just how it arose. The analysis providing this is called a *variance analysis* and is prepared by finding the variance associated with each planned factor in the control plans. This involves taking the flexible budgets, standard costs and control profit budget together with the actual results and computing, factor by factor, the variances arising. Needless to say, the sum of all the variances identified in a variance analysis must equal the profit variance.

9. Chart of profit variances. There is a virtually infinite number of differing kinds of profit variances that can arise in practice. Nevertheless there are some that are common to most organizations and these variances are shown in Fig. 18.1 in their hierarchical form. Note that the main effect of using absorption costing rather than marginal costing is to create an additional series of variances – though, as will be seen in **28**, the sales margin quantity variances arising under the two techniques will differ, since under marginal costing the sales margin is measured in terms of unit contribution, while under absorption costing it is measured in terms of unit profit.

It should also be appreciated that any variance can be found by summing its sub-variances (so that, for example, the direct wages variance can be found by adding the wage rate and labour efficiency variances together).

Absorption variance analysis

We start by looking at the preparation of a variance analysis using the technique of standard absorption costing. To illustrate the mechanics of making the analysis the control plans in the example in 17: **29**, will be used in connection with an assumed set of actual figures for the first control period which are shown below. Whenever the subsequent text refers to an 'actual' amount, it is in the following figures that the required amount will be found.

Actual Profit and Loss Account – Control Period 1

					£	£
Sales: 7,000 cwt Z						136,400

Costs: Materials X   Y

	cwt	£	cwt	£		
Purchases	6,600	27,840	5,000	49,560	77,400	
To stock (at standard)	−500	−2,000	−600	−6,000	−8,000	
Issues	6,100	25,840	4,400	43,560	69,400	

	£
Direct wages: 8,850 hrs	26,800
Factory overheads	46,200
Production royalty	2,000
Cost of production (8,000 cwt Z)	144,400
Less Finished goods stock: 1,000 cwt at £16.20 cwt*	−16,200
	128,200
Marketing overheads	22,100
Cost of sales	150,300 150,300
Actual loss	£13,900

*Note the valuation of stock at standard cost (17: **29**(*d*)).

10. Profit variance. As previously indicated, the profit variance is found by comparing the actual profit with the budgeted profit as shown by the control profit budget for the corresponding period. In our illustration this involves comparing our actual loss of £13,900 as shown above with our budgeted profit of £10,000 as shown in 17: **29**(*f*). The profit variance for control period 1 is, therefore, £23,900A, and it is this amount we need to analyze in our illustrative variance analysis. We will, therefore, take each planned factor in turn and find its corresponding variances.

11. Materials price variance. This arises on the purchase of materials and is found by comparing the actual purchase cost with the purchase cost allowance. This allowance is, of course, what the purchase would have cost if the planned (standard) price had been paid, i.e. it is the actual quantity at the standard price. Since every

£1 over- or under-spent affects the profit by £1 the difference be-tween the actual cost and this allowance gives the materials price variance.

EXAMPLE:

	X	Y
Actual quantity purchased (cwt)	6,600	5,000
Standard price (per cwt) 17: **29**(*d*)	£4	£10
Purchase cost allowance	£26,400	£50,000
Actual cost	£27,840	£49,560
Materials price variance	£1,440A	£440F

This variance is, of course, the responsibility of the buyer.

NOTE: No variance arises on the purchase of more or less materials than planned (other than perhaps minor stockholding cost variances) since the profit is unaffected by such divergences – the excess or deficit merely affecting stock levels.

12. Materials usage variance. This is found by comparing the actual materials usage with the usage allowance and valuing any difference at the standard price of the material.

If the planned quantity of material had been used each time a unit was produced then the total material usage would be equal to the number of units produced multiplied by the standard usage. This, then, is the usage allowance and any usage above or below this allowance will affect the profit to the extent of the value of the over- or under-usage.

EXAMPLE:

	X	Y
Units produced, Z (cwt)	8,000	8,000
Standard usage (17: **29**(*d*))	0.75 cwt	0.50 cwt
Usage allowance	6,000 cwt	4,000 cwt
Actual usage	6,100 cwt	4,400 cwt
Difference	100A cwt	400A cwt
Standard price per cwt (17: **29**(*d*))	£4	£10
Materials usage variance	£400A	£4,000 A

This variance is the responsibility of the manager of the produc-tion department concerned.

13. Materials mix and yield variances. Where materials are planned to be mixed in given proportions and a planned loss on process is laid down, it is useful if the materials usage variance is further analyzed into mixture and yield variances which are computed as follows.

(*a*) *Materials mix variance.* The easiest way to compute this is to find the allowed mix value of the total *input* (in other words, ask yourself what the *actual input would have cost* if the materials had been mixed in the planned proportions) and compare this with the actual value of the input (using standard prices for valuing, of course). Clearly, if the materials had been mixed in exactly the planned proportions these two figures would be identical and, almost equally clearly, every £1 extra of actual value is, in fact, an overspending of £1 and therefore a reduction of the profit by this amount.

So a materials mix variance is computed by taking the difference between the allowed mix value of the input and the actual value.

EXAMPLE:

$$
\begin{array}{lllll}
\text{Total actual input:} & \text{X} & 6{,}100 \text{ cwt at } £4 & = £24{,}400 \\
& \text{Y} & \underline{4{,}400} \text{ cwt at } £10 & = \underline{44{,}000} \\
& & 10{,}500 \text{ cwt} & £68{,}400
\end{array}
$$

Standard cost of 1.25 cwt of input
  mix (17: **29**(*d*)) = £8

∴ Allowed value of input mix of

$$10{,}500 \text{ cwt} = \frac{10{,}500}{1.25} \times £8 \qquad\qquad = \underline{67{,}200}$$

Materials mix variance $\qquad\qquad\qquad$ £1,200A

(*b*) *Materials yield variance.* This is found by comparing the actual yield with the allowed yield and valuing the difference at the standard cost per unit of *output*. The allowed yield is quite simply the actual input multiplied by the standard yield. Note that the difference must be valued at the standard cost per unit of *output* since every unit lost (or gained) here is a unit of output and must be valued accordingly.

EXAMPLE:

Actual input (total)	10,500 cwt
Standard yield (17: **29**(*d*))	80%
Yield allowance	8,400 cwt
Actual yield	8,000 cwt
Difference	400A cwt
Standard cost of output (17: **29**(*d*))	£8 per cwt
Materials yield variance	£3,200A

(*c*) *Cross-check*. Since the mixture and yield variances are sub-variances of the usage variance, the sum of the two former must equal the latter. If they do not the analysis has been made incorrectly.

EXAMPLE:

Mix variance		£1,200A
Yield variance		3,200A
Total		£4,400A
Materials usage variance (**12**):	X	400A
	Y	4,000A
Total materials usage variance		£4,400A

The two totals agree and the analysis is therefore proved arithmetically accurate.

14. Wage rate variance. This is really a price variance in respect of the 'purchase' of labour and is found in exactly the same way as a price variance, i.e. it is the difference between the actual and allowed wages. The allowed wages, of course, are the wages that would have been paid if the standard rates had been paid and are computed by multiplying the actual hours worked by the standard wage rate.

EXAMPLE:

Actual hours worked	8,850
Standard wage rate (17: **29**(*d*))	£3 per hr
Wage allowance	£26,550
Actual wages	£26,800
Wage rate variance	£250A

The personnel manager will normally be responsible for this variance.

15. Labour efficiency variance. This is really a usage variance in respect of the 'usage' of labour time. It is called an 'efficiency' variance since the comparison of actual against planned times is a measure of labour efficiency.

To compute a labour efficiency variance, therefore, one merely finds the allowed time (i.e. how long would have been taken if the planned times had been adhered to) and compares this with the actual time. The difference is then valued at the standard wage rate.

EXAMPLE:

Units produced, Z	8,000 cwt
Standard time per cwt (17: **29**(*d*))	1 hr
Time allowance	8,000 hrs
Actual time taken	8,850 hrs
Difference	850A hrs
Standard wage rate (17: **29**(*d*))	£3 per hr
Labour efficiency variance	£2,550A

The manager responsible for the supervision of the labour will be responsible for this variance.

16. Direct expenses variance. This is no more than the difference between the actual and the allowed direct expenses – the latter being simply the actual number of units produced multiplied by the standard direct expenses shown on the standard cost card.

EXAMPLE:

Units produced, Z	8,000 cwt
Standard direct expense – royalty (17: **29**(*d*))	20p per cwt
Direct expense allowance	£1,600
Actual direct expense	£2,000
Direct expenses variance	400A

17. Overhead expenditure variance. This is found by computing the allowed overhead from the relevant flexible budget and comparing this allowance with the actual overhead incurred.

The only difficulty that may arise in finding this kind of variance could be in computing the allowance. In this regard remember that an overhead expenditure allowance is made up of two parts – a fixed allowance and a variable allowance. The fixed allowance is quite simply the budgeted fixed cost for the period, while the variable allowance is found by multiplying the *actual* units of activity by the standard cost per unit of activity. Adding these two allowances gives the total overhead expenditure allowance and the difference between this and the actual expenditure gives the required overhead expenditure variance (since every £1 overspent is £1 less profit).

EXAMPLE (using the illustrative figures):

	Factory	Marketing dept.
Actual activity	8,850 D.L. hrs	7,000 cwt Z
Standard cost per unit activity (17: **29**(*c*))	£1 per hr	£0.80 per cwt
Variable overhead allowance	£8,850	£5,600
Fixed overhead allowance: one control period (17:**29**(*c*))	£40,000	£20,000
Total overhead allowance	£48,850	£25,600
Actual overheads	£46,200	£22,100
Overhead expenditure variance	£2,650F	£3,500F

The relevant departmental managers will, of course, be responsible for these variances.

As indicated earlier, it sometimes happens in examination questions that the actual fixed and variable overheads are given separately. When this occurs separate fixed and variable overhead expenditure variances can be computed by comparing the given actuals with the corresponding allowances.

EXAMPLE: If the actual factory overheads had been given as £40,200 fixed and £6,000 variable, the following variances could have been computed:

Fixed overhead expenditure allowance (as above):	£40,200
Actual fixed overhead expenditure	40,200
Fixed overhead expenditure variance	200A
Variable overhead expenditure allowance (as above)	8,850
Actual variable overhead expenditure	6,000
Variable overhead expenditure variance	£2,850F

18. Variable overhead efficiency variance. This is perhaps the most complex of the variances. It arises because an expenditure allowance is based on the units of *activity* undertaken, *not* the units of production. Thus if 10 units of activity having a standard cost of £2 per unit of activity are undertaken there will be an expenditure allowance of £20. If then £20 is spent there will be no expenditure variance. But it may be that only 3 units of *production*, each having a standard activity of 2 units of activity, were produced. This means these 3 units of production should have required (have an allowance of) 6 units of activity. Since 10 units of activity were actually undertaken then $10 - 6 = 4$ units of activity were in excess of plan. And as variable costs are incurred on each and every unit of *activity* (as against unit of production) then an excess variable cost equal to the variable costs of these 4 units of activity will be incurred, which will reduce the profit by this amount. (In other words there was an under-recovery of the variable cost of 4 units of activity.) This loss will be the variable overhead efficiency variance (since it arises on account of the inefficient use of overhead facilities).

To find a variable overhead efficiency variance, then, it is necessary to take the following steps.

(*a*) Find the *allowed* activity by multiplying the units of production by the standard activity as laid down in the standard cost.

(*b*) Compare this allowance with the *actual* units of activity undertaken.

(*c*) Value the difference at the *standard cost per unit of activity*.

EXAMPLE:

Actual production, Z	8,000 cwt
Standard activity (17: **29**(*d*))	1 D.L. hr.

Activity allowance 8,000 hrs
Actual activity 8,850 hrs

Difference 850A
Standard cost (17: **29**(*d*)) £1 per hr
∴ *Variable overhead efficiency variance* £850A

This variance will be the responsibility of the manager responsible for the efficient use of the overhead facilities.

NOTE: If activity is measured in cost units (as it is in the marketing budget centre), the allowed units of activity will, in fact, be the actual units produced and so no overhead efficiency variance can arise. In other words, the variance only arises where the overheads are incurred on a basis *other than* costs units and where, therefore, a divergence can arise between the overheads allowed on the basis of activity and the overheads allowed on the basis of cost units (indeed, the variance can be computed using just this approach: e.g. allowed variable overheads on basis of units of activity − allowed variable costs on basis of cost units = (8,850 direct labour hours × £1 standard variable overheads per hour) − (8,000 cwt of Z produced × £1 standard variable costs per cwt) = £8,850 − £8,000 = £850A).

19. Volume variance. In 5: **24**(*b*) it was pointed out that a predetermined overhead recovery rate could fail to recover exactly the actual overheads incurred. This failure arises because either the actual overheads are not identical in amount to that budgeted, or the actual production is not as budgeted, or both. In a variance analysis the first of these differences is measured by the overhead expenditure variance. This leaves the second of the differences still to be accounted for and it is the function of the volume variance to do this. In effect a *volume variance* measures the under- or over-recovery of fixed overheads due to the actual volume of production differing from the planned (note that only the *fixed* overheads are involved since the variable overheads automatically rise and fall with production so that a fall, say, in production is matched by a fall in these overheads − which, by definition, is not the case with the fixed overheads).

To compute the volume variance, the allowed volume (i.e. the budgeted production) is compared with the actual volume and the difference valued at the standard fixed overhead cost per unit of production.

EXAMPLE:

(a) *Factory*

Volume allowance (17: **29**(f))	10,000 cwt
Actual production	8,000 cwt
Difference	2,000A cwt
Standard fixed overhead cost (17: **29**(d))	£4 per cwt
∴ *Factory volume variance*	£8,000A

(b) *Marketing*

Volume allowance (17: **29**(f))	10,000 cwt
Actual sales*	7,000 cwt
Difference	3,000A cwt
Standard fixed overhead cost (17: **29**(d))	£2 per cwt
∴ *Marketing volume variance*	£6,000A

*Marketing overheads are recovered using a *sales* absorption rate (and the volume allowance is, of course, unit sales).

In the case of production a volume variance can arise either because more (or less) labour hours were worked than planned or because the labour force worked more (or less) efficiently, or both. A production volume variance can, therefore, be analyzed into variances measuring the effect of both these factors.

20. Productivity variance. A *productivity variance* (or volume efficiency variance or fixed overhead efficiency variance as it is sometimes called) measures the under- or over-recovery of fixed overheads due to the efficiency of direct labour. Since for every hour worked the labour force should produce its planned hourly production then every hour worked during which production does not materialize results in the under-recovery of one hour's fixed overheads. The productivity variance can, therefore, be calculated by comparing the actual hours worked with the number of hours that should have been worked in view of the actual production (the allowed hours) and valuing the difference at the standard fixed overhead rate per hour.

EXAMPLE:

Allowed hours for 8,000 cwt $Z = 8,000 \times 1$		
(17: **29**(*d*))	=	8,000 hrs
Actual hours		8,850 hrs
Difference		850A hrs
Standard fixed overhead rate per hour		
(17: **29**(*c*))		£4
∴ *Productivity variance*		£3,400A

21. Standard hours production. It will be noticed that in calculating all three of the efficiency variances in the illustration (direct labour efficiency, variable overhead efficiency and productivity) an allowance of 8,000 hours was used. Whenever production overheads are recovered on an hourly basis (which is usually the case when absorption costing is used) it sometimes pays to measure production in terms of allowed hours – and this is particularly so where many different kinds of cost units are produced and a common measure is needed to find the overall production. In such circumstances the allowed hours are called *standard hours* and all production is measured in these hours. In our illustration, therefore, we can say that there were 8,000 standard hours of production.

In passing it may be worth noting that since all the efficiency variances arise from the performance of the direct labour, some authorities hold that all these variances should be referred to as labour efficiency variances.

22. Capacity variance. This measures the under- or over-recovery of fixed overheads due to the actual hours worked differing from the budgeted hours. In our illustration the allowance for this variance is the budgeted hours and the form of computation follows the previous pattern.

EXAMPLE:

Allowance: 120,000 hrs for year	
(17: **29**(*c*)) ÷ 12	10,000 hrs
Actual worked	8,850 hrs
Difference	1,150A hrs

Standard fixed overhead rate per hour
(17: **29**(*c*))   £4
∴   *Capacity variance*   £4,600A

Note that the sum of the capacity variance (£4,600A) and the productivity variance (£3,400A) equals the total factory volume variance (£8,000A).

23. Sales margin selling price variance. This is just another instance of the ordinary price variances discussed earlier. It is therefore found by comparing the actual sales value with the allowed sales value. This allowance is simply the amount one would have obtained if all sales had been at the planned selling price and so is found by multiplying the actual sales quantity by the standard selling price. Again, since every £1 obtained above the planned selling price increases the profit by £1, the difference between the actual and allowed sales values is the sales margin selling price variance.

EXAMPLE:

Actual quantity sold, Z	7,000 cwt
Standard selling price (17: **29**(*d*))	£20 per cwt
Sales value allowance	£140,000
Actual sales value	136,400
Sales margin selling price variance	£3,600A

This variance is, of course, the responsibility of the sales manager.

24. Sales margin quantities variance. This measures the effect on profit of actual sales quantities falling below or exceeding the planned quantities, i.e. budgeted quantities. Since the profit is affected by the profit margin associated with the deficient or excess units, the variance is found by comparing the actual sales quantities with the allowed (budgeted) quantity and valuing the difference at the standard profit.

EXAMPLE:

Sales quantity allowance, Z (17: **29**(*f*))	10,000 cwt
Actual sales quantity	7,000 cwt

Difference	3,000 cwt
Standard margin – profit (17: **29**(*d*))	£1 cwt
Sales margin quantities variance	£3,000A

Normally, this variance is the responsibility of the sales manager. If, however, for some reason he was not provided with sufficient units to sell (e.g. because of production failures), the variance will be charged to whoever and whatever caused the shortfall.

One final point – it should be appreciated that sales margin variances all relate to *margin* variances and not sales value variances (i.e. divergences from planned sales values) since the latter are not profit variances and do not therefore automatically measure the effect on profit of a divergence from plan. As it happens, in the case of the sales margin selling price variance we can use sales values since fortuitously, as has been pointed out, every extra £1 we obtain on the selling price is £1 extra profit. But this, of course, is not so in the case of the sales margin quantities variance for if, in our illustration, we compare the allowed quantity at the standard *selling price* with the actual quantity at the standard selling price we obtain sales values of $10,000 \times £20 - 7,000 \times £20 = 200,000 - 140,000 = £60,000$. This £60,000 is the sales *value* quantities variance but it certainly isn't the sales margin quantities variance.

25. Summary of variances. At the end of the analysis the sub-variances should, of course, equal the profit variance. This will prove the arithmetical accuracy of the analysis.

EXAMPLE:

Variance	£
Materials price (**11**): X	1,440A
Y	440F
Materials mix (**13**(*a*))	1,200A
Materials yield (**13**(*b*))	3,200A
Wage rate (**14**)	250A
Labour efficiency (**15**)	2,550A
Direct expenses (**16**)	400A
Overhead expenditure (**17**): Factory	2,650F
Marketing	3,500F

Variable overhead efficiency (18): Factory	850A
Production volume: Productivity (20)	3,400A
Capacity (22)	4,600A
Marketing volume (19(b))	6,000A
Sales margin selling price (23)	3,600A
Sales margin quantities (24)	3,000A
Profit variance (10)	23,900A

Marginal variance analysis

From the point of view of computing variances the modern technique of variance analysis is not so very different from that of absorption variance analysis. In this brief section those variances which are *not* the same under the two techniques are illustrated.

26. Profit variance. An important point which must not be overlooked when working with marginal variance analyses is that all stocks are valued at standard marginal cost. In the case of the raw materials stocks, the valuations will be the same regardless of which technique is used, but this is not so when it comes to finished goods stocks. And changing the value of the finished goods stocks changes, of course, the *actual* profit for the period which in turn changes the profit variance.

EXAMPLE:

Finished goods:	
1,000 units @ absorption factory standard cost of £16.20 (17: 29(d))	£16,200
@ marginal factory standard cost of £12.20*	£12,200
Reduction in stock value	£4,000

*£16.20 per unit – standard fixed overhead of £4 (17: 29(c)(i)) = £12.20

So the actual profit for the period will be reduced by £4,000, which in this case means the loss will increase from £13,900 to £17,900.

∴ *Profit variance* = 10,000 – 17,900 loss = £27,900A

27. Volume, productivity and capacity variances. Since under marginal costing fixed overheads are not charged in any way to cost units, in a marginal variance analysis the volume, productivity and capacity variances disappear completely. The disappearance of these variances means that the only overhead variances left are the variable overhead efficiency and the overhead expenditure. And in the case of these variances the method of computation remains unchanged.

28. Sales margin quantities variance. Under standard marginal costing the unit sales margin is, of course, the unit standard contribution. In computing the sales margin quantities variance, then, the margin figure used will be the standard contribution. Apart from this, the computation is identical to that illustrated in **24**.

EXAMPLE:

Sales quantity allowance, Z (**24**)	10,000 cwt
Actual sales quantity	7,000 cwt
Difference	3,000 cwt
Standard margin – contribution (17: **30**(*a*))	£7 per cwt
Sales margin quantities variance	£21,000A

29. Summary of variances. As will be appreciated, in view of the small number of differences the summary of the marginal cost variances will be substantially the same as that of the absorption variances.

EXAMPLE:

Summary as in **25** except that the two production volume variances and the marketing volume variance will be excluded (i.e. complete exclusion of variances totalling 3,400A + 4,600A + 6,000A = 14,000A) while the sales margin quantities variance will change from £3,000A to £21,000A, an increase of £18,000A. This means the summary total in **25** (£23,900A) will be adjusted by these amounts, i.e. 23,900A – 14,000A + 18,000A = £27,900A.

And this is the profit variance computed in **26** above.

30. The sales margin quantities variance. Before leaving discussion of the individual variances in a variance analysis the importance of the sales margin quantities variance under the modern control technique should be appreciated, for, measuring as it does the contribution gained or lost as a result of a divergence between the actual and planned sales quantities, by its very nature it must measure (as its counterpart in standard absorption costing fails to do) the full impact on profits of the quantities divergence.

This variance is very much a key variance since the success of an enterprise is closely bound up with the level of its sales. For this reason any adverse amounts should be carefully considered. Although the responsibility for the variance often falls on the sales manager this is not by any means invariably so. If, for example, sales quantities were down because production failed to produce the units to sell then the variance must be charged to the production manager responsible. In such a case it would probably be worthwhile analyzing the variance so that the contribution lost as a result of strikes, absenteeism, breakdowns, etc., could be reported to the production manager.

Progress test 18

Principles

1. What is a profit variance and what determines the name of any given profit variance? (**1, 3**)

2. What is the general procedure for computing a profit variance? (**2**)

3. Why is it usually impossible to segregate an actual semi-variable cost into its fixed and variable components? (**6**)

4. What is the profit variance, how is it computed and how does it relate to a variance analysis? (**7, 8**)

5. How is an overhead expenditure variance computed? (**17**)

6. Explain how a variable overhead efficiency variance can arise. (**18**)

7. What is meant by standard hours production and why is this measure useful? (**21**)

8. Which variances have different values according to whether the analysis is prepared along traditional or modern lines? (**26–28**)

9. What is the significance of the sales margin quantities variance in a marginal costing analysis? (**30**)

Practice

10. Given that the cost standards are 20 gallons and £0.25 per gallon, compute the variances when the actuals are:

    (a) 24 gallons for a cost of £6;
    (b) 20 gallons for a cost of £7;
    (c) 24 gallons at £0.35 per gallon;
    (d) 18 gallons for a cost of £5.

11. Find the variances where the cost standards are 100 direct labour hours and £4 per hour and the actuals are:

    (a) 110 hours for a cost of £385;
    (b) 95 hours for a cost of £367.40.

12. Hydrogen pentoxide is prepared by mixing hydrogen and oxygen in the proportions of 1:5. The standard prices of these gases are £0.50 and £0.05 per cubic foot respectively. During the last production run 10,200 cubic feet of hydrogen was mixed with 57,600 cubic feet of oxygen. Compute the mix variance.

13. Pure wrot is prepared by boiling crude wrot (standard price £0.06 a load) until only 60 per cent of the original input remains. One day last period the process ran too long and a mere 726 loads of pure wrot emerged from an input of 1,500 loads of crude. What was the yield variance?

14. MUD is prepared by mixing M, U and D (standard prices £1, £2 and £3 per tonne respectively) in the proportions of 1:1:3. A standard loss of 20 per cent is allowed. Last period 1,100 tonnes of M costing £1,000, 1,000 tonnes of U costing £2,200 and 2,900 tonnes of D costing £8,888 were processed to give 3,815 tonnes of MUD. Find the variances.

15. A foundry producing castings of a standard alloy uses standard costs. The standard mixture is as follows:

40 per cent material A at £300 per tonne
30 per cent material B at £100 per tonne
10 per cent material C at £420 per tonne
20 per cent scrap metal of this alloy

It is expected that from each charge there will be a 5 per cent loss in melt, 35 per cent will be returned to scrap stock (runners, heads, etc.) and 60 per cent will be good castings. Scrap is credited and charged at the standard average cost of the metal mixture.

In a certain period the following materials are purchased and used:

380 tonnes material A at £310 per tonne
330 tonnes material B at £110 per tonne
90 tonnes material C at £420 per tonne
200 tonnes scrap metal at standard price

From this material, 608 tonnes of good castings are produced, and 340 tonnes of scrap metal are returned to scrap metal stock.

Present information to management, showing standard metal costs, and variances from standard in respect of this period.

(*CIMA*)

16. A sales department measures its activity in terms of sales invoices processed. It plans to average 5 articles per invoice. The standard marginal cost of every article carries the following entry: 'Variable sales dept. overheads: 10p.'

In the last period, 11,340 articles were invoiced using 2,504 invoices for a variable overhead cost of £1,521. Compute the relevant variances.

17. The sales budget of the Table & Chairs Co. Ltd. shows budgeted sales of 4,000 chairs at £5 each and 1,000 tables at £30 each. The standard cost of a chair is £2 and of a table £17. Actual sales for the period were 3,100 chairs for £15,215 and 1,200 tables for £35,682. Find the sales margin selling price and quantities variances.

18. The actual results of the company referred to in Progress test 17, question 13, for the first period were as follows:

		£	£
Sales: 95 15-gallon containers of Z			56,084
Costs: Purchases: A: 2,500 gal		7,720	
Containers: 100		794	
		8,514	
Less Closing stocks:			
A: 320 gal at £3	960		
Containers: 1 at £8	8	−968	
		7,546	
Dept. 1: D. labour, Grade I: 2,941 hrs		8,888	
Grade II: 2,100 hrs		3,124	
Overheads (2,550 process hrs)		18,540	

Dept. 2: D. labour: 1,250 hrs   2,451
            Overheads (401 Ind. lab. hrs)   2,101
Marketing overheads   14,990
                                                            ‾‾‾‾‾‾
                                                            57,640

Less Work-in-progress (Dept.2):
     Z: 140 gal at £24   3,360
     Finished goods stock: Full
         containers: 3 at £414   1,242 −4,602 53,038
                                                         ‾‾‾‾‾ ‾‾‾‾‾‾
         Actual profit   £3,046
                                                                ‾‾‾‾‾‾

Production statistics:
     Dept. 1: 1,610 gal of Z
     Dept. 2: 98 15-gallon containers of Z

There were no opening stocks in any of the stores or opening work-in-progress.

Find the profit variance and prepare a variance analysis.

19. Rework question 18 using a marginal cost form of variance analysis.

20. On the basis of a production/sales level of 10,000 units a month the standard unit cost of a carton of Gimmet which sells for £12 is:

	£
Material: 12 kg at 50p	6.00
Labour: $1\frac{1}{2}$ hrs at £1.60	2.40
Fixed overhead	0.60

The operating statement for November 19–7 was as follows:

	£	£	£
Budgeted profit			30,000
Add favourable variances			
Sales volume margin	1,500		
Materials price	1,268		
Wages efficiency	240		
Fixed overhead volume	300	3,308	

Less adverse variances

Sales price	1,000	
Material usage	400	
Wages rates	780	
Fixed overhead expenditure	200	2,380

Net favourable variance	928
Actual profit	£30,928

Prepare the conventional actual profit statement.

(*ACCA, modified*)

21. A company manufactures a food product, data for which for one week has been analyzed as follows:

Standard cost data:	£
Direct materials: 10 units at £1.50	15
Direct wages: 5 hours at £4.00	20
Production overhead: 5 hours at £5.00	25
	£60

Other overhead may be ignored.
Profit margin is 20% of sales price.
Budgeted sales are £30,000 per week.

Actual data:

Sales	£29,880
Direct materials	£6,435
Direct wages	£8,162

Analysis of variances:

		Adverse	Favourable
Direct materials:	price	585	
	usage		375
Direct labour:	rate		318
	efficiency	180	
Production overhead:	expenditure		200
	volume		375

It can be assumed that the production and sales achieved resulted in no changes of stock.

You are required, from the data given, to calculate: (i) the actual output; (ii) the actual profit; (iii) the actual price per unit of material; (iv) the actual rate per labour hour; (v) the amount of production overhead incurred; (vi) the amount of production overhead absorbed; (vii) the production overhead efficiency variance; (viii) the selling price variance; (ix) the sales volume profit variance.   (*CIMA*)

19

Aspects of profit control

With the mechanics of variance analysis behind us we can now turn to look at what the figures are telling us and what they should be telling us.

Causes of variances

1. Basic variance causes. Variances can arise for all sorts of reasons. Initially, though, the cause of a variance can be analyzed into one of the following categories (and to illustrate each it will be assumed that 10 hours were planned for an operation that in the event actually took 15 hours):

(*a*) *Operating variance.* This is caused by the failure of actual operations to meet a valid plan. This, of course, is the normal cause of a variance and so if the operation in our illustration took 15 hours because of the inefficiency of the operative concerned, the variance arising from the 5 excess hours would be an operating variance.

(*b*) *Planning variance.* This is caused by a planning failure rather than a failure in operations. Such a failure can take one of two forms.

(*i*) *Prediction failure.* Where there is a prediction failure the plan wrongly *predicts* some future value. Thus, the 10 hours planned time could have been a predicted time based on the expected future availability of certain material-handling equipment. If the 5 hours excess time arose because in the event this equipment was not available, then the variance arising is a planning variance. The commonest form of predictive failure relates, of course, to price and wage rate standards since these kind of variances more often result from wrong predictions than from bad buying or poor labour recruitment.

(*ii*) *Modelling failure.* All plans are based on models or mental conceptions of the circumstances that apply in a situation. Thus the plan for 10 hours could have been based on the belief that the operation did not involve a setting-up step when, in fact, it did (and required a total of 5 hours to complete). So when there is a modelling failure the plan wrongly *models* the situation. Clerical slips can be considered a form of this type of failure and one common example is where a material standard fails to include a standard loss, even though such a loss is inevitable.

(*c*) *Measurement error variance.* In practice variances often arise as a result of errors in measurement. Thus our illustrative operation may well have been completed in 10 hours but inadvertently 15 hours were booked to the job.

(*d*) *Random variance.* Actuals very rarely exactly equal plan if only because of chance events. Everybody has peaks and troughs in their work cycle and obviously these can lead to adverse and favourable variances of roughly equal frequency. Such variances are random variances.

Each of these kinds of variances calls for different action. Only the first, the operating variance, calls for action of an operating nature. Planning variances naturally call for improved forecasting and modelling techniques, measurement error variances for improved measuring devices or procedures, while random variances call for no action at all.

For simplicity it will be assumed in the remainder of this book that all variances are operating variances.

2. Causes of operating variances. It was, of course, operating variances that we were analyzing in Chapter 18. To control operating variances it is necessary to have some idea as to just how they arose. The commonest causes include the following:

(*a*) *Direct materials price variance.*

    (*i*) Change in purchase price.

    (*ii*) Change in delivery costs.

    (*iii*) Non-standard material purchased.

    (*iv*) Bad buying.

(*b*) *Direct materials usage variance.*

(*i*) Waste or scrap excessive.

(*ii*) Defective material (e.g. due to deterioration, poor handling, bad buying).

(*iii*) Rejection of completed work necessitating additional material withdrawals from store.

(*iv*) Pilferage.

(*v*) Non-standard material used.

(*vi*) Incorrect booking of material usage.

(*c*) *Direct wage rate variance.*

(*i*) General rise in wage rates.

(*ii*) Individual increase in specific wage rates.

(*iii*) Non-standard grade of employee.

(*d*) *Direct labour efficiency variance.*

(*i*) Slow employee.

(*ii*) Employee delayed by factors outside his/her control (e.g. breakdowns; no materials).

(*iii*) Poor working conditions.

(*iv*) Output restricted by employee.

(*v*) Abnormal length of run.

(*vi*) Employee handicapped by physical disability (e.g. bandaged finger).

(*vii*) Quality of supervision.

(*viii*) Non-standard grade of employee.

(*ix*) Non-standard material used.

(*x*) Non-standard job method used.

(*xi*) Incorrect booking of labour times.

(*e*) *Overhead expenditure variance.*

(*i*) Excessive or under utilization of a service (i.e. wasteful or economical use of service).

(*ii*) Price change for service (e.g. rate per kWh).

(*iii*) Change in nature of service (e.g. using gas for heating in lieu of electricity).

(*f*) *Overhead efficiency variance* (variable and productivity). These variances often arise in conjunction with a labour efficiency variance in which case they will be due to the same causes (*see* (*d*)).

(*g*) *Capacity variance.*

 (*i*) Absenteeism.
 (*ii*) Industrial action.
 (*iii*) Injuries.
 (*iv*) Staff shortages.
 (*v*) Breakdowns.
 (*vi*) Adverse weather.
 (*vii*) Overtime.

(*h*) *Sales margin selling price variance.*

 (*i*) Sales discounts.
 (*ii*) Quantity discounts.
 (*iii*) Sales in non-planned markets (e.g. non-budgeted export sales).

(*i*) *Sales margin quantities variance.*

 (*i*) Abnormal economic conditions.
 (*ii*) Ineffective marketing.
 (*iii*) Competitors' activities.
 (*iv*) Changing consumer tastes.
 (*v*) Deteriorating reputation (e.g. due to poor quality, after-sales service, etc.).
 (*vi*) Production failure due to breakdowns, absenteeism, labour or material shortage, strikes, bad production management, design errors, etc.

3. A variance is not a verdict. A variance is really only a *signal* that something somewhere is not conforming to plan. It is not a *verdict* on anybody or anything. Thus a materials usage variance in department Z does not necessarily mean that there are inefficiencies in department Z's operations.

It probably goes without saying that there is no set procedure that automatically identifies sources and causes of variances – there is only the accountant's experience, intelligence and detailed knowledge of the operations of the organization. Sometimes the source may be far removed from the place where the variance arises, e.g. when an after-sales service variance arises on account of the earlier purchase of sub-standard components, or the cause may be subtle, e.g. when an adverse materials usage variance arises because of unsuspected loss of moisture between weighing the materials on issue and weighing the product on completion. Often no clear answers are possible. No matter, for it is better to report an inexplicable variance than to attribute it to the wrong cause as a result of a superficial interpretation.

4. Interdependence of variances. Variances are frequently interdependent. Thus a favourable wage rate variance that arises from the employment of sub-standard labour will very probably be offset by an adverse labour efficiency variance. In such circumstances it would be absurd to praise the personnel manager while castigating the production manager. Although the ultimate cause of a variance may be revealed by a thorough investigation, it speeds up the accountant's work if he is aware from the beginning of probable linkages between variances. Such an accountant will not be surprised if department A, whose supervisor prides himself on always achieving favourable labour efficiency variances, consistently shows an adverse scrap variance while department B, whose supervisor prides himself on his nil scrap variance, consistently shows an adverse labour efficiency variance.

This interdependence of variances does, as it happens, often have an advantage not usually ascribed to a profit control system for it enables 'trade-offs' to be evaluated. For instance, a sales manager may argue that his new generous discount policy benefits the business by virtue of the extra sales made. By comparing the adverse sales price variance arising from the new discounts with the favourable variances arising from the extra sales, the net gain or loss in adopting this policy can be seen.

General principles of profit control

5. The meaning of 'profit control'.

(a) *Profit control is a control technique.* It is not a cost ascertainment technique, a book-keeping technique, a decision-making technique, or a technique for anything else. And this in turn means that all principles and conventions relating to these latter techniques have no automatic relevance to the control technique.

(b) *Profit control is a management technique.* It involves both an appreciation of the significance of a difference between actual and planned performance and the authority to take corrective action.

Both these functions fall to management, the latter by definition and the former by virtue of the fact that appreciating the significance of such a difference is best made by the person who is specifically responsible for the performance analyzed. The object of profit control, then, is not to enable the books to be balanced or economic returns to be calculated but to enable managers to achieve the profit that they set out to achieve. And the validity of all control principles and procedures must be tested against this objective.

Since profit control is a management technique it follows that it must be developed from a management point of view and not from an accounting point of view, though of course the accountant may very well operate the necessary clerical procedure. This requirement has as an important corollary the fact that in operating the technique *the accountant has to fit in with the manager,* not the manager with the accountant.

6. Profit control and flexibility. It is a matter of common observation that all sorts of things can go wrong with a profit plan. This means that all sorts of divergences from plan can arise. A fundamental feature of any system which aims to quantify these divergences in terms of the effect on profit must, therefore, be flexibility. For this reason, if no other, formulae cannot be the basis of such a system – if they were then almost certainly some situation would arise in practice for which no formula existed (in examinations, of course, the examiners can restrict divergences to those formally recognized). So our profit control technique calls for a flexible strategy that will enable *any* divergence, foreseen or otherwise, to be measured in terms of *the effect on profit.* It is, of course, for this reason that we adopt the 'allowance' approach to computing variances as this gives us just that flexibility (*see* 17 : 11).

7. Control, responsibility and authority. All control ultimately depends upon taking appropriate action. Now action can only be taken by those who are authorized to take it – in an economic enterprise, the managers. So, as we have seen, a profit control system must be designed around the managers who must ultimately achieve the planned profit. And that means it must be designed in terms of the responsibilities and authority of the individual managers.

In view of this, it is important that the system should accurately reflect the organization structure of the enterprise. If, for instance, in a particular enterprise, the marketing manager were responsible for the finished goods store, the profit control system should recognize that fact by ensuring the store control data is reported to the marketing manager. If conversely the store is under the authority of the works manager then it should be to him that the system directs the data.

8. A management technique implies a behavioural context. Management involves people – both the managers and the managed – and where people are involved then all the behavioural implications have to be considered. Unfortunately, the subject of managerial behaviour considerations lies outside the scope of this book and, apart from the few comments below, will not be further discussed. Students nevertheless should be aware of this important aspect of all budgeting and control work in the real, practical world.

There are, however, two points that can be briefly referred to:

(*a*) *Goal congruence.* The goals of individuals, centres and the organization as a whole should all support each other – i.e. all goals should be congruent. Such goals include recognition, status, paths of advancement, training, fringe benefits, job satisfaction and, of course, pay and profits. Often one goal is incompatible with another but as far as possible management should aim to make all goals congruent.

(*b*) *Participation.* People are more motivated and able to work more effectively if they are able to participate in the planning and control of operations. So, again, where possible management should aim at engendering the maximum viable participation. In this connection note that a budget prepared on the basis of participation by the people to be controlled by it is called a *participative budget.*

9. Profit control is a supportive, not punitive, system. A profit control system should be used to *help* managers to achieve their profit plans, not to blame them for their profit failures. The reasons for using the system in this supportive way are as follows.

(*a*) Profit arises ultimately as a result of team-work. Although profit divergences can be allocated to individual managers for *analytical* purposes, the elimination of such divergences is very often a matter of combined efforts. Thus production lost due to slow working may be eliminated by the enterprise adopting a new industrial relations policy.

(*b*) Profit divergences do not always arise in the centre that causes them. For instance, scrap arising in department Z could well be due to poor workmanship on the product in department A. To blame the manager of Z would not only be unjust – it wouldn't even lead to a reduction in the scrap.

(*c*) The raw data from which performance figures are computed are very 'adjustable'. Managers afraid of being blamed can easily manipulate such data so as to throw at least part of the blame off themselves, at the expense, of course, of a proper undertanding of the profit failure. Moreover, if the problems of the enterprise are great enough a punitive system will be so disliked by all the middle managers than an unconscious (at best) conspiracy to destroy the system can form, in which case the system will be destroyed just at the time when it could well be proving its greatest worth.

10. When does a variance arise? Classically this problem occurs in the context of the materials price variance. One view is that it arises on the issue of the materials and the other that it arises on the receipt of the invoice. The test is, of course, which method gives the best control. Now, clearly, the *sooner* management are made aware of a divergence then:

(*a*) the sooner corrective action can be taken;

(*b*) the easier corrective action usually proves to be, since whatever underlay the divergence will probably have not become established, e.g. an informal but less efficient operating method may become formalized if corrective action is delayed too long;

(*c*) the clearer will be the memories and understanding of the situation in the minds of the people involved;

(*d*) the greater will be the sense of immediacy, e.g. it will be less likely that the people concerned will regard the matter as being out of date.

From all this it follows that a variance arises the *moment it is detectable*. Indeed, part of the skill of the accountant lies in being able to devise a procedure that advances the moment of detection.

This means that the relevant details should ideally come to him either the moment a decision is made or the moment an event which will give rise to the variance occurs.

Utilizing this principle it can be seen that both views in the classical debate are wrong, since frequently a material price variance actually arises the moment a purchase order is raised. Similarly, on conclusion of a union wages agreement the wage rate variances relating to all the rates affected and covering the whole of the remainder of the year arise immediately.

Needless to say, this approach to the detection of variances is contrary to the traditional accounting concept of matching income and expenditure. However, if there is to be effective control this different accounting approach must be accepted.

11. Profit centre. This is a *budget centre* to which income as well as costs can be assigned. For example, a product sales section could be designated a profit centre since all the sales that it made relating to the product could be assigned to it along with its costs. The advantage of a profit centre is that the control budget can specify a budgeted net contribution in respect of the centre and the manager can be assessed primarily in terms of his net contribution variance. This, then, enables authority to be delegated to him so that as long as he achieves his budgeted net contribution he is allowed to change such aspects of his plan, e.g. sales price, advertising costs, as he may feel is necessary.

12. Non-standard variances. Finally, given the method we have adopted for measuring variances it should be appreciated that any kind of variance in any kind of circumstances should be computable. This is important because in practice there is really no exhaustive list of cost standards and so there is no exhaustive list of cost variances. But, bearing in mind the principle that all variances are based on a comparison of actual with allowance, and with the examples given in Chapter 18, the student should have no difficulty computing any variance, however unusual. For example, if a sheep-breeder planned a fertility standard of $1\frac{1}{4}$ lambs per ewe, such lambs having a standard value of £40, then if 400 ewes produced 440 lambs during a given period the fertility variance would be computed as follows:

Fertility allowance: $400 \times 1\frac{1}{4}$	500 lambs
Actual fertility	440 lambs
Difference	60 A lambs
Standard value	£40
Fertility variance	£2,400 A

Principle of non-apportionment

If there is perhaps one absolute principle in profit control it is the principle of non-apportionment which states in effect that in profit control *a figure must never be apportioned*. This prohibition extends not only to budget centres but also to time periods and cost units.

As this principle is so implacably opposed to the normal accounting principles its validity in each context is argued in **13–15** below. Note that although the principle is not restricted to the fixed costs, in the very nature of things it is these costs which are almost exclusively involved.

13. Non-apportionment: to budget centres.

13. Non-apportionment: to budget centres. Either the manager of a budget centre can control a given item of expenditure or he cannot. If he cannot it should not be charged to him. If he can it should all be charged to him. For instance, although a night watchman may patrol and protect all the departments in a company his manager has the sole responsibility for that man and his entire wages should, therefore, be charged to that manager. Charging a part to some other managers not only achieves nothing (since those other managers can do nothing about it) but it also dilutes the full impact of the variance on the one manager who can, with the result that control suffers.

There are, of course, occasions when two managers share a responsibility. For example, two budget centres may share the same workshop and so jointly control the heating system. In such a case any heating variance should be charged to the two managers *jointly*. Nothing at all is gained by apportioning either the cost or the variance. Indeed, it can be said that a cost apportioned is a control lost.

14. Non-apportionment: to time periods. Since a variance must be taken at the moment it arises, then any cost associated with a variance must be charged to the period in which the variance arises. So if, say, the annual rent were payable in March, March must carry the full year's rent and any variance, and no attempt must be made to apportion the cost over the other eleven months. (The student should note, however, that this principle is in direct contradiction to that implied in official terminology of the CIMA.)

It is sometimes argued that if the annual costs are not apportioned over time then a profit and loss account cannot be prepared month by month and therefore management will not know if they are operating profitably or not. While the initial contention is correct, the conclusion is wrong. Management's budgeted profit for the year will indicate their target and the cumulative operating profit variance will show them each month the extent to which they have fallen away from that target. Indeed, a strong case can be put forward to show that profit progress is more accurately measured under a profit control system than a conventional accounting system.

Not only is the apportionment of such costs wrong in a control context but also an attempt to make such an apportionment leads to the accountant facing impossible conundrums. Assume that one of his costs is an insurance premium budgeted at £24,000 for the year and payable mid-year. Apportionment then gives £2,000 per month.

The first conundrum the accountant faces is what to record as 'actual' on the first operating statements of the manager responsible for the premium. To show £2,000 on the basis that no other figure is available is to record a pious hope as a hard fact – and if the hope is unrealized the accountant's credibility will suffer.

Imagine now that when the bill comes in it is for £30,000. What does the accountant do now? Re-write the early statements to show a £2,500 actual and a £500 adverse variance (which will discredit the operating statements)? Write off the £6,000 excess relating to the first half of the year and charge a £500 adverse variance for each of the remaining months (in which case the statements will collectively fail to show the full actual premium and variance)? Charge a £1,000 variance to each of the remaining months (which will imply that a manager previously performing well has suddenly become incompetent)?

Yet even if the £30,000 bill were to come in during the first month of the year, the accountant would still have problems. To show a £500 adverse variance month after month would imply a *continuing* failure instead of a once-and-for-all failure on the part of the manager concerned (who would become contemptuous in turn of operating statements, profit control systems and accountants generally). To show the whole £6,000 variance in the first month and then record a £2,000 actual for all subsequent months would, of course, reduce the word 'actual' to a book-keeping fiction.

All these problems, naturally, are avoided if the cost is not apportioned. The plan will then show a £24,000 premium is expected mid-year. If, when the bill comes, it is £30,000, a £6,000 variance is recorded in that same month so that management can see immediately that this item has reduced the hoped-for profit by £6,000 for the year, and so that they can at once consider what action must be taken to avoid a recurrence in the next year. In the other months this item has no control relevance and must therefore be omitted from the records.

15. Non-apportionment: to cost units. Finally, it must be appreciated that the only apportioned costs in a cost unit standard cost are those charged via the fixed overhead rate, since all the other costs are direct, and that the only variances in respect of these costs are all sub-variances of the volume variance. The test of validity, then, is the value of the volume variance in control.

If it is recollected that this variance measures the profit effect of the actual volume diverging from that planned, it will be seen that such a variance has no real value at all. Consider the situation where Sales meet their volume plan but Production manufactures excess units which cannot be sold. The volume variance in such circumstances would be favourable, but have profits really been increased? Of course not; indeed the only practical result will be to create problems in the finished goods store. Conversely, if Production fail to produce the planned units, then Sales could be prevented from achieving the planned sales, in which case there is not only an under-recovery of fixed overheads but also a loss of unit profits, i.e. in total a loss of contribution. So the effect of the method in such circumstances would be to apportion the real lost profit (contribution) between Production and Sales in the ratio of budgeted fixed overheads to budgeted profit!

As is obvious, such an analysis would be nonsensical, and an accountant who insists on such an exercise must not expect his management colleagues to be particularly impressed with either his technique or himself.

It could be that at this point some thoughtful student, reflecting on the capacity variance (*see* 18 : 22), feels that by measuring the effect of a strike on the under-recovery of fixed overheads something of value is obtained. There is an element of truth in this but the student should appreciate that not only are the fixed overheads under-recovered in such circumstances but also the profit on the unsold units is lost. The total loss, then, turns out to be not just the fixed overheads but instead the *contribution* on the unproduced, unsold units and, of course, such a lost contribution is easily computed under a standard marginal costing system.

One final point. If a works manager were deliberately to produce more than the sales department could sell he would receive a favourable volume variance at the same time as he receives a reprimand for pointlessly increasing the level of the finished goods stocks. A control system that credits favourable profit variances to people who engage in unprofitable activities will again quickly earn for itself the degree of contempt it deserves.

Control reporting

Once the accountant has analyzed all control data he can then take the final step in his control function – reporting that data. This in turn will enable the managers to move to their final step – taking action to correct divergences from plans.

Reporting is not just presenting managers with figures. Care needs to be taken in selecting what has control relevance for any individual manager and in the layout of the material selected for reporting.

16. Basic details to be reported. Accounting control information, as we have seen, involves a comparison of actual profit events with the profit plans. In practice, for effective control, the resulting divergences need to be analyzed in terms of:

(*a*) *who* was responsible for the divergence;

(*b*) *where* the divergence occurred;

(*c*) *what* factor diverged from plan, e.g. material usage, selling price, etc.;

(*d*) *how much* the profit was affected by the divergence. This latter information enables the manager to judge the importance of the necessary corrective action.

Note the use of the word 'divergence'. Frequently the figures reported will be variances but additionally the difference between actual and planned resource *quantities* will be needed. It is for this reason that the wider term 'divergences' is used rather than just 'variances'.

17. The principles of divergence reporting. Control not only involves reporting divergences but also taking appropriate action. Such action can only be taken on the basis of appropriately-presented divergence reporting. To avoid either wasting one's own time or misleading managers it should always be remembered that a divergence must:

(*a*) only be computed when such a figure can be usefully used;

(*b*) be computed and presented in the form most likely to enable the receiving manager to use it to make the best decision needed to regain control, i.e. be tailor-made for the situation and the manager;

(*c*) in the case of a variance, be part of an overall framework of variance analysis and reporting, i.e. the variance must have an unambiguous, exclusive and logical 'slot' in the full variance analysis, so that both:

(*i*) the 'width' and 'boundaries' of the variance are defined;

(*ii*) the relationship of the variance to other variances is clear.

For example, a material usage variance measures the value at standard price of the divergence of actual usages from planned usages of all standard materials. It in no way reflects the usage of non-standard material nor the effect on profit of the actual *price* of the usage divergence differing from plan, though in combination with the materials price variance it will indicate the total standard materials variance.

To the extent that a tailor-made variance for one manager in a given situation may fall outside the framework of variances, (*b*) and (c) above are incompatible and it is the mark of good accountants that they can achieve a viable measure of compromise.

18. Controllable and non-controllable factors. Since a manager can only take action in respect of those factors for which he is responsible and over which he has authority – which can be termed *controllable factors* – there is little control value in giving him data relating to other factors. A good profit control system, then, ensures that essentially only data relating to the controllable factors of a given manager is reported to that manager. Note that this does not mean that other kinds of data reported for other reasons should be rigidly excluded. For instance, sales trends could be reported to the works manager so that he can bear such trends in mind when making relatively long-term *planning* decisions.

From this it follows that any variance relating to an uncontrollable factor can be classified as an *uncontrollable variance*. Similarly a variance relating to a controllable factor can be classified as *a controllable variance* and defined as a *variance that relates to a factor that falls under the authority of the person for whom the variance is computed*. It also follows that no manager should be charged with an uncontrollable variance.

The accountant must be very careful to distinguish between controllable and uncontrollable variances. Although the analysis of variances in this context generally needs to do no more than follow the lines of formal authority, problems sometimes arise. Who, for example, would be responsible for the loss incurred as a result of a non-standard operation by a production employee (who had been improperly trained in a training department) on inappropriate material erroneously issued by the stores?

Note, incidentally, that a system of accounting that is designed to present managers with information relating to their individual fields of responsibility is termed *responsibility accounting*.

19. Variance synthesis. So far only the *analysis* has been discussed. But there is a serious disadvantage in making a full analysis and that is that the profit variance may be subdivided to the point where the end result is no more than a large number of relatively insignificant variances. Yet frequently there are times when a number of such variances have a common cause, and it is more meaningful to report these variances as a combined total rather than separately. For example, a strike by a group of employees can give rise to both a sales quantities variance and a number of associated efficiency variances (labour and variable overhead particularly). Collecting all these variances together and reporting them as a single 'strike variance' may well prove the most useful way of reporting them to management. Similarly, the variances arising as a result of government action, e.g. complying with a three-day week decree, can be collected together in the same way.

Clearly, then, good control systems will enable variances to be 'synthesised'. In the main this only involves detecting and adding the appropriate variances, though care must be taken that variance synthesis does not lead to variance double-counting.

20. Departmental operating statement. This is a formal, regular report made at the end of each control period to the budget centre manager outlining that manager's variances and any other control data relating to the control period. It is the one regular document in control reporting and the one upon which all other control reports centre.

The following points should be noted in connection with a departmental operating statement.

(*a*) *Layout.* The layout essentially ensures that the following data is appropriately shown.

(*i*) Name of *budget centre.*

(*ii*) Name of *person responsible.* Action can only be taken by a person, not by a department or a product, and so every statement must name the controlling person. Indeed, every figure on the statement will relate to his performance specifically.

(*iii*) The *period reported on* and the *date reported.* These are both vital pieces of information and must be clearly stated.

(*iv*) *Variances,* shown individually and in total.

(*v*) *Reasons* for variances.

(*b*) *Functions.*

(*i*) *Profit control feedback to the manager concerned.* This is its basic and most important function. It acts as the crucial link between the accountant and the manager concerned in a profit control exercise.

(*ii*) *A chronological record of performance*. Performance assessment over a single control period can often be distorted by a non-recurring difficulty or an event that seriously affects operations in the short term but which is of minor consequence in the long term. A chronological record extending over a number of control periods, therefore, enables a more balanced and accurate assessment of the performance of the manager concerned. Moreover, a sounder interpretation of the more subtle causes of variances can sometimes be made by studying trends over a number of control periods and a file of past departmental operating statements relating to a budget centre can form the basic records for such a trend study.

(*iii*) *Advice to higher management*. Higher management exercises control through the performance of subordinates and so departmental operating statements form a good practical basis for evaluating the actual performance of subordinates in terms of the profit plan. In addition, an intelligent scrutiny of such a statement can often indicate to higher managers where their intervention can overcome a particularly serious or intractable difficulty that has fallen to one of their subordinates whose authority is more limited than their own, e.g. low labour efficiency may possibly be eliminated by the purchase of new plant, or abnormal material usage reduced by introducing an improved training scheme.

(*c*) *Other control data*. There will, of course, be other data that the manager may consider of value. The following are frequently found in a well-designed departmental operating statement:

(*i*) variance percentages;
(*ii*) cumulative variances;
(*iii*) control ratios (*see* **21**);
(*iv*) non-monetary performance measures, e.g. percentage down-time, percentage defectives, ratio seconds to firsts, absenteeism, overtime hours.

(*d*) *Timing of statements*. A departmental operating statement should be presented at the earliest possible moment after the end of the control period.

(*e*) *Prior discussion with managers*. Since a profit control system should be supportive rather than punitive (*see* **9**) departmental operating statements must not be used by higher managers to browbeat their subordinates but as tools to help and guide budget centre managers in their attempts to control their profit performance. So it is vitally important that the statement should be discussed with the manager concerned *before completion* – the purpose of such discussion being:

(*i*) to give the manager early notice of any significant variances;

(*ii*) to give the manager the opportunity to correct erroneous factual data, challenge the logic of possible variance charges, and qualify otherwise misleading variances, e.g. part of an adverse material usage variance may have been due to an unrecorded and unascertained quantity of unused material on the shop floor at the end of the control period;

(*iii*) to give the manager advance notice of the information that his superiors will ultimately have at hand;

(*iv*) to enable any '*Reason*' column on the statement to be completed (since in the first instance only the manager responsible can suggest just why a particular variance arose).

21. Control ratios. These are factor ratios that management often find useful for control purposes. The most important of these, and their methods of calculation, are as follows:

(*a*) Efficiency ratio $= \dfrac{\text{Allowed hours}}{\text{Actual hours worked}} \times 100$

(*b*) Capacity ratio $= \dfrac{\text{Actual hours worked}}{\text{Budgeted hours}} \times 100$

(*c*) Activity ratio $= \dfrac{\text{Allowed hours}}{\text{Budgeted hours}} \times 100$

EXAMPLE: Using the figures in our earlier illustration the following, production control ratios can be computed:

(*a*) Efficiency ratio $= \dfrac{8{,}000}{8{,}850} \times 100 = 90\frac{1}{2}\%$

(*b*) Capacity ratio $= \dfrac{8{,}850}{10{,}000} \times 100 = 88\frac{1}{2}\%$

$$(c) \text{ Activity ratio } = \frac{8,000}{10,000} \times 100 = 80\%$$

22. Cost of variance investigations. Not only must accountants always be aware of the need to investigate variances in order to determine their true cause but they must also bear in mind at all times the need to balance the benefits of the information obtained against the cost of obtaining it. Better to make a reduced profit and be ignorant of the cause of the reduction than to sustain a massive loss that nevertheless can be fully accounted for. And in control work the temptation to spend money on uneconomic analysis is greater than in any other field of accountancy work.

Progress test 19

Principles

1. What are the basic variance causes? (**1**)
2. What are the causes of operating variances? (**2**)
3. What is 'profit control'? (**5**)
4. What is (*a*) a participative budget; (**8**(*b*)) (*b*) a profit centre? (**11**)
5. When does a variance arise? (**10**)
6. What is the principle of apportionment in a profit control system? (**13–15**)
7. What are the principles of control reporting? (**16–19**)
8. What are the features of a departmental operating statement? (**20**)
9. Give the formulae for three control ratios. (**21**)

20

Standard cost accounts

It has already been indicated that the traditional standard costing and budgetary control technique is essentially an accounting technique. It is, therefore, understandable that the culmination of all the analyses looked at so far should be the incorporation of the resulting figures into the traditional cost book-keeping pattern.

1. **Basic principles of standard cost book-keeping.** In traditional standard cost book-keeping the framework of the accounts is the normal cost book-keeping pattern as illustrated in Fig. 7.1. On to this pattern are then grafted variance accounts which record the variances disclosed by the variance analysis. The following are the basic principles underlying the operation of these accounts.

(*a*) Variances are transferred to individual variance accounts.

(*b*) As far as possible, transfers between the main accounts are at standard. (You should envisage these accounts as having such a distaste for actual figures that they shed the variances as quickly as possible so that actuals are thereby converted into standard values.)

(*c*) From (*b*) it follows that variances should be accounted for as near as is practical to the moment of occurrence.

(*d*) Variances are written off to profit and loss at the end of the period.

2. **Flow chart for standard absorption cost book-keeping.** *See* Fig. 20.1. The following points should be noted.

(*a*) Material standards are usually maintained for production materials only. Consequently, purchases must be segregated into standard materials and non-standard materials, the latter comprising mainly consumable and maintenance stores. Non-standard

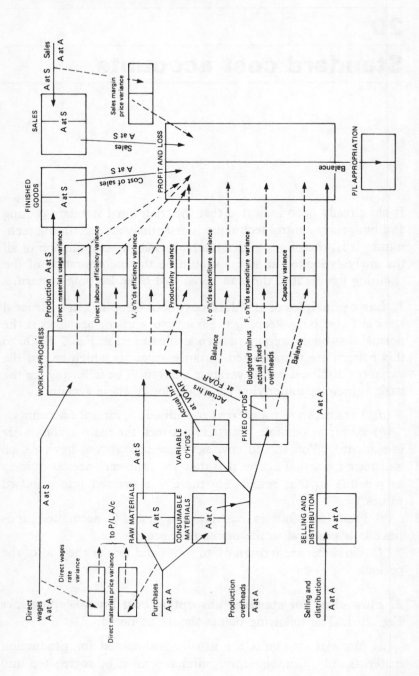

materials are debited to their stores accounts at actual prices and issued using a non-standard issue price method.

(b) The materials price variance on standard materials can be calculated *immediately on receipt of the invoice* by comparing the actual and allowed invoice purchase cost, i.e.:

$$\text{Price variance} =$$
Invoice amount − Invoice quantity at standard price.

This enables the price variance to be taken immediately to the Materials Price Variance account, and the materials charged to the Raw Materials account at the standard price.

(c) On issue, materials are charged to the Work-in-Progress account at standard prices.

(d) The wage rate variance can also be calculated immediately. If desired, the calculation could be made on the payroll itself by inserting alongside the gross wages column two additional columns, thus:

Gross Wages	Allowed wages: Actual hours at standard rate	Difference: Wage rate variance
Totals: Cr. Wages a/c	Dr. Work in Progress a/c	Dr. (or Cr.) Wage Rate Variance a/c

The wage rate variance can be found either in total only or, if desired, for each individual employee.

Figure 20.1 *Flow chart for standard absorption cost book-keeping*

The following abbreviations are used:

A at A = actual quantity at actual price;
A at S = actual quantity at standard price;
VOAR = variable overhead absorption rate;
FOAR = fixed overhead absorption rate.

The flow of variances is indicated by broken lines. The main accounts shed the variances as quickly as possible, converting the actuals to standard figures, and the variances are written off to profit and loss at the end of the period.

*In practice the Variable Overheads account and the Fixed Overheads account will be a single account. They are shown separately here so that the book-keeping pattern can be seen more clearly.

(*e*) The Production Overhead accounts are debited with the actual overheads and credited with the fixed and variable overheads absorbed. Expenditure and capacity variances are taken out at the end of the period.

(*f*) The Selling and Distribution or Marketing Overheads account is traditionally left unchanged in the cost accounts, i.e. the account is debited with the actual overheads as they are incurred and then the total overheads are transferred to the Profit and Loss account at the period end. This means there will be no expenditure or volume variance accounts in respect of these overheads.

(*g*) The following three points should be noted with regard to the Work-in-Progress account.

(*i*) The account is credited with the *actual units produced at the standard cost* as shown on the standard cost card.

(*ii*) As soon as the total production is known (and remember that this figure will be modified by the increase or decrease in work-in-progress over the period – though examiners rarely include this factor in their questions), variances relating to efficiency and usage can be computed and transferred from the Work-in-Progress account to the appropriate Variance accounts.

(*iii*) The balance remaining and carried down on the Work-in-Progress account is the end-of-period work-in-progress valued at standard.

(*h*) All finished goods in the Finished Goods account are carried at standard cost. The standard cost value of the finished goods sold is transferred to the Profit and Loss account.

(*i*) Sales margin selling price variances can be computed at the time of invoicing in the same manner as materials price variances, and can be taken at once to a Sales Price Variance account, the Sales account carrying the necessary double entry. This will leave the Sales account showing the actual sales at standard prices.

(*j*) All variances are transferred to the Profit and Loss account.

(*k*) The final balance on the Profit and Loss account will be the actual profit for the period and will, of course, be transferred to the Profit and Loss Appropriation account.

(*l*) The chart, for reasons of clarity, does not show all variances. However, students should have little difficulty with other variances; e.g. materials mixture and yield variances merely require a sub-division of the Materials Usage Variance account.

3. Worked example of standard cost accounts. On pp. 346–7 are given the cost accounts and accounting entries relating to the variances computed in Chapter 18. It should be appreciated that these accounts are rather more simple than would occur in practice (e.g. there are no opening stocks), and that not all the ledger accounts have been shown (e.g. there are no fixed assets or capital accounts).

4. Standard marginal cost book-keeping. Modern profit control theory is not particularly enthralled by the requirements of a double-entry system and adopts recording techniques of a form that lie outside the scope of this book. When, therefore, the theory is obliged to conform with the conventional book-keeping procedures it merely adopts the approach already illustrated in the earlier paragraphs. In consequence standard marginal cost book-keeping differs from standard absorption book-keeping only in the following respects:

(*a*) *Fixed Overhead accounts.* There is no transfer of overheads from the Fixed Overhead account to the Work-in-Progress account. The only credits to this account are the budgeted fixed overheads, with the double-entry being taken to the P/L account, and the resulting balance on the account, which, of course, is the fixed overhead expenditure variance, being transferred to the Fixed Overhead Expenditure Variance account.

(*b*) *Work-in-Progress and Finished Goods accounts.* The units in these accounts are all valued at standard cost. Under marginal costing no productivity variance can arise and so there is no transfer of any amount out of the Work-in-Progress account in respect of this kind of variance.

(*c*) *Variance accounts.* The Productivity Variance account and the Capacity Variance account are both eliminated from the cost ledger.

(*d*) *P/L account.* This account is debited with a cost of sales at marginal cost and also with the *budgeted* fixed overhead.

5. Implications of transferring variances to profit and loss. When a price variance computed at the time of purchase is transferred to profit and loss it may well contain a favourable variance relating to unissued materials, i.e. an *unrealized profit* is taken. This may also happen with favourable efficiency and usage

Main accounts

Cash

Sales	£136,400	Purchases: X	27,840
Balance c/d	38,100	Y	49,560
		D. wages	26,800
		Factory overheads	46,200
		Royalty	2,000
		Marketing overheads	22,100
		Balance b/d	38,100

Raw Materials (at Standard)

Purchases:		WIP:	
X	26,400	X	24,400
Y	50,000	Y	44,000
		Balance c/d	8,000
Balance b/d	8,000		

Finished Goods

WIP	129,600	P/L (7,000 cwt at £16.20)	113,400
		Balance c/d	16,200
Balance b/d	16,200		

Marketing Overheads

Cash	22,100	P/L	22,100

Royalty

Cash	£2,000	WIP (8,000 cwt at 20p)	1,600
		D. Exs	400

Work-in-Progress

Raw materials:		F.G. (8,000 cwt at £16.20)	129,600
X	24,400	Mix var.	1,200
Y	44,000	Yield var.	3,200
D. wages (at stnd.)	26,550	Labour efficiency var.	2,550
Factory overheads	44,250	V. overhead efficiency var.	850
Royalty	1,600	Prod. var.	3,400

Factory Overheads

Cash	46,200	WIP: overheads absorbed (8,850 hrs at £1 + £4)	44,250
Expenditure var.	2,650	Capacity var.	4,600

Sales

P/L	140,000	Cash	136,400
		Sales price var.	3,600

Variance accounts

Direct Materials Price Variance

Purchase X	1,440	Purchase Y	440
		P/L	1,000

Direct Wage Rate Variance

Cash	250	P/L	250

Direct Expenses (Royalty)

Royalty	400	P/L	400

Factory Overhead Expenditure Variance

P/L	2,650	Factory overheads	2,650

Capacity Variance

Factory overheads	4,600	P/L	4,600

Materials Mixture Variance

WIP	1,200	P/L	1,200

Yield Variance

WIP	3,200	P/L	3,200

Labour Efficiency Variance

WIP	2,550	P/L	2,550

Variable Overhead Efficiency Variance

WIP	850	P/L	850

Sales Margin Price Variance

Sales	3,600	P/L	3,600

Factory Productivity Variance

WIP	3,400	P/L	3,400

Profit and Loss

Finished goods (cost sales)	113,400	Sales (at standard prices)	140,000
Marketing overheads	22,100	Favourable variances:	
Adverse variances:		Factory overhead expenditure	2,650
Direct materials price	1,000		
Direct wage rate	250		
Direct expenses	400		
Materials mixture	1,200		
Yield	3,200		
Labour efficiency	2,550		
Variance overhead efficiency	850		
Productivity	3,400		
Capacity	4,600		
Sales margin price	3,600	Balance – actual loss to P/L Appropriation	13,900

Profit and Loss Appropriation

P/L–actual loss for period	13,900	

variances relating to work-in-progress or unsold finished goods stock.

To allow for this some accountants, and particularly auditors, hold back favourable variances in the Variance accounts until the production to which they relate is sold.

This 'holding back' is achieved by prorating the variances between the closing stock values and the Profit and Loss account in proportion to the extent to which the profit has actually been realized. This, of course, can lead to quite complicated calculations when favourable raw material price variances arise since it calls for adjustments to be made not only to the Raw Materials account but also to the Work-in-Progress and the Finished Goods accounts in respect of products incorporating the materials on which the variances arose.

This complication is a good example of the kind of problems encountered when a single set of accounts is used for more than one purpose. Profit control is essentially a technique for reporting performance to management, not for making an assessment of the enterprise profit on the basis of the normal accounting conventions. If the purpose is the measurement of management performance then all favourable variances must be taken to the Profit and Loss account when they occur since the ultimate profit will be improved by this improved performance, albeit some time may need to elapse before the profit is formally realized. If, however, the purpose is to show the profit available for distribution, the normal conservative accounting convention under which unrealized profits must *not* be taken applies.

6. Profit and loss statement. The normal book-keeping profit and loss statement is one that simply lists income and expenditure to arrive at a net profit. Managers, however, are more concerned to know *where their efforts are failing* rather than money totals. Therefore a statement that highlights the place and consequences of these failings is much more valuable. Budgets and standard costs enable this to be done, since the profit and loss statement can start with the sales at standard prices and, by incorporating all the variances, end with the actual profit. A Profit and Loss account in the form referred to in **4** is, then, much more useful to managers than one in the normal income and expenditure format.

Some managements prefer the statement to start with budgeted sales. This is a doubtful practice, since management's interest should be primarily in profits (sales margins) rather than sales. Moreover, it involves introducing a non-ledger figure and this in turn means that an extra step has to be taken (adding or subtracting the difference between the budgeted and actual sales) to adjust the budgeted sales to the actual sales at standard prices. However, should a manager request his performance to be reported in this form the accountant must comply with his request. In such a case the exact structure of the Profit and Loss account report would need to be tailored to the precise requirements of the manager concerned.

Progress test 20

Practice

1. Last period the Alpha and Beta Company Ltd. budgeted to sell 1,000 Sets for £70,000, but owing to bad trading conditions they only managed to sell 840 for a mere £57,100. Their production, however, was 900 Sets. They had no opening stocks at all, and they had no closing work-in-progress. During the trading period they suffered breakdowns amounting to 25 hours, during which time normal 'direct' wages were paid. To add to their troubles they found 120 MTs broken in the store, apparently due to bad stack-

ing. Other figures relating to the period were as follows:

Purchases (5,000 MTs)	£14,800
Direct wages (4,450 hours)	£9,140 (this includes breakdown hours and pay)
Variable overheads	£4,580
Fixed overheads	£20,900
Selling and distribution costs	£7,000

4,550 MTs were issued to production.

The company operates standard costs (a Set standard cost is shown below) and you are to prepare all cost and variance accounts for the period, including the profit and loss.

Standard Cost Card: 1 Set

	£
Direct materials (5 MTs)	15
Direct labour (5 hours)	10
Variable overheads (varying with production)	5
Fixed overheads	20
Factory standard cost	50
Selling and distribution overheads	8
Total standard cost	58
Standard profit (sales margin)	12
Standard selling price	£70

Appendix 1

Examination technique

To pass any examination you must:

(*a*) have the knowledge;
(*b*) convince the examiner you have the knowledge;
(*c*) convince him within the time allowed.

In the book so far we have considered the first of these only. Success in the other two respects will be much more assured if you apply the examination hints given below.

1. Answer the question. Apart from ignorance, *failure to answer the question is undoubtedly the greatest bar to success.* No matter how often students are told, they always seem to be guilty of this fault. If you are asked for a control report, *don't* give a product cost statement; if asked to give the advantages of standard costs, *don't* detail the steps for computing them. You can write a hundred pages of brilliant exposition, but if it's not in answer to the set question you will be given no more marks than if it had been a paragraph of utter drivel. To ensure you answer the question:

(*a*) read the question carefully;
(*b*) decide what the examiner wants;
(*c*) underline the nub of the question;
(*d*) do just what the examiner asks;
(*e*) keep referring to the question in your mind as you write.

2. Put your ideas in logical order. It's quicker, more accurate and gives a greater impression of competence if you follow a pre-determined logical path instead of jumping about from place to place as ideas come to you. This *initially* requires more time before starting to write, but it is time ultimately well spent.

3. Maximize the points you make. Examiners are more impressed by a solid mass of points than an unending development of one solitary idea, no matter how sophisticated and exhaustive. Don't allow yourself to become bogged down with your favourite hobby-horse.

4. Allocate your time. The marks for questions often bear a close relationship to the time needed for an appropriate answer. Consequently the time spent on a question should be in proportion to the marks. Divide the total exam marks into the total exam time (less planning time) to obtain a 'minutes per mark' figure, and allow that many minutes per mark of each individual question.

5. Attempt all required questions. Always remember that the first 50 per cent of the marks for any question is the easier to earn. Unless you are working in complete ignorance, you will always earn more marks per minute while answering a new question than while continuing to answer one that is more than half done. Thus you can earn many more marks by half-completing two answers than by completing either one individually.

6. Don't show your ignorance. Concentrate on displaying your knowledge, not your ignorance. There is almost always one question you need to attempt and are not happy about. In answer to such a question put down all you *do* know, and then devote the unused time to improving some other answer. Certainly you won't get full marks by doing this, but neither will you if you fill your page with nonsense. By spending the saved time on another answer you will at least be gaining the odd mark or so.

7. If time runs out.

(*a*) If it is a numerical answer, don't bother to work out the figures. Show the examiner by means of your layout that you know what steps need to be taken and which pieces of data are applicable. He is very much more concerned with this than with your ability to calculate.

(*b*) If it is an essay answer, put down your answer in the form of notes. It is surprising what a large percentage of the question marks can be obtained by a dozen terse, relevant notes.

(*c*) Make sure that every question and question part has some answer – no matter how short – that summarizes the key elements.

(*d*) Don't worry. Shortage of time is more often a sign of knowing too much than too little.

8. Avoid panic, but welcome 'nerves'. Being nervous enables one to work at a much more concentrated pitch for a longer time without fatigue. Panic, on the other hand, destroys one's judgement. To avoid panic:

(*a*) know your subject (this is your best 'panic-killer');

(*b*) give yourself a generous time allowance to read the paper – quick starters are usually poor performers;

(*c*) take two or three deep breaths (there are good physiological reasons why this helps);

(*d*) concentrate simply on maximizing your marks – leave considerations of passing or failing until after;

(*e*) answer the easiest question first – it helps to build confidence;

(*f*) don't let first impressions of the paper upset you – given a few minutes, it is amazing what one's subconscious will throw up. This, too, is a good reason for answering the easiest question first; it gives your subconscious more time to 'crack' the difficult ones.

Report-writing in examinations

9. Purpose of report-writing: in practice. In practice, reports are written so that the person reported to receives in a permanent form information which has been selected and presented *with a specific object in mind.*

` Good report-writing involves *clear, logical and attractive presentation of information that is pertinent to the basic objective.* Usually action is taken on the basis of a report, and in order that appropriate action is taken the report must embody these qualities. The extent to which a report aids the achievement of the objective that initially gave rise to its commission is the ultimate measure of the quality of a report.

10. Purpose of report-writing: in examinations. Examiners ask for reports in examinations to see if:

(*a*) candidates appreciate the qualities needed to write a good report and can embody these qualities in their own writing, i.e. it is a test of lucid, logical and attractive presentation and the ability to select the relevant from the irrelevant;

(*b*) candidates know their subject – clearly knowledge (or the converse) of subject matter shows itself in the candidate's report;

(*c*) candidates know how to lay out a report properly.

11. Report layout.

(*a*) *Heading.* A simple heading for an examination report is as follows:

TO: .....(Person's title)..   REPORT REFERENCE: ....

FROM: .....(Person's title)..   DATE: ....

COPIES TO: ......(Persons' titles) ....

TITLE

The 'Copies to' space enables candidates to indicate that they appreciate which people in the organization are likely to be affected by the contents of the report.

Titles are sometimes difficult to compose on the spur of the moment, but the attempt shows the examiner that the candidate is aware of the need of a title for a report.

(*b*) *Reason for report.* If possible the first paragraph should outline the reason for the report. The time available for the question will indicate whether this outline should be given or whether a higher priority should be put on getting down to the subject matter.

(*c*) *Main body.* This will usually be the major part of the examination report and will state the findings and arguments in a lucid and logical manner.

(*d*) *Conclusions and/or recommendations.* Candidates should *never* forget this part of the report. It is absolutely essential that some conclusions and/or recommendations are given. This will indicate the extent to which the candidate is able to appreciate the significance of the information he has reported. Often candidates leave the examiners to dig out the conclusions. To be blunt, the examiners won't do this – they prefer to regard the omission as indicating the candidate's lack of ability to do this himself.

(*e*) *Signature.* A report must be signed. In addition it is usual to add the title of the person signing, e.g. management accountant. Beware of using 'Yours faithfully' (or 'Dear Sir' at the beginning). This only applies to reports to *clients*, and even then can be omitted if it is assumed that a covering letter (not given in the answer, of course) is sent with the report.

(*f*) *Appendices.* These give all the details upon which the main body of the report was built (in practice they often form the bulk of the report). Time in the examination does not usually allow appendices to be given, though use of an appendix to give specimen figures or suggested form design should be borne in mind.

Finally, note that a good report layout requires *all paragraphs to be numbered.*

12. Report-writing technique.

(*a*) *Length.* The shorter a report the better, provided all relevant information is given. Brevity not only saves time, it also improves clarity. If an idea can be given in a sentence it is better understood than if two pages are used to express it. This may be paradoxical but it's a psychological fact. Length only keeps a person thinking about it *longer* (which has been the sole function of the last three sentences).

(*b*) *Paragraphs.* Decide before you start writing what each paragraph will contain. This will aid logical writing.

(*c*) *Style.* Keep sentences short. Good reports state facts and opinions tersely.

(*d*) *Technical jargon.* The reader of the report must always been borne in mind, and jargon that would not be clearly understood by him should not be used. Candidates should check the question carefully to see what level of sophistication the reader may be assumed to have – some examiners make this a major factor in their questions.

(*e*) *Assumptions.* Some reports require assumptions to be made. Others do not as there is enough 'meat' in the question without conjuring up more (though whether the candidate will appreciate this is another matter). As a general rule do *not* make assumptions in your answer unless it is absolutely necessary.

(*f*) *Specimen figures.* If the subject matter allows it, try and give specimen figures. A few simple but well-chosen figures will often make a point much more effectively than a paragraph of writing.

(*g*) *Presentation of data.* When presenting data consider the possible use of tables and graphs. Figures should be represented wherever possible in a comparative form, i.e. in adjacent columns, headed, for example *This year/Last year, Current/Proposed.*

13. Reporting is a form of communication. A report is not an end-product, it is a device for communicating information to somebody who wants to *use* such information. If this person cannot understand it, is misled by it, or is repelled by its appearance so that he cannot get to grips with it, then no matter how accurate and painstaking the collection and analysis of detail, no matter how comprehensive the arguments, no matter how brilliant the conclusions and recommendations, the writer has failed and *all* his work (not just the writing of the report) is to no avail. After all, the writer alone has the choice of matter to be included, its order, and the words used to express it – the onus is on him for the comprehension of the report. Always remember that:

> *If the reader hasn't understood, the writer hasn't reported.*

14. Practise. You should now look at other people's reports, e.g. model answers, and criticize them. Make a start by criticizing this part of the appendix as a *report*. Criticizing others will teach you to look at your own reports with a more critical eye.

Appendix 2
Examination questions

Below are reproduced questions from past examination papers. The following abbreviations are used:

AAT – Association of Accounting Technicians.
ACCA – Chartered Association of Certified Accountants.
CIMA – Chartered Institute of Management Accountants.
ICA – Institute of Chartered Accountants in England and Wales.

1. A large local government authority places orders for various stationery items at quarterly intervals.
 In respect of an item of stock coded A32, data are:

- annual usage 5,000 boxes
- minimum order quantity 500 boxes
- cost per box £2

Usage of material is on a regular basis and on average, half of the amount purchased is held in inventory. The cost of storage is considered to be 25% of the inventory value. The average cost of placing an order is estimated at £12.5.
 The chief executive of the authority has asked you to review the present situation and to consider possible ways of effecting cost savings.

You are required to:

(a) tabulate the costs of storage and ordering item A32 for each level of orders from four to twelve placed per year;
(b) ascertain from the tabulation the number of orders which should be placed in a year to minimise these costs;
(c) produce a formula to calculate the order level which would minimise these costs – your formula should explain each constituent part of the formula and their relationships;
(d) give an example of the use of the formula to confirm the calculation in (b) above;

(*e*) calculate the percentage saving on the annual cost which could be made by using the economic order quantity system;

(*f*) suggest *two* other approaches which could be introduced in order to reduce the present cost of storage and ordering of stationery.   (*CIMA*)

2. (*a*) An importer deals only in one commodity and has recorded the following transactions for the first six months of the year.

Purchases

Date	Quantity Purchased Units	Gross Invoice Value £	Quantity Discount
February 1st	100	30,000	NIL
March 1st	200	60,000	2.5%
May 1st	300	90,000	5%

Sales

Date	Quantity Sold Units	Total Sales Value £
February	75	30,000
May	350	175,000

There was an opening balance at January 1st of 50 units, valued at £12,500.

Required

(*i*) Prepare the stores ledger account for the six months using the perpetual inventory system and the FIFO method of pricing issues.

(*ii*) Prepare a trading account to show the gross profit for the period, using the FIFO method of valuation.

(*iii*) Prepare a trading account to show the gross profit for the period, using the LIFO method of valuation.

(*b*) Production labour has traditionally been regarded as a directly variable cost.

Required
Discuss the factors or circumstances which would make this treatment inappropriate. You may draw on your own experience in answering.

(*AAT*)

3. (*a*) A company is proposing to introduce an incentive scheme into its factory.

Required
Three advantages and three disadvantages of individual incentive schemes.

(*b*) The company is undecided on what kind of scheme to introduce.

Required
From the following information calculate for each employee his earnings,
using

(*i*) guaranteed hourly rates only (basic pay),

(*ii*) piecework, but with earnings guaranteed at 75% of basic pay
where the employee fails to earn this amount, and

(*iii*) premium bonus in which the employee receives two-thirds of time
saved in addition to hourly pay.

Employees

		A	B	C	D
Actual hours worked		38	36	40	34
Hourly rate of pay		£3	£2	£2.50	£3.60
Output (units)	X	42	120	—	120
	Y	72	76	—	270
	Z	92	—	50	—

Standard time allowed (per unit)

X – 6 minutes, Y – 9 minutes, Z – 15 minutes

Each minute earned is valued at £0.05 for piecework calculation.

(*c*) The company has also considered introducing a Measured Day Work
scheme.

Required
A brief summary of the features and characteristics of Measured Day
Work. *(AAT)*

4. Shown below is an extract from next year's budget for a company
manufacturing three different products in three production departments.

Product	A	B	C
Production	4,000 units	3,000 units	6,000 units
Direct Material Cost	£7 per unit	£4 per unit	£9 per unit
Direct Labour Requirements:	hours per unit	hours per unit	hours per unit
Cutting Department:			
Skilled operatives	3	5	2
Unskilled operatives	6	1	3
Machining Department	$\frac{1}{2}$	$\frac{1}{4}$	$\frac{1}{3}$
Pressing Department	2	3	4
Machine Hour Requirements:			
Machining Department	2	$1\frac{1}{2}$	$2\frac{1}{2}$

The skilled operatives employed in the Cutting Department are paid £4 per hour and the unskilled operatives are paid £2.50 per hour. All the operatives in the Machining and Pressing Departments are paid £3 per hour.

	Production Departments			Service Departments	
	Cutting	Machining	Pressing	Engineering	Personnel
Budgeted Total Overheads	£154,482	£64,316	£58,452	£56,000	£34,000

Service department costs are incurred for the benefit of other departments as follows:

	Cutting	Machining	Pressing	Engineering	Personnel
Engineering Services	20%	45%	25%	—	10%
Personnel Services	55%	10%	20%	15%	—

The company operates a full absorption costing system.

Required:

(a) Calculate, as equitably as possible, the total budgeted manufacturing cost of:

(i) one completed unit of Product A, and

(ii) one incomplete unit of Product B, which has been processed by the Cutting and Machining Departments but which has not yet been passed into the Pressing Department.

(b) At the end of the first month of the year for which the above budget was prepared the production overhead control account for the Machining Department showed a credit balance.

Explain the possible reasons for that credit balance.   (ACCA)

5. In order to identify the costs incurred in carrying out a range of work to customer specification in its factory, a company has a job costing system. This system identifies costs directly with a job where this is possible and reasonable. In addition, production overhead costs are absorbed into the cost of jobs at the end of each month, at an actual rate per direct labour hour for each of the two production departments.

One of the jobs carried out in the factory during the month just ended was Job No. 123. The following information has been collected relating specifically to this job:

400 kilos of Material Y were issued from stores to Department A.

76 direct labour hours were worked in Department A at a basic wage of

£4.50 per hour. 6 of these hours were classified as overtime at a premium of 50%.

300 kilos of Material Z were issued from stores to Department B. Department B returned 30 kilos of Material Z to the storeroom being excess to requirements for the job.

110 direct labour hours were worked in Department B at a basic wage of £4.00 per hour. 30 of these hours were classified as overtime at a premium of 50%. All overtime worked in Department B in the month is a result of the request of a customer for early completion of another job which had been originally scheduled for completion in the month following.

Department B discovered defects in some of the work, which was returned to Department A for rectification. 3 labour hours were worked in Department A on rectification (these are additional to the 76 direct labour hours in Department A noted above). Such rectification is regarded as a normal part of the work carried out generally in the department. Department B damaged 5 kilos of Material Z which then had to be disposed of. Such losses of material are not expected to occur.

Total costs incurred during the month on all jobs in the two production departments were as follows:

	Department A £	Department B £
Direct materials issued from stores*	6,500	13,730
Direct materials returned to stores	135	275
Direct labour, at basic wage rate†	9,090	11,200
Indirect labour, at basic wage rate	2,420	2,960
Overtime premium	450	120
Lubricants and cleaning compounds	520	680
Maintenance	720	510
Other	1,200	2,150

Materials are priced at the end of each month on a weighted average basis. Relevant information of material stock movements during the month, for

*This includes, in Department B, the scrapped Material Z. This was the only material scrapped in the month.
†All direct labour in Department A is paid a basic wage of £4.50 per hour, and in Department B £4.00 per hour. Department A direct labour includes a total of 20 hours spent on rectification work.

materials Y and Z, is as follows:

	Material Y	Material Z
Opening Stock	1,050 kilos	6,970 kilos
	(value £529.75)	(value £9,946.50)
Purchases	600 kilos at	16,000 kilos at
	£0.50 per kilo	£1.46 per kilo
	500 kilos at	
	£0.50 per kilo	
	400 kilos at	
	£0.52 per kilo	
Issues from stores	1,430 kilos	8,100 kilos
Returns to stores	—	30 kilos

Required:

(a) Prepare a list of the costs that should be assigned to Job No. 123. Provide an explanation of your treatment of each item.

(b) Discuss briefly how information concerning the cost of individual jobs can be used. (*ACCA*)

6. Kaminsky Ltd. manufactures belts and braces. The firm is organized into five departments. These are belt-making, braces-making, and three service departments (maintenance, warehousing, and administration).

Direct costs are accumulated for each department. Factory-wide indirect costs (which are fixed for all production levels within the present capacity limits) are apportioned to departments on the basis of the percentage of floor-space occupied. Service department costs are apportioned on the basis of estimated usage, measured as the percentage of the labour-hours operated in the service department utilized by the user department.

Each service department also services at least one other service department.

Budgeted data for 1981 are as follows:

			Departments			
	Belts	Braces	Admin-istration	Main-tenance	Ware-housing	Company Total
1. Output and sales (units)						
Output capacity	150,000	60,000				
Output budgeted	100,000	50,000				
Sales budgeted	100,000	50,000				
2. Direct variable costs (£000)						
Materials	120	130	—	20	30	300
Labour	80	70	50	80	20	300
Total	200	200	50	100	50	600
3. Factory-wide fixed indirect costs (£000)						1,000

Departments

	Belts	Braces	Admin-istration	Main-tenance	Ware-housing	Company Total
4. Floor-space (%)	40	40	5	10	5	100
5. Usage of service department labour-hours (%)						
Administration	40	40	—	10	10	100
Warehousing	50	25	—	25	—	100
Maintenance	30	30	—	—	40	100

(*a*) You are required to calculate the total cost per unit of belts and braces respectively, in accordance with the system operated by Kaminsky Ltd.

(*b*) In addition to the above data, it has been decided that the selling prices of the products are to be determined on a cost-plus basis, as the unit total cost plus 20%.

Two special orders have been received, outside the normal run of business, and not provided for in the budget.

They are as follows:

(*i*) an order for 1,000 belts from Camfam, an international relief organisation, offering to pay £5,000 for them;

(*ii*) a contract to supply 2,000 belts a week for 50 weeks to Mixon Spenders, a chain-store, at a price per belt of 'unit total cost plus 10%'.

You are required to set out the considerations which the management of Kaminsky Ltd. should take into account in deciding whether to accept each of these orders, and to advise them as far as you are able on the basis of the information given.

(*c*) 'Normalized overhead rates largely eliminate from inventories, from cost of goods sold, and from gross margin any unfavourable impact of having production out of balance with the long-run demand for a company's products.'

You are required to explain and comment upon the above statement.

(*CA*)

7. (*a*) XY Constructions Limited is building an extension to a college operated by the Education Authority. Work on the college extension commenced on 1st April, 1981 and after one year, on 31st March, 1982, the data shown below were available.

You are required to:

(*i*) prepare the account for the contract for the year ended 31st March, 1982;

(*ii*) show in relation to the contract an extract from the balance sheet as at 31st March, 1982.

During the year:	£000
Plant sent to site	100
Direct materials received at site	460
Direct wages incurred	350
Direct expenses incurred	45
Hire of tower crane	40
Indirect labour costs	70
Supervision salaries	42
Surveyors fees	8
Service costs	18
Hire of scaffolding	20
Overhead incurred on site	60
Head office expenses apportioned to contract	70
Cash received from the Education Authority	1,000

At 31st March, 1982	£000
Value of plant on site	75
Work certified, valued at	1,250
Cost of work not certified	250
Wages accrued	30
Service costs accrued	2
Materials unused on site	40

(b) Discuss the valuation of work-in-progress, with particular reference to contract building work. (*CIMA*)

8. Using the information given below for the month of October, in respect of A Limited, you are required to:

(a) write up the integrated accounts;
(b) prepare a trading and profit and loss account for October;
(c) compile a trial balance as at 31st October;
(d) comment on the difference in the level of stocks and state which administration cost will be increased following the changed levels of stocks.

1. List of balances at 1st October, 1983:

	£000
Fixed assets – production	1,000
Provision for depreciation of fixed assets	400
Material stores control	100
Work-in-progress stock	50
Finished goods stock	20
Debtors	600
Creditors	290
Creditor for P.A.Y.E. and national insurance	85
Wages control – credit balance (accrued direct wages)	20

Cash	5
Bank – overdrawn	300
Share capital	600
Profit and loss appropriation: credit balance	80

2. Transactions for the month of October:

	£000
Received from debtors	380
Paid to creditors	170
Expenses paid by cheque: production	60
administration	40
selling	30
Bank interest on overdraft	10
Paid to creditor for P.A.Y.E. and national insurance	60
Depreciation of fixed assets (for production)	25
Materials received and invoiced	110
Materials price variance, favourable, extracted as materials are received	10
Materials issued to production, at standard prices	80
Materials issued to production maintenance	20
Transfers from work-in-progress to finished goods	230
Sales on credit	310
Sales for cash	10
Production cost of goods sold	200

	Gross £000	P.A.Y.E./ Nat. Ins. £000	£000
Direct wages paid	86	20	66
Direct wages accrued	22	—	22
Indirect wages paid (production)	24	4	20
Administrative staff salaries paid	12	4	8
Selling staff salaries paid	20	4	16
Employer's contribution, national insurance:			
production			9
administration			3
selling			2
Cash paid into bank			13

Production overhead is absorbed on the basis of 150% on direct wages; any under or over absorption is transferred to profit and loss account.

Administration and selling costs are not absorbed into product costs.

(*CIMA*)

9. Product B is made by means of three processes. Material is put into process at the start of process 1 and the output transferred to process 2. The output of process 2 is transferred to process 3 and the completed product of process 3 is transferred to finished goods stock.

The following data for the week ended 31st October, 1980 relating to product B are given below:

Process	Description	Units	Stage of completion %	Cost £
1	Work in process, at start	20	50	270
	Input: Material	270		3,240
	Labour and overhead			840
	Output: Transferred to process 2	290		
2	Input: Material added			530
	Labour and overhead			1,540
	Output: Transferred to process 3	240		
	Work in process, at end:			
	Material added	50	$\begin{cases}50 \\ 80\end{cases}$	
	Labour and overhead			
3	Work in process, at start:	90		
	Transferred cost			2,025
	Labour and overhead		$33\frac{1}{3}$	105
	Input: Labour and overhead			1,015
	Output: Transferred to finished goods stock	300		
	Work in process, at end	30	$66\frac{2}{3}$	
	Finished goods:			
	Stock at start	100		2,700
	Sold	324		

No units were lost in production and the weighted average basis of pricing is to be used.

You are required to prepare for the week ended 31st October, 1980:

(a) the three manufacturing process accounts, showing in each:
  (i) the unit cost;
  (ii) the value of work in process;
  (iii) the cost of production transferred;

(b) the finished goods stock account.   (*CIMA*)

10. (a) Distinguish between job costing and process costing.
  (b) Explain how you would treat the following items in the accounts of

a process costing system:

(i) waste

(ii) scrap

(c) A chemical is produced by passing a basic ingredient through four processes, during each of which direct materials are added. From the information given below for the month of March, you are required to prepare a statement in which each element of cost is analyzed and the output evaluated, and to show the accounts of process 3 and abnormal loss.

Data for process 3 include:

Work in process:

	Opening stock	Closing stock
Units	400	1,000
Degree of completion	%	%
Material X	80	50
Material Y	80	45
Labour	50	30
Overhead	40	25

Cost incurred during the period:

		£
Transfer from process 2	5,400 units	6,240
Material X		2,862
Material Y		944
Labour		468
Overhead		1,398

Transfer to process 4 during the period: 4,550 units

Rejections during the period:

Normal	200 units
Abnormal	50 units

Units rejected had reached the following stages:

	%
Material X	80
Material Y	80
Labour	60
Overhead	40

Rejected units are considered as waste.

The cost per unit in February and March was the same.   (CIMA)

11. A company manufactures two types of industrial sealant by passing materials through two consecutive processes. The results of operating the

two processes during the previous month are shown below:

Process 1
Costs incurred:

Materials 7,000 kilos @ £0.50 per kilo	£3,500	
Labour and Overheads	£4,340	

Output

Transferred to Process 2	6,430 kilos
Defective production	570 kilos

Process 2
Cost incurred:

Labour and Overheads	£12,129

Output

Type E Sealant	2,000 kilos
Type F Sealant	4,000 kilos
By-Product	430 kilos

It is considered normal for 10% of the total output from Process 1 to be defective and all defective output is sold as scrap at £0.40 per kilo. Losses are not expected in Process 2.

There was no work-in-process at the beginning or end of the month and no opening stocks of sealants.

Sales of the month's output from Process 2 were:

Type E Sealant	1,100 kilos
Type F Sealant	3,200 kilos
By-Product	430 kilos

The remainder of the output from Process 2 was in stock at the end of the month.

The selling prices of the products are, Type E Sealant £7 per kilo and Type F Sealant £2.50 per kilo. No additional costs are incurred on either of the two main products after the second process. The by-product is sold for £1.80 per kilo after being sterilized, at a cost of £0.30 per kilo, in a subsequent process. The operating costs of Process 2 are reduced by the net income receivable from sales of the by-product.

Required:

(*a*) Calculate, for the previous month, the cost of the output transferred from Process 1 into Process 2 and the net cost or saving arising from any abnormal losses or gains in Process 1.

(*b*) Calculate the value of the closing stock of each Sealant and the profit earned by each Sealant during the previous month using the following methods of apportioning costs to joint products:

   (i) according to weight of output,
   (ii) according to market value of output.

(c) Consider whether apportioning process costs to joint products is useful. Briefly illustrate with examples from your answer to (b) above.

(ACCA)

12. The manager of a small business has received enquiries about printing three different types of advertising leaflet. Information concerning these three leaflets is shown below:

Leaflet type	A	B	C
	£	£	£
Selling price, per 1,000 leaflets	100	220	450
Estimated printing costs:			
Variable, per 1,000 leaflets	40	70	130
Specific fixed costs, per month	2,400	4,000	9,500

In addition to the specific fixed costs a further £4,000 per month would be incurred in renting special premises if any or all of the above three leaflets were printed.

The minimum printing order would be for 30,000 of each type of leaflet per month and the maximum possible order is estimated to be 60,000 of each leaflet per month.

Required:

(a) (i) Examine and comment upon the potential profitability of leaflet printing. Make whatever calculations you consider appropriate.

(ii) Assuming that orders have been received to print each month 50,000 of both Leaflet A and Leaflet B calculate the quantity of Leaflet C which would need to be ordered to produce an overall profit, for all three leaflets, of £1,800 per month.

(b) It is possible that a special type of paper used in printing the leaflets will be difficult to obtain during the first few months. The estimated consumption of this special paper for each type of leaflet is:

   Leaflet A   2 packs per 1,000 leaflets
   Leaflet B   6 packs per 1,000 leaflets
   Leaflet C   16 packs per 1,000 leaflets

Advise the manager on the quantity of each leaflet which should be printed in order to maximize profit in the first month, if 50,000 of each type of leaflet have been printed, there remains unfulfilled orders of 10,000 for each type of leaflet and there are 170 packs of special paper available for the rest of the month.

(c) 'If the manager of the above business wastes ten packs of special paper then the cost to the business of that waste is simply the original cost of that paper.'

Critically examine the validity of the above statement.   (*ACCA*)

13. Woodwind Ltd manufactures and sells three products, Baubles, Bangles and Beads, holding respectively 10%, 6% and 8% of the national market for them. It has no plans to produce any other product. It is generally believed in the industry that demand for each of the products is little affected by demand for the other two. Like the other smaller firms in the industry, Woodwind Ltd has always followed the prices set by the market leader, Goodman Ltd. Woodwind Ltd is operating at well below full capacity and faces no foreseeable production constraints.

For the year to 30th June 1980 the following historic cost management accounts were produced for Woodwind Ltd. (All the data are in £000.)

	Baubles	Bangles	Beads	Total	Nature of cost (V = variable; F = fixed)
Rent, rates & insurance	602	494	562	1,658	F – allocated by floor area
Direct labour	2,752	1,306	1,465	5,523	V
Indirect labour	882	424	460	1,766	F – allocated by direct labour
Energy	194	192	194	580	F – allocated by cubic space
Materials & supplies	1,568	968	960	3,496	V
Depreciation	1,130	854	730	2,714	F – allocated by plant value
Total manufacturing cost	7,128	4,238	4,371	15,737	
Selling expenses	1,820	916	940	3,676	F – allocated by sales value
Administration	690	260	356	1,306	F – allocated by time spent
Interest	104	80	106	290	F – allocated by asset value
Total cost	9,742	5,494	5,773	21,009	
Sales (less cash discounts)	10,354	5,208	5,344	20,906	
Profit (Loss)	612	(286)	(429)	(103)	
Unit sales (in thousand dozens):					
Actual	2,160	1,034	970	4,164	
Budget	2,000	1,000	1,000	4,000	
Unit selling price per dozen: (before discounts)	£5.00	£5.20	£5.40	£5.15	(average)

Beads have shown a loss in the management accounts for four of the last five years (including the year to 30th June 1980). Bangles showed a small loss in the year to 30th June 1979. Sales in the industry have declined slowly for the past three years. Goodman Ltd has just announced a reduction in the price of its brand of Baubles to £4.50 per dozen, effective immediately.

Woodwind Ltd's marketing director has estimated that, if Woodwind makes a similar price reduction immediately, then its unit sales of Baubles in the year to 30th June 1981 will be 2,000,000 dozen; that if it maintains its price at £5.00 per dozen sales will be 1,400,000 dozen units; and that if the price is dropped to £4.25 per dozen unit sales will be 2,200,000 dozen units. He estimates also that, barring price changes relative to competitors, sales of Bangles and Beads will be 1,000,000 dozen units each in the year to 30th June 1981.

You are required to set out the various issues which the directors of Woodwind Ltd should consider in relation to their production and pricing policies at their meeting to be held on 20th July 1980, and to write a short report to the Board summarizing the advice which you would offer to them.

(CA)

14. The management of Springer plc, is considering next year's production and purchase budgets.

One of the components produced by the company, which is incorporated into another product before being sold, has a budgeted manufacturing cost as follows:

	£
Direct Material	14
Direct Labour (4 hours at £3 per hour)	12
Variable Overhead (4 hours at £2 per hour)	8
Fixed Overhead (4 hours at £5 per hour)	20
Total Cost	54 per unit

Trigger plc, has offered to supply the above component at a guaranteed price of £50 per unit.

Required:

(a) Considering cost criteria only, advise management whether the above component should be purchased from Trigger plc. Any calculations should be shown and assumptions made, or aspects which may require further investigation, should be clearly stated.

(b) Explain how your above advice would be affected by each of the two SEPARATE situations shown below.

(i) As a result of recent government legislation if Springer plc continues to manufacture this component the company will incur additional inspection and testing expenses of £56,000 per annum, which are not included in the above budgeted manufacturing costs.

(*ii*) Additional labour cannot be recruited and if the above component is not manufactured by Springer plc, the direct labour released will be employed in increasing the production of an existing product which is sold for £90 and which has a budgeted manufacturing cost as follows:

	£
Direct Material	10
Direct Labour (8 hours at £3 per hour)	24
Variable Overhead (8 hours at £2 per hour)	16
Fixed Overhead (8 hours at £5 per hour)	40
	90 per unit

All calculations should be shown.

(*c*) The Production Director of Springer plc, recently said:

'We must continue to manufacture the component as only one year ago we purchased some special grinding equipment to be used exclusively by this component. The equipment cost £100,000, it cannot be resold or used elsewhere and if we cease production of this component we will have to write off the written down book value which is £80,000.'

Draft a brief reply to the Production Director commenting on his statement.
                                                            (*ACCA*)

15. (*a*) The following information relates to two hospitals for the year ended 31.12.1985.

	St. Mathew's	St. Mark's
Number of in-patients	15,400	710
Average stay per in-patient	10 days	156 days
Total number of out-patient attendances	130,000	3,500
Number of available beds	510	320
Average number of beds occupied	402	307

Cost Analysis	In-patients £	Out-patients £	In-patients £	Out-patients £
A. *Patient Care Services*				
1. Direct treatment services and supplies (e.g. nursing staff)	6,213,900	1,076,400	1,793,204	70,490
2. Medical supporting services:				
2.1 Diagnostic (e.g. pathology)	480,480	312,000	22,152	20,650
2.2 Other services (e.g. occupational therapy)	237,160	288,600	77,532	27,790

Cost Analysis	In-patients £	Out-patients £	In-patients £	Out-patients £
B. *General Services*				
1. Patient related (e.g. catering)	634,480	15,600	399,843	7,700
2. General (e.g. administration)	2,196,760	947,700	1,412,900	56,700

Note: In-patients are those who receive treatment whilst remaining in hospital. Out-patients visit hospital during the day to receive treatment.

Required:

(i) Prepare separate statements for each hospital for each cost heading:

(a) cost per in-patient day, £ to two decimal places.

(b) cost per out-patient attendance, £ to two decimal places.

(ii) Calculate for each hospital the bed-occupation percentage.

(iii) Comment briefly on your findings.

(b) A transport company operates with one vehicle only, and has produced the following forecast for next year:

Estimated operating kilometres	30,000
	£
Revenue	30,000
Total wages cost	10,000
Total standing costs	6,000
Total vehicle running costs	12,000

Revenue and vehicle running costs are directly variable with operating kilometres.

Required:

(i) Calculate the break even point and margin of safety in kilometres for the forecast period.

(ii) Prepare a table showing the profit or loss at the following levels of activity:

(a) 20,000 kilometres

(b) 30,000 kilometres

(c) 40,000 kilometres

(iii) Calculate the break even point in kilometres if the operating kilometres were forecast to be only 28,500 kilometres and the annual wage costs was cut to £8,000. (AAT)

16. A local authority owns and controls a multipurpose leisure/conference hall with adjacent bars and restaurants, in a seaside holiday resort. The

authority has received requests for the letting of the hall from

(1) the organizers of an international Modern and Latin American dance championship, and
(2) a firm of exhibition organizers which wants to mount an exhibition of hotel and catering equipment.

The estimates of income and costs are shown below.

Dance championship
Dates hall required: Monday 16th May to Saturday 21st May, 1988, inclusive.

Income: £200 per day rent plus 25% of box office takings from visitors who pay £5 entry fee per day to watch the championships. From past experience of running this event, the organizers estimate the number of dance competitors, who do not pay at the box office, will be 1,200 (200 per day) and that there will be 14,000 paying visitors over the six-day period.

30 stalls can be let to traders who use the concourse adjoining the hall. The traders sell dance shoes, clothes, records and videos. Stall rents vary with size but if all are occupied, the rental income received by the authority for the whole period of six days will be £5,000.

Some events are to be filmed for showing on television at a later date for which the authority will receive a fee of £3,000.

Bars and restaurants can expect to take £3 per person per day for *each person using the hall*.

Hotel and catering equipment exhibition
400 stand units can be erected and dates required are Sunday 15th May to Wednesday 18th May, 1988, inclusive. Sunday is the preparation day for the businesses renting stands for the exhibition from the organizers. The exhibition is to be open to the trade and public on the Monday, Tuesday and Wednesday. Stands are dismantled during Wednesday evening.

The exhibition organizers believe that all the stands will be let although some exhibitors will take two or more units to constitute larger stands. Exhibitors' employees average two per stand unit per day with the exception of the preparation day (Sunday) when the average is six employees per stand unit.

Although open to the public, the exhibition is primarily for the trade, i.e. for buyers of hotel and catering equipment, which is what prompted the organizers to select a holiday resort. The exhibition organizers are offering £8,000 rent for the four-day period plus 20% of receipts from visitors. It is expected that 4,600 visitors will each pay £2.50 to enter the exhibition over the three-day period.

It is estimated that all the exhibitors' employees will spend £6 each per day in the bars and restaurants and that each visitor to the exhibition will spend an average of £2.

Authority employees, some of whom are temporary part-time, staffing the hall, bars and restaurants are listed below. Box office staff are engaged on other duties within the hall when it is not open to the public. Assume that the weekly payments are variable with the days the hall is in use and are based on a 6-day working week.

	Weekly wage £	Number required for duty	
		Dance championship	Exhibition
Managers	300	4	2
Box office staff	200	9	6
Attendants/security staff	150	20	20
Restaurant and bar staff	200	10	6
Restaurant and bar staff	120	100	60

Variable costs:
Energy costs $\left.\begin{array}{l}\text{£200} \\ \text{£300}\end{array}\right\}$ *per day the hall is in use*
Cleaning contractors
Employee-related costs are 10% of *total* variable staff costs.

Fixed costs are expected to be incurred as follows:

	Per annum £
Manager and support staff permanently on site	60,000
Electrical, lighting and maintenance staff	100,000
Depreciation on fittings and equipment	80,000
Insurance	20,000

A gross profit of 45% is expected from all bar and restaurant receipts; the gross profit represents sales less cost of food, beverages and drinks.

IGNORE INFLATION AND VALUE ADDED TAX.

You are required to:

(a) prepare a comparative statement showing the income and expenditure relating to letting the hall for

(1) the dance championship
and
(2) the exhibition;

(b) calculate the average surplus contribution per day of use for each proposal;

(c) recommend to the authority which proposal should be accepted, together with *two* reasons supporting your choice;

(d) list *three* factors which the authority should consider – these may not necessarily be of a financial nature.   (*CIMA*)

17. A company manufactures two products. Each product uses two kinds of material and three grades of labour.

The next budget period includes the following:

Budget Period – 12 weeks; 5 days are worked each week and normal attendance is 7 hours per day.

Products

	Fern	Alder
Budget sales (units)	1,500	3,000

Material consumption per product

	Fern	Alder
A (£2 per kilo)	3 kilos	2 kilos
B (£4 per kilo)	3 kilos	1 kilo

Labour cost and utilization

	Fern	Alder
Grade 1 (£3 hour)	2 hours	1 hour
Grade 2 (£4 hour)	2 hours	1 hour
Grade 5 (£5 hour)	1 hour	1 hour

There are employed 16 – Grade 1, 15 – Grade 2, 10 – Grade 3.

Labour is paid a premium of 50% on basic pay for overtime.

Absenteeism and lateness (which is not paid) is expected to be 5% of time available and evenly spread over the three grades.

Labour efficiency is assessed at 75% in normal time but at 100% in overtime.

Budgeted Stocks of products and materials

	Opening	Closing
'Fern'	400	10 days sales
'Alder'	600	30 days sales
Material A	5,000 kilos	20 days usage
Material B	1,000 kilos	20 days usage

There is a 2% loss in material consumption anticipated.

Required for the budget period:

(a) The production quantities for the period.
(b) The direct wages cost budget. Include overtime if necessary.
(c) The direct material cost budget.   (AAT)

18. G.T. Urnside plc, a company which manufactures pressed steel fitments, commenced trading on 1 December 1981. Summarized below is the profit statement and balance sheet after the first year of trading.

G.T. Urnside plc
Summarized Profit Statement for the year ended 30 November 1982

	£000s	£000s
Sales		240
Cost of Sales:		
Direct Materials	60	
Direct Labour	48	
Variable Overhead	30	
Fixed Overhead	70	
		208
Net Operating Profit		£32
Proposed Dividends to Ordinary Shareholders		15
Retained Profit		17
		£32

G.T. Urnside plc
Summarized Balance Sheet as at 30 November 1982

	£000s	£000s	£000s
Issued Share Capital			
108,000 £1 Ordinary Shares			108
Reserves			
Retained Profit			17
Shareholders' Fund			£125
Represented by:			
Fixed Assets			
Plant and Machinery (at cost on 1.12.1981)		120	
Less: Depreciation		24	
			96
Current Assets			
Stocks of Materials		8	
Debtors		40	
Cash		1	
		49	
Less: Current Liabilities			
Creditors	5		
Dividend	15		
		20	
Net Working Capital			29
Net Assets Employed			£125

Shown below are relevant data extracted from the company's budget for the year ended 30 November 1983.

Sales: 1st Quarter £66,000   3rd Quarter £90,000
         2nd Quarter £78,000   4th Quarter £84,000

The weekly sales in each quarter will be constant and, on average, debtors pay eight weeks after goods have been despatched.

The selling prices and product mix will remain the same as the previous year.

Materials:
The price of materials will be 20% lower than the previous year. The weekly purchases of materials in each quarter will be constant, except for the budgeted stock increase in the third quarter shown below. Material suppliers are paid on average four weeks after the goods have been received.

Direct Labour:
Wages will be paid at the 1981/82 level of £12,000 per quarter plus the following changes:

(i) All direct operatives have been awarded a 15% rate of pay increase with effect from 1 December 1982.

(ii) One additional direct operative will be recruited at the beginning of the second quarter, and another direct operative will be recruited at the beginning of the third quarter. Both operatives will be paid £100 per week and will continue to be employed for the remainder of the year. Wages are paid at the end of the week in which they are earned.

Overheads:
Variable overheads vary directly with production activity and there will be no price increases from the previous year. Fixed overheads will increase by £12,000 p.a. and the total amount will be incurred evenly throughout the year. All relevant overheads are paid in cash immediately they are incurred.

Stocks:
Stocks of work-in-progress and finished goods will not be carried. However stocks of raw materials will increase by £3,000 in the first week of the third quarter and remain at £11,000 throughout the remainder of the year.

Capital Expenditure:
Additional equipment costing £20,000 will be purchased and paid for during the second quarter of the year. Depreciation on this equipment will not commence until the following year.

Dividends:
The dividends outstanding will be paid in the first quarter of the year.

Required:
Prepare the company's quarterly cash budgets for the year ended 30 November 1983.

NOTE: It should be assumed there are 12 weeks in each quarter and any other assumptions which you consider to be necessary should be clearly stated.

(ACCA)

19. The following data relate to Product Aye:

Budgeted Data

	1st October to 31st December, 1985			*1st January to 31st March, 1986*		
Sales Division	1	2	3	1	2	3
Sales of Aye	£ 54,000	342,000	228,000	60,000	360,000	240,000
Stocks of Aye: opening units	90	320	260	100	350	250
maximum units	150	500	350	150	500	350

Sales and production occur evenly each month during each budget quarter.

Debtors pay for sales in the month following that when sales occur.

Creditors are paid for materials in the second month following that when purchases occur.

On average, overhead incurred is paid for within the month following that in which incurred.

Wages are paid in the same month as earned.

Cash balance on 31st December, 1985, £(18,000).

Corporation tax of £50,000 is payable in January 1986.

Special advertising campaign expenditure of £60,000 is due in March 1986.

Standard Cost Data

Direct Materials	DM1	10 kilos @ £3 per kilo
	DM2	5 kilos @ £2 per kilo
Direct Wages	DW1	5 hours @ £4 per hour
	DW2	2 hours @ £5 per hour

Production overhead is absorbed as a labour hour rate, i.e. £12 in respect of DW1 and £10 in respect of DW2.

Administration and selling overhead is recovered at 20% of production cost.

Profit is calculated at 10% of selling price.

Direct Materials Data

	Materials	
	DM1	*DM2*
Maximum consumption per week (kilos)	3,600	1,800
Minimum consumption per week (kilos)	2,400	1,200
Re-order quantity (kilos)	20,000	12,000
Stock at 30th September, 1985 (kilos)	24,500	13,650
Stock at 31st December, 1985 (kilos)	23,000	14,400
Lead time from suppliers (weeks):		
Maximum	6	5
Minimum	4	3

A major sales campaign is planned in the budget period beginning 1st April, 1986. In anticipation of an increase in sales, an advertising campaign will commence in the previous quarter. The production director has requested that stocks of raw materials be increased to maximum level by 1st April, 1986 and the sales director has requested that stocks of finished goods be increased to maximum level by 1st April, 1986.

You are required to prepare the following budgets for the three months ending 31st March, 1986:

(*a*) production;
(*b*) purchases;
(*c*) production cost;
(*d*) cash (for each of the three months).   (*CIMA*)

20. Perchance Products Ltd manufacture and sell cassette recorders. Their budgets, standard costs and actual figures for Period 4 were as follows:

	Budget	*Standard*	*Actual*
Sales	15,000 units	£28 each	14,600 units totalling £401,500
Materials		£10 unit	Total £147,460
Wages		£5 unit	Total £72,730
Factory overhead		£6 unit	Total £85,980

	Budget	*Standard*	*Actual*	
Administration (fixed)	£30,000		Total	£29,000
Selling (fixed)	£20,000		Total	£21,000
Selling (variable)		2% sales	Total	£7,960

Required

(a) The budgeted results for period 4.

(b) The variances between actual and standard results for the period in which the manufacturing operations achieved standard efficiency.

(c) A Costing Trading and Profit & Loss Account for Period 4 reconciling the budgeted profit with actual profit achieved. (Note – assume no stocks exist at the beginning or end of period 4.) (*AAT*)

21. The information shown below is an extract from the previous period's budget and standard cost data for the Machining Department in a company manufacturing two products and which operates a full absorption standard costing system.

	Product X	*Product Y*
Budgeted Production	6,500 units	4,200 units
Standard machine hours allowed to process each product in the Machining Department	4 hours	7 hours

The department's overhead is applied to production by means of a standard machine hour absorption rate and this is calculated at the beginning of each period. The variable element of the previous period's absorption rate was £1.50 per standard machine hour and the department's total overheads for that period were budgeted to be £207,750. The budget assumes that one standard machine hour should be produced in one actual hour of machining time.

The actual results in the Machining Department for the previous period were:

Actual machining time	54,000 hours
Production: Product X	7,200 units
Product Y	4,000 units
Actual overheads incurred: Fixed	£120,550
Variable	£87,600

Required:

(a) Calculate the following variances from standard/budgeted cost which occurred in the Machining Department during the previous period:

> Fixed overhead volume variance.
> Fixed overhead expenditure variance.
> Variable overhead expenditure variance.

(b) Discuss in detail the possible reasons for the fixed overhead volume variance.

(c) Calculate the Machining Department's total flexed overhead budget for the actual level of production in the previous period and explain the difference between this total budgeted amount and the total production overhead absorbed by the department in the period. (ACCA)

22. The Finishing Department of a company manufacturing two different products employs 60 direct operatives working a basic 40 hour week. The company operates a standard costing system and the Finishing Department's standard direct labour cost for each of the two products is, Product X £12 per unit and Product Y £2 per unit. The standard wage rate for the operatives in the Finishing Department is £4 per hour and the company offers a guaranteed wage of £160 per week for each direct operative. Overtime premium, which is not included in standard product costs, is paid at time rate plus one third.

The following results occurred in the Finishing Department during the previous two months:

	Month 1	Month 2
Output Product X	2,200 units	2,300 units
Product Y	5,250 units	4,700 units
Gross wages paid to direct operatives	£44,800	£39,600
Productive hours worked by direct operatives	10,800 hours	9,000 hours
Number of hours for which direct operatives were paid: Ordinary time	9,600 hours	9,600 hours
Overtime	1,200 hours	NIL

In the second month all 60 direct operatives were standing idle for 10 hours as a result of equipment breakdowns.

Required:

(a) Calculate the Finishing Department's Productivity (or Efficiency) Ratio for Month 1.

(b) Calculate the efficiency variances, together with any other variances from standard labour cost, which occurred in the Finishing Department during each of the previous two months.

(c) Write up the entries for the first month's wages in the Finishing Department's Wages Control Account and Work in Progress Control

Account, including the entries for the appropriate variances calculated in (b) above.

(d) Consider whether the efficiency variances which you have calculated are likely to measure the net effect on the company's profit of direct operatives being more or less efficient than that specified by the standard.

(ACCA)

23. (a) From three raw materials (Gorgon, Camem and Stil) VLS manufactures a single cosmetic product called Eau de Vie. The standard mix of materials for one batch of output of Eau de Vie is as follows:

			£
Gorgon	100 fl. oz. at	£15.00 per oz. =	1,500
Camem	200 fl. oz. at	£7.15 per oz. =	1,430
Stil	700 fl. oz. at	£0.10 per oz. =	70
	1,000	£3.00	£3,000

Each batch should produce a standard output of Eau de Vie sufficient to fill five hundred bottles.

During June one hundred batches of materials were processed, producing enough Eau de Vie to fill forty-five thousand bottles. The actual consumption and cost of the materials were as follows:

			£
Gorgon	8,000 fl. oz. at	£19.00 per oz. =	£152,000
Camem	20,000 fl. oz. at	£6.85 per oz. =	137,000
Stil	80,000 fl. oz. at	£0.10 per oz. =	8,000
	108,000	£2.75	£297,000

Venuti, Lang and South are partners in VLS. Venuti has been working out the standard cost variances for materials in June. He has calculated *inter alia* that the total variance was £27,000 ADV, the mix variance was £29,000 FAV, and the yield variance was £30,000 ADV. However, he felt unsure of his methods of calculation, and asked Lang to make check calculations of the variances independently.

Lang agreed with Venuti's figures for the total cost and yield variances, but calculated the mix variance to be £53,000 FAV. South was therefore asked to check both sets of calculations, again working independently.

After a few minutes of work South said that he agreed that the total cost variance was £27,000 ADV, and that he agreed with Lang that the mix variance was £53,000 FAV; however, he calculated the yield variance to be £54,000 ADV.

You are required to calculate the total cost, price, quantity, mix, and yield variances (including all workings) as they have probably been worked out by each of

(*i*) Lang and
(*ii*) South.

(*b*) You are required to comment on the significance of mix and yield variances, using the figures from part (*a*) to illustrate your answer if you wish.

(*c*) In many process operations:

(*i*) price variances for materials are isolated when the materials are purchased and placed in inventory, and not at the time of usage, and

(*ii*) only the total batch input of materials is measured, any deviations from the standard mix being accidental and unmeasured.

Assume now that these conditions applied at VLS in June.
You are required to calculate the variance which would be measurable for the month of June, and to suggest how in practice the partners might seek to establish the cause of the variance.   (*CA*)

24. The financial and cost accounts of the MA Manufacturing Company for the year ended 30th September, 1985 have been reconciled as below.

*Financial profit and loss account
for the year ended 30th September, 1985*

	£	£	£	£
Raw materials:				
Opening stock	56,450		Cost of goods	
Purchases	324,560		manufactured	810,000
	381,010			
Closing stock	58,060			
		322,950		
Direct wages		247,320		
Production salaries		86,465		
Indirect wages		42,321		
Depreciation		50,000		
Power		10,642		
Telephone		8,742		
Rates		16,400		
Insurance		6,475		
Miscellaneous		18,325		
		809,640		

Work-in-progress:

Opening stock	18,620			
Closing stock	18,260			
		360		
		810,000		810,000

Finished goods:			Sales	1,103,500
Opening stock	142,350			
Manufactured	810,000			
	952,350			
Closing stock	146,850			
		805,500		
Gross profit c/d		298,000		
		£1,103,500		£1,103,500

Administration expenses		124,620	Gross profit b/d	298,000
Selling and distribution expenses		87,380	Discount received	1,600
Discount allowed		1,240		
Debenture interest		6,360		
Net profit c/d		80,000		
		£299,600		£299,600

Reconciliation of Financial and Cost Accounts
Year ended 30th September, 1985

	£		£
Profit as per financial accounts	80,000	Profit as per cost accounts	84,550
Discount allowed	1,240	Discount received	1,600
Debenture interest	6,360	Difference in stock valuation:	
Difference in stock valuation:		Raw materials: Opening	700
Work-in-progress: Closing	480	Raw materials: Closing	750
Finished goods: Opening	720	Work-in-progress: Opening	620
		Finished goods: Closing	580
	£88,800		£88,800

Data in the cost accounts include:

	£
Direct material price variance	3,120 Adverse
Direct material usage variance	1,280 Adverse
Direct labour rate variance	4,160 Favourable
Direct labour efficiency variance	4,470 Favourable
Production overhead expenditure variance	4,880 Favourable
Production overhead volume variance	1,680 Adverse

You are required, from the above data, to show the following accounts as they should appear in the cost ledger:

(a) stores ledger control;
(b) work-in-progress ledger control;
(c) finished goods ledger control;
(d) profit and loss.   (CIMA)

25. (a) State, and define, Cost Accounting ratios which may be used in the measurement of:
(1) Production, and
(2) Productivity

(b) Illustrate your answer to (a) above by calculating the appropriate ratios from the following data for each department.

(i) Department P	Model A	Model B
Output in units	17,600	16,800
Standard time per unit	9 minutes	16.5 minutes
Time taken in department	6,400 hours	
Budget/output, in standard hours	2,500	4,700

(ii) Department Q	
Output in units	10,500
Standard time per unit	0.9 hours
Time taken in department	12,400 hours
Budget output, in standard hours	12,600 hours

(c) What is the significance of the answers to (b) above?   (AAT)

26. Exe operates an integrated accounting system and prepares its final accounts monthly.

Balances as at 1st October

	£000
Issued share capital	1,500
Profit and loss balance	460
Freehold buildings	1,000
Plant and machinery, at cost	500
Plant and machinery: depreciation provision	300
Motor vehicles, at cost	240
Motor vehicles: depreciation provision	80
10% Debentures	240
Creditors (materials)	144
Creditors (expenses)	36
Stock – raw materials	520
Wages payable	40
Debtors	246
Bank	162
Stock – finished goods	132

Data for the month of October

Materials purchased – 400,000 units at £4.90 per unit
Issued to production – 328,000 units
Paid to creditors – £1,800,000
Direct wages incurred – 225,000 hours at £4.20 per hour
Direct wages paid – £920,000
Production overhead incurred on credit – £1,490,000
Expense creditors paid – £1,900,000
Cash received from debtors – £4,800,000
Sales – £4,875,000
Plant and machinery purchased for cash on 1st October – £100,000
Administration and selling overhead incurred on credit – £895,000
Production and sales – 39,000 units

Additional data

Debenture interest – payable monthly
Depreciation provision – plant and machinery, 20% p.a. on cost
                       – motor vehicles, 25% p.a. on cost
Stocks of raw materials and finished goods are maintained at standard
There are four working weeks in the month of October
The operation of motor vehicles is regarded as a cost of selling

Standard data

Direct material price – £5.00 per unit
Direct material usage – 8 units per product

Direct wages – £4.00 per hour
Direct labour – 6 hours per product
Production overhead – absorbed at 150% of direct wages
Gross profit – calculated at $16\frac{2}{3}$% of selling price
Budgeted output – 10,000 units per week.

You are required to:

(*a*) calculate the appropriate variances for October;
(*b*) show the accounts for October as they would be expected to appear in the ledger;
(*c*) prepare a profit and loss statement for October, together with a balance sheet as at the end of that month. (*CIMA*)

Appendix 3

Suggested answers

Progress test 2

9. (a) FIFO: (40 at £25 + 40 at £30) – (30 at £25 + 10 at £20 + 20 at £30) = £600. Alternatively 20 at £30.

(b) LIFO: (40 at £25 + 40 at £30) – (30 at £25 + 30 at £30) = £550. Alternatively 10 at £25 + 10 at £30.

(c) Weighted average: Receipts 1/6/ $\quad$ = 40 × £25 = £1,000
Issues 2/6/ $\quad$ = 30 × £25 = $\quad$ 750

Balance in
stock: $\quad$ 10 units for $\quad$ 250
Receipts 8/6/ $\quad$ = 40 units for 1,200

$\qquad$ 50 $\qquad$ £1,450

∴ New average price $= \dfrac{£1,450}{50} = £29$

∴ Value of 20 units closing stock = 20 at £29 = £580

10. In this situation there are in effect two prices: £10 and £10 less 2 per cent = £9.80. In the EOQ formula, therefore, S will be either 25 per cent of £10 = £2.50 or 25 per cent of £9.80 = £2.45. And the first step is to compute the EOQ associated with each price and see what quantities are involved. We have, then:

$$\text{EOQ at £10} = \sqrt{\dfrac{2 \times 105 \times 60,000}{2.5}} = 2,245 \text{ units.}$$

$$\text{EOQ at £9.80} = \sqrt{\dfrac{2 \times 105 \times 60,000}{2.45}} = 2,268 \text{ units.}$$

Now the EOQ for the £9.80 price is way below the quantity discount level and so cannot be realized. And since the total cost curve rises continuously beyond this point (*see* Fig. 2.2), the attainable EOQ for this price is at the discount level of 14,000 units.

Given that we now have two EOQs, 2,245 and 14,000 units, the next step is to compute the total costs involved for a year at both levels. And these are:

Year's costs with EOQ of 2,245 units = Purchasing costs of £105 × 60,000/2,245 + holding costs of £2.5 × 2,245/2 = 2,806.50 + 2,806.50 = £5,612.50

Year's costs with EOQ of 14,000 units = Purchasing costs of £105 × 60,000/14,000 + holding costs of £2.45 × 14,000/2 − discount of 2 per cent on 60,000 at £10 = £450 + £17,150 − 12,000 = £5,600.00

In theory, then, a re-order level of 14,000 rather than 2,245 units saves £12.50 a year. Clearly, however, when the difference in costs is as trivial as this the decision will be made on the basis of some factor other than cost.

Progress test 3

13.

		X	Y
(a)	Total time allowance	$189 \times \frac{1}{3} = 63$ hrs	$204 \times \frac{1}{4} = 51$ hrs
	Less time taken	45 hrs	39 hrs
	Time saved	18 hrs	12 hrs
∴	Bonus payable	$18 \times \frac{1}{2} \times £4 = £36$	$12 \times \frac{1}{2} \times £4 = £24$
(b)	Basic week's pay	$42 \times £4 = £168$	$42 \times £4 = £168$
	Overtime	$3 \times 1\frac{1}{2} \times £4 = £18$	Nil
∴	Gross wage payable	$36 + 168 + 18 = £222$	$24 + 168 = £192$
(c)	Good units made	$189 - 6 = 183$	$204 - 4 = 200$
∴	Wage cost per good unit	$\dfrac{£222}{183} = £1.213$	$\dfrac{£(192 - 12)^*}{200} = 90\text{p}$

*Assume 3 hours at £4 per hour booked to dayrate work.

Progress test 5

9.

Overhead Analysis and Overhead Absorption Rates.

Overhead	Basis of apportionment	Total £	Total Units	Rate/unit	Maintenance £	Maint. Units	Stores £	Stores Units	General £	Gen. Units	Machine X Units	Machine X £	Machine Y Units	Machine Y £	Assembly Units	Assembly £	Packing Units	Packing £
Indirect wages and supervision	Allocation	204,000			22,500		11,500		24,250			38,000		43,500		41,250		23,000
Maintenance wages	Allocation	52,000			5,000		2,500		4,500			10,000		20,000		5,000		5,000
Indirect materials	Allocation	127,750			9,000		6,750		4,000			27,000		36,000		18,000		27,000
Power	Effective HP	60,000	100	£600	6,000	10	—	—	—	—	40	24,000	40	24,000	—	—	10	6,000
Rent and rates	Area (000 sq ft)	80,000	50	£1600	4,800	3	8,000	5	3,200	2	10	16,000	7½	12,000	15	24,000	7½	12,000
Lighting and heating	Area (000 sq ft)	20,000	50	£400	1,200	3	2,000	5	800	2	10	4,000	7½	3,000	15	6,000	7½	3,000
Insurance	Book values (£000s)	10,000	400	£25	1,500	60	250	10	250	10	120	3,000	160	4,000	20	500	20	500
Depreciation	Book values (£000s)	200,000	400	£500	30,000	60	5,000	10	5,000	10	120	60,000	160	80,000	20	10,000	20	10,000
Total		**753,750**			**80,000**		**36,000**		**42,000**			**182,000**		**222,500**		**104,750**		**86,500**
Services:																		
Maintenance	Maintenance wages		40,000*	£2†	−80,000						10,000	20,000	20,000	40,000	5,000	10,000	5,000	10,000
					Nil		36,000		42,000										
Stores	Direct labour hours (000s)		300	£120			36,000				100	12,000	75	9,000	75	9,000	50	6,000
							−36,000												
General	Direct labour hours (000s)		300	£140					42,000		100	14,000	75	10,500	75	10,500	50	7,000
									−42,000									
Total		**£ 753,750**			**Nil**		**Nil**		**Nil**			**228,000**		**282,000**		**134,250**		**109,500**
Hours (machine/labour)												50,000		60,000		75,000		50,000
Overhead absorption rate (per machine/direct labour hour)												£4.560		£4.700		£1.790		£2.190

*Wages allocated in second line to non-service departments sharing apportionment (see question)

†i.e. £2 maintenance overhead per £1 maintenance wages.

Progress test 6

7. The first step is to calculate the unknown rates as follows. *Materials:* Weighted average price of issue to job 111 = average price after purchase on 24th April =

$$\frac{(100 - 40) \times £2 + £240}{(100 - 40) + 100} = £2\tfrac{1}{4}.$$

Labour: Total wages paid excluding special overtime:

A. Able: $(40 + 8 \times 2) \times £4 = £224$.
B. Baker: $(40 + 10 \text{ hrs normal O/T} \times 2) \times £4.50 = £270$.
∴ Chargeable labour rates:

A. Able: $£224/48 = £4\tfrac{2}{3}$.
B. Baker: $£270/50$ (normal) $= £5.4$.

Overheads: Dept. X: $\dfrac{£40,000}{20,000} = £2$ per direct labour hour.

Dept. Y: $\dfrac{£100,000}{100,000} = £1$ per direct labour hour.

Sales Dept.: $\dfrac{150,000}{3,000,000} \times 100 = 5\%$ factory cost.

Now the job cost can be prepared as follows.

Job cost – Job 111

	Rate	£
Materials: 20 units PQ	£2¼	45
Labour: Dept X, 9 hrs	4⅔	42
Dept Y, 5 hrs	5.4	27
2 hrs O/T	9	18
Overheads: Dept. X, 9 hrs	2	18
Dept. Y, 7 hrs	1	7
Direct expenses: Storage box		3
Factory cost		160
Selling overheads: 5% factory cost		8
Total cost		168
Profit		32
Selling price		£200

8(a). *SSAP 9:*

CONTRACT 158 A/C (CLIENT AZA)

	£		£
Prepayments b/d	11,000	Accruals b/d	37,000
Stock at site b/d	124,000	Profit in suspense b/d	382,267
Plant at site b/d	205,000	Stock at site c/d	61,000
Work in progress b/d	371,000	Plant at site c/d	195,000
Materials purchased	92,000	Work in progress c/d	112,000
Site wages	16,000	Cost of work certified	422,000[2]
Site expenses	2,000		
Sub-contract work	3,000		
Head office overheads	2,000		
Accruals c/d	1,000		
Profit in suspense c/d	382,267[1]		
	1,209,267		1,209,267
Cost of work certified b/d	422,000	Profit in suspense b/d	382,267
P/L on Contracts	145,411[3]	Work certified – AZA a/c	500,000
Profit in suspense c/d	314,856[3]		
	882,267		882,267
Stock at site b/d	61,000	Accruals b/d	1,000
Plant at site b/d	195,000	Profit in suspense b/d	314,856
Work in progress b/d	112,000		

(1) The profit in suspense previously carried down from the earlier year's Profit and Loss section must be reversed before the Profit and Loss section can be started.

(2) The balance on the account must be the cost of work certified.

(3) Profit apportionment:

		£
Total contract cost: Cost of work certified – year 1 (**18**)		7,080,000
year 2		422,000
Total cost of work certified		7,502,000
Work in progress		112,000
Cost of work done		7,614,000
Cost to complete		300,000
Rectification costs		700,000
Total estimated contract cost		8,614,000

$$\text{Total attributable profit} = (9,500,000 - 8,614,000) \times \frac{7,614,000}{8,614,000}$$

$$= £783,144$$

So period profit = 783,144 − 637,733 (*see* **18,** note 1(*a*)) = 145,411.

And profit in suspense = balancing figure = £314,856

(*b*) *Traditional:* If the accounts were kept using the traditional method of ascertaining profit then the Current section would only change to the extent that the profit in suspense on both sides of the account would be a different figure – in this case £408,000 (*see* **18,** note 1(*b*)). The Profit and Loss section would be as follows:

Cost of work certified b/d	422,000	Profit in suspense b/d	408,000
P/L on contracts	8,500*	Work certified – AZA a/c	500,000
Profit in suspense c/d	477,500*		
	908,000		908,000

The Future section would, of course, be the same as in (*a*) except for the profit in suspense figure of £477,500.

*Profit ascertainment: Work certified – year 1	£8,100,000
year 2	500,000
Total value of work certified	8,600,000
Cost of work certified (*see* (*a*)(3))	7,502,000
Profit	1,098,000

Total attributable profit $= \frac{2}{3} \times 1,098,000 \times \dfrac{7,290,000}{8,600,000}$ (**18**) = £620,500

So period profit = 620,500 − 612,000 (*see* **18,** note (*b*)) = £8,500

And profit in suspense = balancing figure = £477,500

Extract from Balance Sheet under SSAP 9.

	£
Cost to date	7,614,000
Plus attributable profit	783,144
	8,397,144
Less cash received and receivable	7,740,000*
Work in progress	657,144

*£8,600,000 work certified less 10%

In normal circumstances the total attributable profit under the traditional method would give a far too conservative estimate of the profit earned for a contract which is virtually complete and will make a large estimated profit. However in this instance, in view of the client's request for a slow-down and the fact that no further payments have been received an attitude of caution does seem to be indicated. Since the total cost to date (£7,614,000) is greater than the actual cash received to date (£7,290,000) it would appear to be prudent in this particular instance to lean towards the traditional profit rather than SSAP 9.

9. The following is an alternative system of job costing for the Thorough Garage.

(a) The service manager is given permission to quote the price of all minor work, on the basis of either a set of standard charges or his own estimate.

(b) A single standing order number is raised for *all* such work.

(c) Employees are instructed to book all time and materials on such work to this order number. This will simplify workshop recording and analysis, since any employee who spends all his time on a succession of minor jobs will simply book the whole of his time (and materials used) to the one order number by means of a single entry.

(d) An account is opened for this order number and all materials, labour and direct expenses booked against the number, together with the appropriate overheads, are debited to this account. In addition, all sales are credited.

(e) At the end of each costing period the balance on this account (apart from any work-in-progress, which should be insignificant) is the overall profit or loss on minor work. As long as this balance figure is reasonable, there is no real need for further details of individual jobs, since the service manager is ensuring that all costs are covered and a reasonable profit is being obtained on this work as a whole.

Progress test 7

7. *Materials Control Account*

	£		£
4/5/-2: Balance b/d	9,834	4/5/-2: Adjustments:	
		Work-in-progress	
Adjustments:		(Job 819)	60
Work-in-progress		Loss on breaking	
(Job 312)	40	bulk	12
Creditors	400	Factory overheads	10
		Selling overheads	20
		Balance c/d	10,172
	10,274		10,274
4/5/-2: Balance b/d	10,172		

8. Accounts and trial balance for Tiny Ltd.

FINANCIAL LEDGER

Creditors Control

Cash	1,500	Balance	2,000	
Discounts	100	Purchases (cost		
Balance c/d	2,400	control)	2,000	
	4,000		4,000	
		Balance b/d	2,400	

Debtors Control

Balance	1,000	Cash	2,000
Sales		Discounts	150
(cost control)	2,500	Balance c/d	1,350
	3,500		3,500
Balance b/d	1,350		

Bank

Balance	1,000	Creditors	1,500
Debtors	2,000	Wages (cost	
		control)	1,000
Balance c/d	500	Gen. operating	
		expenses (cost	
		control)	1,000
	3,500		3,500
		Balance b/d	500

Fixed Assets

Balance	3,000	Depreciation	30
Additions (cost		Balance c/d	3,470
control)	500		
	3,500		3,500
Balance b/d	3,470		

Capital

	Balance	10,000

Discounts Allowed

Debtors	150	P/L	150

Discounts Received

P/L	100	Creditors	100

Cost Control

Balance	7,000	Debtors	2,500
Creditors	2,000		
Wages	1,000	Fixed assets	500
Gen. operating			
expenses	1,000	Balance c/d	8,630
Depreciation	30		
Notional			
rent (P/L)	100		
Profit (P/L)	500		
	11,630		11,630
Balance b/d			
RM	1,000		
WIP	2,630		
FG	5,000		
	8,630		

Financial P/L

Discounts		Notional	
allowed	150	rent written	
Net profit to		back	100
appropriation	550	Cost profit	
		(cost control)	500
		Discounts	
		received	100
	700		700

P/L Appropriation

	P/L	550

COST LEDGER

Stores

Balance	2,000	WIP	3,000
Purchases	2,000	Balance c/d	1,000
	4,000		4,000
Balance b/d	1,000		

Overhead Control

Gen. operating		WIP	1,130
expenses	1,000		
Notional			
rent	100		
Depreciation	30		
	1,130		1,130

Capital Expenditure

WIP	500	Fixed assets	500

Notional Rent

Financial P/L	100	Overheads	100

Sales

P/L	2,500	Debtors	2,500

Finished Goods

Balance	3,000	Cost of sales	
WIP	4,000	(P/L)	2,000
		Balance c/d	5,000
	7,000		7,000
Balance b/d	5,000		

Cost P/L

Finished		Sales	2,500
goods	2,000		
Cost profit			
c/d	500		
	2,500		2,500
Financial P/L	500	Cost profit b/d	500

Work-in-Progress

Balance	2,000	Finished	
Wages	1,000	goods	4,000
Raw		Capital	
materials	3,000	expenditure	500
Overheads	1,130	Balance c/d	2,630
	7,130		7,130
Balance b/d	2,630		

Trial Balance – Tiny Ltd.

as at 31/1/..............

Capital			10,000
Creditors			2,400
Debtors		1,350	
Bank			500
Cost control:			
RM	1,000		
WIP	2,630		
FG	5,000	8,630	
Fixed assets		3,470	
P/L appropriation			550
£		13,450	13,450

9. Reconciliation Statement

	£	£
Profit as per cost accounts:		19,770
Add:		
Selling expenses difference £(7,500–7,100)	400	
Discounts received (not in cost accounts)	260	
Profit on sale of land (not in cost accounts)	2,340	3,000
		22,770

Subtract:

Closing stock difference £(4,280–4,080)	200	
Works expenses difference £(12,130–10,500)	1,630	
Administration expenses difference £(5,340–5,000)	340	
Depreciation difference £(1,100–800)	300	2,470
Profit as per financial accounts		£20,300

10. (a) There are two strange features about the data in this question. First, the sum of the direct wages given (15,236+5,230+2,670=£23,136) and the total gross wages paid (17,646+4,364=£22,010) differ by £1,126, i.e. £1,126 more direct wages were booked to work than were paid for. Second, the closing balance on a first draft of the Work-in-progress Control account is: 19,210 balance b/d+26,350 stores+15,236 direct wages+22,854 overheads (150% direct wages) − 62,130 transfers to finished goods= £21,520, yet the stock value of the work-in-progress is £24,360, i.e. an extra £2,840.

Now, it is very unusual either to book more time to work than is paid for or even to find a stock value so much in excess of what was expected. Unfortunately, though, the question does not give enough information as to the possible reason for these discrepancies.

However, doing what we can in the absence of other data, it may be argued, albeit very tentatively, that there is a clue in the fact that direct wages is charged from work tickets – not time sheets. If these work tickets actually accompany the work (see 3:**26**(a)) then the £1,126 discrepancy could relate to work, with its accompanying work tickets, overlooked at the end of the previous period (if the accountant had been absent for some time the fact that the direct wages failed to balance at that time may not have been noticed). This being so, the following adjustments would need to be made:

(i) The direct wages booked to this month's costs is the wages paid for, i.e. 22,010–(5,230 + 2,670) = £14,110, and hence the overheads are 14,110 × 1.5 = £21,165.

(ii) The value of the overlooked work should have been included in the opening work in progress balance of £19,210. Now, if the ratio of material used to direct wages is constant (and the odd coincidence that all valuations of work are close to a multiple of just under £2,500 suggests that near identical batches are being processed), then since £14,110 direct wages call for £26,350 materials, work involving £1,126 direct wages would probably have a material content of some 26,350 × 1,126/14,110 = £2,103. So the total cost of the overlooked work would be 1,126 + 1,126 × 1.5 + 2,103 = £4,918, i.e. the opening work in progress balance would be 19,210 + 4,918 = £24,128.

(*iii*) This adjustment to the Work-in-progress account would result in a final account balance of:

24,128 + 26,350 + 14,110 + 21,165 − 62,130 = £23,623.

Comparing this with an actual valuation of £24,360 shows a much more credible gain of £737.

Although perhaps very subjective the accounts in the answer have been prepared on the basis of the above reasoning. (This analysis is, almost certainly, more than could be undertaken under examination conditions. Students, then, whose own answers incorporate the figures given in the opening paragraph can regard their work as being acceptable, though they must decide for themselves how far their own treatment of the discrepancies would meet critical appraisal.) And these accounts are shown below.

Note, incidentally, the large under-recovery of £1,872 on the overheads as shown in the Production Overhead Control account. £1,689 of this is due to the assumption of overlooked work, i.e. a mere £183 would have been under-recovered otherwise. Yet the larger figure makes good sense since a quarter of the direct wages paid was for idle time! Indeed, if there had been no idle time and no capital work the overheads would have been 2,100 + 3,280 + 4,232 + 12,200 = £21,812 on direct wages of £14,110, i.e. 155%, which is close to the overhead absorption rate. So idle time would have been a much smaller *budgeted* item (if it had been budgeted at all) − and, this being so, a large under-recovery would be expected in a period with a high rate of idle time. So this, too, is consistent with the possibility of overlooked work.

(*b*) The following aspects of the accounts should be investigated:

(*i*) The possibility of work being overlooked at the period end.

(*ii*) The manner in which direct wages paid for and direct wages booked can be reconciled.

(*iii*) The reason for the very high idle direct wages costs.

(*iv*) The reason for the very large increase in the stock shown on the Stores Ledger Control account.

(*v*) The absence of any materials being booked to capital equipment produced (and whether there could be a link between this and (*iv*)).

(*vi*) The absence of any pre-payments or accruals at the end of the period under review.

(*vii*) The staffing levels required. (If £4,918 worth of finished work incorporated £1,126 direct wages −*see* (a(ii)) above − then the month's cost of sales of £59,830 would incorporate 59,830 × 1,126/4,918 = £13,700 direct wages, i.e. only 62 per cent of that actually paid for (£22,010). Note, too, that if idle time is excluded, the overheads amount to £21,800 and if these overheads are more or less as expected, then to obtain an overhead absorption rate of 150 per cent on direct wages the direct wages would need to be about £14,500, i.e. acceptably close to the £13,700 just calculated. So direct wages do seem to be higher than they should be.)

Stores Ledger Control A/c

	£		£
Bal b/d	24,175	Issues: WIP	26,350
Purchases	76,150	O'h'ds	3,280
		Bal c/d	70,695
	100,325		100,325
Bal b/d	70,695		

Work in Progress Control A/c

	£		£
Bal b/d	19,210	FG	62,130
Overlooked work	4,918	Contra	1,450
Stores	26,350	Bal c/d	24,360
Contra	1,450		
D. wages	14,110		
O'h'ds (150% DW)	21,165		
P/L – Stock gain	737		
	87,940		87,940
Bal b/d	24,360		

Finished Goods Control A/c

	£		£
Bal b/d	34,164	P/C-COS	59,830
WIP	62,130	Bal c/d	36,464
	96,294		96,294
Bal b/d	36,464		

Production Overhead Control A/c

	£		£
Pre-payment b/d	2,100	WIP	21,165
Stores	3,280	Capital equip.	4,005
Ind. wages	4,232	P/L: o'h'ds u-absorbed	1,872
Idle time	5,230		
Other o'h'ds	12,200		
	27,042		27,042

P/L A/c

	£		£
FG-COS	59,830	Sales	75,400
Selling & distrib.	5,240	WIP – Stock gain	737
O'h'ds u-absorb	1,872		
Bal c/d – Profit	9,195		
	76,137		76,137
		Profit b/d	9,195

Overlooked Work A/c

	£		£
Direct wages	1,126	WIP	4,918
O'h'ds	1,689		
Materials	2,103		
	4,918		4,918

Notes on double-entry for Overlooked Work A/c:

WIP: The £4,918 is debited to WIP Control A/c as shown.

Direct wages: There must be a debit balance on the Wages A/c of this amount, so £1,126 credit to Wages will off-set this.

Overheads: £1,689 more should have been shown as recovered in the *previous* period's accounts, so credit for this goes to P/L Appropriation.

Materials: The debit for the materials would have been made in the previous period's WIP A/c so that month's P/L A/c would have shown £2,103 too little profit. The double-entry, then, goes to the P/L Appropriation.

Progress test 8

4.

Cost element	Opening WIP	Period cost	Total cost	Complete units	Work-in-progress			Total equivalent units	CPU	WIP value
					Units	%	Equivalent			
	£	£	£						£	£
Material	29,600	112,400	142,000	28,000	12,000	100	12,000	40,000	3.550	42,600
Wages	6,600	33,400	40,000	28,000	12,000	$33\frac{1}{3}$	4,000	32,000	1.250	5,000
Overhead	5,800	30,200	36,000	28,000	12,000	$33\frac{1}{3}$	4,000	32,000	1.125	4,500
Total	42,000	176,000	218,000						5.925	52,100

Total value completed output = 28,000 at £5.925 = £165,900

(Input/output cross-check: £165,900 + £52,100 = £218,000.)

5. From the information in the answer to Question 4 above, the 8,000 units lost can only affect the completed units.

Now value of 8,000 units = 8,000 × £5.925 = £47,400.

∴ Extra cost per unit to be charged to remaining completed good

units $= \dfrac{£47,400}{20,000} = £2.370.$

∴ Complete cost per unit = £5.925 + £2.370 = £8.295.

The work-in-progress value remains the same, as such work has not reached the rejection point and cannot, therefore, carry any of the costs of such losses.

Progress test 9

6. Total joint cost = £31,200 + £13,800 = £45,000.

	Product A	Product B
Sales	£38,000	£42,000
Selling costs	5,000	20,000
Net realizable value	33,000	22,000
Joint cost apportionment (ratio of 3 : 2)	27,000	18,000
Profit	£6,000	£4,000

7. The solution to this problem breaks down into the following steps:

(*i*) *Net realizable value of BP9.*

	£	£
By-product units, 420:		
Sales at £9 each		3,780
Subsequent process costs at £2 each	840	
Selling and distribution expenses	420	1,260
Net realizable value		£2,520

(*ii*) *Production statistics.*

		Process	
	I	II	III
Normal loss	10%	5%	10%
Input	10,000	→8,800	→8,400
Normal loss	−1,000	−440	−840
Expected output	9,000	8,360	7,560
Actual output	8,800 ──	8,400 ──	7,000
Abnormal loss (gain)	200	(40)	560
Unit scrap value	£1	£3	£5
Scrap value normal loss	£1,000	£1,320	£4,200

(*iii*) *Process costs.*

		Process	
	I	II	III
	£	£	£
Direct materials introduced	20,000		
Transferred from previous process		→52,800	→100,800
Direct materials added	6,000	12,640	23,200
Direct wages	5,000	6,000	10,000
Direct expenses	4,000	6,200	4,080
Overheads: 400% D. wages*	20,000	24,000	40,000
Total cost	55,000	101,640	178,080
Less scrap value normal loss (from *ii*)	−1,000	−1,320	−4,200
Expected cost	54,000	100,320	173,880
CPU: expected cost ÷ expected output (from (*ii*))	6	12	23

Answer to Question 7(iv), Progress Test 9. Process accounts

Process	I Units	I £	II Units	II £	III Units	III £
Materials introduced/transferred	10,000	20,000	8,800	52,800	8,400	100,800
Direct materials added	—	6,000	—	12,640	—	23,200
Direct wages	—	5,000	—	6,000	—	10,000
Direct expenses	—	4,000	—	6,200	—	4,080
Overheads	—	20,000	—	24,000	—	40,000
Abnormal gain	—	—	40	480	—	—
	10,000	55,000	8,840	102,120	8,400	178,080

Process:	I Units	I £	II Units	II £	III Units	III £
Finished output transferred	8,800	52,800	8,400	100,800	7,000	158,480
BP9: NRV	—	—	—	—	—	2,520
Scrap value – normal loss*	1,000	1,000	440	1,320	840	4,200
Abnormal losses	200	1,200	—	—	560	12,880
	10,000	55,000	8,840	102,120	8,400	178,080

Abnormal losses account

Process:			Sales	
I	1,200		Sales I	200
III	12,880		III	2,800
			Net loss to P/L	11,080
	14,080			14,080

*Credited to Sales I, Sales II and Sales III.

Abnormal gains account

Process II	480		Sales II (lost sales due to abnormal gain)	120
			Net gain to P/L	360
	480			480

BP Account

Transferred from Process III	2,520		Sales BP9	3,780
BP process costs	840			
Selling and distribution	420			
	3,780			3,780

	£	£	£
Valuations: Abnormal loss (gain) (CPU × units in (*ii*))	1,200	(480)	12,880
Units transferred (CPU × units in (*ii*))	£52,800┘	£100,800┘	†

★ $\dfrac{£84,000 \text{ O'h'ds}}{£21,000 \text{ D. wages}} \times 100 = 400\%$

	£
†Process III: Value of finished units = 7,000 at £23	161,000
Less net realizable value of BP9 (from (*i*))	−2,520
	£158,480

(*iv*) *See* Table on p.401.

Progress test 10

7. The first step is to identify those levels of activity that lie outside the relevant activity range.

Period	Interviews conducted (*No.*)	Analyses prepared (*pages*)
1	6,290★	310
2	4,550	200★
3	6,200	600★
4	4,630	480
5	6,200	400
6	3,800	440
7	3,560★	440
8	4,770	330
Total	40,000	3,200
Mean	5,000	400
Mean + 25%	6,250	500
Mean − 25%	3,750	300

★Levels found to lie outside the relevant activity range and so ignored in the analysis.

The second step is to sketch roughly the two scattergraphs resulting from using each of the possible activity measures and to see which measure is the more closely associated with the cost. Such sketches at once show that number of interviews conducted is the better activity measure of the two.

The third step is to prepare more carefully the scattergraph showing cost plotted against number of interviews conducted. The line of best fit is then drawn on the graph. From this (or by computing the regression line) it can be seen that there is a fixed cost element of about £10,300 (computed, £10,350) and a variable cost per interview element of about £2 (computed, £2.09).

The final step is to compute the required predicted cost for period 9 as follows (using computed figures):

Predicted cost = $10,350 + 2.09 \times 4,000 = £18,710$

NOTE: If the interviews conducted are added to the pages of analysis prepared to give an artificial activity unit then an even better activity measure results since analyzing the cost in this situation (again after excluding levels outside the relevant range) gives a scattergraph with a perfect straight line fit of the points. From this graph it will be seen that there is a fixed cost element of £10,000 and a variable cost element of £2 per activity unit. Applying these new costs to the period 9 expectations gives a predicted cost of $10,000 + 2 \times (4,000 + 480) = £18,960$.

Though in the normal way interviews conducted and pages prepared cannot be added, if it so happens that together they provide a variable that is highly correlated with cost then they can legitimately be added together for the purpose of creating an activity unit.

8. (a) graph (v); (b) graph (iv); (c) no graph; (d) graph (vi); (e) graph (vii); (f) graph (ii); (g) graph (viii); (h) graph (iv); (i) graph (iii); (j) graph (i).

9. (a) When the throughput is only such that the time allowed equals the total time worked or less, no bonus is payable. Above that, the bonus paid is half an hour every hour of time allowed. Consequently, the cost curve is akin to a penalty variable cost curve (see **13**(e)).

(b) The total cost of labour per hour of work done in this situation falls continuously though at an ever decreasing rate and never to below a cost per hour equal to one-half of the hourly rate of the people employed.

Progress test 12

7.

Alternative	Existing machine*	New machine*
Cash in:†		
Receipts from production	£50,000	£60,000
Residual value	4,000	2,000
From sale of existing machine	–	10,000
	+£54,000	+£72,000
Cash out:		
Cash running costs	45,000	30,000
Purchase of new machine	–	30,000
	–£45,000	–£60,000
Net cash flow	+£9,000	+£12,000

*Take one alternative at a time and consider what cash would actually flow in and out if that alternative were the one selected.
†Take all figures over the full life of the project, i.e. five years.

Since the net cash flow from the new machine is higher than that from the existing, the correct decision is *to replace the existing machine.*

It should be noted that the book value of £24,000 for the existing machine does not enter the computation anywhere. It is important to appreciate that book values relate to book-keeping only and *have no relevance whatsoever in decision-making.* Only actual current and future economic values should be used in this type of work.

8. This is essentially a differential cost problem.

(*a*) Under these circumstances 10,000 lb of A which would have been sold for 10p lb will be sold for 95p lb, i.e. the extra income will be 95p – 10p = 85p lb. However, the order will require extra subsequent costs being incurred of £5 + £5 + £5 = £15 per 50 lb of A = 30p lb.

$$\therefore \text{ Net gain per lb} = 85p - 30p = 55p \text{ lb}$$
$$\therefore \textit{Order should be accepted.}$$

Additional profit resulting will be 10,000 × 55p = £5,500. The minimum price would be direct costs plus loss of 'scrap' sales income = 30p + 10p = 40p lb.

(*b*) Under these circumstances the 10,000 lb of A will need to come from extra processing.

Now a batch of 150 lb input gives 50 lb of A.

$$\therefore \quad \frac{10,000}{50} = 200 \text{ batches will need to be processed.}$$

Production schedule:

Product	lb per batch	Output from 200 batches
A	50	10,000 lb
B	45	9,000
C	45	9,000
Scrap	10	2,000
		20,000 lb

And the extra joint cost incurred will be:[*]

Per batch: Material 150 lb at $33\frac{1}{3}$p lb = £50
Labour £(12.5 + 11.25 + 11.25) = £35 [†]

£85

For 200 batches: $200 \times £85 = £17,000$
$\therefore$ Total extra cost = £17,000 + Subsequent costs of
10,000 lb A at 30p lb = £20,000

However, extra income is only:

From sales of A: 10,000 lb at 95p   = £9,500
From sales of B, C and Scrap: 20,000 lb at 10p = £2,000

£11,500

Now this £11,500 extra income is less than the extra cost.

$$\therefore \quad \textit{Order should not be accepted.}$$

If the order were accepted the minimum price would need to exceed the 95p offered by an amount that would just allow the 'loss' suffered at 95p to be recovered.

---

[*]Since the costs are joint, if one is incurred all are incurred. As we are only interested in *extra* costs, there is no point in apportioning the joint cost.
[†]If the material charges to the three products are added they will be found to total £17.50 + £19.25 + £12.25 = £49. So the process scrap sale of 10 lb at 10p lb = £1 has been deducted from the material input cost – i.e. no process costs are apportioned to the scrap. The total batch labour cost, then, is the sum of the three labour figures given.

Now 'loss' is £20,000 − £11,500 = £8,500

Over 10,000 lb, this is $\dfrac{£8,500}{10,000}$ = 85p lb

∴ Minimum price = 95p + 85p = £1.80 lb

(c) Again, the 10,000 lb of A will need to come from extra processing and production, and total extra joint costs will be as in (b). However, all C and 6,750 lb of B can be sold at the standard selling prices. Therefore:

Extra income:

A 10,000 lb at 95p lb	=	£9,500
B { 6,750 lb at £$\dfrac{55}{45}$ lb	=	8,250
2,250 lb at 10p lb	=	225
C 9,000 lb at £$\dfrac{35}{45}$ lb	=	7,000
Scrap: 2,000 lb at 10p lb	=	200
		£25,175

Extra costs:

Joint	=	£17,000
Subsequent:		
A 10,000 lb at 30p lb	=	3,000
B 6,750 lb at £$\dfrac{14}{45}$ lb	=	2,100
C 9,000 lb at £$\dfrac{10}{45}$ lb	=	2,000
		£24,100

The extra income is therefore greater than the extra costs.

∴ *Order should be accepted.*

Additional profit resulting = £25,175 − £24,100 = £1,075

Minimum price: In these circumstances the price could only be lowered until the £1,075 vanished. Over 10,000 lb of A this is £1,075 ÷ 10,000 = 10.75p per lb

∴ Minimum price would be 95p − 10.75p = 84.25p lb

9. In the situation in question the following figures will remain un-

changed whether the new machine is purchased or not: the total contract income; the cost price of the existing machine (£22,000); the fixed production and selling overheads (£40,000 and £80,000); the variable selling overheads. The decision, therefore, can be made by ascertaining which is the lower of the remaining two sets of costs, i.e.:

	Existing machine £	New machine £
Direct material, per unit	1.50	$1.57\frac{1}{2}^{(a)}$
Direct labour, per unit	1.00	$0.80^{(b)}$
Variable production overheads (60% direct labour)	0.60	0.48
Total variable cost per unit	3.10	$2.85\frac{1}{2}$
∴ Total variable cost for 200,000 units	620,000	571,000
Additional machine purchase costs	$0^{(c)}$	$31,000^{(d)}$
Residual machine value	−2,000	0
Total differential cost	£618,000	£602,000

∴ Since new machine has the lowest differential cost it should be purchased.

NOTES
  (a) £1.50 + 5 per cent.
  (b) If 25 per cent more units can be produced per hour, then cost drops by 20 per cent (not 25 per cent).
  (c) No *additional* cost for keeping existing machine.
  (d) £36,000 − £5,000 trade-in allowance.

10.

Alternative: Volume of production and sales p.a. (units):	Old Product 5,000	New Product 20,000*
Income per year	£200,000	£320,000
Direct material cost per year	£20,000	£120,000

*Since the labour time per unit of the new product is only a quarter that of the old, four times as many units can be made in a year.

Additional fixed cost per year	–		12,000	
	20,000	20,000	132,000	132,000
Net differential income*		£180,000		£188,000

*No other figures are needed to determine the net differential income as all other amounts (labour and normal fixed costs) remain unchanged. The unrecovered tooling cost is quite irrelevant (though if the tools had any scrap value this would have been a credit to the *new* product).

Since new product shows highest net differential income it should be manufactured in lieu of the old product.

11. Limit of own production – 200 tonnes material = 100 halves.

	Both halves made		R.h. halves bought	
Alternative:				
Sales	100 units		200 units	
Sales at £200 per unit		£20,000		£40,000
Assembly costs at £20 per unit	£2,000		£4,000	
Transport costs	–		400	
	2,000	2,000	4,400	4,400
Net differential income* (excluding cost of bought halves)		£18,000		£35,600

*Casting costs do not enter the analysis for whichever alternative is selected they will be the same, i.e. 200 halves will be cast in either event.

Since the relative differential income when the halves are bought (excluding purchase price) is 35,600 – 18,000 = £17,600, then the foundry could afford to pay up to £17,600 for these halves.

∴ since 200 right-hand halves will be required, maximum price will be 17,600/200 = £88 per r.h. half.

12. The existence of hours as a key factor in this question indicates that a solution could be approached by maximizing the contribution per hour. However, a quicker way is to apply a somewhat more sophisticated differential costing technique.

First note that it always pays the company to manufacture a component rather than sub-contract it and have idle time, since the marginal costs of all components are less than the sub-contract prices. Therefore, whichever components are sub-contracted, profit is only maximized when the factory is working at its capacity of 50,000 hours. This in turn means that whatever sub-contracting is done, the combined labour and variable overheads will *always* be $50,000 \times (£4.40 + £1.60) = £300,000$. If this figure is added to the fixed cost of £140,000 we see that whatever alternative is selected we will always have constant costs of £440,000 in respect of labour and overheads, and therefore these factors can be ignored in our analysis.

All this means that we need only take into consideration material costs and sub-contract prices. Note next that if the company makes a component as against sub-contracting it, the only additional cost will be the material cost and so the only saving will be the difference between the material cost and the sub-contract price. Such a saving, however, is only obtained at the expense of using valuable key factor hours. This shows that profit will be maximized *by maximizing the savings per hour*. This approach will underlie our solution to this question.

(*a*) Note that currently the sub-contracted price of a complete suite $[(1 \times 200) + (2 \times 80) + (4 \times 60) = £600]$ exactly equals the selling price. If, then, we sub-contract all the components the sales income will exactly cover our sub-contract costs no matter how many suites are sold. Let us assume we adopt this approach and at the same time have the factory *working at capacity producing nothing*. Our factory costs will clearly be our constant cost of £440,000 (no material costs will be incurred in such a situation) and our loss, therefore, also £440,000.

Next let us compute the saving we can make by manufacturing components instead of sub-contracting them and find the saving per hour (remember material costs only are the additional factory costs incurred):

	Settee	Armchair	Armless chair
Sub-contract price saved	£200	£80	£60
Direct material cost incurred	£80	£40	£44
Saving per component	£120	£40	£16
Hours required per component	10	5	1
Saving per hour	£12	£8	£16

Making armless chairs maximizes our saving. However, only $8,000 \times 4 = 32,000$ chairs are required to meet current sales. These chairs will use only 32,000 of our 50,000 hours and so 18,000 hours can be allocated to the next most profitable alternative, namely manufacturing settees. In 18,000 hours 1,800 settees will be made, leaving 6,200 to be sub-contracted.

The company therefore should manufacture 32,000 armless chairs and 1,800 settees, and should sub-contract 6,200 settees and 16,000 armchairs.

(*b*) (*i*) Profit = Saving from manufacture *less* constant costs. Now savings while manufacturing armless chairs and settees are at £16 and £120 per component respectively. Therefore profit at current level of sales:

$$(32,000 \times £16) + (1,800 \times £120) - £440,000 = \underline{\underline{£288,000}}$$

(*ii*) If sales are unlimited then profit is maximized by manufacturing armless chairs only. Since the saving per hour is £16, the 50,000 hours available will give a total saving of £800,000 which, after deduction of constant costs of £440,000, leaves a profit of £360,000.

(*c*) If the selling price drops to £560 then it is no longer true that the selling price of a suite exactly equals its sub-contract cost, and indeed, since we make £40 less contribution per suite, selling 8,000 units would lead to £320,000 less contribution – i.e. it would wipe out all the profit. Now, in this situation we need to see what would happen if we gave up selling one suite. First, note that this would release 4 hours of labour (4 chairs at 1 hour each). These hours we could then devote to reducing the sub-contracted work – for a settee not sub-contracted we would save $\frac{4}{10} \times (200 - 80) = £48$ and for an armchair $\frac{4}{5} \times (80 - 40) = £32$. In this case, then, we'd elect to make 0.4 of a settee and save £48.

Next, we need to compute the loss of contribution from the sale we have given up. Since this particular sale would have involved a sub-contracted settee the contribution lost is $560 - (200 + 2 \times 80 + 4 \times 44) = £24$. This loss is only half the saving so the sacrifice is profitable. And if it's profitable for one sale it's profitable for all sales involving sub-contracted settees. So we can improve the profit by making all our own settees as well as armless chairs.

The analysis continues at the next level, i.e. where we are sub-contracting armchairs only. Now the contribution per suite is $560 - (80 + 2 \times 80 + 4 \times 44) = £144$. If here we give up selling a suite we gain 10 settee hours $+ 4 \times 1$ armless chair hours $= 14$ hours, which allows us to make 14/5 armchairs and so save $\frac{14}{5} \times (80 - 40) = £112$. In this case, though, the savings do not match the lost contribution of £144 and so we will continue to sub-contract armchairs.

Finally, if we are making settees and armless chairs which together require 14 hours per suite we can only manufacture 50,000/14 = 3,571 suites (with 6 hours spare). So the profit earned will be:

$$3,571 \times (560 - (80 + 2 \times 80 + 4 \times 44)) - 440,000 = \underline{\underline{£74,224}}$$

(actually, £74,260 since the labour and variable overhead for the 6 saved hours won't need to be paid for)

> NOTE: The solution indicates that in the new situation our most profitable course of action is to reduce sales from 8,000 suites to 3,571, i.e., unusually, profit is maximized by cutting sales by over 50 per cent!

13. (a) If the machine were sold to VW Ltd then AB would sacrifice the following opportunity costs relating to disposals:

Sale of P to scrap merchant		£6,000
Sale of Q to scrap merchant	£4,000	
Less Preparation costs – 120 × £3	360	3,640
Scrapping of R		−1,200[(i)]
Sale of design and specifications		3,000
		£11,440

Also by converting rather than scrapping AB will incur the following additional opportunity costs:

Conversion materials used ex stock – cash sacrifice to be made on replacement	£7,600
Contribution from work that would otherwise be done in Department L – 3 × 4 × 300 × £2.50	9,000
Direct labour and variable overheads in Department M	0[(ii)]
	£16,600

Finally, AB will incur the following normal future costs on conversion:

Marginal costs:	
Department L Direct labour – 3 × 4 × £300	£3,600[(b)(iii)]
Identifiable fixed costs:	
Temporary supervision	1,800
	£5,400

Summary:

Opportunity costs:	
Arising from scrapping machine	£11,440
Arising from converting machine	16,600
Future costs to be incurred	5,400
Total cost of converting machine for sale to VW Ltd	£33,440
∴ Minimum price that AB should accept for the machine =	£33,440

NOTES:

(*i*) Since selling the machine to VW Ltd will result in this disposal cost being avoided, then the £1,200 is a negative opportunity cost. (*ii*) Since the direct labour in this department has spare time during which nothing else can be done but must nevertheless be paid for, the opportunity cost of using this labour is zero (*see* also (*b*)(*ii*)).

(*b*) The following assumptions have been made.

(*i*) The only disposal cost of the machine is the cost of scrapping the type R material, e.g. there would be no costs of scrapping the machine.

(*ii*) Variable overheads continue to be incurred even when the direct labour is idle.

(*iii*) The £2.50 per £1 of labour figure given in (*c*) of the question is a contribution towards the variable as well as the fixed overheads.

Although the style of the question indicates that the examiner is probably looking for an opportunity-costs form of solution, it should be noted that a differential cash flow format could possibly be a simpler approach. Certainly such an approach avoids mixing different kinds of costs which the student may well find confusing. Below, then, the answer is re-presented using this format.

Machine Scrapped

Differential Cash Flow In[i]		*Differential Cash Flow Out*	
Sale of P	£6,000	Preparation costs of Q	£360
Sale of Q	4,000	Scrapping of R	1,200
Sale of design and specifications	3,000		
Added value from Dept L	12,600[ii]		
	25,600		£1,560

Net cash flow   £ + 24,040

Machine Converted

Differential cash flow out:	
Future cash to be spent replacing materials	£7,600
Temporary supervision	1,800
Net cash flow	£ − 9,400

Differential Net Cash Flow

Machine scrapped	£ + 24,040
Machine converted	− 9,400
Differential NCF	£33,440

∴ If the cash flow in from sale to VW Ltd does not reach £33,440, it is more profitable to scrap the machine than to convert it.

NOTES:

(*i*) *Differential* cash flow, i.e. any cash flow that remains unchanged whether machine is scrapped or converted is ignored. Since all direct labour and variable overheads fall into this category they are excluded along with the fixed overheads.

(*ii*) Perhaps the only figure that really calls for careful thought. It is made up of the direct labour (3 × 4 × £300 = £3,600) and the contribution loading (3,600 × £2.50 = £9,000) that would be charged to other customers in respect of the work that would be displaced by the conversion alternative, i.e. if the conversion were to be carried out this cash flow in would not arise.

Progress test 13

9. Trading and profit and loss accounts: (*a*) fixed overhead is absorbed; (*b*) fixed overhead charged against sales. (Stock details would normally have been omitted from the cost statement and the cost of sales calculated directly, but are included here for comparative purposes.)

	Per unit (£)	Quarter 3			Quarter 4		
		Units	£	£	Units	£	£
(*a*) Sales	1.00	28,000		28,000	32,000		32,000
Production costs:							
Variable	0.65	34,000	22,100		28,000	18,200	
Fixed	0.20	34,000	6,800		28,000	5,600	
		34,000	28,900		28,000	23,800	
Plus Opening stock	0.85	Nil	−		6,000	5,100	
		34,000	28,900		34,000	28,900	
Less Closing stock	0.85	6,000	5,100		2,000	1,700	
Costs of sales	0.85	28,000	23,800	23,800	32,000	27,200	27,200
Gross profit	0.15	28,000		4,200	32,000		4,800

	Per unit (£)	Quarter 3 Units	£	£	Quarter 4 Units	£	£
Selling and administration costs				2,100			2,100
Less Under-(over-) absorption of fixed production overhead							
Absorbed			6,800			5,600	
Budgeted			6,000	(800)		6,000	400
Net profit				£2,900			£2,300
(b) Sales	1.00	28,000		28,000	32,000		32,000
Production costs:							
Variable	0.65	34,000	22,100		28,000	18,200	
Plus Opening stock	0.65	*Nil*	–		6,000	3,900	
		34,000	22,100		34,000	22,100	
Less Closing stock	0.65	6,000	3,900		2,000	1,300	
Marginal cost of sales	0.65	28,000	18,200	18,200	32,000	20,800	20,800
Contribution	0.35	28,000		9,800	32,000		11,200
Fixed costs:							
Production			6,000			6,000	
Selling and administration			2,100	8,100		2,100	8,100
Net profit				£1,700			£3,100

10. (*a*) In view of the scarcity of labour, labour hours are obviously a key factor. Since any new work undertaken by the company will entail diverting labour from the standard product (for which there is a heavy demand) the first thing that must be done is find the contribution per hour sacrificed by such a diversion:

Standard product

Selling price of product		£60
Marginal cost: Materials	£24	
Labour: 2 hrs at £3	6	30
Contribution		30
Contribution per labour hour		£15

(*b*) The next step is to determine whether to make or buy the special component in the event of accepting the contract:

Make cost for component:

Materials	£120
Labour: 12 hrs at £3	36
Opportunity cost: 12 hrs at £15	180
Total	£336

Since this component can be purchased for only £300, the company should buy it rather than make it.

(c) Knowing the component will cost £300, the cost of the contract can now be computed:

Contract cost:

Materials	£1,140
Special component	300
Labour: 200 hrs at £3	600
Opportunity cost: 200 hrs at £15	3,000
Total	£5,040

Since the total cost, including lost contribution from the 100 standard units to be displaced, is less than the contract price of £5,400, the contract should be accepted.

(d) *Conclusion.* Management, therefore, will be advised to accept the contract and buy the component from an outside supplier. Company profit as a result will be £5,400 − £5,040 = £360 higher.

NOTE: The fixed costs given in the question are, in fact, irrelevant to the solution. Indeed, since labour is a key factor and will always be used to its maximum, the total company wage bill will be the same whatever production is undertaken, i.e. the wages and fixed overheads can both be regarded as a committed cost to be covered by the sales less the materials. Using this approach, the opportunity cost per labour hour in respect of the standard product is (£60 − 24)/2 = £18. Hence the opportunity cost of the special component is £120 + 12 × £18 = £336 and the contract cost is £1,140 + £300 + 200 × 18 = £5,040 − as before, though more simply calculated.

11.

	Staked tomatoes	Ground tomatoes	Cucumbers	Green beans
Boxes per acre	700	200	150	300
Income per acre:	($)	($)	($)	($)
Price per box	3.86	3.86	4.56	5.68
Income per acre	2,702	772	684	1,704
Marginal cost per box:				
Harvesting and packing labour	0.80	0.72	1.00	1.20
Transport and export	1.30	1.30	1.00	2.40
Marginal cost per box	2.10	2.02	2.00	3.60
Marginal cost per acre:				
Marginal cost per acre for boxes	1,470	404	300	1,080
Materials	189	74	63	108
Growing labour	224	152	93	132
Marginal cost per acre	1,883	630	456	1,320
∴ *Contribution per acre*	819	142	228	384

These figures show that staked tomatoes are the most profitable. However, on 70 acres only cucumbers and ground tomatoes can be grown. The figures show that cucumbers are the more profitable of these two latter products.

Ideally, then, the farmer should concentrate on staked tomatoes and, where these cannot be grown, cucumbers. Market policy, though, requires him to produce a minimum of 5,000 boxes of each product. His profit, then, is maximized by growing up to 5,000 boxes of ground tomatoes on part of the 70 poor acres and cucumbers on the remaining balance, and similarly growing up to 5,000 boxes of green beans on the 240−70 = 170 other acres and staked tomatoes on the balance of these acres. His production, then, will be scheduled as follows:

	Total acres available	*Low contribution production*		*High contribution product*		
		Boxes per acre	Acres required for 5,000 boxes	Acres available	Boxes per acre	Boxes
Green beans/ staked tomatoes	170	300	17[*]	153	700	107,100
Ground tomatoes/ cucumbers	70	200	25	45	150	6,750

[*]Rounded up to complete acre.

It is now possible to complete the workings and answers; (*i*) and (*ii*) are given in the table below:

	(*i*) Area to be cultivated (*acres*)	(*ii*) Profit	
		Contribution per acre ($)	Total contribution ($)
Staked tomatoes	153	819	125,307
Ground tomatoes	25	142	3,550
Cucumbers	45	228	10,260
Green beans	17	384	6,528
Total	240		145,645
Less Fixed costs:		$	
Growing		36,000	
Harvesting		12,000	
Transport and export		12,000	
General administration		40,000	
Notional rent		12,000	112,000
Profit			$33,645

Progress test 14

6. (*a*) Contribution = £5 − £3 = £2 unit.

∴ No. of units to give contribution equal to fixed costs

$$= \frac{10,000}{2} = 5,000 \text{ units} = \text{B/E point.}$$

£40,000 sales must come from $\frac{40,000}{5} = 8,000$ units.

∴ Contribution, 8,000 × £2 = £16,000
Less fixed costs   = £10,000

Profit   £6,000

(*b*) Contribution = £80,000 − £60,000 = £20,000.

∴ P/V ratio $= \frac{20,000}{80,000} = 25\%$.

∴ Contribution from B/E sales = 25% × 60,000 = £15,000.
∴ Fixed cost = £15,000.
∴ Profit = contribution − fixed costs = £20,000 − £15,000 = £5,000.

(*c*) Since profit = contribution − fixed costs, then contribution = profit + fixed costs, i.e. in this case contribution = £5,000 + £15,000 = £20,000. At the break-even point contribution from sales equals fixed costs. As the £20,000 contribution came from £60,000 sales, then £15,000 contribution will come from sales of $\dfrac{£15,000}{£20,000} \times £60,000 = £45,000.$

Therefore, break-even point = £45,000

(*d*) At break-even point the contribution equals the fixed costs. Therefore £80,000 sales would bring in a contribution of £20,000 and so the P/V ratio is 25 per cent. With a P/V ratio of 25 per cent, sales of £100,000 will bring in a total of £25,000 contribution; and after deducting fixed costs of £20,000 the profit remaining is £5,000.

(*e*) Again sales of £20,000 brings a contribution equal to the fixed costs, i.e. £10,000. Therefore the P/V ratio is 50 per cent. Since profit is all the contribution earned above the break-even point, the £5,000 profit equals the contribution from sales, above break-even. With a P/V ratio of 50 per cent, a contribution of £5,000 is earned from £10,000 sales. Therefore total sales are £10,000 + sales at break-even = £10,000 + £20,000 = £30,000.

7. (*a*) (*i*) The total costs for the two periods can be plotted at 10,000 and 12,000 units respectively. By joining these points and extending the line to the *y* axis, the fixed cost is found to be £28,000. Alternatively, the fixed cost can be found as follows:

	Period 1	Period 2	Difference
Total material, labour and overheads	£93,000	£106,000	£13,000
Production (units)	10,000	12,000	2,000

∴   2,000 extra units incurred additional (i.e. variable) cost of £13,000.

∴   10,000 units have a variable cost of $\dfrac{13,000}{2,000} \times 10,000 = £65,000.$

But the *total* cost of 10,000 units = £93,000 (*see* above).
∴   The fixed cost must be 93,000 − 65,000 = £28,000.

(*ii*) See chart below which shows that the B/E point is 8,000 units.
(*b*) See chart below where:

(*i*) new break-even = 8,800 units;
(*ii*) The plan will obviously not be worth operating as long as the new total cost exceeds the old. This situation holds until the indifference point is reached, i.e. where the two cost curves cross. The graph shows that this does not occur until the activity reaches 11,600 units. Therefore, unless a

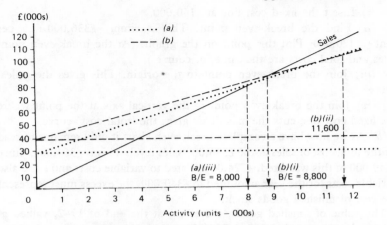

minimum sales of 11,600 units can be achieved the new plan should not be adopted.

NOTE: In examinations the examiners almost invariably want mathematical-type questions answered on a basis of pure break-even theory.

8. This problem is solved by taking the following steps.

(a) Prepare the break-even chart with appropriate axes (see chart below) in the following manner.

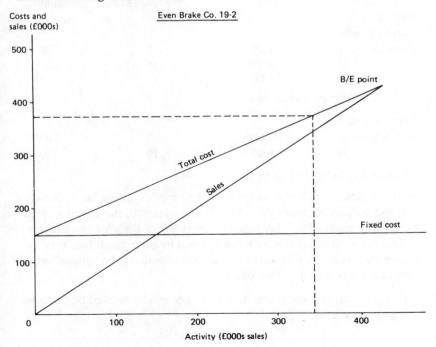

(*i*) Insert the fixed cost line at £140,000.

(*ii*) Find the break-even point. This is simply £336,000 + 25 per cent = £420,000. Plot this point on the graph. (At the break-even point sales and total costs are the same, of course.)

(*iii*) Join the break-even point to the origin. This gives the 'sales' curve.

(*iv*) Join the break-even point to the vertical axis at the point where the fixed cost line cuts the axis. This gives the 'total cost' curve.

(*b*) As we now have a complete break-even chart it only remains to read off the total cost of sales at the £336,000 sales level. This is £364,000. Since £140,000 of this was fixed, £224,000 related to variable costs and since also variable costs for the year amounted to £340,000, the excess must represent the cost of finished goods stock.

The value of finished goods, therefore, at the end of 19–2, valued at marginal cost was £340,000 – £224,000 = £116,000.

9. The answer here depends upon the number of units involved. It is therefore necessary to find the points of indifference, noting that at the very lowest numbers A's quote is the best and that it always pays to take a lower variable cost quote *providing* that the actual quantity will exceed the point of indifference.

Supplier	Extra fixed cost (£)	Variable cost savings per unit (£)	Point of indifference (units)
Start with A and consider switch to: B	1,000	5	200
C	3,000	10	300
D	5,000	15	$333\frac{1}{3}$

∴ Over 200 units, switch to B.

Then consider switch to: C	2,000	5	400
D	4,000	10	400

∴ Over 400 units, switch to D.

So if the actual number is under 200, the supplier should be A; between 200 and 400, the supplier should be B; and over 400, the supplier should be D. Regrettably for C his quote is never better than his competitors.

This problem could also have been solved by plotting all four total cost curves and then selecting at the actual level of activity the supplier whose cost curve was lowest at that point.

NOTE: In this case the points of indifference will be marked by the crossing of the curves.

10. First, find the selling price:

Last period (9,000 units sold):

	£
Variable costs at £5 each	45,000
Fixed costs	20,000
Total cost	65,000
Loss	2,000
∴ Sales	£63,000

$$\therefore \quad Selling\ price = \frac{£63,000}{9,000} = \qquad £7\ unit$$

Next, the basic planned contribution:

Fixed cost	£20,000
Planned profit	£4,000
Planned contribution	£24,000

Proposal A. This proposal will increase variable cost per unit by £0.50.

∴ Contribution per unit: up to 12,000 = £7 − £5.50 = £1.50;
over   12,000 = £7 − £6.50 = £0.50.

∴ First 12,000 units will give a contribution of 12,000 × £1.50
= £18,000.

This leaves £6,000 to be found, and at £0.50 per unit this means an

additional $\dfrac{£6,000}{0.50}$ = 12,000 units must be sold, i.e. a total of 24,000 units.

∴ Increase is 24,000 − 9,000 = 15,000 units, i.e. $\dfrac{15,000}{9,000} \times 100 = 166\frac{2}{3}\%$

increase in sales.

Proposal B. This proposal, through the increase in fixed costs, will increase planned contribution by £2,000 to £26,000.

Now contribution per unit: up to 12,000 = £7 − 5 = £2;
over   12,000 = £7 − 6 = £1.

∴ First 12,000 units will give a contribution of 12,000 × £2 = £24,000.
This leaves £2,000 to be found, and at £1 per unit this means an additional 2,000 units must be sold, i.e. a total of 14,000 units.

∴ Increase is 14,000 − 9,000 = 5,000 units, i.e. $\dfrac{5,000}{9,000} \times 100 \approx 55\frac{1}{2}\%$

increase in sales.

Proposal C. Dropping selling price by £0.50 results in contribution per unit dropping £0.50 at all levels. This, of course, is equivalent to increasing variable cost by £0.50, i.e. the consequences are the same as in A.

∴ Increase in sales = $166\frac{2}{3}\%$.

Proposal D. New contribution per unit (below 12,000)
$$= £7 - £4 = £3.$$

∴ Contribution from sales of 9,000 units = £27,000.
This is £3,000 above planned contribution.

∴ Fixed machine costs can rise by a maximum of £3,000.

11. Cost of a set of tyres: our vehicle $4 \times £9 = £36$;
his vehicle $6 \times £8 = £48$.

(*a*) Cost of tyres per 1,000 miles:
our vehicle $£36 \div 6 = £6$;
his vehicle $£48 \div 10 = £4.80$.

∴ His customer saves $£6 - £4.80 = £1.20$ per 1,000 miles on tyres but pays $£999 - £900 = £99$ more for the vehicle.

∴ No. of miles customer must travel at a saving of £1.20 per 1,000 miles to recoup the £99 extra vehicle cost $= \dfrac{99}{1.2} \times 1,000 = 82,500$ miles. At this distance, then, customer is indifferent as to which vehicle he buys.

(*b*) If the vehicle life is 120,000 miles and his customer changes his tyres every 10,000 miles then he will have a total cost for 120,000 miles of

$$£999 + \frac{120,000}{10,000} \times £48 = £1,575.$$

∴ Total cost to our customer must not exceed £1,575. Now since £900 is spent on the vehicle $1,575 - 900 = £675$ is available for tyres, which, at £36 a set, allow for $\dfrac{675}{36} = 18.75$ sets*. And since these must cover 120,000 miles the life of a set must be $\dfrac{120,000}{18.75} = 6,400$ miles.

If the sales manager were to include a free set of tyres in the price of £900, then our customer would still have £675 available for tyres which would again buy 18.75 sets. However, since the vehicle starts with a complete set of tyres there will be a total of 19.75 sets to cover the 120,000 miles – meaning each set requires a life of $\dfrac{120,000}{19.75} = 6,076$ miles.

---

*It is assumed that the last set of tyres, still having a quarter of their life left, can be transferred to another vehicle.

Progress test 16

8. *4-week profit budgets:*

	A £	B £
Sales at £5 per unit	250,000	500,000
Less total costs:		
Direct materials, 50% sales	125,000	250,000
Direct labour at £100 for 200 units	25,000	50,000
Indirect wages – 4 weeks at £100 per man a week	8,000	14,000
Power	5,000	10,000
Maintenance	15,000	25,000
Distribution	10,400	14,800
Selling costs $2\frac{1}{2}$% sales	6,250	12,500
Depreciation	5,000	5,000
Other fixed costs	15,000	15,000
Total costs	£214,650	£396,300
Budgeted profit	£35,350	£103,700

9. Work sheet (*i*)

	Month				
	1	*2*	*3*	*4*	*Total*
Sales: Barrels					
silcpercys (*ii*)	10,000	15,000	20,000	25,000	70,000
Value (£50 + 20%)	£600,000	900,000	1,200,000	1,500,000	4,200,000
FG month end:					
(*iii*) Barrels	10,000	15,000	20,000	0	
FG stock change:					
Barrels	–5,000	+5,000	+5,000	–20,000	
Production (sales +					
stock change)	5,000	20,000	25,000	5,000	55,000
Purchases: (*iv*)					
Barrels sowzeers	100,000	20,000	120,000 (*v*)	0	240,000
Value (£5 + 20%)	£600,000	120,000	720,000	0	1,440,000
Marketing costs					
(£5,000 + 1%					
sales)	£11,000	14,000	17,000	20,000	62,000
Sales at 5%					
discount (70%)	£420,000	630,000	840,000	1,050,000	2,940,000
Other sales (30%)	£180,000	270,000	360,000	450,000	1,260,000

Profit budget for first four months.

		£	£
Sales: 70,000 barrels* silcpercys at £60			4,200,000
Less discount, 5% of 70% of £4.2m			− 147,000
			4,053,000

			£	£
Costs: Purchases: 240,000 barrels* sowzeers at £6			1,440,000	
Plus 100,000 barrels opening stock (old B/S)			500,000	
	340,000		1,940,000	
Less	120,000* barrels closing stock at £6		− 720,000	
	220,000		1,220,000	

	£
Direct wages: 55,000 barrels silcpercys* at £12 (*vi*)	660,000
Variable overheads: 50% direct wages (*vii*)	330,000
Fixed overheads: $66\frac{2}{3}$% direct wages (*viii*)	440,000
Total production cost: 55,000 barrels silcpercys	2,650,000
Plus Opening stock: 15,000 barrels silcpercys	675,000
Manufacturing costs of sales: 70,000 barrels silcpercys	3,325,000
Marketing contract costs*	62,000

	£
Total costs of sales	3,387,000
Budgeted profit	£666,000

*See work-sheet.

Cash budget.

	Month			
	1	2	3	4
	£	£	£	£
Receipts				
Debtors taking 5% discount, 70% previous month's sales*	140,000 (*ix*)	420,000	630,000	840,000
Less 5% discount	−7,000	−21,000	−31,500	−42,000
	133,000	399,000	598,500	798,000
Debtors not taking discount, 30% of sales 2 months previous*	30,000 (*ix*)	60,000 (*ix*)	180,000	270,000
Total	163,000	459,000	778,500	1,068,000

Payments

RM creditors, previous month's purchases*	400,000 (x)	600,000	120,000	720,000
Direct wages, £12 per barrel produced*	60,000	240,000	300,000	60,000
Variable overheads, 50% previous month's wages	20,000 (x)	30,000	120,000	150,000
Fixed overheads (excl. rent and deprec.), previous month	41,667 (x)	50,000	50,000	50,000
Rent	–	–	110,000	–
Marketing cost, 1 month in advance*	14,000	17,000	20,000	8,000 (xi)
Plant and equipment	–	–	–	100,000
Total	535,667	937,000	720,000	1,088,000
Excess receipts over payments	(372,667)	(478,000)	58,500	(20,000)
Opening cash balance	500,000 (x)	127,333	(350,667)	(292,167)
Closing cash balance	127,333	(350,667)	(292,167)	(312,167)

*See work-sheet.

Budgeted balance sheet.

	£	£
Assets		
Plant and equipment (900,000 + 100,000)		1,000,000
Less depreciation ($\frac{1}{3} \times$ 10% of £900,000 + £360,000)		−390,000
		610,000
Stocks: RM, 120,000 barrels* sowzeers at £6	720,000	
FG, nil (*iii*)	0	720,000
Debtors: Entitled to 5% discount (month 4 sales)	1,500,000	
Not entitled to discount (30% month 3 sales)	360,000	
	1,860,000	
Less provision for discount (5% of 70% of £1.5m)	−52,500	1,807,500
Prepayments: Marketing costs (*xi*)		8,000
Cash (*xii*)		(312,167)
		£2,833,333
Financed by:		
Head office: Opening balance (*x*)		2,014,833
Plus profit (*xiii*)	666,000	
Plus overhead suspense (*xiv*)	122,500	788,500
Accruals: Variable overheads (50% £60,000 D. wages, month 4)		30,000
		£2,833,333

*See work-sheet.

NOTES (lower case letters refer to question):

(*i*) In any extensive budget exercise it usually proves useful to prepare a work-sheet which lays out the basic operating data.

(*ii*) The planned annual sales must be the old 80,000 + 25 per cent = 100,000 barrels of silcpercys (*a*). These will divide up over the months as follows (*b*):

Month 1	10%	10,000 barrels
2	15%	15,000
3	20%	20,000
4	25%	25,000
5	5%	5,000
6 – 12	25%	25,000

(*iii*)(*g*).

(*iv*) Production two months hence (*d*) × 4 (since 4 barrels of sowzeers are needed to make 1 barrel of silcpercys, see *Profit and Loss* in question).

(*v*) Purchases equivalent to sales in months 5–12 (*f*) = (5,000 + 25,000) (*ii*) × 4 = 120,000 barrels.

(*vi*) £10 per barrel (*Profit and Loss* in question) + 20 per cent (*c*).

(*vii*) The *Profit and Loss* in question shows that the variable overheads were 50 per cent of the direct wages. Since both are to increase as a result of inflation by the same percentage this proportion will remain unchanged.

(*viii*) The old fixed overheads were £500,000 excluding £200,000 for depreciation and rent. Inflation will increase these by 20 per cent to £600,000, and adding back the unaffected £200,000 gives a total overhead of £800,000. At the same time the approximate direct wages for the year will be 100,000 (*ii*) × £12 (*vi*) = £1,200,000 ('approximate' since the 100,000 is the budgeted sales and not the budgeted production which will be slightly different if any change in the year-end finished goods stock is planned).

(*ix*) The old balance sheet debtors divide as follows:
Paying in month 1 – 70% of £200,000 + £30,000;
Paying in month 2 – 30% of £200,000.

(*x*) See old balance sheet.

(*xi*) Sales for month 5 will be 5,000 (*ii*) × £60 = £300,000. Therefore £5,000 + 1 per cent sales = 5,000 + 3,000 = £8,000. This, of course, is a prepayment.

(*xii*) From cash budget.

(*xiii*) From profit budget.

(*xiv*) Probably the most difficult figure in the exercise. The point here is that the profit budget was charged with fixed overheads absorbed on a basis of production whereas for the balance sheet they have to reflect the time periods in which the overheads are incurred, i.e. the prepayments and accruals. Probably the best way to do this is to prepare the fixed overhead account. Bearing in mind that the fixed overheads consist of the regular monthly cash overheads, rent and depreciation this account will look as follows:

Fixed Overheads Account

Opening B/S: Rent	27,500	Opening B/S: Accrual	41,667
Cash payments:		P/L (Profit budget)	440,000
Month 1	41,667		
Months 2,3,4,	150,000		
Rent	110,000		
Depreciation (4			
months)	30,000		
Balance: Suspense c/d	122,500		
	481,667		481,667
		Suspense b/d	122,500

At the *year* end the balance on this account will be one month's accrued fixed overheads and 3 months' prepaid rent (in a budgeting exercise there is no under- or over-absorption of overheads, of course).

Progress test 17

11. (*a*) Control plans:
Flexible budget: Dept 1:

Budgeted activity – 25,000 process hours

Overhead	Budget	Fixed	Variable	Variable per process hour
	£	£	£	£
Fixed	55,000	55,000	–	–
Variable	125,000	–	125,000	5
	180,000	55,000	125,000	5

Standard fixed overhead rate: £55,000/25,000 = £2.20 per process hour.

Flexible budget: Dept. 2:

Budgeted activity – 4,000 indirect labour hours

Overhead	Budget	Fixed	Variable	Variable per ind. lab. hr.
	£	£	£	£
Fixed	14,000	14,000	—	—
Variable	8,000	—	8,000	2
	22,000	14,000	8,000	2

Standard fixed overhead rate: £14,000/4,000 = £3.50 per indirect labour hour.

Flexible budget: Marketing:

Budgeted activity – 1,000 containers

Overhead	Budget	Fixed	Variable	Variable per container sold
	£	£	£	£
Fixed	60,000	60,000	—	—
Variable	50,000	—	50,000	50
	110,000	60,000	50,000	50

Standard fixed overhead rate: £60,000/1,000 = £60 per container.

Standard cost – 1 15-gal container of Z.

		£
Dept. 1:	D. mats: 20 gal of A at £3 per gal	60
	D. lab.: Grade I 30 hrs at £3 per hr	90
	Grade II 20 hrs at £1.50 per hr	30
	V. overheads: 25 process hrs at £5 per hr	125
	F. overheads: 25 process hrs at £2.20 per hr	55
	Standard cost: 15 gal Z*	360
Dept. 2:	D. mats: 1 container at £8	8
	D. lab.: 12 hrs at £2 per hr	24
	V. overheads: 4 hrs at £2 per hr	8
	F. overheads: 4 hrs at £3.5 per hr	14
	Standard factory cost: 1 15-gal container Z	414

Marketing: V. Overheads	50
F. Overheads	60
Standard total cost	524
Standard profit	76
Standard selling price	£600

*Standard yield 75 per cent. Note that the standard cost of output is £360/15 = £24 per gal Z.

Control profit budget for year   £

Budgeted profit: 1,000 15-gal containers Z at £76 profit
each   76,000

(b) *Control profit budget for first period*

£

Budgeted profit ($\frac{1}{10}$ of year): 100 15-gal containers Z at
£76 profit each   7,600

Progress test 18

10. NOTE: Standard price for usage column: £0.25 per gal.

		Price	*Usage*
(a)	Allowance	24 × £0.25 = £6	20 gal
	Actual	£6	24 gal
	Difference	—	4A gal
	Variance	*Nil*	£1A
(b)	Allowance	20 × £0.25 = £5	20 gal
	Actual	£7	20 gal
	Difference	£2A	—
	Variance	£2A	*Nil*
(c)	Allowance	24 × £0.25 = £6.00	20 gal
	Actual	24 × £0.35 = £8.40	24 gal
	Difference	£2.40A	4A gal
	Variance	£2.40A	£1A
(d)	Allowance	18 × £0.25 = £4.50	20 gal
	Actual	£5.00	18 gal
	Difference	£0.50A	2F gal
	Variance	£0.50A	£0.50F

11. NOTE: Standard rate for labour efficiency column: £4 per hr.

	Wage rate	Labour efficiency
(a) Allowance	$110 \times £4 = £440$	100 hrs
Actual	385	110 hrs
Difference	£55F	10A hrs
Variance	£55F	£40A
(b) Allowance	$95 \times £4 = £380$	100 hrs
Actual	367.40	95 hrs
Difference	£12.60F	5F hrs
Variance	£12.60F	£20F

12. Standard cost 6 cu ft HO_5:

	£
1 cu ft H at £0.50	0.50
5 cu ft O at £0.05	0.25
6	£0.75

Actual input at standard price:

	£
10,200 cu ft H at £0.50	5,100
57,600 cu ft O at £0.05	2,880
67,800	£7,980

Allowed cost of 67,800 cu ft input =

$$\frac{67,800}{6} \times £0.75 = \quad £8,475$$

Materials mix variance £495F

NOTE: Favourable mixture variances should not really be allowed to occur; they do not so much indicate a saving as an adulterated product (since an excessive quantity of the cheaper component has been allowed into the final product).

13. Standard cost of Input:

		p
	1 load pure wrot:	
	1 load crude wrot at £0.06 per load	6
Standard loss 40%	0.4 load	—
Standard yield 60%	0.6 load	6

$\therefore$ Standard cost per load pure wrot $= \dfrac{60}{0.6} =$ 10p

Allowed output for actual input of 1,500 loads of
crude wrot $= £1,500 \times 60\%$ = 900 loads
Actual output 726 loads
Difference 174 loads

$\therefore$ *Yield variance* = 174 loads pure wrot at 10p per load = £17.40A

£

NOTE: Cross-check: Cost of input: 1,500 at £0.06 = 90.00
Allowed value of output:
726 at £0.10 = 72.60
Excess value of input over
output £17.40

14. Standard cost card for MUD: £
1 tonne M at £1 1
1 tonne U at £2 2
3 tonnes D at £3 9
5 tonne input 12
−1 tonne 20% loss —
4 tonnes (80% yield) MUD £12

$\therefore$ 1 tonne MUD has standard cost of £12/4 = £3.

	Allowed cost	*Actual cost*	*Price variance*
	£	£	£
Actual mix at standard prices:			
M 1,100 tonnes at £1	1,100	1,000	100F
U 1,000 tonnes at £2	2,000	2,200	200A
D 2,900 tonnes at £3	8,700	8,888	188A
5,000 tonnes	£11,800	£12,088	£288A

Allowed cost of 5,000 tonnes of input =

$\dfrac{5,000}{5} \times £12$ = £12,000

$\therefore$ *Materials mix variance* = £200F

Allowed yield from 5,000 tonnes input
$= 5,000 \times 80\% =$ 4,000 tonnes
Actual yield = 3,815
Difference 185A

$\therefore$ *Yield variance* = 185 tonnes at £3 = £555A

$\therefore$ *Total material variance* $= £288A + £200F + £555A = $ £643A

NOTE: Cross-check: Total actual cost = £12,088
Allowed cost of actual output = $3,815 \times £3 = $ £11,445

Total variance £643A

15. *Standard cost card for input of 100 tonnes:*

		£
A	40 tonnes at £300 per tonne	12,000
B	30 tonnes at £100 per tonne	3,000
C	10 tonnes at £420 per tonne	4,200
Scrap	20 tonnes at £240* per tonne	4,800
	100 tonnes (at £240)	24,000
	−5 5% loss	—
	95	24,000
Scrap:	−35 tonnes returned at £240 per tonne	8,400
	60 tonnes (standard yield 60%)	£15,600

Standard cost per tonne of good casting $= \dfrac{£15,600}{60} = £260$

* To find scrap price per tonne, let $x = $ average alloy price.
$\therefore$ Total cost $= (12,000 + 3,000 + 4,200 + 20x) = 19,200 + 20x$
$\therefore$ Average alloy price $= (19,200 + 20x) \div 100 = 192 + 0.2x$
$\therefore$ $x = 192 + 0.2x$ $\therefore$ $0.8x = 192$ $\therefore$ $x = 240$.

Variances

Material	Actual quantity (tonnes)	Standard price (£)	Allowed cost (£)	Actual purchase cost (£)	Price variance (£)
A	380	300	114,000	380 × £310 = £117,800	3,800A
B	330	100	33,000	330 × £110 = £36,300	3,300A
C	90	420	37,800	90 × £420 = £37,800	Nil
Scrap	200	240	48,000	200 × £240 = £48,000	Nil
	1,000		£232,800	£239,900	£7,100A

		£
Allowed cost of 1,000 tonnes of input = 1,000 × £240 =		240,000
Actual cost (at standard prices) of input (as above)	=	232,800
∴ *Materials mix variance*		£7,200 F

Yield:	£	£
Allowed yield from 1,000 tonnes input:		
Good castings: 60% = 600 tonnes		
at £260	156,000	
Scrap: 35% = 350 tonnes at £240	84,000	240,000
Actual yield:		
Good castings: 608 at £260	158,080	
Scrap: 340 at £240	81,600	239,680
∴ *Yield variance*		£320A

NOTE: Separate scrap and yield variances can be calculated, but since scrap and good castings are partially linked in so much that a lower yield of good castings will tend to result in a higher production of scrap, and vice versa, it is probably better to recognize this association by computing a single overall yield variance.

Summary (for presentation to management):

	£	£	£
Actual cost of purchases			239,900*
Less Value of scrap produced:			
340 tonnes at £240			81,600
			158,300

Variance:	*Favourable*	*Adverse*	
Price: A		3,800	
B		3,300	
Mixture	7,200		
Yield		320	
Totals	7,200	7,420	220A
Allowed cost of actual good castings: 608 tonnes at £260			£158,080

*See 'Actual purchase cost' column in table above.

16.

	£
Variable overhead allowance for 11,340 articles	
= 11,340 × 10p =	1,134
Actual overhead cost	1,521
Total overhead variance	£387A

Analysis of variance: £
No. of invoices allowed for 11,340 articles
                        = 11,340 ÷ 5 =   2,268
Actual no. of invoices   2,504

Difference (excess invoices)   236

Standard variable cost per invoice   50p*
∴ *Variable overhead efficiency variance* = 236 × 50p =   £118A

Expenditure allowance for 2,504 invoices
                        = 2,504 × 50p* = 1,252
Actual expenditure   1,521

∴ *Overhead expenditure variance*   £269A

*If each article has a standard variable overhead of 10p and if 5 articles are planned per invoice, then the standard cost per invoice (i.e. unit of activity) is 50p.

17.	Chairs	Tables	Total (£)
Allowed sales value	3,100 × £5	1,200 × £30	
	= £15,500	= £36,000	51,500
Actual sales value	£15,215	£35,682	50,897
∴ *Sales margin price variance*	£285A	£318A	£603A
Allowed (budgeted) sales quantities	4,000	1,000	
Actual sales quantities	3,100	1,200	
Differences	900A	200F	
Standard profit	£3	£13	
∴ *Sales margin quantities variance*	£2,700A	£2,600F	£100A

18. (The student should refer to the control plans detailed in the answer to question 11 of Progress test 17.)

Profit variance	£
Budgeted profit	7,600
Actual profit	3,046
Operating profit variance	£4,554A

Variance analysis
Materials price variance:

	A		Containers	
	£		£	
Allowed cost of actual purchases	2,500 gals		100 conts.	
	A × £3 = 7,500		× 8	= 800
Actual cost	7,720			794
Materials price variance	£220 A			£6F

Materials usage variance:

A: Allowed usage for 1,610 gal $Z = \dfrac{1,610}{15} \times 20$ $= 2,146\frac{2}{3}$ gal
   Actual usage = 2,500 − 320 $= 2,180$ gal

   Excess usuage $33\frac{1}{3}$ gal

   Standard price   £3
∴ *Materials usage variance (A)* = $33\frac{1}{3} \times £3$ = £100A

Containers: Allowed usage for 98 15-gal
              containers   = 98 containers
           Actual usage = 100 − 1 = 99

           Excess usage   1

           Standard price   £8
∴ *Materials usage variance (containers)* = £8A

Z: Allowed usage for 98 15-gal
     containers = 98 × 15   = 1,470 gal
   Actual usage = 1,610 − 140 = 1,470 gal
   Difference   *Nil*

∴ No materials usage variance in respect of Z arises.

Wage rate variance:

	Dept. 1		Dept. 2
	Grade I	Grade II	
Allowed wages	2,941 hrs ×	2,100 hrs ×	1,250 hrs ×
	£3 = £8,823	£1.50 = £3,150	£2 = £2,500
Actual wages	£8,888	£3,124	£2,451
∴ *Wage rate variance*	£65A	£26F	£49F

Labour efficiency variance:

	Grade I	Grade II
Dept 1:		
Allowed hrs for 1,610 gal Z	$\dfrac{1,610}{15} \times 30 =$	$\dfrac{1,610}{15} \times 20 =$
	3,220	$2,146\frac{2}{3}$
Actual hrs	2,941	2,100
Difference (saving)	279	$46\frac{2}{3}$
Standard wage rate	£3	£1.50
∴ *Labour efficiency variance*	£837F	£70F

Dept 2:	
Allowed hrs for 98 15-gal containers	
Z = 98 × 12 =	1,176
Actual hrs	1,250
Excess hrs	74
Standard wage rate	£2
∴ *Labour efficiency variance*	£148A

Overhead expenditure variance:

	Dept. 1	Dept. 2	Marketing
Activity measure	Process hrs	Ind. lab. hrs	Containers
Actual units of activity	2,550	401	95
Standard variable overhead per unit(a)	£5	£2	£50
Variable overhead allowance	£12,750	£802	£4,750
Fixed overhead allowance(b): ($\frac{1}{10}$ budgeted for year)	£5,500	£1,400	£6,000
Total overhead allowance	£18,250	£2,202	£10,750
Actual overhead	£18,540	£2,101	£14,990
∴ *Overhead expenditure variance*	£290A	£101F	£4,240A

Variable overhead efficiency variance:
Dept 1: Allowed activity for 1,610 gal Z =

$$\frac{1,610}{15} \times 25 =$$ 2,683$\frac{1}{3}$ process hrs

      Actual activity   2,550 process hrs

      Saving   133$\frac{1}{3}$ process hrs

      Standard variable cost per process
        hour   £5

   ∴ *Variable overhead efficiency*
       variance (Dept. 1)   £666$\frac{2}{3}$F

Dept 2: Allowed activity for 98 15-gal
         containers = 98 × 4   =   392 ind. lab. hrs
         Actual activity   401 ind. lab. hrs

         Excess activity   9 ind. lab. hrs
         Standard variable cost per ind.
         lab. hr   £2

∴ *Variable overhead efficiency*
    variance (Dept. 2)   £18A

NOTE: No variable overhead efficiency variance can arise in the case of the Marketing Department since activity is there measured in cost units.

Fixed overhead variances:

	Dept. 1	*Dept. 2*	*Marketing*
Activity measure	Process hours	Ind. lab. hours	Containers
Budgeted activity	2,500	400	100
Actual activity	2,550	401	95
Difference	50F	1F	5A
Stnd. overhead rate	£2.20	£3.5	£60
Capacity variance	£110F	£3$\frac{1}{2}$F	£300A
Actual production	1,610 gals	98 containers	Not applicable – activity measure same as cost unit (*see* note to **18**)
Allowed hours	$\frac{1,610}{15} \times 25$	98 × 4	
	= 2,683$\frac{1}{3}$	= 392	
Actual hours	2,550	401	
Difference	133$\frac{1}{3}$F	9A	
Stnd. overhead rate	£2.20	£3.50	
Productivity variance	£293$\frac{1}{3}$F	£31$\frac{1}{2}$A	

Sales margin variances:

			£
Price:	Allowed sales value for 95 15-gal		
	containers = 95 × £600	= 57,000	
	Actual sales value	56,084	
	∴ *Sales margin selling price variance*	£916A	

Quantity:	Allowed sales quantity(c)	100 15-gal containers
	Actual sales quantity	95
	Deficit	5
	Standard profit	£76
	∴ *Sales margin quantity*	
	variance	£380A

NOTES:

(*a*) *See* flexible budgets.

(*b*) On basis of ten control periods for the year.

(*c*) *See* control profit budget for first period (*see* answer to 11(*b*), Progress test 17).

SUMMARY:

Variance		£	£
Materials price:	A	220A	
	Containers	6F	214A
Materials usage:	A	100A	
	Containers	8A	108A
Wage rate:	Dept. 1, Grade I	65A	
	Dept. 1, Grade II	26F	
	Dept. 2	49F	10F
Labour efficiency:	Dept. 1, Grade I	837F	
	Dept. 1, Grade II	70F	
	Dept. 2	148A	759F
Overhead expenditure:	Dept. 1	290A	
	Dept. 2	101F	
	Marketing	4,240A	4,429A
Variable overhead efficiency:	Dept. 1	$666\frac{2}{3}$F	
	Dept. 2	18A	$648\frac{2}{3}$F
Total variable cost variances			$3,333\frac{1}{3}$A
Capacity:	Dept. 1	110F	
	Dept. 2	$3\frac{1}{2}$A	
	Marketing	300A	$186\frac{1}{2}$A
Productivity:	Dept. 1	$293\frac{1}{3}$F	
	Dept. 2	$31\frac{1}{2}$A	$261\frac{5}{6}$F
Sales margin:	Selling price	916A	
	Quantity	380A	1,296A
Profit variance			£4,554ADV

19. (*a*) Standard variable cost of 1 15-gal container of Z (*see* answer to question 11(*a*), Progress test 17):

Dept. 1: Variable cost of 15 gallons Z: $60 + 90 + 30 + 125$	£305*
Dept. 2: Variable costs: $8 + 24 + 8$	40
Marketing: Variable costs	50
Total variable costs	395
Standard margin – contribution	205
Standard selling price	£600

*Standard yield 75%. Note that the variable standard cost of output is

$$305/15 = £20\tfrac{1}{3} \text{ per gal Z.}$$

(*b*) Amendment to actual profit and loss statement in question 18:

WIP variable cost Dept. 2: 140 gallons Z at $£20\tfrac{1}{3} = £2,846\tfrac{2}{3}$
FG variable cost: 3 full containers at $£(305 + 40) = £1,035$

So actual profit = $3,046 - (3,360 - 2,846\tfrac{2}{3}) - (1,242 - 1,035) = £2,325\tfrac{2}{3}$

(*c*) The variances are all the same as those in question 18 save for the following:

Profit variance = $7,600 - 2,325\tfrac{2}{3} = £5,274\tfrac{1}{3}\text{A}$

Sales quantity variance = 5 containers at a standard
contribution of $£205 = £1,025\text{A}$

(*d*) Variance summary:

Total variable cost variances as in Progress test 18, answer 18, up to and including Variable Overhead Efficiency variance		3,333$\tfrac{1}{3}$A
Sales Margin variances: Selling price (as before)	916A	
Quantity – 5 containers at £205 margin	1,025A	
		1,941A
Profit variance		£5,274$\tfrac{1}{3}$A

20. NOTE: This question and the next involve what can be termed 'reverse' analyses, i.e. the end result of a conventional analysis is given and the question calls for information that in practice would be available before the analysis began. This type of problem, testing as it does the student's grasp of the principles involved, is popular with examiners. Finding the answers, though, essentially calls for no more than finding the missing figures in either of the following equations:

Variance = £(Allowance – actual)
Variance = (Allowance – actual)units × standard cost.

In the working sheet that follows the 'actual' figure is the last to be computed. Note that the non-monetary actuals are needed in order to compute the monetary actuals at later points on the sheet.

Note	Cost element	Variance	Stnd. cost	Difference	Allowance	Actual
(a)	Fixed overhead volume	£300	60p	500 units	Budgeted quantity = 10,000	10,500 units
	Fixed overhead expenditure	£(200)			10,000 × 60p = £6,000	£6,200
(b)	Material usage	£(400)	50p	(800) kg	10,500* × 12 kg = 126,000 kg	126,800 kg
(c)	Materials price	£1,268			126,800* × 50p = £63,400	£62,132
(b)	Wages efficiency	£240	£1.60	150 hrs	10,500* × 1½ = 15,750 hrs	15,600 hrs
	Wages rates	£(780)			15,600* × £1.60 = £24,960	£25,740
(d)	Sales volume margin	£1,500	£3	500	Budgeted quantity = 10,000	10,500
	Sales price margin	£(1,000)			10,500* × £12 = £126,000	£125,000

*From 'Actual' column.

NOTES:

(a) Since the material usage and wages efficiency variances depend upon the actual volume of production, this variance needs to be computed first.

(b) To find the materials price and wages rates allowances it is necessary to know the actual material usage and labour hours, so these variances must be computed first.

(c) It is assumed that there is no change in the raw material stocks.

(d) Again, to find the sales price allowance it is necessary to know the actual sales quantity, so this variance must be computed first. Note, too, that since the actual sales quantity equals the actual production there has been no change in the finished goods stocks.

Actual profit statement:

	£	£
Sales		125,000
Cost: Purchases	62,132	
Wages	25,740	
Fixed overheads	6,200	94,072
Actual profit (as per question)		£30,928

21. (*See* note at introduction to question 20.)
Unit selling price = £60 + 20% of selling price = £75.
So budgeted sales and production = 30,000/75 = 400 units.

Working sheet:

Line	Cost element	Variance	Stnd. cost	Difference	Allowance	Actual
(a)	Overhead volume	£375F	£25	15 units	Budgeted prod. = 400	415 units
(b)	Overhead expend	£200F			Budgeted overhead 400 × 25 = £10,000	£9,800

(c)	Material usage	£375F	£1.5	250 units	$415 \times 10 = 4,150$	3,900 units
(d)	Labour efficiency	£180A	£4	45 hrs	$415 \times 5 = 2,075$	2,120 hrs

In answers below italicized numbers are taken from the question and letters refer to lines in the working sheet.

(i) <u>415 units</u> (a)

(ii) Actual profit = Sales – (materials + wages + overheads)
$$= 29,880 - (6,435 + 8,162 + 9,800(b)) = \underline{\underline{£5,483}}$$

(iii) $6,435/3,900(c) = \underline{\underline{£1.65}}$

(iv) $8,162/2,120(d) = \underline{\underline{£3.85}}$

(v) $\underline{£9,800(b)}$

(vi) Overhead absorbed = $2,120(d) \times £5 = \underline{\underline{£10,600}}$

(vii) Standard hours produced = $415(a) \times 5$ *hours* = 2,075 hrs
Actual hours worked $= 2,120(d)$
∴ production overhead efficiency variance= $(2,120 - 2,075)$
$$\times £5 = \underline{\underline{£225A}}$$

(viii) Allowed sales value = $415(a) \times £75 = £31,125$
∴ sales price variance = $31,125 - 29,880 = \underline{\underline{£1,245A}}$

(ix) Allowance = 400 units. Actual = 415(a) units.
∴ sales quantity variance = $(415 - 400) \times (£75 - £60) = \underline{\underline{£225F}}$

Progress test 20

1. The cost and variance accounts in answer to this question are given on the following pages. The letters in brackets refer to the explanatory notes given below. (It should, perhaps, be pointed out that providing the basic principles are not violated there are valid alternative ways of making some of the minor book-keeping entries.)

MAIN ACCOUNTS

Raw Material Stores

Purchases(a)		WIP(b)	£13,650
	£14,800	Breakages	360
Price var.	200	Balance c/d	990
	£15,000		£15,000
Balance	990		

Work-in-Progress

Materials	£13,650	Finished	
Direct wages	8,850	goods(g)	£45,000
Variable		Materials	
overheads	4,500	usage	
Fixed		var.(h)	150
overheads	17,700		
Efficiency			
vars.(i)			
Labour	150		
Product-			
ivity	300		

MAIN ACCOUNTS

Direct Wages

Cash	£9,140	Wages rate var.(c)	£240
		Breakdowns(d)	50
		WIP(e)	£8,850

Variable Overheads

| Cash | £4,580 | WIP(f) | £4,500 |
| | | Expenditure var. | 80 |

Fixed Overheads

Cash	£20,900	WIP(k)	£17,700
		Expenditure var.(l)	900
		Capacity var.(m)	2,300

Finished Goods

WIP	£45,000	P/L(j)	£42,000
		Balance c/d	3,000
	£45,000		£45,000
Balance	3,000		

Selling and Distribution Overheads

| Cash | £7,000 | P/L(n) | £7,000 |

Sales

| P/L | £58,800 | Cash | £57,100 |
| | | Price var.(o) | 1,700 |

VARIANCE ACCOUNTS

Direct Materials Price

| P/L | £200 | RM stores | £200 |

Breakages

| RM stores | £360 | P/L | £360 |

Direct Wages Rate

| Direct wages | £240 | P/L | £240 |

Capacity

| Fixed overheads | £2,300 | Breakdowns(p) | £100 |
| | | P/L | 2,200 |

Breakdowns

| Direct wages | £50 | P/L | £150 |
| Capacity var. | 100 | | |

Fixed Overhead Expenditure

| Fixed overheads | £900 | P/L | £900 |

Variable Overhead Expenditure

| Variable overheads | £80 | P/L | £80 |

Direct Labour Efficiency

| P/L | £150 | WIP | £150 |

Productivity

| P/L | £300 | WIP | £300 |

Direct Materials Usage

| WIP | £150 | P/L | £150 |

Sales Margin Price

| Sales | £1,700 | P/L | £1,700 |

Profit and Loss Account

Cost of Sales:		Sales	£58,800
FG	£42,000		
Selling and			
distribution	7,000		
Adverse		Favourable	
variances:		variances:	
Breakages(*q*)	360	Direct	
Direct wages		materials	
rate	240	price	200
Breakdowns(*q*)	150	Direct labour	
Capacity	2,200	efficiency	150
F. overhead			
expenditure	900	Productivity	300
V. overhead			
expenditure	80		
Direct material			
usage	150		
Sales margin			
price	1,700		
Net profit to			
appropria-			
tion	4,670		

Profit and Loss Appropriation

	P/L	£4,670	

NOTES: The following explanatory notes are given for the benefit of the student checking his or her answer.

(*a*) 'Actual' figures shown in this account for simplicity.

(*b*) 4,550 at £3.

(*c*) £9,140 – 4,450 at £2.

(*d*) 25 hrs at £2.

(*e*) 4,425 at £2.

(*f*) 900 at £5. (The allowance here is not based on hours but on production in accordance with the note on the standard cost card.)

(*g*) 900 at £50.

(*h*) Allowed usage (900 × 5) – 4,550 = 50 at £3.

(*i*) (900 × 5) – 4,425 = 75 hours at appropriate rate.

(*j*) Standard cost of sales, i.e. 840 at £50.

(*k*) From the standard cost card the fixed overhead absorption rate is clearly £4 per hour. Therefore since 4,450 – 25 hours' breakdowns = 4,425 hours went to production, the WIP charge is 4,425 at £4.

(*l*) Budgeted fixed overheads clearly must have been $1,000 \times £20 = £20,000$ (i.e. budgeted sets × overheads per set). Therefore expenditure variance = $£20,000 - £20,900$.

(*m*) 5,000 budgeted hours – 4,425 hours spent on production, at £4.

(*n*) By tradition no variance extracted, although if the question had indicated the degree of variability of this cost it would have been advisable to see if a variance could be calculated and extracted.

(*o*) $£57,100 - (840 \text{ at } £70)$.

(*p*) Fixed overheads chargeable to breakdowns: 25 at £4. (This step is optional.)

(*q*) Since no breakages or breakdowns were planned these costs are, in effect, variances and so have been included among the variances.

Index

M&E Handbooks

Law

Business and Management

Advertising/F Jefkins
Basic Economics/G L Thirkettle
Basic of Business/D Lewis
Business and Financial Management/B K R Watts
Business Mathematics/L W T Stafford
Business Systems/R G Anderson
Data Processing Vol 1: Principles and Practice/R G Anderson
Data Processing Vol 2: Information Systems and Technology/R G Anderson
Human Resources Management/H T Graham, R Bennett
International Marketing/L S Walsh
Managerial Economics/J R Davies, S Hughes
Marketing/G B Giles
Marketing Overseas/A West
Modern Commercial Knowledge/L W T Stafford
Modern Marketing/F Jefkins
Office Administration/J C Denyer, A L Mugridge
Operational Research/W M Harper, H C Lim
Production Management/H A Harding
Public Administration/M Barber, R Stacey
Public Relations/F Jefkins
Purchasing/C K Lysons
Retail Management/R Cox, P Brittain
Selling: Management and Practice/P Allen
Statistics/W M Harper
Stores Management/R J Carter

Accounting and Finance

Auditing/L R Howard
Basic Accounting/J O Magee
Basic Book-keeping/J O Magee
Company Accounts/J O Magee
Company Secretarial Practice/L Hall, G M Thom
Cost Accounting/W M Harper
Elements of Banking/D P Whiting
Elements of Insurance/D S Hansell
Finance of Foreign Trade/D P Whiting
Investment: A Practical Approach/D Kerridge
Investment Appraisal/G Mott
Management Accounting/W M Harper
Practice of Banking/E P Doyle, J E Kelly
Principles of Accounts/E F Castle, N P Owens

Humanities and Science

European History 1789–1914/C A Leeds
Land Surveying/R J P Wilson
World History: 1900 to the Present Day/C A Leeds